Esoteric Buddhism in China

THE SHENG YEN SERIES IN CHINESE BUDDHIST STUDIES

THE SHENG YEN SERIES IN CHINESE BUDDHIST STUDIES
Edited by Natasha Heller and Jimmy Yu

Funded jointly by the Sheng Yen Education Foundation and the Chung Hua Institute of Buddhist Studies in Taiwan, the Sheng Yen Series in Chinese Buddhist Studies is dedicated to the interdisciplinary study of Chinese language resources that bear on the history of Buddhism in premodern and modern China. Through the publication of pioneering scholarship on Chinese Buddhist thought, practice, social life, and institutional life in China—including interactions with indigenous traditions of religion in China, as well as Buddhist developments in South, East, and Inner/Central Asia—the series aspires to bring new and groundbreaking perspectives to one of the most historically enduring and influential traditions of Buddhism, past and present.

Yoshiko Ashiwa and David L. Wank, *The Space of Religion: Temple, State, and Buddhist Communities in Modern China*
Huaiyu Chen, *In the Land of Tigers and Snakes: Living with Animals in Medieval Chinese Religions*
John Kieschnick, *Buddhist Historiography in China*
Chün-fang Yü, *The Renewal of Buddhism in China: Zhuhong and the Late Ming Synthesis*, Fortieth Anniversary Edition
Erik J. Hammerstrom, *The Huayan University Network: The Teaching and Practice of Avataṃsaka Buddhism in Twentieth-Century China*
Dewei Zhang, *Thriving in Crisis: Buddhism and Political Disruption in China, 1522–1620*
Geoffrey C. Goble, *Chinese Esoteric Buddhism: Amoghavajra, the Ruling Elite, and the Emergence of a Tradition*
Jan Kiely and J. Brooks Jessup, editors, *Recovering Buddhism in Modern China*
Jiang Wu and Lucille Chia, editors, *Spreading Buddha's Word in East Asia: The Formation and Transformation of the Chinese Buddhist Canon*
Erik J. Hammerstrom, *The Science of Chinese Buddhism: Early Twentieth-Century Engagements*
N. Harry Rothschild, *Emperor Wu Zhao and Her Pantheon of Devis, Divinities, and Dynastic Mothers*
Paul Copp, *The Body Incantatory: Spells and the Ritual Imagination in Medieval Chinese Buddhism*
Beverley Foulks McGuire, *Living Karma: The Religious Practices of Ouyi Zhixu (1599–1655)*
Koichi Shinohara, *Spells, Images, and Maṇḍalas: Tracing the Evolution of Esoteric Buddhist Rituals*
Michael J. Walsh, *Sacred Economies: Buddhist Business and Religiosity in Medieval China*

ESOTERIC BUDDHISM IN CHINA

Engaging Japanese and
Tibetan Traditions, 1912–1949

WEI WU

COLUMBIA UNIVERSITY PRESS *NEW YORK*

Columbia University Press
Publishers Since 1893
New York   Chichester, West Sussex
cup.columbia.edu
Copyright © 2024 Columbia University Press
All rights reserved
Library of Congress Cataloging-in-Publication Data
Names: Wu, Wei (Scholar on religion), author.
Title: Esoteric Buddhism in China : engaging Japanese and Tibetan traditions, 1912–1949 / Wei Wu.
Description: New York : Columbia University Press, 2024. | Series: The Sheng Yen series in Chinese Buddhist studies | Includes bibliographical references and index.
Identifiers: LCCN 2023034126 (print) | LCCN 2023034127 (ebook) | ISBN 9780231200684 (hardback) | ISBN 9780231200691 (trade paperback) | ISBN 9780231553742 (ebook)
Subjects: LCSH: Tantric Buddhism—China—History—20th century.
Classification: LCC BQ8912.9.C5 W82 2024 (print) | LCC BQ8912.9.C5 (ebook) | DDC 294.3/9250951/0904—dc23/eng/20230807
LC record available at https://lccn.loc.gov/2023034126
LC ebook record available at https://lccn.loc.gov/2023034127

Cover design: Chang Jae Lee
Cover image: Tsongkhapa Hall in Jinci Monastery, photo courtesy of Wei Wu

Contents

Acknowledgments vii

Map xi

Introduction 1

ONE Chinese Buddhism in Transition 26

TWO The Lamas and the Rituals 48

THREE Esoteric Buddhism for Laypeople 73

FOUR Debates on Esoteric Buddhism 95

FIVE The Path to Enlightenment 121

SIX Tibetan Buddhism Among Han Chinese 148

Conclusion 181

List of Chinese Characters 187

Wylie Transliteration 201

CONTENTS

Notes 203

Bibliography 265

Index 295

Acknowledgments

My interest in the project can be traced back to my sophomore year at Peking University in Beijing where I took an introductory course on Chinese Buddhism in 2003. I became fascinated by Chinese Buddhist philosophy and occasionally attended student events. When an earnest friend invited me to a weekly Buddhist reading group, I was surprised to find that the group was deep into discussing *The Great Treatise on the Stages of the Path to Enlightenment* (Ch. *Puti dao cidi guanglun*, Wylie: *Lam rim chen mo*), a commentary composed by the fourteenth-century Tibetan master Tsongkhapa and translated in 1934 by the Chinese monk Fazun. The reading group had been studying the text for years by the time I met them.

I was surprised as much by their dedication as by their choice. Why read a Tibetan commentary, not a Chinese one? I knew from the introductory course that the Chinese Buddhist canon offered a rich body of Buddhist literature, including profound philosophical works produced by ancient Chinese writers of the Tiantai school and the Huayan school. And the Chan tradition and the Pure Land tradition prevailed as the major forms of Buddhism in China. Given the availability of Chinese Buddhist teachings and practices, what were these Chinese Buddhist students looking for in Tibetan Buddhism? And what did they find? How did they understand Tibetan Buddhism in juxtaposition with Chinese Buddhism? What did they make of the differences in doctrines and practices?

ACKNOWLEDGMENTS

For over a decade, such questions energized me. They prompted me to visit temples and sacred sites in Beijing, Shanghai, Sichuan, Zhejiang, Hubei, Gansu, and Mount Wutai, and to meet many Chinese men and women, monastics and laity, devoted to Tibetan Buddhism. The questions compelled me to do graduate study at the University of Hong Kong and later at Princeton University, and they became the focus of my doctoral dissertation, which explored the intellectual and social history of Chinese Buddhism with a particular focus on the reception of Tibetan Buddhism by Chinese Buddhists in the early twentieth century.

I feel incredibly fortunate for the support I have received throughout the years at Princeton University. I would first like to express my deepest gratitude to my advisor, Stephen F. Teiser. He has been a constant source of guidance, support, and encouragement in my research and writing. His critical insight always refined my approaches and brought my discussion back to the big issues. I also benefited immensely from other members of my committee. I am particularly grateful to Jacqueline Stone for sharing her wisdom in research. I also benefited from the knowledge of Jonathan Gold, whose excellent advice and criticism propelled me to think with greater clarity. Janet Chen lent her expertise in historiography and offered helpful advice on visiting municipal archives. This project would have been impossible without the intellectual generosity and personal kindness of my mentors.

I would like to express my appreciation to Susan Naquin, Benjamin Elman, and Elaine Pagels for sharing their insights on my project at various stages. My gratitude also goes to a host of scholars, particularly Ester Bianchi, Fabienne Jagou, Shen Weirong, James Benn, Gray Tuttle, Gregory Adam Scott, Erik Hammerstrom, Chen Jinhua, Stefania Travagnin, Elena Valussi, Rongdao Lai, and Erik Schicketanz, all of whom provided thoughtful comments and intellectual inspiration. My thanks also go to Ulrike Guthrie and Merrick Lex Berman, who helped me to improve the presentation of the project. I also want to thank my teachers at the University of Hong Kong, particularly Kakkapalliye Anuruddha, K. L. Dhammajoti, Jingyin, Y. Karunadasa, Guangxing, and Gereon Kopf for their encouragement.

I received great assistance during my visits to Wutai, Beijing, Shanghai, Zhejiang, and Chengdu in 2009 and 2013. I am profoundly grateful to Ven. Jiexin, who generously shared a wealth of materials about Nenghai that she amassed and helped me to gain access to several religious sites. Hu Qixiu,

ACKNOWLEDGMENTS

Hu Zihu's granddaughter, recalled her grandfather's enthusiasm for Buddhism and his patronage of Buddhist endeavors. Liu Wei shared with me materials about the history of the Beijing Lay Buddhist Society. I thank Fang Guangchang, Zhanru, Lou Yulie, and Chen Bing for their helpful suggestions.

I am deeply grateful to the series editors, Dan Stevenson and Jimmy Yu, for their constant support. Their editorial suggestions improved this work tremendously. Their insight played a significant role in reshaping the book's arguments and presentation. A special thanks goes to Lowell Frye of Columbia University Press for his precise advice. Thanks are due to Leslie Kriesel for overseeing the editorial work in its final stages, to Mary Bagg for copyediting, and to Alexander Trotter for preparing the index. I also offer my gratitude to all the anonymous reviewers and readers for their substantive and constructive comments. I alone take responsibility for its errors and shortcomings.

My appreciation also extends to my friends, including Ethan Lindsay, Bryan Lowe, April Hughes, Jolyon Thomas, Douglas Gildow, Takashi Miura, Kwi Jeong Lee, Timothy Benedict, Daniel Burton-Rose, Kyle Bond, Jessica Zu, Pascal Wenz, Minhao Zhai, and Kentaro Ide. Their comments helped me to think through my subject and keep my curiosity piqued. Other friends, too numerous to name, also offered encouragement and comments.

Princeton University's Graduate School, Institute for International and Regional Studies, Center for the Study of Religion, and East Asian Program offered generous funding for my fieldwork. ACLS/Robert H. N. Ho Family Foundation fellowship advanced my writing. I also received generous support from Emory University. Emory University Research Committee Grant, Scholarly Writing and Publishing Fund, Program to Enhance Research and Scholarship are indispensable for the completion of the manuscript.

I want to express my heartfelt thanks to my colleagues in the Department of Religion at Emory University. They provided collegial support and intellectual stimulation. I benefit from the advice of my colleagues, particularly Sara L. McClintock, María Carrión, Gary Laderman, Joyce Burkhalter Flueckiger, Bobbi Patterson, Tara Doyle, Devaka Premawardhana, and Ellen Gough. I am thankful to Eric Reinders, who read my draft and provided thought-provoking suggestions.

ACKNOWLEDGMENTS

Finally, I am enormously thankful to my parents, Guojin Wu and Xiu'e Chen. The book is dedicated to them with my deepest gratitude. I also thank my husband, Jinsong Chen, for his unwavering support of my intellectual pursuit. Jinsong has provided invaluable emotional and technical support over the years, including fixing all sorts of computer problems. I am grateful for his being at my side throughout the journey.

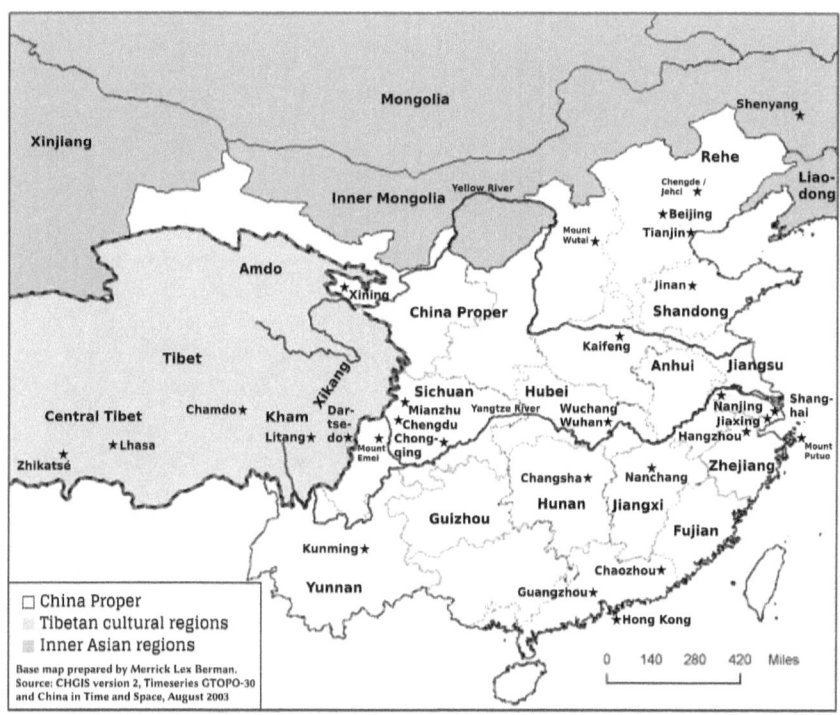

FIGURE 0.1 Esoteric Buddhist Activity in China: The base map was prepared by Merrick Lex Berman. The boundaries were based on the PRC digital presentation of the Qing Empire in 1820. Some territories and boundaries are disputable. The sources for drawing the map include the China Historical Geographical Information System (CHGIS) version 2, Timeseries GTOPO-30, August 2003; and CHGIS version 2, China in Time and Space, August 2003.

Esoteric Buddhism in China

Introduction

THIS BOOK EXPLORES the rise of esoteric Buddhism during the Republican era (1912–1949) in China proper. It particularly focuses on the cross-cultural religious communication that occurred when Chinese Buddhists were challenged by discourses of nation-building and religious reform.[1] From the late nineteenth century on, China witnessed great changes in its politics, economy, and culture, and its religious communities adopted various initiatives in response. Dynamics set in motion during this period greatly transformed the Chinese religious landscape, chief among them the spread of esoteric Buddhism. With the fall of the Qing, Buddhists not only lost imperial patronage but also faced a declining monastic economy and challenges from antireligious campaigns. To rejuvenate Chinese Buddhism in such a context, some Han Buddhists looked to Japan, Tibet, and other traditions outside China. This rich array of ideas and practices had a lasting impact on Chinese Buddhism. While conducting research for this book, I examined the various currents and developments of esoteric Buddhism in Chinese society, as well as the Chinese Buddhists' engagement with the newly translated ideas and practices.

The history of esoteric Buddhism in modern China has captured scholarly attention for over half a century. Within religious studies, Holmes Welch and other scholars have investigated the attempts by Buddhist leaders to advance cross-cultural religious communication.[2] Dongchu, Chen Bing, Deng Zimei, and Mei Jingxuan investigated the rise of esoteric Buddhism

INTRODUCTION

as expressed in two trends: the introduction of Japanese Tendai and Shingon Buddhism since the 1910s, and learning from Tibetan Buddhism since the 1920s.[3] Gray Tuttle and other historians have focused on Tibetan Buddhism's political impact, especially how Buddhism has served as a tenuous political link between China proper and Tibet after the collapse of the Qing.[4] More recently, Ester Bianchi, Fabianne Jagou, Joshua Esler, and others have researched the contemporary encounters between Chinese Buddhism and Tibetan esoteric Buddhism in Taiwan and the mainland.[5] Yet little scholarship has focused on the doctrinal, ritual, and institutional dimensions of early interactions between Chinese, Japanese, and Tibetan Buddhism. The lack of analysis concerning the actual interplay between them means that the dialectical aspects of the movement are unexplored, and the ways in which Tibetan and Japanese Buddhist traditions have shaped the modern Chinese religious landscape have been deeply underestimated. My study looks at the Chinese translation and interpretation of esoteric Buddhist doctrines, practices, and modes of institutional organization to argue that a creative synthesis occurred. I also examine the forces shaping the transmission of such ideas and practices, with an emphasis on the Chinese side of the equation. I show that the introduction of esoteric Buddhism reflected, and in turn influenced, dynamics in Chinese Buddhist communities in the first decades of the twentieth century and after.

Ann Swidler's repertoire theory defines culture as a "tool kit" containing symbols, habits, skills, rituals, stories, and worldviews that people use in a varied configuration to construct their own interpretations. It thus provides a useful framework to analyze the Chinese reception of Japanese and Tibetan esoteric Buddhism.[6] The repertoire framework emphasizes cultural variety and the variable ways people use culture.[7]

But here the reader may wonder, why the "repertoire theory" and not another model? After all, there are numerous methodical frameworks available to describe cross-cultural religious transmission. Each model has its particular history, emphasis, and constraints. One such model—syncretism—has been widely used in the study of religion, especially in Christian missiology. Broadly speaking, syncretism describes the process of a religion engaging and mixing with another culture or cultures. In the mid and late twentieth century, with the rise in scholarship on the spread of Christianity in Asia and Africa, some scholars criticized the syncretism model as static, ahistorical, and pejorative, accusing it of falsely presupposing a reified,

INTRODUCTION

stereotypical religious body being transplanted, thereby implying a hierarchy of the original religion over its later forms in other cultures.[8] They proposed other notions—such as inculturation, indigenization, and contextualization—to describe the integration of the transmitted religion with the realities of its changing contexts.[9] While these various models are often used interchangeably to refer to similar situations, they are in fact each loaded with quite particular meaning and address the various facets of cross-cultural religious transmission. Donald K. McKim, for example, asserts that indigenization implies the local expression of something that, has come from somewhere else.[10] Choki Coe emphasizes that religion is always developing in changing contexts.[11] And according to Aylward Shorter, "inculturation" suggests "an on-going dialogue between faith and culture or cultures" that accentuates "the creative and dynamic relationship" between the religion and cultures.[12]

Despite their contributions, these approaches should be used with caveats. Some scholars caution that like the syncretism model, the various alternatives can perpetuate the dualistic differentiation of the imported religion and the local context. The Kenyan philosopher John Mbiti highlights that Africans have always practiced Christianity with reference to their African religious backgrounds rather than Western norms.[13] And the Ghanaian theologian Kwame Bediako also advocates for the translatability of Christianity in Africa, showing that Christianity has been articulated into a plurality of cultural contexts.[14] Their research has warned against presupposing that a static religion with an unchanging core can be uprooted and transplanted into another evolving culture.

Other cultural studies have broadened the discussion by questioning the dichotomous taxonomies of religion and culture. They maintain that as an evolving process, a religion is constantly intermingling with cultural systems. Andrew Walls, examining the tensions between the universalizing features of religion and the cultural particularities, claims that local cultures strengthen the faith shared across the different cultures.[15] Kathryn Tanner, noting the internal conflicts in a culture, highlights the ubiquitous presence of cultures in faith.[16] She has shown that every religion is always interweaving with the surrounding cultures, and that its cross-cultural spread constitutes a part of its ongoing history and helps to shape its distinctiveness.[17] Tanner and Wall's research has warned us against the pitfalls of reifying both the religion and the cultures in question.

INTRODUCTION

I use the repertoire framework for the basis of my study in *Esoteric Buddhism in China* because it helps to analyze an ever-changing religion in ever-changing contexts, and because it can refer to the roles of agents as well as circumstances. As Robert Campany has noted, when studying interreligious interactions, we should not personify the religions or treat them as monolithic wholes.[18] Instead of suggesting an encounter between two discrete cultural bodies as if these cultures were static entities unchanged through their interactions, the repertoire model locates agency in the people and attends to their strategic actions as conditioned by the cultural resources available to them.

Repertoire

The repertoire framework emphasizes the evolving process of cross-cultural transmission, the human agency in interpretation, and the cultural circumstances that condition the interpretation.[19] The approach assumes that religions are products of human minds and bodies, and hence contingent upon all the complexities that those minds and bodies—individually and socially—entail. People are constantly changing in response to circumstances, and the religions that they live and embody are also necessarily changing. As Ann Swidler has noted, culture influences people's actions by providing a repertoire of resources, from which people select certain elements to construct "strategies of actions" to solve different sorts of problems.[20] Such a repertoire of resources emphasizes that the ways in which people enact cultural styles, habits, rituals, symbols, skills, and customs vary. People select different parts of the repertoire to form a strategy of action in a particular situation.[21]

Building upon the scholarship of Ann Swidler and Robert Campany, I adopt a more historical and dynamic perspective of cultural repertoire in *Esoteric Buddhism in China*, tracing how people themselves adopted a repertoire over four decades. The cultural repertoire I examine in this book encompasses not only various Buddhist texts, practices, and traditions, but also elements from Chinese culture, history, and contemporary discourses, particularly those relevant to modernity and the way Chinese Buddhists responded to it. This approach emphasizes the role of human agency in the historical process of interpretation, where an agent formulates their interpretative strategy by drawing on selected parts of the repertoire. Thus it offers several advantages.

First, viewing the repertoire as a shifting collection with permeable boundaries, it enables us to avoid being caught up by the normative categorizations that distinguish "true" or "authentic" esoteric Buddhism from locally restrictive accretions and allows us to analyze changes over time: how human agents adopt different interpretative strategies, and how their interpretations are contingent on specific circumstances. For example, Buddhist sources, such as canonical scriptures and commentaries, are important parts of the repertoire, but they are not static, closed, or exclusive. Buddhist sources are shaped by specific contextual experiences in history and also require interpretation in the present context. People's interpretation and selected use of its components can lead to changes in the repertoire, with some ingredients gaining or losing importance over time and some being reevaluated or questioned.

In this study, "esoteric Buddhist resources" include not only the newly translated Japanese and Tibetan esoteric Buddhist texts, ideas, rituals, and practices, but also the esoteric teachings found within the Chinese Buddhist canon, as well as various rites and practices that have been a part of Chinese traditions since ancient times. During the modern era, Chinese individuals sparked an interest in esoteric Buddhism, drawing renewed focus on the esoteric scriptures and commentaries in the Chinese Buddhist canon. Some Chinese scholars advocated works of the eminent esoteric masters of the Tang dynasty (618–907), in particular, as reliable sources. Thus, the esoteric Buddhist resources, and the entire repertoire, are subject to transformation through the ongoing human experience and have the potential to integrate new elements and meanings, enhancing the repertoire's overall diversity.

Attending to the active roles of human agents in translation and interpretation, the repertoire framework in this book implies a succession of contacts and interpretative actions during which new meanings are created, highlighting how cultural repertoires shape people's interpretative strategies and the meaning they generate. In doing so, this method reflects a dual commitment, as described by Stephen Bevans, both to "the experiences of the past" as recorded in scriptures and defended in traditions, and to "the experiences of the present," that is, the context in which people live.[22] In this study, my subjects' prior knowledge of Chinese Buddhism and their visions of Buddhism in a modern world preconditioned their reception of esoteric Buddhism. Aware of the tensions in the Chinese context, they strategically synthesized the teachings and practices to adapt esoteric Buddhism to the Chinese milieu.

During the years from 1912 to 1949, Chinese individuals understood the intricacies of esoteric Buddhism within a specific context, which was shaped by their personal and collective experiences, cultural background, encounters with historical events, contemporary intellectual discourses, and political trends.[23] Their interpretations were influenced not only by external factors such as dramatic social changes, but also by personal ones, including their concerns, needs, feelings, intellectual training, linguistic capacity, and knowledge of the varied Buddhist resources. In emphasizing human agency, the extent of their access to and strategic use of the available repertoire, this approach underscores the diversity and historical contingency of their interpretations.

The introduction of Tibetan and Japanese esoteric Buddhism was conditioned by the situation of early twentieth-century Chinese Buddhists, who were particularly challenged by discourses of nation-building and religious reform.[24] With the decline of the Qing dynasty and the establishment of the Republican regime in 1912, Buddhist monks faced the loss of imperial patronage, the collapse of the monastic economy, and the impact of new ideologies.[25] The intellectuals debated how to build a modern China that was radically different, and many perceived Buddhism and other religions as superstitious and outdated symbols of the past. Government threats of property confiscation and anti-superstition movements propelled the monastic priesthood to redefine itself. In response, beginning in the 1910s, the monk Taixu 太虛 (1890–1947) and other Buddhist leaders initiated a series of reforms to modernize Buddhism.[26] As part of his vision of how to revive Chinese Buddhism, Taixu urged the revival of the teachings of all eight sects of the Tang dynasty, an era in which Buddhism reached its peak.[27] He considered the reintroduction of the lost teachings (especially the esoteric teachings) from other non-Chinese traditions of great importance for the restoration of Chinese Buddhism. The introduction of esoteric Buddhism, therefore, constituted part of the broader Buddhist endeavor to reformulate Buddhism for the modern era. For example, in 1924, Taixu and his disciple Dayong 大勇 (1893–1929) founded a Tibetan college (Zangwen xueyuan 藏文學院) in Beijing. The next year, Dayong led a group of twenty-five Buddhists

INTRODUCTION

to study Tibetan Buddhism in temples in Kham and later in central Tibet. Some of his party, including Fazun 法尊 (1902-1980) and Nenghai 能海 (1886-1967), received years of formal training in Tibetan seminaries in Lhasa. After returning to their home communities in the 1930s, they devoted themselves to the spread of Tibetan Buddhism by establishing seminaries and temples, translating texts, producing commentaries, and giving lectures. They also introduced certain doctrines as special inspiration to Chinese Buddhist communities. Nenghai founded a Tibetan Gelug (Wylie: Dge lugs) lineage in Sichuan, promoting Tibetan Buddhism to the followers through a network of branches in Chengdu, Chongqing, Shanghai, and Mount Wutai. Understanding their endeavor as part of a greater, evolving enterprise offers us a new framework through which to perceive Chinese Buddhist modernism.

The repertoire model highlights the importance of people's choices and motivations in selecting and using different elements, which can shape their interpretative strategies. For example, the agendas of the monastic and lay Buddhists differed, influencing their decisions to promote or reject certain esoteric ideas or practices. This is evident in their debate over the authority of lay teachers in the 1920s.

Moreover, the different availability of esoteric Buddhist resources also shaped the various interpretations among Chinese Buddhists. Certain individuals had greater access due to factors such as their proficiency in Tibetan or Japanese languages, ability to travel and attend relevant seminaries, or opportunities to directly interact with esoteric masters. On the other hand, the enthusiasts who lacked knowledge of the original languages had to rely on translated works as their primary source of information. Many people did not have the privilege of receiving formal training or getting access to certain types of esoteric Buddhist practices. The limited information could potentially lead to their narrow, skewed, or biased understanding. But as esoteric Buddhist resources became more accessible to Chinese enthusiasts—a result of the growing translation and publication of the esoteric masters and the circulation of their texts in Chinese cities, as well as the increased opportunities to encounter them—their popularity and influence increased. As a result of a changing historical trajectory, there was a noticeable expansion of esoteric practices among many Chinese Buddhists from the 1910s to the 1940s. Taking a historical approach allows us to identify both thematic continuities and discontinuities over time.

INTRODUCTION

Another advantage of the repertoire concept concerns its ability to preserve the insight into the way that the imported religion and the host culture are both altered in this encounter. Erik Zürcher, Kenneth Ch'en, Nicolas Standaert, John Kieschnick, and Pierce Salguero have shown just how complex the interplay of cross-cultural religious transmission is.[28] Unlike when Buddhism entered China in the first century CE or when missionaries brought Christianity to China in the Ming and Qing dynasties (1368–1911), however, Tibetan and Japanese esoteric Buddhism entered China proper with ideas and practices that were not completely alien to the Han Chinese.[29] Tibetan, Japanese, and Chinese Buddhist traditions agreed on the fundamental assumptions and traced many common teachings to Śākyamuni Buddha. Modern interpreters have often highlighted such common orientations and doctrinal substructures to reduce resistance to the incoming ideas and practices, making the transmission of esoteric Buddhism different from the earlier cases.

Yet esoteric Buddhism nonetheless underwent strategic transmutations in doctrines, praxis, and institutional formations to adapt to norms in the Chinese Buddhist world. For example, drawing on prior knowledge of Chinese Buddhism, Han Buddhists translated Tibetan texts selectively. They emphasized what they regarded as the distinct aspects of Tibetan teachings while highlighting the shared assumptions. In practice, on the one hand, the clergy modeled themselves upon Tibetan monastic training and followed Tibetan traditions in their rituals. On the other hand, they consciously maintained the Chinese monastic codes in their daily practices, rather than supplanting them with precepts prevalent in Tibet. These initiatives facilitated the spread of teachings and won followers. An analysis of the various groups and their interpretations, especially a case study of the lineage founded by Nenghai, would help to reveal these strategic transformations of Tibetan Buddhism.

The repertoire framework emphasizes how the Chinese cultural norms conditioned the interpretative strategies used by Han individuals and groups. They selectively drew on a repertoire of meanings available to them—such as their understanding of the Chinese Buddhist past, the expectations of its role in society, and knowledge of the different ideological discourses—to influence their experience of esoteric Buddhism.

In the late 1910s, Taixu, Dayong, and others aspired to import Japanese esoteric Buddhism to revive Chinese Buddhism. But they soon found that

INTRODUCTION

Japanese Buddhism had transformed over the course of the centuries rather than remain a static and timeless source of knowledge. Dismayed, they hoped to be freshly inspired by Tibetan esoteric Buddhism, which they had once dismissed as a degenerate form of Buddhism. Meanwhile, the ninth Panchen Lama (1883–1937) and other masters attracted significant numbers of followers in Chinese cities. Many communities emerged in association with esoteric Buddhism in the 1930s, and the temples and lay societies provided a space for the different groups to showcase their knowledge and praxis.

The repertoire framework highlights both the tensions on the ground and the historical contingencies that conditioned the transmission. It helps to reveal the ways in which certain agents appropriate, assimilate, or reject a certain idea. In the early twentieth century, Chinese Buddhists faced a major challenge in how to explain the diversity and conflicts of the Buddhist teachings. When Chinese Buddhists borrowed extensively from the Japanese and Tibetan traditions, they needed to account for the divergences. In spite of some advocates' efforts, Chinese Buddhists' attitudes toward esoteric Buddhism ran the gamut from complete adoption to complete rejection. Some new ideas were subject to the close scrutiny of Buddhist intellectuals, and gradually penetrated broader Chinese Buddhist society, whereas other ideas were found by Buddhist intellectuals to be in fundamental conflict with the established standpoints of dominant Chinese Buddhist schools such as Huayan, Tiantai, Pure Land, and Chan. Crossing regional and cultural borders, Dayong, Fazun, Nenghai, and their peers brought new knowledge to their home communities. But in bringing that new knowledge home, they also transformed it, in the process making it more compatible with the established Chinese Buddhist cultures. Emphasizing the human agents' strategies of actions and the circumstances in which they are shaped, the repertoire framework allows us to explore the varied ways in which Chinese Buddhists received and transformed esoteric Buddhism.

The Chinese Buddhists contested the doctrines, customs, rituals, and praxis of various sources. Lacking a centralized interpretative authority, they generated a plurality of discourses. Their contentions reveal as much as their agreements. On the one hand, the shared Indian origins and the Mahāyāna ideal of universal salvation provided common ground. On the other hand, given its broad array of ideas and practices, the compatibility of the esoteric teachings became prominent in the polemics. The conflict was evident in a series of debates in the 1920s and 1930s. While the layman

Wang Hongyuan 王弘願 argued for the superiority of Zhenyan esoteric Buddhism, Dayong, Chisong 持松, and other monks found Wang's claim contradictory to the principle of doctrinal inclusiveness held by the Chinese Tiantai and Huayan schools. In terms of practice, Pure Land practitioners questioned the necessity of the Tibetan lamas' reincarnation, insisting that Amitābha Buddha's land of bliss would be a favorable destiny for all. Meanwhile, Chan Buddhists confronted the ancient Tibetan philosophers' rejection of sudden enlightenment—a central teaching in Chan Buddhism.

Following the Chinese scholarly tradition of doctrinal classification (*panjiao* 判教), some Buddhists tried to systemize the plural teachings and advocate for their coherence. They used different systemization methods and reference points. While some tapped into the intellectual resources of the Tiantai and Huayan schools, others employed interpretive tools from Japanese and Tibetan Buddhist scholasticism. As a result, their responses to esoteric teachings were manifold and often conflicting. They discussed comparable ideas from various sources, striving to find consistency and coherence between them. In the process they brought into conversation the literature of Chinese Buddhism, Japanese Buddhism, and Tibetan Buddhism. This introduction ushered in an unprecedented era of intellectual exchange in Chinese Buddhist history. The combining of old religious elements in new contexts and in response to new forces resulted in reinterpretations and new syntheses.

The repertoire framework moreover reveals why the Chinese Buddhist groups or individuals promoted certain components or aspects of esoteric Buddhism. For example, they turned to esoteric Buddhism for varied reasons, including the need to "restore" Chinese esoteric Buddhism (chapter 1), the belief in its more effective rituals to attain mundane and ultimate goals (chapters 2 and 3), a scholarly framework to systematize the wide range of Buddhist teachings (chapters 4 and 5), and an inclusive institutional structure to combine doctrines and practices (chapter 6). They drew from an array of religious meanings available to them to explain their ritual choices (chapters 1 and 3), doctrinal propositions (chapters 2, 4, and 5), and institutional innovation (chapter 6).

This dynamic and dialectical process entailed an ongoing confluence of ideas and practices, and the interpretations and negotiations of different groups. Going beyond the conventions, the Chinese Buddhists derived knowledge from various sources to apprehend the Buddha's true meanings. At

INTRODUCTION

the same time, they struggled to comprehend the disagreements of the various traditions that developed at different times and in different contexts. Intellectual innovations emerged out of this evolving process of translation and interpretation. *Esoteric Buddhism in China* provides a fuller account of that history of translation and interpretation by considering and accounting for the different groups and their interactions, as well as the social forces that conditioned their communications.

Introducing Nenghai

Nenghai served as a Kuomintang (KMT) battalion commander in Chengdu following the 1911 Revolution. After becoming a fully ordained monk in 1924, he headed to Ganzi 甘孜 (Wylie: Dkar mdzes) to study Tibetan.[30] For three years beginning in 1928, he studied Gelug teachings with the renowned Khangsar Rinpoche (1888–1941) at Drepung Monastery in Lhasa. Returning to Shanghai in 1932, he initiated a new lineage, which would later become the most influential Tibetan Buddhist lineage founded by a Han Chinese.[31] Beginning in the 1930s, he presided over seven temples and attracted followers from all over the country. Despite bans on religion during the Cultural Revolution (1966–1976), the lineage recovered in the 1980s and now thrives with more than twenty affiliated temples in Mount Wutai, Sichuan, Zhejiang, and other provinces.[32]

The introduction was rarely a homogeneous process, and the beginning stages were in particular ridden with conflict. In 1936, four years after returning from Tibet, Nenghai accepted an offer to become abbot at the Thatched Cottage of Vast Salvation (Guangji maopeng 廣濟茅蓬) on Mount Wutai (Wutaishan 五臺山) and started to guide disciples to perform tantric practices that he had learned in Tibet. Yet in the winter of that year, dissension between Nenghai's followers and other resident monks—mainly about monastic management and the esoteric practices—became so pronounced that Nenghai had to leave.

Two years later, Nenghai began his own enterprise and founded a lineage at the Monastery of Approaching Compassion (Jincisi 近慈寺) in Chengdu. Various monastic and lay organizations invited Nenghai to conduct rituals and deliver lectures.[33] Seven branches were incorporated into the lineage and attracted monastic and lay disciples. Moreover, at the height of Jinci

INTRODUCTION

Monastery's flourishing in the 1940s, a large translation center (*yijing yuan* 譯經院) was established there. These extraordinary successes raise the question: What strategies did Nenghai take to accommodate the Tibetan teachings to practices in China proper?

Interactions Among Chinese, Japanese, and Tibetan Buddhists

The Chinese Buddhist world was multiple rather than monolithic. Attitudes toward the Tibetan branch of Buddhism, particularly its tantric components, ranged from support to denunciation. In a narrow sense, Tantric Buddhism refers to systems of practices that derived from "tantra"—basic texts that differ from Mahāyāna literature in terms of effecting rapid transformation through visualization, symbols, and rituals.[34] In a broader sense, Tantric Buddhism can refer variously to one of its complex dimensions. Thus Charles Orzech, Richard Payne, and Henrik H. Sørensen suggest that the words "tantric" or "esoteric" should be contextualized because they describe such a wide range of phenomena.[35] Here I show that the ambiguity of "*mijiao* 密教" (which could be rendered as secret teachings, Tantric Buddhism, or esoteric Buddhism) allowed twentieth-century Buddhists much flexibility in interpreting it to a Chinese audience. Instead of providing a precise definition for that category, I explore what Chinese Buddhists understood and promoted as *mijiao*. I treat the terms "Tantric Buddhism" and "esoteric Buddhism" as interchangeable synonyms, but I tend to use "esoteric Buddhism" when I need to emphasize how it contrasts with "exoteric Buddhism" (*xianjiao* 顯教) or the traditional Mahāyāna teachings.

In the late nineteenth century, when Japanese missionary monks spread Japanese Buddhist teachings to China, and when Buddhist intellectuals like Yang Wenhui 楊文會 (1837–1911) started to contact Buddhists abroad, Chinese Buddhists pursued the study of Japanese Tantric Buddhism.[36] Through the efforts of the early exegetes, a plurality of interpretations emerged. These interpretations explained the newly imported esoteric knowledge in relation to the more familiar ideas of Chinese Buddhism. But some pioneers were dissatisfied with Japanese esoteric Buddhism and shifted their interest to Tibetan Tantrism in the 1920s.[37] Such pioneers typically believed that Tibet had inherited the sacred legacy originating in India and that it preserved much of the mature teachings of Tantrism.[38] Others found Tibetan

[12]

INTRODUCTION

Tantrism to be a decadent form of Buddhism, a mixture of magic and Brahmanism.³⁹ Yinshun 印順 (1906–2005), for example, denounced certain later forms of tantric practices developed in Indian Buddhism as "superstitious, debauched, and decadent" and "offering no benefit for mind or body."⁴⁰ Between these two extremes lay a spectrum of opinion. Yet dissension regarding the authority and authenticity of Tantric teachings—which constituted a large body of the introduced texts and practices—never abated among Chinese Buddhists. In Buddhist periodicals published during the Republican era, we find numerous essays written by the enthusiasts and critics defending their respective positions. The controversy involved not only monastic and lay leaders but also ordinary followers from a wide range of backgrounds.

To show that different Chinese groups viewed and interpreted esoteric Buddhism in a variety of ways, I examine diverse voices in the Chinese Buddhist communities, including those of advocates, opponents, and the ensuing controversies between them. An analysis of such materials indicates not only that perceptions and levels of knowledge about esoteric Buddhism differed among Chinese Buddhists, but also that their opinions changed as that knowledge and information accumulated over time. Their interpretations were informed not only by their religious needs but also by their social circumstances. For example, propositions made by the Chinese advocates were not always in line with the original Japanese or Tibetan standards. These discrepancies should not be dismissed as misunderstandings. As Robert Campany's study of the influence of Buddhism on Chinese Daoism shows, ancient Daoists appropriated Buddhist concepts, values, and conventions to create narratives to meet their needs in a particular context. Some of the Daoist interpretations may look like misunderstandings when measured against the norms of Buddhist teachings. But when examined in the particular circumstance, many seeming discrepancies can be explained as the Daoists' strategic reinterpretation.⁴¹ For the same reason, I investigate the Chinese interpretations of the Tibetan and Japanese esoteric teachings in the local circumstances rather than against the norms in Japan or Tibet. Doing so shows how the expectations, assumptions, and aspirations of the different agents influenced their interpretations.

The rise of the modern notion of Buddhism as a "world religion" also altered Chinese Buddhists' conception of Tibetan Buddhism.⁴² Following the 1893 World's Parliament of Religions in Chicago, Chinese Buddhists began to conceive of Buddhism as a world religion consisting of various branches that developed in different contexts. This conception helped to create a pan-Asian Tibetan-Sino religious identity among many Buddhists.[43] The Chinese perceived Tibetan Buddhism, as well as Japanese and Chinese Buddhism, as shared branches growing out of an original truth. From this perspective, esoteric Buddhism was a complex interplay of customs, beliefs, and rituals shared across the spectrum of Buddhism. For the Buddhist reformer Taixu, the revival of Chinese Buddhism entailed the restoration of an "esoteric sect" of the Tang dynasty through reintroducing esoteric Buddhism from non-Chinese Buddhist traditions.

Following Holmes Welch's discussion of the rise of esoteric Buddhism, scholars have uncovered more facets of Japanese and Tibetan Buddhism in twentieth-century China.[44] Chen Bing, Deng Zimei, Mei Jingxuan, Huang Ying-chieh, Françoise Wang-Toutain, and Ester Bianchi have written about the major figures and their roles in promoting esoteric teachings.[45] Gray Tuttle has investigated the role of Tibetan Buddhism in the making of the modern nation-state after the collapse of the Qing dynasty.[46] And Martino Dibeltulo has detailed the ways in which European philology altered Chinese Buddhists' conceptualization of Tibetan Buddhism.[47]

In *Esoteric Buddhism in China* I raise new questions and draw on untapped resources. For example, scholars have rarely discussed what the Han pilgrims wanted to learn, and what they sought from Japan and Tibet. So I ask: After they entered the Chinese priesthood, what dissatisfied these Han pilgrims about Chinese Buddhism, and what did they think other Buddhist traditions could offer in its place? Which elements did they choose to follow, and which ones did they ignore? To penetrate the process of reinterpretation and reconstruction of traditions requires analyzing the specific ideas, practices, and institutions they adopted. Finally, how do we understand their experience in the larger context of pan-Asia Buddhist reform movements in the twentieth century?

Some scholars have characterized the transmission as fundamentally a Tantric Buddhist movement, and indeed tantric texts constituted a large portion of the translated corpus.[48] As Chen Bing and Deng Zimei estimated, in the Republican period, the Buddhists translated two- to three-hundred types of mantras and tantric manuals from Tibetan to Chinese.[49] For unlike some Buddhist intellectuals who discredited devotional practices as superstitions, Dayong, Nenghai, and other promoters never tried to deemphasize rituals.⁵⁰ Daily mantra chanting, making offerings to deities, and attending tantric ceremonies were indispensable practices for both clergy and laity in Nenghai's lineage. For them, personal experience in ritualistic practices reinforced doctrinal learning. Nonetheless, exoteric or nontantric components were also essential elements in the translation and interpretation.

In addition to tantric practice, the philosophical richness of Tibetan Buddhism also drove Chinese Buddhists to pursue formal training in Tibetan seminaries. Dayong, Fazun, and Nenghai highly appreciated the sophistication of Tibetan commentarial tradition. They translated and preached on several important commentaries that constituted the foundation of Tibetan Buddhist scholasticism.⁵¹ Their experience reflects the difference in textual traditions in the two cultural circumstances: Tibetan Buddhist canonical texts outnumber Chinese Buddhist canonical texts by a third.⁵² This difference is attributable in large part to the thriving commentarial and tantra traditions in Tibetan Buddhism: the number of commentaries in the Tibetan Buddhist canon is double that in the Chinese Buddhist canon, and many Tibetan tantric texts are not available in the Chinese canon.⁵³

Scholars have investigated important intellectual trends in the late Qing and Republican era, but rarely in Chinese Buddhists' discussion of Tibetan commentaries.⁵⁴ Some Tibetan Buddhist philosophical classics were only introduced to China during this period. A case in point was some Chinese Buddhist leaders' promulgation of *Lamrim Chenmo* (*Great Treatise on the Stages of the Path to Enlightenment*, henceforth the *Great Treatise*, Wylie: *Lam rim chen mo*, Ch. *Puti dao cidi guanglun* 菩提道次第廣論), which was composed by the Gelug founder Tsongkhapa (1357–1419) and translated into Chinese by Fazun in 1934. Taixu, Fazun, and Nenghai valued this treatise for systemizing Buddhist doctrines and providing specific instructions for practitioners with a range of capacities.⁵⁵

Although translation facilitated religious exchange, the processes of interpretation and reinterpretation also played a part. By incorporating both Tibetan and Chinese teachings, the Han Buddhists managed to reorganize esoteric Buddhist knowledge into a system compatible with the Chinese Buddhist tradition. For example, based on the framework of a staged path to enlightenment, Nenghai created a graduated training program to educate his disciples.⁵⁶ In actual practice they used not only the newly imported Tibetan literature but also the traditional Chinese works as a guide. Nenghai's teachings and practices were therefore inclusive and syncretic, and they cannot be characterized simply as "Tibetan" or "Tantric."

The creative and syncretic nature was obvious in Nenghai's institution building. While Nenghai promulgated the Gelug teachings, he strived to build and maintain close connections with the local Chinese Buddhist community. In the system of clerical training he created, education began with the general courses open to all monastic members and led to the esoteric practice that was reserved exclusively for authorized practitioners.[57] In the lectures, he often downplayed the doctrinal conflicts between the Chinese and Tibetan Buddhist teachings. He insisted on vegetarianism and continued to observe the Dharmagupta Vinaya (Sifenlü 四分律, Four-Part Vinaya) that dominated in Chinese monasticism, rather than Mūlasarvāstivādin Vinaya that prevailed in Tibet.[58] His erudition in Buddhist knowledge, his close interaction with the local Buddhist community, and his ability to build an institution to accommodate disciples of different needs were all conducive to the founding of his lineage.

I therefore explore in this book the multifaceted ways in which different parties in Republican-era China have perceived, identified, and appropriated Tibetan and Japanese esoteric Buddhist ideas and practices. More specifically, I show how this reception was shaped by the profound transformations that came with certain Han Chinese people's embrace of "modernity." Insofar as my focus in this book is the representation and engagement of esoteric Buddhist practices on the part of Chinese-speaking Buddhists, Chinese language source materials remain the principal medium. I investigate Chinese Buddhists' reception, discussion, and reformulation of what they perceived as important in esoteric Buddhism. In so doing, I also seek to reconstruct the various Buddhist environments, regimes of cultural practice, modalities of sociohistorical imaginary, and societal circumstances at large, through which representative forms of Chinese Buddhist accommodation and transformation of esoteric Buddhism were generated.

To those ends, I draw on a wide range of previously unexplored Chinese sources. During the period under study, Chinese individuals obtained esoteric Buddhist knowledge through various means, including reading translated texts, attending sermons, patronizing ritual ceremonies, joining societies, meeting the masters, having dialogues with other Buddhists, and more. The Chinese writings and publications can inform and illustrate the conditions

INTRODUCTION

under which esoteric Buddhism was interpreted in certain contexts. For example, chapter 1 and chapter 3 explore a variety of materials (including speeches, periodical articles, letters, advertisements, memoirs, and commentaries), the contents of which provide direct insight into the transcultural and translingual interactions that took place between influential Tibetan lamas (the ninth Panchen Lama, Norlha Lama, and others) and the different Chinese groups (monks, laypeople, politicians, warlords, educators, and others) who came into contact with them. The sources in question allow me to investigate how Tibetan Buddhist ideas and practices were selectively communicated to, circulated among, and interpreted by the Chinese recipients. Also, to understand Nenghai's interpretation of the Tibetan doctrines, my study focuses on a specific genre of Chinese writing—lecture notes (*biji* 筆記, also rendered as *ji* 記 or *jiangji* 講記). These notes were written by Nenghai or made by his disciples during the sermons, and with Nenghai's approval were circulated among the disciples as a learning guide. A reading of the notes helps us to understand the ways in which Nenghai interpreted the Tibetan Buddhist teachings for his disciples, many of whom had some prior knowledge of Chinese Buddhism and were confused about the divergences. I emphasize his representation of the distinctive features of Tibetan Buddhism and his strategy to explain the doctrinal and praxis conflicts. I also employ memoirs, biographies, and letters to help recover the thought and activities of Nenghai and his contemporaries.[59] The recent publication of the Buddhist periodicals of the Republican era enabled me to trace the early history of the main figures in detail, and to investigate the contests between proponents and critics in the 1920s and 1930s.[60] My study also relies on my visits to private collections and archives in China in 2009 and 2013. Interviews with Nenghai's Dharma descendants provided information about recent developments in the lineage. I gained access to the unpublished manuscripts of Nenghai in temples at Mount Wutai, Sichuan, and Zhejiang. Archives in Beijing and Sichuan provided me with information to contextualize the rise of esoteric Buddhism in the first decades of twentieth-century China and to show more specifically the ways in which the transmission of Tibetan Buddhism enriched Chinese Buddhism—doctrinally, ritually, and institutionally—and thus influenced the religious landscape of modern China. My research on the interactions between Buddhist traditions also aims to shed light on cross-cultural and transregional religious transmission.

INTRODUCTION

Rethinking Buddhist Modernity

The transmission of esoteric Buddhism provides a new lens through which we can view Buddhist modernity in China. In the second half of the twentieth century, Buddhist modernism and its key aspects began to attract scholarly attention. In Heinz Bechert's pioneering work on Buddhist modernity, for instance, he focused on demythologization—the shift away from rituals and the deemphasis on image worship—characterized the movement of modernization in Burma and Ceylon.[61] Scripturalism—the emphasis on rational reasoning and study of canonical texts, as well as a central emphasis on meditation, was a concurrent trend that gained momentum in many Buddhist communities in Asia.[62] By locating Buddhism in the larger social context, scholars provided in-depth analyses of the phenomena across Asia, such as Engaged Buddhism in southeast Buddhist traditions, Humanistic Buddhism in Taiwan, and Nichiren Buddhism in Japan.[63] These works add greatly to our understanding by documenting the interplay between Buddhist modernism, social reforms, and nationalist movements in Asia.

More recently, David McMahan has adopted Charles Taylor's theory to examine the impacts of modernity on Buddhism in Asia and in the West. According to Taylor, the modern world rests on three sources of morality and identity: the Protestant Reformation, the Enlightenment, and Romanticism. The Protestant Reformation challenged the authority of a hierarchical church and rejected external mediation, calling instead for the devotee's inner commitment; the Enlightenment advanced reasoning as the basis of human inquiry; and Romanticism affirmed inner feelings as a natural and valuable source of knowledge. These three trends together constituted the moral frameworks that underlie the development of religions in the past five centuries.[64] In *The Making of Buddhist Modernism*, McMahan refers to Taylor's theory to show that Buddhism also transformed itself to cope with these trends of the modern West. For example, following the discourses of Enlightenment, many Buddhists attempted to purge the superstitious and mythological components from Buddhism, which resulted in the trends of deritualization and demythologization in many Asian Buddhist traditions.[65] McMahan's study greatly deepened the discussion of Buddhist modernity by showing how the broader cultural and moral patterns that emerged in modernity facilitated the reinvention of Buddhism in many Asian and Western countries.

INTRODUCTION

The transforming Chinese Buddhism shared many features of Buddhist modernity in other regions of Asia. Numerous scholarly works have explored the common trends that emerged in Chinese Buddhism in addition to demythologization and scripturalism, such as the rise of the laity, participation in social welfare, and engagement with science and technology.

Modernity helps to elucidate various dynamics that influenced the Chinese reception of esoteric Buddhism. In this book I examine factors such as monastic institutional reform, the active involvement of the laity, the emergence of Buddhist publications, and the scholarly study of Buddhism. Many of these aspects are related to scientific rationalism, one of the main trends that McMahan identifies as shaping Buddhist modernism.[66] The circulation of information through publications led to an unprecedented awareness among many Chinese individuals of the plurality of Buddhist teachings in the 1920s and 1930s, and Chinese Buddhist scholars engaged in debates over esoteric Buddhist ideas and practices. Their discussions reveal a spectrum of attitudes toward the imported ideas, with some scholars expressing skepticism and others assuming an embracing stance. The discussion also sparked an inquiry into the doctrinal, ritual, and institutional aspects of these ideas, which were frequently compared to those in the established Chinese Buddhist traditions. My investigation highlights that many Chinese Buddhists tended to approach esoteric Buddhism with a rational perspective.

But Chinese Buddhism also exhibited many coexistent and conflicting trends, some of which challenged (and exposed the inefficiency of) common assumptions about Buddhist modernity. One apt example is the increasing practice of esoteric rituals at a personal and communal level in the first decades of the twentieth century. On the one hand, echoing the modern trope of demythologization, the Republican government launched campaigns of iconoclasm to replace religious affiliation with national passion in the 1920s.[67] The local governments attacked religions as outdated and as a hindrance to nation-building. In many cities and towns, the believers were mobilized to discard their "superstitious" ritualistic practice. Based on these nationalistic discourses, the Buddhist critics who suspected the authenticity of esoteric Buddhism took a solid stand against its rituals. They rejected the use of violent, sexual, or vigorous images in esoteric rituals, claiming that involvement with mystery would only perpetuate a negative image of Buddhism.

INTRODUCTION

On the other hand, the public performance of esoteric rituals provoked great interest among many Buddhists. From the 1920s to the late 1940s, Tibetan ritual specialists and their disciples in Beijing, Shanghai, Hangzhou, and many other cities openly performed massive ceremonies. These rituals attracted people of all kinds, ranging from high-ranking officers and businessmen to students and housewives. For example, the ninth Panchen Lama Thubten Choekyi Nyima presided over the Kālacakra Vajra Dharma-Ceremony in the imperial palace in Beijing in 1932, which attracted one hundred thousand people.[68] Another Kālacakra Vajra ceremony in Hangzhou in 1934 was also widely reported, with over seventy thousand attending the event.[69] The public display of esoteric rituals helped to popularize the practice of Tibetan esoteric Buddhism. The devotees claimed that esoteric rituals provided a more effective means to attain this-worldly and transcendent ends, from personal success in mundane affairs to the altruistic goal of liberating all sentient beings from suffering. The popularity of these ceremonies suggested that miracles and efficacy remained strong motivations for people to participate in Buddhist activities.

To many adherents, esoteric teachings were the chief appeal of Tibetan and Japanese Buddhism. The adherents devoted themselves to the translation of ritual texts, learning about them from Buddhist teachers, and becoming empowered to perform the rituals. As a result, the influx of esoteric Buddhist ideas and practices helped to generate diverse forms of rituals. Chapters 1 and 2 focus on esoteric rituals as a way of introducing Tibetan and Japanese Buddhism. Esoteric rituals performed at personal and communal levels, where mythology and efficacy continued to draw adherents to religion, challenged the general assumption about Buddhist modernism in Asia. In contrast to the demythologizing and deemphasis of rituals that characterized many modern forms of religions, esoteric rituals constituted a substantial part in the rise of Tibetan and Japanese Buddhism in modern China. By referring to the traditional Buddhist theories and the newly emerged nationalistic discourses, adherents developed a variety of discourses to justify embracing them. Their daily practices and important discussions demonstrate the transformation of esoteric Buddhism in modern China.

Another noticeable trend in Buddhist modernism is the emphasis on meditation as a central practice of Buddhism. Although recent scholarship has shown that historically meditation did not occupy a dominant place in monastic life, some influential Theravada and Zen Buddhists in the nineteenth and twentieth centuries promoted meditation as a core of Buddhism. According to scholars such as McMahan and Robert Sharf, this focus on inner experience can be understood as a modern response to rationalism and the influence of Romanticism.[70] McMahan points out that decontextualization, individualization, and psychologization of meditation have transformed it from a practice deeply embedded in Buddhist cosmology, ethics, and community to a technique prioritized by many Buddhists in Asia and the West, but divorced from its original contexts.[71]

In contrast, when learning esoteric meditation, Chinese practitioners generally did not prioritize it as separate from other traditional practices. Instead, they tended to situate their understanding of the recently learned esoteric meditation within traditional Buddhist frameworks of cosmology, ethics, and community. Many Chinese Buddhists drew heavily from the available legacy and cultural traditions of Chinese Buddhism. They saw esoteric meditation as a means to serve the shared goals of Mahāyāna Buddhism, with doctrines such as enlightenment, bodhisattva ideal, and skillful means playing an essential part in this understanding. Buddhist cosmology, including the idea of rebirth in six realms, as well as the soteriological aims such as liberation from cyclic existence and universal salvation, continued to influence the Chinese Buddhists.

Moreover, many Chinese practitioners of esoteric Buddhism combined meditation and commentarial literature. Similar patterns can be found in other regions of Asia. For example, as Erik Braun has shown, Ledi Sayadaw, a Burmese monk who pioneered the Insight movement in the late nineteenth century, promoted meditation alongside the study of Pali Buddhist commentaries.[72] Likewise, Dayong, Fazun, Nenghai, and other Chinese adepts introduced esoteric meditation alongside Tibetan commentarial works, especially those related to the stages of the path to enlightenment. They also believed that these commentaries provide valuable knowledge to assist their meditative practice.

These examples complicate the commonly held narratives of Buddhist modernism and reveal a diversity of forms. As McMahan has noted, Buddhist modernity is not homogeneous but shaped by historical and cultural factors.[73] In *Esoteric Buddhism in China* I affirm this idea by illustrating how human agents in specific contexts selectively appropriate a configuration of elements from a repertoire to construct various discourses. As a result, the Chinese reception of esoteric Buddhism simultaneously displays certain patterns of modernity while also countering them.⁷⁴ Along with modernity's role in shaping all religious phenomena in modern Asia, the Buddhists' prior knowledge of Chinese Buddhist traditions and the tensions in the immediate circumstances also deeply influenced their reception.

Comparison and Representation of Esoteric Buddhism

Beyond addressing the rise of esoteric Buddhism in modern China, I also look more broadly at the Chinese Buddhists' engagement with Tibetan and Japanese Buddhism. How was their interpretation a powerful source in helping them to cope with a rapidly changing context? Which parties played important roles in the translation and interpretation? How was it influenced by their understanding of Chinese reality? Decisions on what to appropriate and what to reject were contingent on their acknowledgment of the previously dominant rites and customs, theories, and practices, as well as their views of what was lacking in Chinese Buddhism. Together, these discourses provide a portrait of the introduction of esoteric Buddhism and form a basis for us to discuss the factors that shaped this process.

To emphasize the dialectical process of interpretation, I examine various groups' representations of esoteric Buddhism in their specific cultural contexts beginning with the earliest pioneers who introduced Japanese and Tibetan esoteric Buddhism in the late 1910s and early 1920s. Chapter 1 investigates Taixu and Dayong's initiatives in introducing esoteric Buddhism in the 1910s and 1920s. In 1915, in Taixu's famous blueprint "The Reorganization of the Sangha System," he envisioned a systematic introduction of esoteric Buddhism from non-Chinese traditions as part of the larger project of reviving Chinese Buddhism. He imagined a revival of Chinese Buddhism that would restore the eight mainstream schools of the Tang dynasty, the era in which Buddhism came to prominence in ancient China. A school to be revived was the Zhenyan school (Zhenyanzong 真言宗) or Kaiyuan school (Kaiyuanzong 開元宗), which was known for esoteric teachings but had declined after the ninth-century persecution.⁷⁵

Taixu's reformative discourse provided a powerful rationale for introducing Japanese and Tibetan Buddhist traditions into China. In the early 1920s, his disciple Dayong traveled to Japan with several monks to study esoteric rituals, hoping to bring back the lost teachings. But as their knowledge of

INTRODUCTION

Japanese Buddhism increased, Taixu and Dayong were struck by the transformations that Buddhism had undergone in Japan over the centuries. Dayong suggested that Tibetan Buddhism preserved esoteric teachings in a much richer and more intact format. With support from the lay patrons, Taixu and Dayong therefore built a Tibetan college in Beijing in 1924, aiming to prepare students to learn and to translate aspects of Tibetan Buddhism. The next year, Dayong and his students traveled to pursue learning at Tibetan temples. Among them, Fazun and Nenghai translated a number of Tibetan commentary texts and greatly expanded the scope of philosophical communication between the two traditions.

Analyzing the conflicting discourses regarding the legitimacy of esoteric rituals, chapter 2 investigates the religious and political trends that shaped Chinese Buddhists' reception of esoteric rituals. The dissemination of esoteric Buddhism was concurrent with Chinese Buddhism's transformation when Chinese Buddhists endeavored to adapt their tradition to a dramatically changing society. After the collapse of the Qing dynasty, the Republican government unified religious and political goals by building connections with Tibetans through Buddhism. Panchen Lama's exile to China proper inspired particular interest among some Chinese Buddhists in the 1920s and 1930s. At the same time, Chinese Buddhism faced attacks from the radical nationalistic intellectuals in anti-superstitious campaigns. In this chapter I suggest that the proponents of esoteric practices faced internal and external pressures to justify their acts. When they joined the efforts to appropriate nationalistic discourses to substantiate the social function of Buddhism against criticism from radical intellectuals, they simultaneously strived for a lessening of suspicion from other Chinese Buddhists. When they struggled to defend their beliefs by separating "Buddhism" and "superstition," they also generated meanings to define esoteric Buddhism as a system of authentic Buddhist teachings. They found theoretical grounds not only in the modern concepts such as "world religion," but also in the traditional Chinese Buddhist history and philosophy.

The rise of esoteric Buddhism intertwined with concurrent dynamics in the Chinese Buddhist community, including the ascendance of lay Buddhism. In chapter 3 I look at the history of important lay individuals and organizations as a means to explore the cooperation and conflicts between various Buddhist groups. From the 1910s onward, the idea that esoteric Buddhism offered a more effective method to enlightenment had special significance in the introduction of Tibetan Buddhism. A wide variety of esoteric texts in translation and lectures given by charismatic Tibetan religious teachers added to the appeal of this form of Buddhism. Many followers believed that they could realize enlightenment more quickly through the use of spells, hand signs, and ritual diagrams. More than simply patronizing the esoteric activities, lay Buddhists were actively involved in their introduction by translating, preaching, and performing rituals. In addition, lay supporters opened several lay societies in Beijing, Tianjin, Guangzhou, Shanghai, Wuhan, Jiangxi, and Hong Kong that served as important platforms to facilitate communications between different Buddhist traditions.

As more and more texts and rites were translated and performed, a growing sentiment emerged regarding the divergences. The Chinese Buddhists keenly disputed the imported knowledge, and this greatly galvanized intellectual developments. Advocates suggested that esoteric Buddhism, if properly appropriated, could do much to further the spiritual goals of personal and universal salvation. Critics, however, rejected esoteric Buddhism not only on ritualistic grounds but also on doctrinal and moral grounds. Much of their unease with esoteric Buddhism involved suspicion of the origin of the esoteric rituals and the theories behind them. They raised issues of authenticity and congruence, seeing certain elements as evidence of esoteric Buddhism's mixing with non-Buddhist, degenerate practices.

As I show in chapter 4, a debate on the categorization of esoteric Buddhism provided the most pronounced example of the doctrinal controversy about esoteric Buddhism in the 1920s. The debate involved Taixu, Wang Hongyuan, and other important Buddhist thinkers who tried to compare esoteric Buddhism with the prevalent Chinese traditions, such as Huayan, Tiantai, Chan, and Pure Land. The importation of esoteric Buddhist knowledge galvanized intellectual creativity in the Chinese Buddhist communities. Various groups interpreted the myriad esoteric ideas and practices differently, their views preconditioned by their prior knowledge of Chinese Buddhism and the current concerns of the Buddhist community. The binary concepts of "esoteric Buddhism" and "exoteric Buddhism" were particularly susceptible to redefinition and renegotiation by Chinese Buddhists, who disputed the validity of "esoteric Buddhism" as a taxonomic category in contrast to "exoteric Buddhism." Looking into the most debated issues, I analyze how the concepts of esoteric Buddhism and exoteric Buddhism were contested in Chinese Buddhist community to reveal the tensions in the translative and

INTRODUCTION

interpretative process, as well as the shaping forces in the doctrinal interaction between Chinese and non-Chinese Buddhist traditions.

The transmission of esoteric Buddhism involved an interpretative process by which Chinese Buddhists continuously generated meanings for the newly obtained teachings. The proponents of esoteric Buddhism not only learned and translated texts but also had to adjudicate the doctrinal conflicts with the preexisting Chinese Buddhist philosophical structures. Chapter 5 shows that proponents of esoteric Buddhism also applauded Tibetan commentaries for offering a practical framework for approaching many important scriptures that were available in the Chinese Buddhist canon. In chapter 5 I examine innovations and doctrinal interpretations in which certain Tibetan elements were represented as particularly inspirational to Chinese Buddhists. Nenghai presented *lamrim*, or stages of the path to enlightenment, as an alternative framework by which to integrate scholarly learning and meditative practice. His representation can be understood as a response to the tensions in the modern Chinese Buddhist community regarding the proper relation between study and practice.

Chapter 6 presents a case study to illustrate the dynamics of the introduction of esoteric Buddhism on Buddhist institutions in modern China. I examine the Gelug lineage founded in Chengdu by Nenghai, which was constituted of ethnically Han Chinese devotees. By tracing the founding history of Jinci Monastery in the 1930s and 1940s, I investigate the adaptation of Tibetan Buddhism to the local Buddhist community. Using Nenghai's works, biographies, and Buddhist periodicals as my basis, I show how Nenghai and his disciples created an institution with elements from both Tibetan and Chinese Buddhist traditions, which helped to maintain the lineage's distinctions while sustaining a close connection with the larger Chinese Buddhist community. I also demonstrate in chapter 6 how many Chinese Buddhists tried to rationalize such a synthesis by referring to the traditional Chinese Buddhist philosophy. Instead of describing esoteric Buddhism in general terms, I suggest that their forms and expressions were inflected by various particular discourses and considerations, and that in this process, the notion of esoteric Buddhism assumed a variety of meanings at different time periods and in different cultural circumstances. These meanings may be specific to certain groups and reflect the cultural contexts with which they identified. The Buddhist groups' varying attitudes to esoteric Buddhism reveal the different visions of Chinese Buddhism at a modern time.

ONE

Chinese Buddhism in Transition

AT DAWN ON October 9, 1932, the serenity of the Forbidden City in Beijing was broken by a raucous crowd in the Hall of Supreme Harmony (Taihedian 太和殿). The grandiose hall had long served as the ceremonial center of imperial power: this was where the Ming (1368–1644) and Qing (1644–1911) emperors had held their enthronements. After the collapse of the Qing dynasty and a short-lived restoration of the monarchy in 1915 the hall remained quiet for a long time. An elegant arch had been set up over the red-carpeted entrance, and the hall had been adorned with flowers. When a limousine arrived, a massive crowd hustled to see the guest: the ninth Panchen Lama, who at that time was in exile in China proper and held the second highest rank in the Gelug school of Tibetan Buddhism after the Dalai Lama. The lama was ushered into a yellow sedan-chair, and two attendants carried him up to the magnificent hall. His seat in the western chamber had been thoughtfully arranged, covered with yellow embroidered cushions and silk carpets that had once belonged to the Qianlong Emperor.[1]

The Panchen Lama had been invited to preside over a massive and lengthy public ritual called the Kālacakra Vajra Dharma-Ceremony (Shilun jingang fahui 時輪金剛法會) intended to serve religious as well as political ends. Over the next ten days, the Panchen Lama and thirty-two assistant monks chanted mantras, performed hand mudrās, and built a sand maṇḍala to "pacify calamities and protect the state." They also conferred initiation rituals that admitted disciples into esoteric Buddhist practices. Newspapers reported that attendance was unprecedented, reaching one hundred thousand. The guests included some of the most powerful military and political leaders in the city, some of whom received initiations from the lama.[2]

Subsequently, the Beijing Kālacakra Vajra Dharma-Ceremony was widely publicized, and the Panchen Lama's fame spread among the Chinese. In 1934, he was invited to the Temple of Hidden Efficacy (Lingyinsi 靈隱寺) in Hangzhou to host another Kālacakra Vajra Dharma-Ceremony, attracting seventy thousand attendees.[3] Kālacakra is an advanced esoteric ritual based on the vision of Shambhala Kingdom, a Buddhist pure land where a powerful Dharma king and his invincible army reside. The initiation empowers recipients to practice the Kālacakra tantra to achieve Buddhahood. Some Chinese Buddhists became enamored with Tibetan esoteric liturgy, finding it more systemized and comprehensive than the conventional Buddhist practices in China. They proclaimed that Tibetan esoteric rituals can not only bring favorable results in the mundane world, but also provide a more promising path toward spiritual salvation. A monk named Changxing 常惺 touted the superiority of the Kālacakra ceremony by comparing it to several traditional rites in China:

> Exoteric and esoteric teachings in the western frontiers are more comprehensive than we have.... From the 1911 Revolution to the present, war, flood, and drought continuously plagued the country. Our clergy occasionally performed the traditional Rite for the Deliverance of Creatures of Water and Land [*shuilu fahui* 水陸法會] to pacify the dead, but the effect was finite. With the blessing of the Kālacakra deities, the dead can be reborn in Shambhala and attain salvation. Moreover, even visitors attending the Kālacakra ceremony out of curiosity rather than seeking to learn Dharma, on hearing the bell or glancing at the maṇḍala, will have accumulated sufficient merit to be reborn in the Shambhala Kingdom.[4]

The Chinese Buddhists' fascination with tantric rituals was accompanied by heightened criticism from other Buddhists. In spite of the extraordinary public attendance, the 1934 ceremony drew censure from Buddhist and non-Buddhist writers. The Buddhist authors doubted the authenticity of Tibetan esoteric Buddhism, viewing the imagery as a mixture of Indian and Tibetan cults. An editorial in the *Voice of Sea Tide* dismissed Shambhala Kingdom as a fable circulated among the Tibetans, suggesting that, with questionable provenance, Tibetan esoteric rituals could not embody Śākyamuni Buddha's original teachings.[5] Simultaneously, outside the Buddhist fold, secular writers lambasted the participation of the high officials in the ceremony. Acknowledging the politicians' intention to strengthen ties with the Tibetans by endorsing the ceremony, the writers reprimanded them for participating in rituals. The *China Times* (*Shishi xinbao* 時事新報) derided the attempt by some politicians to connect religious rituals with a national agenda. An editorial mocked the political patrons—such as Minister Dai Jitao 戴季陶 and his notion of "saving the country through scriptures and mantras," envisioning instead a modern nation-state relying on science and institutional reforms. The editorial states:

> The Tibetans sincerely worship Buddha, but we are just fawning on Buddha. The Tibetans believe in Buddha but we are just cheating ourselves. Can the chanting at the West Lake of Hangzhou be heard at the remote border? The high elites of the Republican nation swarmed to the religious ceremony. Are they insinuating to the common, uneducated people that the resolution to the international and domestic calamities is not science or self-strengthening, but prostration in the wafting smoke of incense?[6]

The dissonant responses to tantric rituals reveal the tensions in the appropriation of Tibetan Buddhism in early twentieth-century China. The introduction of esoteric Buddhism was concurrent with the modern transformation of Chinese Buddhism. When Buddhist reformers adapted their tradition to a dramatically changing society, many sought spiritual solutions from non-Chinese Buddhist traditions. The importation of esoteric Buddhist teachings and practices, however, should not be conceptualized as the transplantation of an intact, holistic cultural body from the Tibetan plateau or the Japanese islands to China proper. Rather, as I argue, in an on-going process between various agent groups, the practices and theories were being constantly reinterpreted in the specific circumstances. In this chapter I further explore the rise of esoteric Buddhism and its effects in the Chinese Buddhist communities in the 1910s and 1920s. The conceptualization of "esoteric Buddhism" was elusive and subject to interpretation by different actors throughout the process. This lengthy negotiation was not only contingent upon Chinese Buddhists' preconceived knowledge of Buddhist teachings, but also rested on their very understanding of Chinese Buddhist history, as well as the challenges faced by Buddhism in a modern era.

Chinese Buddhism in Transition

The 1911 Revolution brought the collapse of the Qing dynasty and ended two millennia of imperial rule in China. Nonetheless, the newly founded Beiyang government failed to unify the nation, and warlord battles caused regional disorder before the Northern Expedition in 1927. Vincent Goossaert and David Palmer have explored how ideologies of constructing a consolidated state affected government policies and the religious landscape in the late Qing and Republican periods.[7] Yoshiko Ashiwa and David Wank have examined how neologism "religion" (zongjiao 宗教), imported during the late Qing from Europe and Japan, eventually resulted in the formation of five officially recognized religions in modern China: Buddhism, Daoism, Islam, Protestantism, and Catholicism.[8] To exclude superstition and folk beliefs from officially approved religious activities, reformers attempted to sort a wide range of previously undistinguished practices into one of two categories, either "religion" or "superstition." In this way, the revolutionary intellectuals convinced the government that the religious paradigm should be organized to accommodate the state-making process.

Between 1911 and 1927, the central government in Beijing carried out a series of legal and administrative measures to tighten control over religion. As a response, the Buddhist reformer Taixu and other leaders started to consolidate the Buddhist institution while lobbying the state to protect religious freedom. In 1912, a group of Buddhists established the first national Buddhist association, the Chinese Buddhist Federation (Zhonghua fojiao zonghui 中華佛教總會), to coordinate the efforts of twenty-two provincial branches and more than four hundred sub-branches.[9] Nonetheless, instead of acknowledging the legitimacy of the Buddhist federation, the Beiyang government issued the "Provisional Regulations on Temple Management" (Simiao guanli zanxiu tiaoli 寺廟管理暫修條例) in 1913, which allowed local governments to confiscate temple properties that depended on public donations for construction and maintenance. The regulation resulted in the closure of many temples and the disbanding of clergy.

Compared to the tightening control over religion in general, the state policy toward Tibetan temples was more favorable partly as a result of increasing frontier tensions. The collapse of the Qing dynasty led to the repatriation of the imperial troops from Lhasa in 1912. More broadly, the Republic of China's nationalistic rhetoric and feeble military power failed to hold together the former territories of the Qing. Buddhism, therefore, became an alternative way to cement links and advance rapprochement between Tibet and China.[10] Despite the revolutionaries' fervor to sever all ties with the past, the state selectively maintained the Qing court's conciliatory policy toward senior Mongolian and Tibetan lamas. For instance, Changkya Khutukhtu (Zhangjia Hutuketu 章嘉呼圖克圖, 1891–1957), the spiritual head of the Gelug lineage of Tibetan Buddhism in Inner Mongolia, was one of the most esteemed lamas in the Qing court and had served as a preceptor to the Qing emperors. After 1912, the Republican state continued to confer honorable titles on him. With state support, Changkya Khutukhtu secured his prestige and position of power, maintaining command over Gelug temples in Inner Mongolia, Beijing, Rehe, and Mount Wutai.

Aware that the state selectively supported Tibetan Buddhism, some Chinese Buddhist leaders sought to align their appeals of religious protection with the ideology of nation-building. When lobbying the Beiyang government, they also tried to leverage Changkya Khutukhtu's influence to protect monastic properties from state confiscation. In 1913, Daoxing 道興 and Daojie 道階—vice president and secretary of the Chinese Buddhist Federation—met with Changkya Khutukhtu in Beijing. They invited him to join and lead the federation as its president.[11] In a subsequent statement addressing all its provincial branches, the federation proclaimed that Han Buddhists should usher in "an era of religious coalition" with the Tibetans and Mongolians under Sun Yat-sen's principle of "five races under one union (wuzu gonghe 五族共和)."[12] Changkya Khutukhtu joined the monks in filing a petition to the state council, urging President Yuan Shikai 袁世凱 to protect Buddhist temple properties.[13] After the Buddhists' protests and negotiations, in 1913 the state finally supported the federation's charter and recognized its legal status.

Although the Chinese Buddhist leaders were keen to cooperate with a few high-ranking lamas in leveraging the interests of Chinese Buddhist institutions, they showed little interest in learning Tibetan Buddhist teachings. And the most popular Chinese Buddhist periodicals published in the 1910s contain little discussion of Tibetan Buddhism. In contrast, in the late nineteenth and the first two decades of the early twentieth century, some Chinese Buddhist scholars were actively importing Buddhist knowledge from Japan, including knowledge of esoteric Buddhism.

Yang Wenhui, named the "father of Chinese Buddhist revival" by Holmes Welch, played an important role in exposing Chinese Buddhists to non-Chinese Buddhist traditions in the late Qing.[14] To recover the canon lost during the Taiping Rebellion (1850–1864), Yang Wenhui introduced scriptures from Japan and reprinted them, which greatly helped to promote cultural communication between Japanese and Chinese Buddhists.[15] The canon used in Japan was largely written in Classical Chinese, which helped the Chinese learn Japanese Buddhist teachings. Yang's student Taixu, inspired by his teacher and eager to revive Chinese Buddhism through various avenues, became one of the most important Buddhist reformers to shape the modern Chinese Buddhist landscape. Following in his teacher's footsteps, Taixu expanded contacts with non-Chinese Buddhist traditions; accentuating Japanese esoteric Buddhism as a treasure that originally derived from ancient China, Taixu envisioned introducing it as a part of his vision to revive Chinese Buddhism. Frustrated by the state's tightening of religious policy in 1915, Taixu crafted a blueprint for strengthening Chinese monastic institution in the "Reorganization of the Sangha System" (Zhengli sengqie zhidu lun 整理僧伽制度論).[16] For Taixu, a revival of Chinese Buddhism (Zhendan fojiao 震旦佛教) entailed restoring the eight philosophical schools of the Tang dynasty (618–907), when Buddhism came to prominence in ancient China.[17] One school to be revived was the Kaiyuan school (Kaiyuanzong), also known as the Zhenyan school (Zhenyanzong) or Esoteric school (Mizong 密宗).[18] In Taixu's view esoteric Buddhism had been transmitted from India to China, then to Japan—and though the practice of esoteric Buddhism had declined in India and China, its legacy was maintained in Japanese Buddhism. So to fully revive the original Chinese esoteric school, Taixu proposed to reintroduce the lost teachings from Japan.

Taixu identified "the three esoteric masters of Tang dynasty"—Śubhakarasiṃha (Shanwuwei 善無畏), Vajrabodhi (Jingangzhi 金剛智), and Amoghavajra (Bukong 不空)—as the patriarchs of the Kaiyuan school.[19] In 804, a Japanese monk named Kūkai 空海 (774–835) traveled to the capital of Tang to study under Master Huiguo 惠果 (746–805) and returned to Japan as a legitimate Dharma successor. While Chinese esoteric Buddhism suffered from persecution and declined in the ninth century, Shingon Buddhism developed into one of the largest Buddhist traditions in Japan with a base monastery at Mount Kōya.[20] Taixu outlined the transmission history as follows:

In the fourth year of the Kaiyuan period of Tang dynasty (716), Master Śubhakarasiṃha brought Indian scriptures to the capital, Chang'an, and translated the esoteric scriptures. Master Yixing 一行 received all his knowledge. At the same time, Vajrabodhi and his disciple Amoghavajra also arrived. The emperor respected them as if they were buddhas. The school soon declined. So in *Fozu tongji* 佛祖統紀 [*Comprehensive Record of Buddhas and Patriarchs*] written by Zhipan 志磐, the author claimed that all esoteric scriptures had been destroyed in the religious persecution during the late Tang. The esoteric teachings currently prevail in Japan. What we Chinese call *yuqie* 瑜伽 [yoga] rites are only remnant rituals infused with folk chanting formed in the Song dynasty. Esoteric teachings practiced in the Yuan, Ming, and Qing imperial courts derived from Mongolian and Tibetan lamas, so they were not the same as the Kaiyuan tradition [*fei fu Kaiyuan zhi jiu* 非復開元之舊]. The teachings were preserved fully intact only in Japan. If we receive and follow [the Japanese teachings], we can restore the school.[21]

Because he viewed Japanese Shingon as a successor to the ancient Chinese Kaiyuan school (or Tang esoteric school, Tangmi 唐密), Taixu encouraged importing Japanese esoteric Buddhism as a way to revive the ancient Chinese esoteric school. But introducing Tibetan esoteric Buddhism was not in his blueprint because Taixu regarded the Tibetan practice as divergent from the Kaiyuan tradition. For Taixu, although the Yuan and Ming emperors patronized esoteric Buddhism at the imperial courts, the practice transmitted by the Tibetans and Mongolian lamas was different from that of Kaiyuan tradition. Why the divergence? In a later article, Taixu attributed the variances to the expansion of Tibetan Buddhism in the thirteenth century, and he criticized its rampant transmission and loose disciplines:

In the Yuan dynasty, the prestige of the Imperial Preceptor Phagpa went with the Mongolian armies, and the Red School of Tibet expanded as far as to Europe. With the expansion, the transmission became unregulated and practices became mixed. It became aberrant and erroneous. Seeing its corruption, the Hongwu reign (1368–1398) forbade the Tibetan esoteric practice.... On the other hand, while the practice of the Kaiyuan [esoteric] system completely perished in the central land [China], it thrived in Japan. For a thousand years it flourished there, in a continuous and unbroken line.[22]

So Taixu did not deny the Indian provenance of Tibetan esoteric Buddhism, but he did question the alterations developed in its later expansion.[23] As Roy Rappaport has pointed out, the idea of "invariance" principally accounts for the cogency of religious systems, particularly concerning the tradition of rituals. The apparent invariability of the liturgy indicates the changelessness of the canonical information embodied in the rituals; therefore, because it serves to anchor the sacred, this stasis is essential to the ritual specialists' acceptance of it.[24] For Taixu, the proliferation of Tibetan esoteric Buddhism had led to its mixture with non-Buddhist elements. In contrast, Chinese esoteric teachings, he believed, had been transmitted intact to Japan and thus passed down from generation to generation.

Hence, in the late 1910s and early 1920s, Taixu was optimistic about reviving Chinese esoteric Buddhism by introducing Japanese esoteric Buddhism rather than by communicating with Tibetan esoteric Buddhism. In his view, proper transmission became an important indicator of the authenticity of the teachings. To this end, Taixu stressed the significance of *abhiṣeka* rituals (*guanding* 灌頂, empowerment) in ensuring the proper transmission of esoteric teachings from ancient Indian patriarchs to the Chinese and then to the Japanese. *Abhiṣeka* is a gateway ceremony that admits a candidate into the esoteric community and authorizes the candidate to perform esoteric practices.[25] The ceremony requests the presence of a spiritual master (*a she li* 阿闍黎, *ācārya*) who has himself been consecrated and authorized to perform esoteric rituals and employ mantras. This guru-to-disciple inauguration rite ensures there is the requisite religious authority to transmit the teachings from generation to generation in an unbroken lineage.

Given the importance of an authorized *ācārya* in *abhiṣeka* rites, Taixu highlighted the guru-to-disciple authorization in restoring Chinese esoteric Buddhism. For Taixu, among the eight schools of Tang, the esoteric school and the Chan school were distinctive for the crucial role teachers played in their transmission. Unlike the other six philosophical schools that were based on doctrinal learning, the esoteric Kaiyuan school and the Chan school required direct master-to-disciple transmission to ensure the restoration of Chinese Buddhism.[26] In the planned restoration, the two schools needed teachers more than the other six schools did:

> The eight schools differed in two aspects. First, their patriarchs differed in terms of their origins; only the patriarchs of Kaiyuan and Chan came from India, while

all other patriarchs were Chinese. The Chan school and the esoteric school had to have Indian patriarchs because they were the strictest in requiring direct transmission [of the teachings] from a master. Abhiṣeka is a prerequisite for practicing esoteric rituals, hence the esoteric school was rigid in guru-to-disciple transmission. The school now prevails in Japan, and the Japanese esoteric practitioners also revere the three masters of the Kaiyuan period. The tenets of Chan [are passed down through] special transmission outside the doctrine, [through] mind sealing the mind, and do not establish words, which makes teacher-to-disciple transmission essential for Chan as well.... The other six schools rely on the sūtra, vinaya, and śāstra, and they do not require personal transmission [of the teachings].[27]

Without mentioning any specifics of esoteric teachings, it seems that Taixu was not driven by a faith in the soteriological or philosophical distinction, but rather by an almost self-evident narrative of reviving Chinese Buddhism. Constituting a part of the glorious legacy from the Tang dynasty, the esoteric school must be rejuvenated to restore Chinese Buddhism to its fullness. Without an examination of the doctrines, Taixu also asserted that the teachings of the three masters of Tang dynasty were "correct."[28] Even though the school failed to survive in China, its unique master-to-disciple transmission (*shicheng* 師承) ensured that the teachings were passed down in an unbroken lineage in Japan. Hence, Chinese Buddhists could expect to reestablish the line by receiving empowerment from the Japanese teachers. Therefore, in the 1910s, Taixu included the import of Japanese esoteric Buddhism in his project to revive Chinese Buddhism. But as the divergences unfolded and the conflicts exposed, Taixu adjusted his plan by considering Tibet as a richer source of inspiration.

The Rising Interest in Esoteric Buddhism

Although Shingon Buddhism had undergone a millennium of change in Japan, Taixu assumed its reintroduction in the late 1910s and early 1920s would be an unproblematic, direct revival of the ancient Chinese esoteric Buddhism it was based on. Some Chinese Buddhists grew interested in studying the teachings of the Zhenyan (Shingon) Buddhist school, notably the layman Wang Hongyuan, who was one of the pioneers in translating them.[29]

In 1918, Wang came across the *Essentials of Esoteric Buddhism* (*Mikkyō kōyō* 密教綱要, hereafter abbreviated as the *Essentials*) written by Gonda Raifu 権田雷斧 (1846–1934), chief priest of the Buzan sect of Shingon Buddhism.[30] This book recapitulates the historical and doctrinal developments of esoteric Buddhism in India, China, and Japan, with an emphasis on the Tang-era doctrinal tenets of Kūkai, particularly his theories on the differentiation of esoteric teachings and exoteric teachings. Wang's translation of the book exposed Chinese Buddhists to a set of notions and practices established by Kūkai and other Japanese masters.[31] Taixu credited Wang's translation with drawing Chinese Buddhists' attention to esoteric Buddhism, saying that "my interest and the countrymen's attention to esoteric Buddhism (*mizong*) began with Wang's translation of the *Essentials*."[32] Taixu's praise helped to promote the book's circulation. He invited Wang to publish more of his translation on the *Voice of the Sea Tide*, a major Buddhist periodical for which Taixu acted as the chief editor.[33] From the 1920s to the 1940s, the periodical grew to be one of the most influential Buddhist print media, providing a platform for dialogues between esoteric proponents and dissenters.

When doctrinal translation increased the publicity of Zhenyan Buddhism, rituals also brought it greater visibility. Wang's translation inspired enthusiasm among some Buddhists and he attracted a group of followers in his hometown of Chaozhou 潮州 (Guangdong Province). Within a few years, dissatisfied with merely studying the theories, Wang and his followers yearned to learn the esoteric praxis, which entailed their obtaining empowerment from a legitimate Japanese master. In June 1924, Wang invited Gonda to Chaozhou to give empowerment to the enthusiasts. During the week-long ceremony at the Creation Era Temple (Kaiyuansi 開元寺), Gonda initiated Wang and hundreds of monastic and lay Buddhists to two core forms of Shingon esoteric practices: the Womb Realm (Skt. *garbhakoṣadhātu*; Ch. *taizangjie* 胎藏界) and the Diamond Realm (Skt. *vajradhātu*; Ch. *jingangjie* 金剛界).[34] After two years of practicing the preliminary techniques, Wang strived to be an *ācārya* himself, which entailed obtaining more advanced authorization. In 1926, Wang traveled to Japan to receive full initiation from Gonda, which then allowed Wang to perform esoteric rites as an *ācārya*.[35] Like Wang, several monks also traveled to Japan to receive training in esoteric practice; among the most famous were Dayong, Chisong, and Xianyin 顯蔭.[36]

Dayong, a disciple of Taixu, visited Mount Kōya with Chisong in 1922 to study with Kaneyama Bokushō 金山穆昭 (1875–1958). Both Dayong and

Chisong received the title of *ācārya*. When Dayong returned to China in 1923, he was warmly welcomed and invited by Buddhist temples and seminaries in Wuhan, Hangzhou, and Beijing to deliver talks. Dayong performed a preliminary initiation ritual named the eighteen-method (Jūhachidō 十八道) for hundreds of Buddhists.[37] Chisong became the abbot at the Temple of Precious Efficacy (Baotongsi 寶通寺) in Wuhan in 1924. Over the next decade, by conducting initiation ceremonies to thousands of devotees, Chisong developed the temple into a center for spreading Japanese esoteric teachings in central China. After the temple was destroyed by war in 1937, and prior to his death in 1972, Chisong continued to promote esoteric Buddhism, only this time from his new bases at the Temple of Saintly Immortals (Shengxiansi 聖仙寺) and the Temple of Silent Peace (Jingansi 靜安寺) in Shanghai.

The expansion of Zhenyan Buddhism in the early 1920s not only created a sensation among the Buddhists but also triggered a debate regarding its doctrines and patterns of practice. Because Wang Hongyuan was a layman, the initiation he provided to monks and nuns challenged monastic authority. In addition, some Chinese Buddhist leaders were annoyed when Japanese monks violated the fundamental monastic disciplinary codes, and Chinese philosophers struggled with new doctrines that were incompatible with the traditional framework. In chapter 4 I analyze these tensions in greater detail.

With more knowledge of Zhenyan Buddhism revealed, some early supporters changed their attitude and became suspicious. From the mid-1920s on, Taixu no longer credited Japanese esoteric Buddhism (Rimi 日密 or Dongmi 東密, Eastern Esoteric Buddhism) with being a pure successor of Tang esoteric Buddhism (Tangmi). In dismay, Taixu moved away from the earlier plan of restoring the ancient Kaiyuan school solely by reintroducing esoteric Buddhism from Japan. In a 1925 article to assess "the current revival of esoteric Buddhism in China," Taixu castigated the behavior of some Japanese and Tibetan esoteric Buddhists:

> The transmission [ritual] conducted by Gonda Raifu [in Chaozhou] last year was ridiculous. The transmission not only contravened Buddha's Vinaya and the patriarchs' pure regulations, but also contradicted the conventional method of esoteric transmission in Japan.... Also, the Tibetan and Mongolian lamas, dressed in lay attire, publicly consumed meat and alcohol, and despised the disciplinary practice that was cherished in Chinese tradition.... In the long run, before we attain the true essence of esoteric practice and achieve the amazing

outcome, Buddha's Vinaya and the patriarchs' pure regulations will have turned into dust, which will leave long-lasting harmful impacts on the human mind. We should be cautious about the danger.[38]

Despite his outspoken remarks about seemingly transgressive behaviors, Taixu never meant to abandon the introduction of esoteric Buddhism altogether. The revival of Chinese esoteric Buddhism remained integral to Taixu's plan. He nevertheless proposed to build Chinese esoteric Buddhism (Zhongmi 中密) by adopting aspects of Japanese as well as Tibetan esoteric Buddhism (Zangmi 藏密), on the assumption that these esoteric practices would be integrated with conventional Chinese disciplinary norms, and that their transmission should be under control. He contended, "[We shall] fully study Japanese and Tibetan esoteric Buddhism and assimilate them into a form of Chinese esoteric Buddhism."[39] He emphasized that the "assimilation" (tonghua 同化) must be "incorporated into Chinese disciplinary norms and doctrinal teachings."[40] Thus, sometime around 1924 or 1925, Taixu modified his vision, aiming to build Chinese esoteric Buddhism based on elements from Japanese and Tibetan esoteric practice, Chinese disciplinary codes, and doctrinal teachings.[41]

As Taixu incorporated Tibetan Buddhism into his vision, his followers also started to realize the rich offerings available to those with Tibetan Buddhist literacy. The growing interest in doctrinal learning and praxis generated a need for formal education. The renewed orientation led to the building of Tibetan College in Beijing in 1924 and a group trip headed toward Lhasa in 1925.

The Founding of the Tibetan College

As the enthusiasts explored their interest in Japanese esoteric Buddhism, some of them learned across the different traditions and shifted their inquiry to Tibetan esoteric Buddhism. Why the shift? It seems particularly surprising, especially because by the late 1910s Dayong and other converts were showing barely any interest in Tibetan esoteric Buddhism or hinting that an organized effort to pursue a formal study of it was underway. Instead, after the introduction of Japanese esoteric Buddhism in the 1910s and the early 1920s, the contention regarding its divergent teachings led them to scrutinize esoteric Buddhism more profoundly. As the Chinese Buddhists explored the historical evolution of esoteric Buddhism, the distinction of Tibetan esoteric Buddhism became more and more obvious to them.

Esoteric Buddhism bases its practice on a group of texts known as tantras. Tantras appeared in India before the third century and their composition continued until the twelfth century when Buddhism in India disappeared.[42] When tantric teachings were transmitted to China and later to Japan, esoteric Buddhism was in its early stages. Tibetan Buddhism inherited aspects from Indian Buddhism in the eighth to the twelfth centuries, thereby preserving a large number of the extant tantras. As a result, a multitude of tantras—especially the later ones—survived in the Tibetan canon but not in the Chinese canon.[43] More than 450 tantras were found in the "Kangyur" section of the Tibetan canon, otherwise known as "the collection of words of Buddha," and 2,400 texts survived in tantric section of the "Tengyur" or "the collection of commentaries."[44] According to a recent comparative study by Kanben, the Tibetan Buddhist canonical texts outnumbered the Chinese canonical texts by one-third, and the number of Tibetan commentary texts was twice that of the Chinese commentary texts.[45]

Moreover, the Tibetan canon contained tantras that emerged in the later phase of Indian Buddhism, and most of these tantras were missing in Chinese and Japanese Buddhism. These later tantras were liturgically complex and considered to be profound teachings in Tibetan traditions. In Tibet, a common classification of the tantras was the four-fold divisions: Kriya, Carya, Yoga, and Anuttarayoga ("highest yoga").[46] Compared to the first three divisions that emerged earlier, the highest yoga did not become apparent until the eighth century or later. The highest yoga was rich in ritualistic forms and expressions, marked with the emphasis on a group of cosmic buddhas and deities, and the use of sexuality and impure substances.[47] Although the Chinese tantric translation contained counterparts of the first three divisions, it didn't include many tantras of the highest yoga. In contrast, Tibetan Kangyur contained about 120 tantras classified in the highest yoga.[48] Even though tantras of the highest yoga—such as the Kālacakra tantra—were regarded as the highest teachings in Tibetan traditions, they were not available in the Chinese or Japanese traditions.

Buddhist periodicals of the 1920s increasingly provided information about Tibetan Buddhist history and culture. The writers extolled the richness of Tibetan esoteric Buddhism and emphasized its multitude of advanced tantras. For example, a monk named Fandeng deemed Japanese esoteric Buddhism to be not as "complete" as its Tibetan counterpart and praised Tibet as esoteric Buddhism's greatest source.[49] Another monk named Huizhong also considered Japanese esoteric Buddhism less intact, arguing that Tibet's geographical adjacency to India allowed it to keep all the teachings in their entirety.[50]

Tibetan monks in Beijing and other cities also provided instruction to the enthusiasts, which helped to widen their understanding of esoteric Buddhism. Lama Bai Puren 白普仁 at Yonghe Temple (Yonghegong 雍和宫, literally, Palace of Peace and Harmony) in Beijing was one of the most active among them. From the early eighteenth century onward, Yonghe Temple—a royal temple of the Qing—was managed by Mongolian and Tibetan monks of the Gelug lineage. While the Manchu and Mongolian believers patronized this temple, there was little extant record to document its interaction with the Han believers. In the 1920s, the temple had Lama Bai Puren as its abbot, who was known for ritualistic expertise. In chapter 2 I provide a detailed account of his interaction with the various Chinese parties.

In 1924, Dayong went to study esoteric teachings with Lama Bai Puren in Beijing.[51] According to Taixu, Dayong then resolved to pursue further study in Tibet.[52] In a letter to his monastic friend Xianyin, Dayong enthusiastically explained why his interest shifted from Japanese to Tibetan esoteric Buddhism: "[Not only does] Tibetan Buddhism fully conserve the appearance and essence of esoteric Buddhism, providing complete aspects [xiang 相] and functions [yong 用]; [but] their extant scriptures, as well as books of medicine and arts, exceed tens or hundreds of times the extant Chinese translations. They are all transmitted in unbroken lines [from the Indian masters]."[53] He wanted to depart for Lhasa to study immediately. However, Lama Bai and the lay supporters persuaded him to nurture a group of fellows and travel together, hence leading to the founding of the first formal educational institution for enthusiasts.[54]

With support from Taixu and Lama Bai, Dayong opened the Tibetan College in Beijing's Compassionate Cause Temple (Ciyinsi 慈因寺) in the fall of 1924. The college was funded by Taixu's and Dayong's lay supporters, many of whom were core members of the Beijing Lay Buddhist Society.[55] The stated aim of the college was to equip the students with Tibetan language skills and prepare them for further study in Tibet.[56] In September 1924, the college welcomed the first batch of more than thirty students. They studied Tibetan for three hours a day, instructed by a bilingual teacher from the Kham region.[57] Dayong suggested they receive language training for three years in Beijing, then they would set off to study at a Tibetan seminary in Lhasa.[58]

When establishing the college, Taixu and Dayong not only articulated their aspiration to introduce Tibetan esoteric teachings, but they also expressed an interest in exploring its exoteric or Mahāyāna teachings. In the college's advertisement to recruit the first batch of students in 1924, the organizers extolled Tibetan Buddhism for its richness of both esoteric and Mahāyāna teachings. The advertisement especially highlighted a large number of scriptures and commentaries that were not available in Chinese, claiming that they were "vast and systematic," and "far exceed[ed] those available in Chinese and Japanese."[59]

The fact that the college founders highlighted this shows that some Chinese Buddhist leaders recognized the value of the whole body of Tibetan Buddhist literacy, not just its esoteric contents. Around the mid-1920s, more and more Buddhist writers were discussing the richness of scriptural and commentary resources of Tibetan Buddhism. The Yonghe Temple in Beijing, especially its catalog of the Tibetan canon, allowed Chinese Buddhists to have a glimpse of Tibetan Buddhist literature. For example, according to a memoir by his disciples, Nenghai first became intrigued by Tibetan Buddhism after reading the catalog in Yonghe Temple.[60] Wang Yuji 王與楫, the president of the Shanghai Lay Buddhist Society, who was interested in the Yogācāra teachings of Mahāyāna Buddhism, likewise mentioned the influence of the catalog on him. In a letter to welcome the ninth Panchen Lama in 1925, Wang listed the titles of more than ten major commentaries in the Yonghe Temple catalog, adding that these Yogācāra commentaries were not available in the Chinese Buddhist canon. Being curious about the Yogācāra tradition—and having heard that a much larger body of Yogācāra teachings was conserved in Tibet—Wang asked the Panchen Lama to promote both esoteric Buddhism and Yogācāra Buddhism when visiting Beijing.[61]

After it opened, Tibetan College provided a platform to facilitate communication between the Chinese enthusiasts and the Tibetan lamas who were visiting Beijing. In addition to its regular courses, the college often invited Tibetan masters to give lectures. For example, Dorje Chopa (Duojie Jueba 多傑覺拔), a renowned Gelug scholar, offered esoteric initiations to the students on his visits. Several students developed their faith in him and respected him as their spiritual guru. They began writing to him and their communication lasted for many years.[62]

The 1925 visit of the ninth Panchen Lama also brought greater visibility to Tibetan Buddhism in the public arena in Beijing. The thirteenth Dalai Lama's reform initiatives increased suspicion among the leaders, resulting in the ninth Panchen Lama's flight to Inner Mongolia in 1924.[63] With internal tensions increasing among the Tibetan leaders in the early 1920s, the Beijing government sought to advance its political agenda by cementing connections with the exiled lamas.

The Panchen Lama's arrival generated much enthusiasm among Dayong and his students. Ahead of the lama's arrival, Dayong invited his representative Khenpo Wangdu to give a talk.[64] Dayong appealed to him to increase communication between Chinese and Tibetan Buddhists. For example, Dayong asked the Panchen Lama to provide language education for the Tibetan monks living in Beijing, saying that with increased language skills, the Tibetan monks would be able to communicate more effectively with Chinese enthusiasts. In response, Khenpo Wangdu delivered a positive message, claiming that the Panchen Lama shared the same concern about enhancing communication. He added that the lama was planning to open a seminary where the Tibetans could study the Chinese language and the Chinese could learn Tibetan. And the lama also planned to invite between one and two hundred Chinese students to study in the temples in central Tibet.[65]

In the spring of 1925, political authorities and crowds of the faithful welcomed the Panchen Lama to Beijing. He lived in a former royal residence in suburban Beijing, and it was reported that every day over a thousand believers came to pay homage and receive blessings from him. After contacting his representative, Dayong and his disciples also came to pay homage and had a special meeting with the lama. Following the Tibetan tradition, the dialogue began with their offering of flowers and a ceremonial scarf to the lama. After the Han monks prostrated themselves to pay respects, the lama blessed them one by one by touching their foreheads. Then he delivered a sermon on esoteric Buddhism and introduced some basic knowledge, such as its relevance to exoteric Buddhism, the foundation of textual study and disciplinary training, and the prerequisite of ethical conduct for spiritual cultivation.[66] The lama praised the students for learning the Tibetan language and Tibetan Buddhism, and his supportive message ignited their hope of pursuing a study in central Tibet.

The building of the Tibetan College reflected a rise of interest in Tibetan Buddhism among Buddhist intellectuals in the 1920s. The clear shift in interest among Dayong and his followers showed that for them, Tibetan esoteric Buddhism was a conscious choice they made after deliberately comparing the three Buddhist strands. While they had gained initial knowledge about esoteric teachings through Japanese Buddhism, they then opted for Tibetan esoteric Buddhism, which they regarded as being more advanced. With the growing influx of knowledge, this tendency to learn new teachings by contrasting with previously assimilated knowledge continued over the next decades. In chapter 5 I show that this dynamic created a culture of religious diversity, with both cooperation and a degree of tension existing simultaneously among the competing groups.

Seeking Dharma from Tibet

The original goal of the Tibetan College was to provide a three-year language training course in Beijing. Within a few months of paying homage to the Panchen Lama, however, Dayong and twenty-two students left Beijing, perhaps because the Panchen Lama's encouragement may have elevated Dayong's hopes of getting a thorough and systematic education in a Tibetan seminary, one through which they would grasp the depth and breadth of Tibetan Buddhism in a way that they couldn't in their home community at that time. Known as the "group for seeking Dharma from Tibet" (*ruzang qiufa tuan* 入藏求法團), they headed toward Tibet in the summer of 1925; the anticipation of war in north China was also a factor in their decision.[67]

Dayong's supporters felt as thrilled as he did about the endeavor. Prior to the group's departure, several articles in Buddhist periodicals applauded the journey as comparable to the ordeal of the legendary master Xuanzang 玄奘 in the Tang dynasty, who traveled to India to carry back scriptures.[68] The writers optimistically predicted that, by transmitting Tibetan esoteric teachings to fill a gap in the Chinese Buddhist canon, Dayong and his cohort would make an incredible contribution to Chinese Buddhist literacy, just as Master Xuanzang did a millennium ago.[69]

In addition, the community had been supporting their endeavors since the formation of the college. The Beijing lay Buddhist society provided an initial grant for the group's trip, and its leaders founded a special committee to run a fund-raising campaign over the next years.⁷⁰ On the travels from Beijing to Hubei and Sichuan, the group also received assistance from the local lay Buddhist societies; the Sichuan Buddhist Society (Sichuan foxuehui 四川佛學會) for example, collected donations for them when the group passed through Sichuan in 1925. On the way, the group grew larger when joined by some newcomers—five from Hubei Province, eight from Sichuan.⁷¹

Yet however fervently Dayong and his peers yearned to study in Lhasa, they had trouble getting permission. After the Lhasa government severed its contact with the Beiyang government after the collapse of Qing, it became frustratingly difficult for Han travelers to enter. Tensions persisted after battles broke out on the borders in 1917 and 1918.⁷² In the winter of 1925, Dayong and his disciples reached Kangding 康定 (Wylie: Dar rtse mdo; Dartsedo), a small town in the Kham region, where they asked for permission to enter. The Lhasa government declined their request. They consequently stayed in the Ganzi region, hoping that "the Tibetan government would clear [themselves of] suspicion and the situation [would] become more favorable."⁷³ The group resided at Drakkar Temple (Zhajiasi 札迦寺), where the members continued to sharpen their language skills. They also learned several commentaries, including *Lamrim Chenmo*, from the senior lamas at the temple. From time to time, they visited the renowned Tibetan masters in the vicinity to learn scriptures.

With the grant drying up and the uncertainty about their passage looming, ten members withdrew. The group shrunk to seventeen people by the autumn of 1926.⁷⁴ Dayong wrote to the Beijing patrons to ask for more financial support. Some letters they wrote home in the mid to late 1920s were published in Buddhist periodicals; they give us a glimpse into the struggles of the group, as well as how they shared their experience of Tibetan Buddhism with fellow believers back home. The correspondence between the group and the home supporters also reveals many previously unknown facts about their interactions with the Tibetans at the border.

For years, Dayong pleaded for travel permission, but the Lhasa government remained suspicious of the request. In July 1928, after about three years of waiting, Dayong re-sent an application to the Dalai Lama, along with gifts and ten taels of silver, requesting entry into a seminary in Lhasa to study Buddhism. In return Dayong received only a rejection letter in the name of the Dalai Lama, with gifts of amulets and blessed Tibetan medicine. The stated explanation for the rejection was the "ambiguous negotiation between

China and Tibet" and the "suspicion felt by many Tibetan people."[75] Facing financial challenges and frustrated by the repeated denial of entry, Dayong wrote to the lay supporters in Beijing urging them to work toward a solution.

Despite the difficulties, Dayong reaffirmed his commitment and tried to convince his supporters that they could still achieve their goal through alternative means. In a previous letter, Dayong had stated that Tibetan seminary training was distinctively systematic, with its curriculum ranging from exoteric Buddhism to esoteric Buddhism, from discipline to commentary and scriptural study, from doctrinal learning to meditative training. Given such a broad scope, Dayong estimated that the team should anticipate spending at least ten years at a seminary in Lhasa.[76] But given the unexpected delay at the border, Dayong proposed an adjusted plan. In a letter to Hu Zihu 胡子笏, a leader of the Beijing Lay Buddhist Society, Dayong suggested that the team should accommodate to the circumstance and strategize learning at the temples in Ganzi. Since their arrival at Kangding, Dayong and his students studied with Lama Jampa and lived in a private temple owned by the lama.[77] Over the years, they had forged a close relationship with the local Tibetan masters.[78] Dayong believed that they could offer the students an equally rigorous and well-structured education by instructing them in the core curriculum of the major Tibetan seminaries.[79] Also, he contended that, without a commitment to provide service as required in the Lhasa seminaries, the students would enjoy plenty of undistracted time to immerse themselves in the teachings offered in these local temples.[80]

Likewise, other members showed resilience in adjusting their learning plans. Their firsthand witness provided important information for the home community. In general, they spoke positively about Tibetan Buddhism and tried to dispel prejudices. For example, the monk Wuyi 悟一 wrote to Taixu to share his excitement about the scriptural richness of the Tibetan Buddhist canon. In a letter from 1926 he detailed the organization of the canon and its main contents: the "Kangyur" included Buddha's discourses of over 100 volumes, the "Tengyur" contained over 220 volumes of Indian commentaries by ancient Indian philosophers, and the canon also provided over 2,000 types of works by Tibetan masters. Wuyi noted enthusiastically, "these texts are profoundly vast," and emphasized that the Tibetan canon conserved more Indian commentaries than the Chinese Buddhist canon did. He was satisfied with temple life, saying that the Tibetan temples were well organized and the teachers erudite. With an emphasis on the disciplines, the Tibetan monks of the Gelug tradition received better education in ethics than the average Chinese monks did, and they strictly followed the monastic codes.[81]

Like Dayong and Wuyi, other members of the group also revered their Tibetan masters. Wuyi and two other monks, for example, went to study for months with Thubden Geshe on a mountain near Kangding. According to Wuyi, Thubden Geshe was a degree holder from Lhasa, "knowledgeable and strict about the disciplines."[82] Another monk Fazun was impressed by Amdo Geshe, a visitor to Drakkar Temple, from whom he learned many commentaries and also received over forty types of esoteric initiations.[83] After Amdo Geshe moved to a temple in Changdu 昌都 (Wylie: Chab mdo), Fazun and three other monks also went there to follow him in 1930.[84]

The bonds with the Tibetan masters of the Kham region were crucial for the aspirants' learning. In the memoirs, the monks expressed their gratitude for their teachers in Kham, who generously offered guidance and assistance. Indeed, with help from these teachers, a few monks finally got the chance to enter Tibetan seminaries after years of attempting to do so. Nenghai and his peer Yongguang 永光 were an example.[85] Nenghai and Yongguang went to study esoteric rituals with Jamyang Chopel Rinpoche in Litang 理塘 (Wylie: Li thang) in 1927. According to a memoir, Jamyang Rinpoche was known as a pious pilgrim, who had prostrated himself for over two thousand miles from Lhasa to the sacred Mount Wutai. When teaching Nenghai esoteric practices, Jamyang Rinpoche urged him to pursue scholarly study in a Tibetan seminary, predicting that Nenghai would one day widely spread Tibetan Buddhism to Chinese Buddhists. To help Nenghai, he wrote to Khangsar Rinpoche at Drepung Seminary in Lhasa to ask for assistance. In the summer of 1928, Nenghai and three other monks disguised themselves as Tibetan pilgrims, arriving in Lhasa in September 1928. He later spent four years studying with Khangsar Rinpoche at Drepung Seminary.[86] Likewise, after accompanying Amdo Rinpoche to Lhasa, Fazun and three other monks also made entry to Drepung Seminary in the autumn of 1930.[87] By 1931, eight monks from Dayong's team had arrived in Lhasa to pursue study.[88]

Dayong and his cohorts' endeavor was an extraordinary one. The team made an organized effort to travel a long distance to acquire teachings from Tibetan Buddhist tradition, a feat that was very rare in Chinese Buddhism prior to the time. Their perseverance showed that some Chinese Buddhists were committed to acquiring a well-rounded understanding of Tibetan Buddhism. And such an attempt was made possible through the cooperation of the monks, the lay patrons, and the Tibetan lamas.

Unfortunately, Dayong never did reach Lhasa; he died in Drakkar Monastery in September 1929 at the age of thirty-seven.[89] After his passing, some members continued studying with the local teachers in Ganzi, and some went back to their home community to teach Tibetan Buddhism. Together with those who entered Lhasa, they also became important figures in the rise of Tibetan Buddhism among the Chinese Buddhist communities in the 1930s and the 1940s, as the next chapters reveal. Meanwhile, the Panchen Lama and other Tibetan lamas continued to play an active role in increasing the visibility of Tibetan Buddhism in Chinese Buddhist communities. From the 1920s to the 1940s, they performed a series of esoteric ceremonies, translated tantric texts, and conferred initiation to a large number of enthusiasts. Although the Tibetan lamas and the Chinese adherents collaborated to introduce Tibetan Buddhism, they faced suspicion from Buddhist and non-Buddhist critics. These discordant voices reflect diverse views about Tibetan Buddhism and help us to discern the conflicting interests and purposes held by the various social groups in the transmission.

Conclusion

The situation of early twentieth-century Chinese Buddhists, who were particularly challenged by the discourses of nation-building and religious reform, eased the introduction of esoteric Buddhism to China proper. Existing knowledge about Chinese Buddhism's past and their vision of Buddhism in modern times preconditioned their reception of non-Chinese Buddhist teachings. In the late 1910s and the early 1920s, Taixu and his fellow Buddhist intellectuals believed that Japan preserved the esoteric teachings that had been transplanted directly from the three masters of the Tang dynasty. Importing Japanese esoteric Buddhism was for them tantamount to restoring the ancient Chinese esoteric school and thus considered a huge success.

In the early days of their efforts, Taixu and his closest disciples regarded Japanese esoteric Buddhism as a resource for rejuvenating Chinese esoteric Buddhism. As their awareness of the historical transformation of esoteric Buddhism grew, they also wanted to introduce esoteric Buddhism from beyond East Asia. In the mid-1920s, Taixu, Dayong, and their peers became convinced that Tibetan Buddhism, Chinese Buddhism, and Japanese Buddhism shared one origin in the historical Buddha, and Tibetan Buddhism conserved far richer esoteric teachings than the other two traditions. This belief led to an organized effort to systematically transmit Tibetan Buddhism. The opening of the Tibetan College and the attempt to obtain formal training at Tibetan seminaries displayed the enthusiasts' dedication to learning and introducing Tibetan Buddhism. Their attempts were facilitated by the guidance and assistance of Tibetan religious teachers.

The influx of ideas and practices also reshaped the Chinese Buddhists' understanding of esoteric Buddhism. The advocates were challenged to prove its authenticity and validity to the critics in their home community, who had been suspicious of its origin and ritual expressions. They also needed to clarify the taxonomic category of esoteric Buddhism, justify its different ritualistic forms, and explain the doctrinal divergence.

Perceptions of esoteric Buddhism became more divided when Buddhists defended their beliefs against the criticisms of secular intellectuals. In the wake of the anti-superstition campaigns, as the secular revolutionaries attempted to exterminate superstitious elements from public life to build a modern nation, the Buddhists had to defend their beliefs and practices by establishing distinctions between religion and superstition. They thus sought to formulate theories to explain the ritualistic functions. In the 1920s and 1930s, when highly publicized lamas and their ceremonial activities attracted mass audiences, their teachings drew skepticism from secular and Buddhist critics. Esoteric rituals, therefore, created a domain in which various Chinese social parties contested the role of "esoteric Buddhism" in public life.

TWO

The Lamas and the Rituals

ON THE AFTERNOON of April 1, 1926, a ship arrived at the port of Nanjing, the capital of Jiangsu Province in eastern China. A middle-aged Mongolian monk disembarked, escorted by other lamas. City officers along with hundreds of cheering people warmly welcomed Lama Bai Puren, the abbot of the Yonghe Temple in Beijing. To music performed by a military band, he and the other lamas took their seats in sedans, and were carried to Vairocana Temple (Pilusi 毗盧寺), a major temple in Nanjing.[1]

Lama Bai came to Nanjing to perform the Dharma Ceremony of Golden Light (Jinguangming fahui 金光明法會) as a prayer for peace, part of his 1926 tour to southern China. In the following months, he conducted ceremonies in five provinces in the Yangtze River basin: Jiangsu, Zhejiang, Jiangxi, Hubei, and Hunan.[2] Traditionally among China's most prosperous areas, these regions endured a series of battles among warlords between 1916 and 1927. Sun Chuanfang 孫傳芳—the commander of the allied armies of five provinces, along with the governors of Hunan, Jiangsu, Jiangxi, and Zhejiang—had invited Lama Bai as a way to begin to reestablish peace in the region.[3] After defeating the enemy troops of the Feng clique (Fengxi 奉系) in Zhejiang in October 1925, Sun consummated his power. As ruler of a vast territory in the lower Yangtze plain, Sun invited Lama Bai to "pray for peace over the five provinces" by performing Golden Light ceremonies in all the provinces' major cities. So it was that in 1926 Lama Bai performed a series of large-scale ceremonies in Beijing, Nanjing, Wuhan, Changsha, and other cities.

Nonetheless, not everyone welcomed Lama Bai and the ceremony. While the officers and faith adherents promoted esoteric rites as an effective means to advance social welfare, nonbelievers attacked this approach, understanding it as backward and futile, and they lambasted their politicians for reverting to superstition and irrationality. So although Sun and other top-ranking officers patronized the esoteric Buddhist ceremonies, they faced fierce opposition from dissenters, radical writers, and students.

The suspicion and protest were most evident in Hunan Province, where the dissenters asked the government to evict the lamas. In January 1926, Hunan's governor Zhao Hengti 趙恒惕 invited Lama Bai to conduct the Golden Light Ceremony at Changsha, the capital of Hunan, with the stated goal of "eliminating calamities" and "bringing bliss" to the people. A Buddhist committee was formed to oversee the ceremony, with a budget of twenty thousand yuan partially intended for renovating the Opening Bliss Temple (Kaifusi 開福寺), where Lama Bai and his peers were due to perform rituals over forty-nine days.[4] Reports document that the various rituals drew large crowds. For example, the rite of initiation into the practice of Medicine Buddha (Yaoshifofa 藥師佛法) attracted thousands who believed that it would help to protect them from disease and epidemics.[5]

While the ceremony elicited many positive headlines in Buddhist periodicals, it likewise elicited many critiques from nonbelievers for whom the ceremonies affirmed their conviction that superstition was still rampant, and that the government's patronage was counterproductive.[6] At the provincial council meetings, several councilors expressed indignation at the government's engagement. In January 1926, Hunan Province was hit by famine and drought. Thousands of people suffered from hunger, with over eighty-thousand refugees fleeing to Changsha.[7] The councilors claimed that, given the severity, the politicians should refrain from funding the ceremony and instead allocate the resources to help the victims directly.[8] Councilor Ma Xuchang voiced his opposition: "At the city station, you can see thousands of refugees leaving the disaster-stricken areas and swarming into the capital. They are dying from hunger and cold. Instead of doing something to relieve their plight, the government is squandering a large amount of wealth to receive Lama Bai, isn't it very inappropriate?"[9] Councilor Ye Dequan went on to urge the governor to oust Lama Bai and use the reception funds to resolve the locals' plight.[10] Following the councilors' lead, some student organizations protested against the governor's patronizing the ceremony.

Prior to the lama's arrival, the students had put up posters and distributed pamphlets on the streets outside the temple. As officers tailing them removed the posters and pamphlets, the students organized a strike. On the day following Lama Bai's arrival, the student union urged protesters to take to the streets to demonstrate.[11]

Lama Bai Puren's 1926 Golden Light Dharma Ceremonies exemplified the many ceremonial assemblies conducted by Tibetan and Mongolian lamas in Chinese cities from the 1920s to the 1940s. Widely publicized, these ceremonies drew great crowds and became venues through which esoteric rites entered the public view. The responses to their performance ranged from support to indifference to total rejection. Such widely different assessments of (and attitudes toward) the esoteric rituals reflected the different groups' varied understanding of the role and impact of rituals in specific social-historical settings. Without much discussion of their transcendent meanings, the enthusiasts and the critics diverged primarily on the relevance of religious rites in secular life. At a time when many areas were afflicted by war, famine, and epidemics, a ritual was assessed according to its utility in meeting real needs. Analyzing the voices of different parties and their interactions with each other helps unpack and explain the tension in the reception of esoteric rituals among the Chinese general public.

Drawing from influential newspapers like *Shenbao* and *Shishi xinbao*, as well as from Buddhist periodicals, I create in this chapter a profile of how various Chinese groups regarded the lamas and their rites.[12] I consider their expectation and needs, and the social processes by which the interpretations were formulated and circulated. To that end, I focus on the following questions: Given the many ritualistic options available to Chinese Buddhists, why did the adherents opt for the newly-introduced esoteric rites? In what ways did the lamas instruct their disciples on the esoteric Buddhist knowledge and practice they were witnessing? At a time when secular critics dismissed these rites as synonyms with the superstition that must be discarded, how did the Buddhists defend their beliefs and practices? What kinds of factors shaped the representations of esoteric Buddhism? Analyzing the largest ceremonies, as well as the controversy they provoked, will help to reveal the tensions between the competing narratives that underlie the introduction of esoteric Buddhism.

As many scholars have shown, rituals and liturgy are defining parameters of esoteric Buddhism. According to Robert Sharf, esoteric Buddhism is a new technology of rituals to facilitate widely circulated Mahāyāna aims.[13] Mudrā (hand gesture), mantra (spell), and maṇḍala (symbolic diagrams) constitute the hallmarks of esoteric practice.[14] In the early decades of the twentieth century, the Chinese patrons invited Tibetan and Mongolian specialists to perform rituals for a variety of supramundane and secular purposes. By attracting broad attention, these highly publicized rituals became an arena for contesting esoteric Buddhism. I approach the subject of esoteric rituals in Chinese cities with the assumption that transmission is a performative process. Although Tibetan and Mongolian lamas mostly followed the instructions of age-old manuals in carrying out the rituals, new meanings were also generated in different contexts of performance. The presentation of the esoteric ritual was a dialectical process—with different groups debating subjects that were themselves shifting over time. As Catherine Bell has pointed out, ritual practice is highly situational and strategic, and ritual bodies are produced in interaction with a structured and structuring environment.[15] While the lamas performed rituals following a set of codified patterns, interpretation of rituals was contingent upon the rituals' immediate context and carried the imprint of specific interpreters. Hence, despite the duplication of formality, performing a ritual in Chinese communities was not a simple translation or repetition of a Tibetan Buddhist liturgy. Ritual performers and interpreters never acted autonomously, separate from their context. When facing skepticism from Chinese Buddhist critics and secular writers, adherents of esoteric ritual not only justified it on grounds of Buddhist doctrines, but also strived to align their interpretation with national discourses. The conflicting discourses embodied the multiple voices disputing the role of Buddhism in Chinese society in modern times, especially as evidenced by its ritualistic components.

The Panchen Lama

The ninth Panchen Lama played an important part in drawing public attention to Tibetan Buddhism. When he fled to Beijing in 1924, the capital of the republic was in political chaos. After the collapse of the Qing dynasty in 1911, the Beiyang army commander Yuan Shikai took over the presidency of the republic. Yuan's military clout allowed the government to assert authority over fractional cliques, thus maintaining peace for years. But following

Yuan's death in 1916, political disintegration resulted in the rise of many regional warlords who fought each other for supremacy from 1916 to 1927. In October 1924, as Feng Yuxiang 馮玉祥 seized the capital and overturned the central government led by Cao Kun 曹錕, the coup reshuffled power among the authorities. With the defeated Zhili 直隸 army retreating to the south, Duan Qirui 段祺瑞 became the acting chief executive of the republic.

The ninth Panchen Lama's arrival in China was reported as a historic event. The last time he had visited Beijing was in 1780, when the sixth Panchen Lama Lobsang Palden Yeshe (1738–1780) met with Emperor Qianlong at the height of the Qing dynasty. After 1911, the Beiyang government struggled to strengthen contact with the Tibetans and the Mongolians at the borders. At a time when the state authorities were trying to increase contact with neighboring peoples in the frontier regions, the ninth Panchen Lama's arrival in Beijing had a far-reaching impact on the Sino-Tibetan relationship. Some historians consider his flight from Tibet as the catalyst that opened the door for the Republican government's intervention in Tibet's religious-political affairs.[16]

On the ninth Panchen Lama's arrival in Beijing, the Beiyang government seized the opportunity to integrate him into the state system. From February to April 1925, to deal with the aftermath of the coup, Duan's new government called a two-month meeting to restart negotiations among the competing forces.[17] The Panchen Lama was invited to join the meeting, and he delivered a talk on "dispersing the calamity of war." Echoing the meeting's theme of peace through a ceasefire, the Panchen Lama called for peace and restated Sun Yat-sen's principle of "five races under one union," calling for harmony among the various ethnic groups.[18] When the state took steps to associate religion overtly with politics, the Panchen Lama seized the opportunity to reassert his power. He met with Duan several times to seek assistance in returning to Tibet.[19] With support from the Mongolian and Tibetan Ministry (Mengzangyuan 蒙藏院)—a government body that supervised borderland issues—he also attempted to enhance communication between the Chinese and the Tibetans.[20] In 1925, it was reported that the Panchen Lama was working with Xiong Xiling 熊希齡, a politician and philanthropist, to build a school to provide language education.[21] The Panchen Lama suggested inviting two hundred Tibetan Mongolian youth to study Chinese in Beijing, and offering Mongolian and Tibetan courses to two hundred Han students.[22] To launch the program, he invited the educator Tao

Xingzhi 陶行之 to open a Chinese language class to a dozen of the young lamas in his company.[23]

In addition to his involvement in education, the Panchen Lama interacted directly with the Tibetan Buddhists in Beijing and Mongolia. Aside from routine chanting and praying, the Panchen Lama met daily with visitors to bless them. The number of daily visitors ranged from dozens to hundreds, many of whom traveled a long distance to Beijing from Mongolia where Tibetan Buddhism prevailed.[24] The Panchen Lama also met with Chinese intellectuals, to whom he often preached on harmony between the five ethnic groups.[25]

By liaising with other religious groups, the Panchen Lama expanded his influence outside the Buddhist communities. In Beijing, he joined the collective effort of religious groups to advocate for the role of religions in advancing peace. On April 12, 1925, Gilbert Reid, a former US Presbyterian missionary and founder of the International Institute of China (Shangxiantang 尚賢堂), invited the Panchen Lama to give a talk on the Yingtai 瀛臺 island at Zhongnanhai 中南海, a former imperial garden in Beijing.[26] Over 1,500 visitors came to the gathering to "catch sight of the Panchen Lama." The jubilant crowds were mainly Westerners and adherents of various faiths including Christianity, Catholicism, Orthodox Catholicism, Daoism, and Islam.[27] By preaching on the Buddhist principle of living a wholesome life, the Panchen Lama repeated the peace message and highlighted the moral role provided by religion in society.[28] His presence, through political and religious activities, was widely reported and put him in the national headlines in 1924 and 1925.

The Panchen Lama's influence extended beyond the capital. After the meeting, he started a two-month pilgrimage and traveled 900 miles south to Putuo Mountain (Putuoshan 普陀山). Located on an island in the East China Sea, Putuo was believed to be the sacred residence of Bodhisattva Avalokiteśvara—an influential deity in both Chinese and Tibetan Buddhist traditions. In 1924 and 1925, Zhejiang Province was undergoing a series of battles between the Zhili clique (Zhixi 直系) and the Feng clique. Sun Chuanfang, a warlord of the Zhili clique, was expanding his territories in Zhejiang. In early 1925, with support from Duan's new government, Sun assumed the position of the superintendent (duban 督辦) of Zhejiang Province but still faced a military challenge from the Feng in Shandong and Jiangsu. Sun welcomed the visit of the Panchen Lama, in particular hoping that the lama would "bring blessing and subdue calamities."[29]

On April 27, the Panchen Lama left Beijing for Zhejiang. He had with him over thirty lamas and was accompanied by the Chinese officers from the Mongolian and Tibetan Ministry.[30] At a time of volatile politics and regional battles, his visit generated great enthusiasm among politicians and Buddhists. In Shandong and Jiangsu, large crowds waited to greet him at the stations where his train stopped, cheering as he smiled and waved to them.[31] Along the way, the Panchen Lama met privately with top-ranking officers in Shandong, Jiangsu, and Zhejiang.[32] On his arrival in Hangzhou, the capital of Zhejiang, Sun gave him a warm welcome. When the Panchen Lama left for Putuo Island, Sun even dispatched two warships to escort the lama's convoy.[33]

In addition to meeting the regional military heads, a major part of the trip was meeting the Buddhists in southeast China. Buddhism thrived in Zhejiang and Jiangsu, and the tour allowed the Panchen Lama to communicate with influential lay and monastic leaders. At Putuo Island, he was received at the Temple of Dharma Rain (Fayusi 法雨寺) with a "banquet for one thousand monks" (qianseng zhai 千僧齋) and a welcome speech by Yinguang 印光, a respected monk known for disseminating Pure Land teachings.[34] In Shanghai, the Buddhists organized a large reception for the Panchen Lama, which drew over five hundred attendees from lay Buddhist societies, Buddhist associations, and charitable organizations.[35]

The Buddhist leaders applauded the Panchen Lama's promotion of Buddhism and his pursuit of peace. Some of them took the opportunity to seek his support for the reformative initiatives. Qinghai 清海, the president of the Chinese Buddhist Federation, invited the Panchen Lama to join the effort of rejuvenating Chinese Buddhism through strengthening its monastic education. The Panchen Lama assured Qinghai that he shared the same concern about monastic education, saying that he had already been working with Buddhists to explore ways to promote education in Beijing.[36] In his speech highlighting the common origin of Tibetan and Chinese Buddhism, the Panchen Lama called for collaboration among the Buddhist groups. He referred to the slogan "five races under one union," arguing that more than advocating political and ethnic harmony, the slogan also suggested an embracing of religious harmony. Hence, by emphasizing the shared belief of the two traditions, and by referring to the national discourse, the Panchen Lama was claiming a foundation by which to foster fraternity and cooperation among Buddhists.

The Panchen Lama's visit to Beijing and southern China was significant in the transmission of Tibetan Buddhism. By interacting with the various parties and seeking common ground, he advocated for and exemplified the role of Buddhism in advancing harmony and peace. Moreover, he indicated that Buddhism could serve as a resource to overcome conflicts and division through a commitment to build goodwill and rapport among the various parties. These ideas provided a theoretical ground for the performance of large-scale ceremonies by Tibetan and Mongolian lamas, as lay patrons invited them to pray for peace. The highly publicized ceremonies helped to generate and reinforce a stereotype depicting Tibetan Buddhist masters as ritual specialists, which not only brought them faithful followers but also drew criticism from those who questioned the relevance of religious rites in modern society. These ceremonies, therefore, provided a site for many parties to contest the engagement of the lamas in social life, and they offer us a lens through which to consider the conflicts in the Chinese reception of esoteric Buddhism.

The Ceremonies in Dispute

The rising trend of large-scale esoteric ceremonies in Chinese cities was noteworthy in the dynamics of modern Buddhism, and it might challenge some of the common presumptions about Buddhism in Asia and beyond. In response to scientific and rationalistic critiques, many Buddhist traditions adapted to modernist mores by deemphasizing or individualizing the performance of rituals in the nineteenth and twentieth centuries. This trend of de-ritualization took on various forms in Asian Buddhist movements. Japanese Buddhist apologists, for example, downplayed the ritualistic elements of the Zen tradition and highlighted the immediacy of experience.[37] Likewise, some modern Shingon exegetes purged mythological elements to shift the focus to doctrinal learning instead.[38] The Chinese Buddhist reformer Taixu coined the term "humanistic Buddhism" to denounce the monks' preoccupation with funerary rituals and call attention to the need to address this-worldly concerns.[39] The same trend of de-ritualization continued and constituted part of the post-war expansion of Tibetan Buddhism in the West. As shown by David McMahan, Tibetan teachers and their Western followers created a new form of the Buddhist tradition, in which meditation and philosophical learning overtook rituals as the central practices.⁴⁰

By contrast, rituals markedly constituted part of Tibetan esoteric Buddhism and were important in its transmission in modern Chinese cities. In the eyes of many believers, Tibetan lamas were more than scholars, meditators, or revealers of ultimate truth: they were respected as ritual specialists capable of invoking efficacious results. This image of Tibetan Buddhist masters was largely forged and intensified through the ceremonies conducted to meet certain needs in the particular social milieu.

After 1916, division among warlords continued until the Nationalist army unified the fragmented areas in 1928. With cities and towns devastated, numerous lives lost, epidemics and famine rampant, many people clung to faith to counter the disorder and uncertainty produced by wars. The residents, preoccupied with anxiety, sought assistance from divine power. During this period, Buddhists organized many ceremonial assemblies (*fahui* 法會) to pacify calamities (*xizai* 息災). Believers often resorted to Buddhist teachings to explain how these ceremonies functioned to ameliorate catastrophes. Buddhist cosmology explains that human weaknesses cause three kinds of calamities: anger causes war, ignorance causes epidemics, and craving causes famine.⁴¹ According to the doctrine of karma, people's vocal, behavioral, and mental actions would cause corresponding results. If a group of human agents jointly engage in a bad action, their shared karma (*gongye* 共業) would call forth unfavorable results shared among them. Accordingly, the best way to bring an end to calamities was to rid oneself of anger, ignorance, and craving. Within this framework, ceremonies functioned to purify people's minds and to gain protection from deities, thereby alleviating calamities.⁴² With this conviction, the believers were keen to organize ceremonies to counter the hardships in life, which were aggravated by wars and disasters.

Lama Bai Puren, born in Rehe in the eastern Mongolian area, was one of the most famous esoteric ritualistic specialists among Chinese Buddhists. His followers' articles on him were possibly the earliest surviving records about a famous lama's interaction with the Chinese laypeople in the time period. An article titled "A Record of Lama Bai's Dissemination of Dharma," written by his disciples in Tianjin, described Lama Bai as an exceptional practitioner and powerful ritual specialist.⁴³ He became a novice monk at Yonghe Temple in Beijing at the age of eight. During the anti-Christian Boxer

Uprising (1899–1901), the British-French army took over Beijing in August 1900, leading to the flight of the Qing royal family westward. Following the rulers, the lamas at the royal temple also fled. Lama Bai fled to Mount Wutai, a sacred mountain that was widely believed to be the abode of the bodhisattva Mañjuśrī in both the Chinese and the Tibetan Buddhist traditions. He cultivated his faith diligently and made significant spiritual progress. It was said that every day he prostrated himself five thousand times to a pagoda that conserved sacred relics. On the day when he completed one hundred thousand prostrations, auspicious light shined from beneath the pagoda, which his later disciples interpreted as a testimony of his faith. Another day, Lama Bai encountered an old man, whom he later believed to be a human manifestation of the bodhisattva Mañjuśrī, and from whom he received esoteric teachings.[44] By highlighting Lama Bai's spiritual achievement and experience of mystical revelation, such anecdotes helped to create an image of a capable and mystical master.

The Han disciples valued his miraculous power, and stories about his efficacy circulated widely. An article highlighted his prophetic ability, saying that after he successfully predicted the career of a Mongolian officer in Heilongjiang in 1909, many Mongolians became his followers.[45] Another article credited the ebbing of a disastrous flood in suburban Beijing in 1914 to his use of esoteric rites to subdue an evil dragon in West Hill.[46] And several articles applauded his efficacy in healing, praying for rain, and pacifying the deceased.[47] These circulated tales helped to build faith among his followers, who extended his fame by organizing, attending, and recording ceremonies.

Lama Bai was best known for his skills in conducting Golden Light ceremonies, which were related to the teachings in the Golden Light Sutra (Skt. Suvarnaprabhāsottama Sūtra; Ch. *Jinguangming jing* 金光明經), an Indian Mahāyāna scripture. This scripture depicts a reciprocal relationship between the Buddhists and the secular kings: the kings protect the Buddhist monastic community and its teachings, and the Buddhist monastics, by upholding the teachings of the scripture, generate merits to sustain and promote the social order.[48] Hence, by emphasizing the divine power in protecting the country and the kings, the scripture was historically important in East Asia and provided theoretical grounds for Buddhists to engage in social and political crises.

Myths surrounded Lama Bai's reception of the Golden Light teaching. Unlike the Kālacakra ceremonies held by the Panchen Lama, the Golden

Light practice is not based on the advanced tantra or the central deities of the Gelug tradition. Why did Lama Bai choose to transmit it? The disciples believed that Lama Bai received inspiration from a deity in a dream.[49] An article documents that, worried by the political situation in Beijing, Lama Bai allegedly practiced the rite of the divine generals of the Medicine Buddha during a meditation retreat in West Hill.[50] One night, he dreamed of a deity, who gave him a scripture and told him that it was "most suitable for this time." After he woke up, he found that a copy of Golden Light Sutra had been placed on his table. Thereafter, Lama Bai reprinted the scripture to circulate among the disciples, and performed ceremonies based on its teaching.[51] This narrative emphasizes that Lama Bai was circulating what he and his disciples considered the most appropriate needed by the Chinese situation. This strategy of highlighting the usefulness of a particular ritual was commonly used by the advocates.

Although Lama Bai had established his reputation as a ritual specialist among the Chinese Buddhist communities in Beijing, the Panchen Lama's visit helped to boost his influence. After the Panchen Lama arrived in Beijing in 1925, Lama Bai cultivated a close relationship with him and provided support at many events. For example, when the Panchen Lama gave empowerment and taught mantras to the Han disciples, Lama Bai assisted by providing an additional sermon to explain the practice.[52] Following the Panchen Lama, Lama Bai traveled to southern China in the summer of 1925. At the invitation of the Buddhists, he brought a group of twenty-three lamas from Yonghe Temple to perform the Golden Light ceremonies for seven days in Shanghai and three days in Hangzhou. He prayed for the souls of the soldiers fallen in battle to be at peace, and he prayed for peace for the living.[53] These trips and activities increased his visibility in the southern Chinese Buddhist communities.

Thanks to the fame he accrued for his ritual efficacy, Lama Bai attracted some of the most powerful military men in China. Several rival warlords competed to invite Lama Bai to conduct the Golden Light ceremonies. For example, Sun Chuanfang, who attributed his military success to Lama Bai's 1925 ceremony in Hangzhou, was eager to bring him back to repeat the same ceremony in his territories.[54] In the early spring of 1926, invited by Duan Qirui—then the provisional chief executive of the republic, Lama Bai led 108 lamas in conducting the Golden Light Ceremony at Yonghe Temple for twenty-one days, intending to bring peace to the nation. In the late 1920s,

Lama Bai's schedule was full of conducting ceremonies in the north and the Yangtze River basin. Capable of mobilizing significant resources for large-scale ceremonies, the warlords and politicians' endorsement contributed to boosting the Lama's presence in the public sphere.

On Sun Chuanfang's invitation in late spring 1926, Lama Bai visited the southern provinces and conducted Golden Light ceremonies for large crowds. To maximize the efficacy of the ceremonies, Sun and his allies along the lower Yangtze River cooperated with the lama, for example by supplying an enormous amount of funding and labor to ensure the performance of these rituals. Prior to Lama Bai's arrival, a special committee was set up in Nanjing, through which the members coordinated all the event affairs with the regional organizers.[55] Moreover, while the event encouraged public donations, political leaders and Buddhist individuals provided important financial support. The patrons included the governors Xia Chao 夏超 of Zhejiang, Zhao Hengti of Hunan, Chen Taoyi 陳陶遺 of Jiangsu, Li Dingkui 李定魁 of Jiangxi. According to one report, Governor Xia Chao of Zhejiang Province purchased a lot by the scenic West Lake and planned to donate 100,000 yuan to build a temple for Lama Bai, anticipating that if given a permanent site the lama would promote the Golden Light practice widely in the south.[56]

In addition to financing, the participating governments issued temporary regulations to invoke faith among the people. On Lama Bai's arrival, Sun ordered the five provinces to close their slaughterhouses and forbid the killing of animals for three days to "show our sincerity."[57] In the announcement, Sun and Governor Chen Taoyi of Jiangsu Province referred to Buddhist karmic doctrine to call for the people's cooperation. They demanded that the residents act with benevolence—a vital theme of the ceremony:

> All sentient beings are suffering, and misfortune is occurring everywhere in the world. If we reflect on the fundamental cause of the wars, we will find that it is because of killing and craving. From the beginning to the end of the ceremony, killing will be strictly forbidden for three days. From the birds in the sky, to the oysters in the river, let them live their lives and don't hurt them. . . . Lama Bai will initiate the Golden Light ceremony in Nanjing and dispel the disaster on behalf of all the people in our provinces.[58]

While the highest-ranking leaders in the area invited the lama to perform the rites, the common attendees also came to him to receive a blessing for their individual needs, such as their health, wealth, and careers. For example, after the three-day Golden Light ceremony at Vairocana Temple in Nanjing, at the request of the lay Buddhists, Lama Bai conducted a rite to deliver their deceased ancestors.[59] Before leaving Nanjing in late April, accompanied by Governor Chen Taoyi, Lama Bai went to the Efficacious Valley Temple (Linggusi 靈谷寺) to chant sutras for rain.[60]

The political leaders' attitude influenced their subordinates, including Buddhists and nonbelievers. Wherever Lama Bai and his company visited, the hosts demonstrated the utmost reverence and hospitality toward them. The local Buddhists helping with the logistics tried their best to welcome and honor the lamas. For example, when performing the Golden Light ceremony in Jiaxing 嘉興 County in the south of Shanghai in June 1926, the Buddhists arranged for the lamas to reside in the Perfect Solemnity Temple (Jingyansi 精嚴寺). The organizers feared that "our food may not meet the taste of the lamas," so they quickly hired a dozen cooks from Shanghai to prepare delicate banquets.[61] The county government closed the local meat market for four days, forbade fishing, and adorned the temple.[62] On the day of the lamas' arrival, the temple was so packed with excited crowds that a few attendees had to climb over the temple's stove to get a glimpse of the lamas; the peddlers in neighboring blocks also multiplied their profits that day.[63] An observer recalled: "The greeting was livelier than the day when Commander Sun himself visited our town!"[64]

But in contrast to the leaders' and the enthusiasts' support, some local people resisted the performance of ceremonies, especially in Hunan Province, where Lama Bai faced strong opposition. Whereas the governor and city officers endorsed the Buddhist ceremony as a way to deal with the aftermath of famine and war, provincial councilors and students rejected such a message, leading to the students' strike against the lama's visit. The critics reprimanded the governor's patronage, requesting that the government expel the lamas and use the grant to rescue the refugees. In response, the organizers published a statement arguing that the ceremony was funded by local Buddhists rather than public monies. The organizers emphasized that the Buddhists shared the same set of concerns as the critics did, and that the goal of the ceremony was likewise to relieve the victims' suffering.[65] In spite of the opposition, and thanks to the support of politicians and believers, Lama Bai's ceremony still drew a huge number of attendees in Hunan.

Lama Bai's experience reflected the conflicts in many large-scale ceremonies performed by the Tibetan and Mongolian lamas in Chinese cities. When China was going through tumultuous times, many people sought solace and consolation in religion. One noticeable feature of the calamity-pacifying ceremonies from the 1920s to the 1940s was the involvement of esoteric Buddhist teachers. Lay Buddhist associations often invited ritual specialists to host ceremonies; the lamas were among the most popular and received many invitations. Norlha, a high lama of the Nyingma school from the Kham region, who had been exiled to Beijing after years of being imprisoned in Lhasa, performed a series of ceremonies in Shanghai, Guangzhou, and Hong Kong in the early 1930s.[66] His consecration rite at the Great Buddha Temple (Dafosi 大佛寺) in Guangzhou in 1933 drew two thousand recipients.[67] Dorje Chopa also presided over the Southwest Peace Ceremony (Xinan heping fahui 西南和平法會) and conducted esoteric rites to bring peace to the residents of Sichuan, Guizhou, and Yunnan.[68] The laypeople's support therefore greatly helped to promote the presence of esoteric Buddhism in the major cities.

Consequently, advertisements announcing that the lamas would be "performing esoteric rituals (*xiu mifa* 修密法)" appeared in Buddhist periodicals and newspapers. In Chinese Buddhist traditions, the most common ceremonies included chanting the names of Buddhas and bodhisattvas, chanting *dhāraṇī*, chanting scriptures, and conducting rituals. Tibetan esoteric rituals were more sophisticated and involved a complex mixture of chanting spells, making hand signs, and visualization. Given their complexity, some adherents believed that the esoteric rites were especially effective in invoking divine help to meet mundane needs.

When a severe drought hit northwest China in 1928 causing famine *and* widespread death, the Northeastern Charity Alliance (Huabei cishan lianhehui 華北慈善聯合會) organized a calamity-pacifying ceremony to pray and raise funds for the victims. Lama Bai Puren led 108 lamas in chanting the *Jinsheng dhāraṇī* (*Jinsheng tuoluoni* 金勝陀羅尼) of the Golden Light Sutra for forty-nine days.[69] An organizer of this ceremony named Weiyin explained why they chose esoteric rituals to be performed rather than conventional Chinese Buddhist rites. The organizer acknowledged that the Golden Light Sutra, the Humane Kings Sutra, and several other scriptures intended to pacify diseases were available in the Chinese canon.[70] But Weiyin maintained that Chinese exoteric Mahāyāna Buddhism did not provide corresponding rituals for these scriptures, whereas the liturgical programs in esoteric Buddhism were more complete and hence could be applied in varying situations. The organizers believed that if the rituals were "conducted properly in accord with the deities' original vows," the deities would respond to the prayers.[71] This pattern, by connecting the esoteric rituals to the existing scriptures and doctrines in the Chinese tradition, was remarkable in their writings. That is, even though certain scriptures were also available in the Chinese canon, the Chinese Buddhist patrons chose esoteric rites: they not only believed that the esoteric rituals were more systematic but also deemed that the lamas were particularly well trained in ritual skills—factors that would help to ensure efficacy in obtaining the collective benefits promised in the scriptures.

The case of Lama Bai and his ceremonies demonstrates that the popularity of the ceremonies has two dimensions, one sociopolitical and the other religious, and that the two often converge. At a time of political instability, religion provided solace to many, including the most powerful and ordinary people. When the politicians collaborated with the Tibetan masters to strengthen connection with the Tibetans, some of them actively patronized and participated in the ceremonies, which helped to expand the influence of esoteric Buddhism among the Chinese. Meanwhile, the Chinese Buddhists and the lamas found common ground for working together. While Chinese Buddhist leaders sought support from the Panchen Lama and other lamas in monastic education and protecting temple properties, local Buddhists provided labor, space, and funds to support the lamas. The sociopolitical and religious trends continued to interact and influenced the public perception of esoteric Buddhism. After the Nationalist army reunited the fragmented areas in 1928 and founded a new central government in Nanjing, tensions mounted between the critics and the promoters, leading to a series of clashes about the roles of the lamas and their rituals in modern society.

Buddhism and the Anti-Superstition Campaign

After the completion of the Northern Expedition and the unification of southern and eastern China in 1928, the central government in Nanjing advanced the discourse of state-building and intensified many policies it had established in the early years of the republic. On the one hand, in an attempt to strengthen the connection with the Tibetans, the Nanjing government officially integrated the Tibetan high-ranking lamas into the state system. On the other hand, in spite of the government's favorable attitude toward the Tibetan Buddhist leaders, the overall tightening control over religions (as shown in the anti-superstition campaigns) also influenced public opinion about Tibetan Buddhism. While the two discourses were both serving the agenda of nation-building, they sometimes undermined and contradicted each other, generating opposing views regarding esoteric Buddhism.

In the 1930s, some high-ranking officers in the Nanjing government proposed to engage Buddhism in the nation-making project. As demonstrated by Gray Tuttle's research, Dai Jitao, a Buddhist and a senior Nationalist party member, was one of the most active politicians in linking political and religious projects. Dai proposed that by connecting the government with peoples in the borderlands of Manchuria, Mongolia, and Tibet, Buddhism could serve the revolutionary discourse for making a united, modern state.[72] In 1931, the Nanjing government awarded the Panchen Lama the honorary title of Protector of the Nation (Huguo 護國), and in 1932 appointed him as Propagation Envoy to the Western Borderland (Xichui xuanhuashi 西陲宣化使).[73] It appointed Norlha, another lama exiled to Beijing, as Propagation Envoy to the Western Kham (Xikang xuanweishi 西康宣慰使) in 1935.[74] The Panchen Lama, the Changkya Qutughtu, and the Norlha Lama accepted official positions at the Mongolian and Tibetan Affairs Commission, and the Panchen Lama and Norlha received support in their attempts to return to their home communities in Tibet.[75]

Meanwhile, during the late 1920s and early 1930s, the government was tightening its control over religions through anti-superstition campaigns. Both Rebecca Nedostup and Prasenjit Duara have shown how Republican leaders attempted to replace religious affiliation with national passion through campaigns of iconoclasm and nationalist mobilization.[76] The advocates associated magic and superstition with an outdated past and insisted such practices be discarded. To build a modern nation-state, it was essential to instruct people to suspend all irrational activities. By distinguishing objects, practices, and institutions of religious worship from superstition, the government tried to reconcile modernist ideals with traditionally sanctioned institutional religions. In December 1928, the state issued "Standards for Preserving and Eliminating Gods and Shrines" (Shenci cunfei biaozhun 神祠存廢標準), which divided gods and temples into two categories: those to be preserved and those to be eliminated. Claiming that superstition hindered social development, the state intended to suppress superstitious worship and to extend rights to what it considered legitimate religions.[77] All heretical cults and shrines were ordered to be closed, but temples established for the worshipping of ancient saints and temples established by religions of pure principles (*shendao shejiao zongzhi chunzheng* 神道設教, 宗旨純正) were exempt.[78] Based on the 1928 "Standards," campaigns were launched in various regions to purge irrational beliefs and superstitious practices from public life.

Although these campaigns openly and more narrowly targeted heretical cults and superstitious activities, local offices exploited the opportunity to attack Buddhist and Daoist institutions. In many cities and towns, secular intellectuals established anti-superstition societies to force the Buddhist and Daoist clergy to abandon their "superstitious" practice. Some local elites, by defining "superstition" as "meaningless religious activities," interfered in the Buddhist and Daoist performance of rites. For instance, the Beijing anti-superstition committee lobbied the government to urge the clergy to transform all temples into buildings for public use.[79] In Hubei, some local elites banned the hiring of the clergy to conduct funeral rites and forced nuns and monks to return to secular life.[80] In Anhui, to eliminate the convention of hiring clergy to chant scriptures at funerals, the provincial government levied a "superstition tax" (*mixin juan* 迷信捐) on Buddhist funeral services, claiming that "inviting monks to chant scriptures is a superstitious action, because it is meaningless; and such heresy only confuses the public and therefore must be phased out through taxation."[81] The anti-superstition society in Zhejiang, after extending the category of superstition to include common religious activities such as "bowing for repentance," "praying to gods," and "chanting spells," singled out Buddhist and Daoist ceremonies as particularly harmful. Daoist seasonal rites of renewal (*jianjiao* 建醮), ceremonies for the deliverance of creatures of water and land (*shuilu fashi* 水陸法事), and Buddhist ceremonies for chanting scriptures (*songjing fahui* 誦經法會) were all reprimanded for filling communal life with irrationality and superstition.[82] Therefore, the ambiguity existing around the category of superstition left substantial leeway for regional and local officers to intervene in the religious and economic affairs of Buddhism and Daoism.

To defend the temple properties, Taixu and other Buddhist leaders tried in their own ways to demarcate "religion" from "superstition." In 1928, Taixu proclaimed that the government's categorization in the "Standards" was confusing and unsystematic.[83] Other Buddhist writers also responded by differentiating the "true belief" (zhengxin 正信) from "superstition" (mixin 迷信, which means "illusory belief"), claiming that true belief would dispel doubts, cultivate goodness, and purify the mind. Therefore, they argued, religious belief could serve the good of society, whereas superstition was harmful because it spread irrational ideas and misleadingly influenced people's actions.[84]

Given the wide overlapping spectrum, the ritual became an important site of contention for differentiating religion from superstition. When aggressive intellectuals dismissed all forms of ritual programs as superstitious on the premise that they were irrational and meaningless, Buddhism had to justify and rationalize its use of rituals. A monk named Jiezong claimed that Buddhism was free of superstition, which he defined as the cult worship of "demons in grotesque shapes and appearances," spirit writing, and spells and mantras.[85] His definition represented a common argument among the Buddhists who emphasized the doctrinal and nonritualistic aspects of Buddhism. But Jiezong's claim was invalid, for it downplayed the prevalent practice of chanting spells and mantras in the Chinese Buddhist tradition. And his definition was less relevant for Tibetan Buddhism: its deities were often depicted with a wrathful appearance; certain of its concepts, such as "nonduality," were expressed through artistic portrayals of deities engaging in sex with their consorts; and its spells and mantras were central to esoteric Buddhist praxis.

Another strategy to defend Buddhism was to generate new meanings for the rituals undergoing dispute rather than deemphasizing their ritualistic components. Some Buddhists grounded the rituals in Buddhist principles by highlighting their underlying religious significance. For example, the rites of releasing burning-mouth hungry ghosts (fangyankou 放焰口), including scripture chanting and penitential offering (jingchan 經懺), contained components that secular critics would label as "superstitious," such as bowing for repentance and chanting spells. The Buddhists acknowledged this and resorted to Buddhist doctrines to legitimize these activities. In one journal article, for instance, the author referred to the esoteric doctrine of "three mystical associations of body, speech, and mind" (sanmi xiangying 三密相應) to explain the use of mantra and mudrā (magic spells and symbolic gestures) in the rites. He argued that because the performers were fully aware of the significance of the rituals, the chanting and bowing of Buddhist liturgical masters were not "meaningless" activities but rather revealed their compassionate intention to benefit the suffering sentient beings. The behavioral patterns looked similar, but a monk's bowing to a Buddha's statue was different from a "foolish person's" bowing to an idol. The former was imbued with religious meaning, while the latter was mere flattery of ghosts and spirits.[86] Another author also suggested that Buddhist rituals were justified since they were undertaken with a fitting intention and mindset. A religious ritual and superstitious behavior might appear to be similar, but a religious ritual was guided by a set of systematic theories and therefore it informed and was informed by rationality.[87]

Adherents had to defend the esoteric rituals against the charge of superstition. They not only faced sarcasm from the secular critics, but also encountered discord in Buddhist communities when some Buddhists opposed esoteric rites in light of their alleged ambiguous origin and the transgressive content. In the face of these accusations, the adherents attempted to rationalize the rituals by offering a doctrinal justification and by relating them to national discourses. The tension between proponents and critics of esoteric rituals became more obvious when some politicians adopted Buddhist rituals as a way to serve the nation in the 1930s.

Chanting Mantras to Protect the Country

We have already seen how state leaders welcomed the Panchen Lama, as did some Chinese Buddhist leaders, who regarded the lama's political leverage as an important opportunity to negotiate for the interests of Buddhists. The Buddhists also ardently assisted in arranging the Panchen Lama's visits to Shanghai and Zhejiang in 1925. The reciprocal relationship between the Panchen Lama and the Chinese Buddhist leaders continued to develop after the founding of the Nationalist government in Nanjing.

In May 1931, the Panchen Lama attended the National People's Convention (Guomin huiyi 國民會議) in Nanjing at the invitation of Chiang Kai-shek, the chairman of the Nationalist government of China. On behalf of the Buddhists, the Panchen Lama's representative urged the government to return all confiscated temple properties to the clergy. The Panchen Lama also requested that the government issue a memorandum warning all regional offices and armies not to infringe on temple properties or they would be punished. In August 1931, the Nanjing government issued an administrative order urging the army not to "borrow" or "confiscate" temples, which Holmes Welch interpreted as "the high-water mark in governmental recognition of Buddhist property rights."[88] In turn, as studied by Gray Tuttle, the merging of secular and religious systems in 1931 signaled the state's transition from an anti-superstition position to embracing an officially approved Buddhism, including Tibetan Buddhism.[89]

Indeed, this order signaled the Nationalist government's guarantee to protect temples from rampant harassment by military forces. But antisuperstition discourses formed in the preceding years did not fade away. Many secular writers doubted the intervention of religion in the public affairs of a modern world, and some Buddhists remained suspicious of Tibetan Buddhism as an authentic legacy of Indian Buddhism. The divisions manifested in the continuing dissensions over the "state-protection calamity-pacifying ceremonies" (*huguo xizai fahui* 護國息災法會) throughout the 1930s and 1940s, when Buddhists organized ceremonies to protect the country from wars.

On September 18, 1931, the Japanese army invaded the northeastern part of China and presented a looming threat to the vast regions south of the Great Wall. Given the crisis, Minister Dai Jitao of the Examination Ministry proclaimed that religion could transform citizens and bring peace to the country in disastrous times. He advanced the slogan that "scriptures and mantras save the country (*jingzhou jiuguo* 經咒救國)," and invited monks from Mount Baohua (Baohuashan 寶華山) to chant the Humane Kings Sutra.[90]

The state's changing policy toward Buddhism, the pending threats of the Japanese invasion, and the high officials' patronage stimulated a dramatic increase in public religious ceremonies in central and eastern cities in the early 1930s. Some Buddhists quickly adopted Dai's notion to justify the performance of ceremonies. Lay Buddhists invited Tibetan, Mongolian, and Japanese esoteric masters to conduct rituals in Beijing, Shanghai, Nanjing, Hangzhou, Wuhan, Changsha, and Chengdu. For example, under the name of protecting the country, they organized Golden Light ceremonies in Beijing, and White Parasol (Baisangai 白傘蓋) rituals and Yamāntaka rituals in Wuhan in 1932.[91] Among these esoteric ceremonies, the largest were Kālacakra ceremonies presided over by the Panchen Lama. The 1932 Kālacakra ceremony at the Forbidden City of Beijing attracted an estimated

100,000 attendees, and the 1934 Kālacakra ceremony in the Temple of Hidden Efficacy in Hangzhou drew 70,000 attendees.[92]

Nonetheless, Dai's notion of "saving the country through scriptures and mantras" drew scornful remarks from his critics. In newspapers, discordant voices opposed the politicians' attempted use of Buddhist rituals to rescue the country. Secular writers criticized the government's concession to the Japanese and interpreted the promulgation of religious rituals as evidence of the politicians' appeasement. Many authors urged the state to take down-to-earth military actions to defeat the Japanese, rather than pray for divine protection. The famous writer Lu Xun 鲁迅 (1881–1936) ridiculed the politicians, declaring that "saving the country through scriptures and mantras" was merely a Don Quixote–like fantasy. "Chanting the mantra of Golden Light for hundreds and thousands of times," he added, "would not cause an earthquake to sink the Japanese islands."[93] In the *New Life Journal*, another writer mocked the attendees who were jostling with one another to be blessed by the Panchen Lama at the Hangzhou Kālacakra ceremony. Depicting the rituals as "mere gimmicks," the author was disappointed by such a "meaningless and much-vaunted ceremony."[94]

The politicians' engagement in these ceremonies also gave the critics plenty of ammunition. For the opponents, Dai's message of "saving the country through scriptures and mantra" revealed the politicians' lack of administrative competency and deficit in rationality. Opponents attacked the ceremonies as futile and demoralizing in popular newspapers. One author mocked, "if scriptures and mantra could save our country, playing games would save the country as well, so would dancing."[95] Another visitor to the Beijing Kālacakra ceremony articulated his indignation after seeing that Dai Jitao presented the gift of an umbrella to the Panchen Lama: "Looking at the name tag 'from Disciple Dai Chuanxian' on the umbrella, I could not believe my eyes. We, ordinary people, place hope in the high officers, trusting that they will relieve our plight and suffering. And this is all Minister Dai would do to save us!"[96]

Likewise, in an article titled "Beating the Ghosts," the author mocked the patrons, saying that "the slaves of the gods and ghosts are trying to transform us into slaves of gods and ghosts!"[97] Another visitor derided the Kālacakra ceremony as "a farce of praying for peace." He described how the lamas were reciting mantras that "perplexed audiences," and "thousands of pious men and women were just listening to a hubbub of chanting without knowing a word." In his eyes, religious rituals contributed little to pacify the pending threats of war, so he lamented the ignorance of the audience and the uselessness of the ceremony: "Alas! I feel so ashamed and upset. It is like after foreign bandits sliced off our ears and broke our legs, we are still numbly praying to the deities for salvation!"[98]

The esoteric ceremonies not only drew criticism from secular writers, but also drew persistent suspicion from some Chinese Buddhists. Unlike the non-Buddhist authors who ridiculed the notion of "saving the country through scriptures and mantra," most Buddhists did not question the logic of appealing for divine help to serve secular purposes. Actually, it was common for the Chinese Buddhists to pray for celestial blessings to pacify the human mind and bring peace to the world during disastrous times.[99] In the conventional ceremonies, the clergy led their followers in chanting the names of Buddhas and bodhisattvas, reading scriptures, prostrating themselves, repenting, and releasing life to save the nation from a dreadful fate.

Instead of questioning the relevance of rituals per se, the Chinese Buddhist critics questioned the efficacy of esoteric rituals from two angles: the origins of the esoteric rituals, and the performers in following the moral disciplines. In their view, the transgressive components revealed the non-Buddhist provenance of the esoteric rituals, and the ritual specialists of flawed morality would also fail to take on the sacred duties. An editorial in the *Voice of the Sea Tide* dismissed the concept of the Shambala Kingdom as a myth originating in Tibet rather than in India.[100] Other critics cast doubt on the morality of some esoteric specialists, and their judgments were based on the conventional modes of behavior for the Chinese monastics, which had been developed and standardized on Chinese soil over more than a millennium. Adhering to different Vinaya (a collection of disciplinary codes) and cultivated in different cultural and environmental circumstances, Tibetan and Mongolian monks did not follow some of the Chinese Buddhist customs, such as vegetarianism. To the Buddhist critics, the esoteric practitioners flouted the Chinese monastic behavioral customs, which made them less capable in setting a moral example for the lay followers and conducting sacred rituals to appeal for celestial protection.[101]

In response, other Chinese Buddhists defended the lamas and their rituals. Taixu published an article titled "Kālacakra Ceremony in Contentious Debate" in an effort to establish the authentic provenance of Tibetan esoteric rituals. Many esoteric Buddhists believed that Kālacakra scriptures were revealed by Nāgārjuna in an iron tower in south India, which antiesoteric opponents dismissed as a myth without historical grounding. Taixu resorted to Chinese canonical tradition and pointed out that some widely circulated Mahāyāna scriptures also had mythological origins.[102]

Another monk named Changxing wrote in the *Voice of the Sea Tide* to advocate for the Kālacakra tantra. He began the article by naming the splendid legacy of Chinese esoteric Buddhism, emphasizing the Tang-dynasty esoteric master Yixing to exemplify the efficacy of esoteric ceremonies in securing favorable outcomes in ordinary life. He then proceeded to extol the incomparable richness of Tibetan esoteric teachings, the Kālacakra tantra in particular.[103] In the early 1930s, although Taixu, Changxing, and other Buddhist writers had noted that Tibetan esoteric Buddhism developed theories and practices distinct from ancient Chinese ones, they defended Tibetan esoteric Buddhism for its doctrinal and ritualistic authenticity. Their evaluation was based on their belief in a glorious past of esoteric Buddhism in ancient China, together with their confidence that Tibetan Buddhism conserved more advanced and richer esoteric teachings than those preserved in Chinese and Japanese Buddhism. In spite of the divergences, they believed Tibetan Buddhism could still provide inspiration for rejuvenating Chinese Buddhism. Hence, to Taixu and other writers, their positive remarks on Tibetan esoteric rituals were based on their understanding of Chinese Buddhist history, as well as their intention to deal with the challenges in Chinese Buddhist communities and restore Chinese Buddhism.

In short, after the founding of the central government in Nanjing in 1928, the state's religious policy was directed by nationalistic discourses, which greatly affected the public view of the lamas and their rituals. Some politicians integrated the high-ranking lamas into the state system and promoted Buddhist ceremonies as a way to address social crises. Some Buddhist and non-Buddhist writers criticized the performance of esoteric ceremonies, but their arguments were grounded in different reasons. For the non-Buddhist authors, they questioned the relevance of religious rituals in secular life, arguing that performing rituals would undermine the enterprise of nation building. The Chinese Buddhist critics assented to perform rituals and align them with the nationalistic discourse of protecting the country, but they were divided over the acceptance of esoteric rituals. Different Buddhist parties drew upon Chinese Buddhist history and conventions to lend support to their claims, but they came to different conclusions about the origins and expressive forms of Tibetan esoteric rituals. These voices together revealed the conflicting attitudes of the various social parties toward Tibetan esoteric Buddhism, especially its distinct ritual components, and reflected the sociopolitical and religious factors that shaped their understanding.

Conclusion

Esoteric Buddhism derived its popularity in part from the way that rituals offered people consolation during tumultuous times. Available evidence suggests that ceremonies were important for the early spread of Tibetan Buddhism to the south, where Chinese Buddhism traditionally dominated. Facing the threats of wars, famine, and epidemics, the ceremonies provided a sense of comfort to the faithful.

Ceremonies were embedded within the larger context of discourse concerning modernity and nation building. As ritual specialists carried out these ceremonies and rites according to handed-down patterns and expressions, new interpretations emerged. The ceremonies provided a continuous opportunity for questioning the role of religion in modern society. For the Chinese, this negotiation involved a reevaluation of the Buddhist tradition and its position in modernity. The definitions of religion and superstition were also subject to public discussion, shaping the expressions of the Buddhist ideas and patterns of practice that were carried forward in the ongoing debates.

The public display of Buddhist ceremonies and the responses they provoked also provide entry points into investigating the conflicts generated by the competing goals of different social groups. The sociopolitical and religious trends intertwined and jointly drove the discussion of Buddhist ceremonies throughout the Republican period. In response to the sarcasm from radical writers as well as the suspicion from Buddhist critics, the advocates of esoteric Buddhism had to defend their beliefs and practices reflectively. They often grounded their arguments on their preceding knowledge of Chinese Buddhist history and the shared Mahāyāna soteriology.

The connection forged and strengthened over the ceremonies also reflected the rich communications between the lamas and the Chinese followers. These interactions enabled a reciprocal exchange in which the lamas provided knowledge to the earnest disciples, and the disciples helped the masters to adjust to the Chinese Buddhist context. The followers also disseminated the teachings by providing translation, funding, and organizing ceremonial activities. Through such collaborations, the masters learned about the expectations of the Chinese Buddhists as well as how best to respond to their needs and concerns.

THREE

Esoteric Buddhism for Laypeople

TIBETAN AND MONGOLIAN lamas in the 1920s had already attracted a growing number of followers in Chinese cities, but with the religious plurality of the 1930s and 1940s Chinese Buddhists were increasingly exposed to more than one tradition. Members of the laity who were motivated by spiritual instruction approached, studied, and compared these different practices, interpreting esoteric Buddhism in various ways. In this chapter, I focus on the learning processes of Buddhist laypersons who engaged with and adopted esoteric Buddhism, the Buddhist societies they created to support it, and the multiple roles of laywomen. To investigate the contribution of lay translators, I use *The Tibetan Book of the Dead*, a text that had been translated into multiple languages. I also uncover the views of the laity by examining Buddhist periodicals, biographies, and translated works produced by them.

Lay Buddhist Societies

In the late nineteenth and early twentieth centuries, the laity assumed active roles in Buddhist affairs in China. While many Buddhists were loosely bound to communities, some organizations had clearer, more established rules and regular routines. A survey in 1928 documented more than 250 Buddhist organizations (*fojiao jiguan* 佛教機關) in fifteen provinces. Lay societies thrived in the south, with about 200 scattered in the seven provinces on the Yangtze River.¹ Though they were present in rural areas, cities hosted the majority, and unsurprisingly, the major societies were found in centers of dense population. After all, such groups required large numbers of people for their communal activities. Some societies focused on conventional Buddhist practices, such as chanting Buddha's name. This constituted routine practice for the members of lotus societies (*lianshe* 蓮社), halls for the chanting of Buddha's name (*nianfo tang* 念佛堂), and societies of pure karma (*jingye she* 淨業社). Other Buddhists drawn to philosophical study joined societies centered on Buddhist teaching, which were usually known as assemblies of Buddhist studies (*foxuehui* 佛學會) or assemblies for the research of Buddhist studies (*foxue yanjiuhui* 佛學研究會). Taking advantage of the rising printing industry, some organizations were dedicated to the production and circulation of Buddhist texts, and hence were called places of scriptural circulation (*fojing liutongchu* 佛經流通處) or places for reading scriptures (*yuejingchu* 閱經處 or *yuelansuo* 閱覽所). Lay societies showed clear signs of their vitality in modern Chinese Buddhism.

Some of these societies helped to promote esoteric Buddhism. In a general sense, they can be classified in terms of their mission: those that advanced esoteric Buddhism as part of a broad range of programs; and those that chiefly or solely highlighted the promulgation of esoteric Buddhism. Most of the general activities of the first type were indistinguishable from those of other traditional lay societies. One discernable difference, however, concerned the way they integrated esoteric activities with ongoing conventional projects and sponsorship of masters from different backgrounds. Varied in form and content, the esoteric components were evident in their invitations to esoteric teachers to give talks, their patronage of esoteric rituals, their funding of research trips or study groups, and their publication of the newly translated esoteric texts.

A typical society of this kind was the Beijing Lay Buddhist Society (Jushilin 居士林). It was founded by Cui Yunzhai 崔雲齋 and Ding Xuqiu 丁潊秋 in 1926 in the Garden of Nurturing Spring (Yuchunyuan 毓春園) in suburban Beijing.² It had an affiliated office in the central area of the city, less than two miles west of the Forbidden City. The convenient location provided an accessible venue for urban dwellers, and its events often attracted a considerable number of attendees.³ Financially, the society ran on the profits from a privately owned woodland, the rental from a few offices, and the donations of its members. Its declared mission comprised religious and philanthropic dimensions. One regular form of programming was holding Dharma lectures: the society held more than thirty lectures on Sundays in the first three years. It also offered charitable services for the community, such as providing cowpox vaccinations for the poor in the spring and offering free tea to travelers in the summer.[4]

In 1929, when Hu Zihu became the president of the society, his religious disposition influenced its orientation. Born to a rich family in Hubei Province in central China, Hu rose to political power after the collapse of the Qing dynasty. After the outbreak of the Wuchang Uprising that marked the outbreak of the 1911 Revolution, Hu was appointed minister of finance in the Hubei military government. He later served as secretary of the interior in Hunan Province in 1914 and as governor of Fujian Province in 1917. Yet in spite of his success, his fortunes and disposition changed as a result of his son's premature death, and this finally led him to turn to religion. Hu became a loyal disciple of Taixu, firmly advocating Taixu's reforms, especially in Buddhist education. He supported initiatives to advance the education of the laity, and as a result of such support, the first women's Buddhist seminary (*nüzi foxueyuan* 女子佛學院) was opened in Beijing in 1931. His three daughters and other women studied Buddhist classics there under prominent monks and scholars.[5] In 1940, Hu presided over the Propagation Seminary of Mahāyāna Buddhism (Dasheng Fojiao Honghuayuan 大乘佛教弘化院) to educate the clergy of many hereditary temples (*zisun miao* 子孫廟) in Beijing.[6]

In addition to these projects for general Buddhist education, Hu became interested in the attempts of Taixu and Dayong to restore Chinese esoteric Buddhism by importing esoteric teachings from Japan and Tibet. This project would have been impossible without support from lay patrons. With funding from Hu and Yang Mingchen 楊明塵, Taixu and Dayong founded the Tibetan College in Beijing in 1924. The students there received training in the Tibetan language, and the school fully covered their tuition, meals, and lodging.[7] The next year, when Dayong and the students set out for Tibet, Hu and other patrons founded an organization called Beijing Supporters' Association for the Pursuit of Dharma in Tibet (Beijing liuzangxuefa houyuanhui 北京留藏學法後援會) to coordinate support for the endeavor.[8]

Hu's reform tendencies and his inclusive attitude influenced the direction of the Beijing Lay Buddhist Society, as reflected in its diversification of events in the 1930s. In 1930, Hu changed its name to Beiping Lay Buddhist Society of North China (Beiping huabei jushilin 北平華北居士林).⁹ The articulated principles of the organization were to "promote Dharma and bring salvation to sentient beings."¹⁰ After assuming the presidency of the society, Hu continued to patronize Taixu and his reforming activities. In 1930, when Taixu's monastic reform was frustrated in the south, Hu invited him to Beijing. The society published a small booklet titled "Why Should We Welcome Master Taixu?" (Weishenme yao huanying Taixu fashi 為什麼要歡迎太虛法師) as a way of advocating openly for Taixu.¹¹ Hu also patronized Taixu's building of the World Buddhist Institute (Shijie foxueyuan 世界佛學苑) at the Temple of Cypress Forest (Bailinsi 柏林寺) in 1930.¹² After coming to Beijing, Taixu gave regular talks at the society. Other frequent speakers included famous Buddhist leaders such as Changxing, Cizhou 慈舟, Tanxu 倓虛, and Zhengguo 正果.¹³

Dharma lectures remained routine activities and included esoteric elements. Hu's enthusiasm for esoteric Buddhism persisted into the 1930s and 1940s, and he supported the monks who returned from study in Tibet. Nenghai, one of the monks who went to Tibet, returned to Shanghai in 1932. Hu invited Nenghai to Beijing to give lectures. Nenghai also composed chanting manuals for the society, including *Putitang risong* 菩提堂日誦 (Daily chanting at the Hall of Bodhi) and *Guiyi faxin sheyao song* 皈依發心攝要誦 (Compendium of verses for taking refuge and making vows). The society published the two texts in 1934.¹⁴ In addition to writing manuals for devotional practice, Nenghai spoke on Tibetan Buddhist doctrines. In 1935, he delivered a series of talks on the Tibetan doctrine of the stages of the path to enlightenment (*lamrim*). Nenghai's lectures constituted some of the earliest recorded sermons on *lamrim* teaching in the Chinese Buddhist communities in the modern period. A layman named Ren Dingxun 任定詢 took notes on the lectures, and they were circulated among lay and monastic disciples both in and outside Nenghai's lineage as a guide to *lamrim* teaching.¹⁵ With support from patrons like Hu, Nenghai's presence provoked interest in Gelug teachings among the society members. A report detailed that, "through Master Nenghai's lectures on the stages of the path to enlightenment," the society members "learned about Tsongkhapa, who was really the second Dharma King."¹⁶ The following year, the society organizers built a hall at the society dedicated to the veneration of Tsongkhapa, in which a statue of Tsongkhapa was established for permanent worship.¹⁷

ESOTERIC BUDDHISM FOR LAYPEOPLE

Hu's efforts to advance esoteric Buddhism went beyond the confines of Beijing's urban settings. In 1934, when Nenghai moved to Mount Wutai, Hu's family followed him there. In 1939, Hu established the Sino-Tibetan College (Hanzang xueyuan 漢藏學院) in the Temple of Manifested Efficacy (Xiantongsi 顯通寺) at Mount Wutai to promote the translation of Tibetan works. Hu's three daughters learned the Tibetan language and later taught basic Tibetan courses there. Hu and his family followed Nenghai and other Tibetan masters until Hu passed away at Mount Wutai in 1943.[18]

The Beijing Lay Buddhist Society was one of the organizations that contributed to the spread of esoteric Buddhism in modern China. Societies that ran on a similar model included the Shanghai Lay Buddhist Society (Shanghai fojiao jushilin 上海佛教居士林), the Buddhist Association of True Beliefs in Hankou (Hankou fojiao zhengxinhui 漢口佛教正信會), the Chongqing Society of Buddhist Studies (Chongqing Foxueshe 重慶佛學社), the Chengdu Society of Buddhist Studies (Chengdu foxueshe 成都佛學社), and others. Elite members like Hu Zihu played a significant role in supporting esoteric Buddhism in urban societies. The integration of esoteric components may have originated primarily from the ardor of a handful of principal patrons rather than the interests of the participants in general. The patrons provided a public space for esoteric Buddhist teachers to articulate religious stands, perform rituals, and present themselves to a broad Chinese audience. Support from these societies allowed them to disseminate their teachings and enhance their influence in the Buddhist communities.

Lay societies of another kind were more outspoken about their mission of promulgating esoteric Buddhism. Their activities accorded well with the ideals developed by esoteric teachers. One representative society of this type was founded by Wang Hongyuan, the controversial advocate of Zhenyan Buddhism. Wang proclaimed the superiority of esoteric Buddhism over exoteric Buddhism (see chapter 1); he was consecrated by Japanese Shingon master Gonda Raifu and received the title of *ācārya* in 1926. After returning to his hometown in Chaozhou in Guangdong, Wang established the Society of the Restoration of Chinese Esoteric Buddhism (Zhendan mijiao chongxinghui 震旦密教重興會). The society published a bimonthly periodical titled *Records of Sermons About Esotericism* (*Mijiao jiangxi lu* 密教講習錄), which circulated Wang's translations and interpretations of Zhenyan teachings.[19] Wang attracted a number of disciples in Guangdong Province, and similar societies flourished in nearby counties. In 1934, Wang's followers established the Shantou Society of the Restoration of Esoteric Buddhism (Shantou mijiao chongxinghui 汕頭密教重興會) in a nearby county. Within a few months it had grown to about two hundred members.[20] Its stated mission was to "study Buddhism and promulgate the Zhenyan school of esoteric Buddhism" (*yanjiu foxue, chanyang mijiao Zhenyanzong* 研究佛學, 闡揚密教真言宗).[21] The Shantou society also published a periodical titled *Buddhist Monthly of the Light of the World* (*Shideng foxue yuekan* 世燈佛學月刊).[22] Wang's influence expanded to the neighboring Jiangxi Province. An enthusiast named Zhou Zhicheng 周志成 founded the Fengcheng Esoteric Lay Buddhist Society (Fengcheng mizong jushilin 豐城密宗居士林) in 1935, where the members gathered regularly to practice Zhenyan meditation.[23]

Societies that specifically articulated the promotion of esoteric Buddhism as their goal were far fewer in number than the societies that pursued it along with other activities. In fact, some lay Buddhists refused to identify their organization as being based on esoteric Buddhism, even though they devoted themselves primarily to esoteric practice. For example, Zhao Jianji 趙見幾, a founder of the Zhenyan Lay Buddhist Society (Zhenyanzong jushilin 真言宗居士林) in Hong Kong, attempted to open an affiliated branch in Guangzhou with the same name. But the members of Guangzhou were reluctant to accept that appellation because it indicated an exclusive connection to esoteric Buddhism. Feeling that the connotation of the name was "too narrow," the members rejected the proposal. Even though they were interested in learning esoteric knowledge, some members chose to continue with conventional practices such as chanting Amitābha Buddha's name and practicing Chan meditation. In contrast to the Zhenyan Lay Buddhist Society, the members preferred to adopt the Vihāra of Understanding and Practice (Jiexing jingshe 解行精舍) because it suggested a much broader perspective on Buddhist knowledge and practice.[24]

In general, lay organizations showed a syncretistic and inclusive attitude in promoting esoteric Buddhism. They valued esoteric components as an addition to traditional practice rather than as a complete replacement. While lay societies of the two types contributed to the spread of esoteric Buddhism, their approaches demonstrated different interpretations in relation to prevailing teachings and practices in Chinese Buddhist settings. In the cities, these lay societies became important centers for the spread of esoteric Buddhism. By coming to lectures, reading circulated texts, and attending events and activities, the enthusiasts sustained and intensified their interest in esoteric Buddhism.

The Lay Practitioners

The lay societies' promotion of esoteric Buddhism led to questions regarding the laypeople's learning process. How did they interact with the esoteric masters? In what ways did they obtain esoteric Buddhist knowledge and techniques? After receiving initiation into certain esoteric practices, how did the laypeople continue with the daily practice? Investigating the learning process of the laypeople as they interacted with the Tibetan and Mongolian lamas during the Dharma ceremonies offers some insight on these questions. Among the events organized by lay Buddhist societies, ceremonies were particularly important for the transmission of esoteric Buddhism, and this involved the collaborative effort of the lamas and the lay patrons. Especially at the consecration ceremonies, after Chinese participants received initiation to an esoteric practice, they also acquired knowledge about the specifics of certain esoteric practices. Based on the oral instruction given by the lamas, some lay assistants made an extra effort to translate, collate, and circulate manuals for esoteric practice, which further expanded the influence of esoteric Buddhism.

Lama Bai Puren, the abbot of the Yonghe Temple in Beijing, was one of the most active esoteric teachers in the 1920s. The records of his Han disciples were among the earliest surviving accounts about their experience of Dharma ceremonies in the period, therefore providing a useful example through which to examine the transmission of esoteric teachings to the laypeople at ceremonies. Lama Bai gained national fame after his 1926 tour, during which he conducted a series of ceremonies in the south (see chapter 2). On that tour, he developed a reciprocal relationship with the laity, including some top-ranking politicians and warlords.[25] After the establishment of the Nanjing government in 1927, many military and political leaders retired and moved to Tianjin, a city adjacent to Beijing. After founding Tianjin Lay Buddhist Society (Tianjin fojiao jushilin 天津佛教居士林) in the summer of 1928, the lay patrons invited Lama Bai to conduct a Golden Light Ceremony and to teach them esoteric practice, which he did in October 1928.[26] After the ceremony, the society published the *Special Issue on the Tianjin Golden Light Dharma Ceremony* (*Tianjin jinguangming fahui tekan* 天津金光明法會特刊). It not only provides details about the ceremony's procedure and the lama's sermon, but also includes manuals to guide the recipient's practice. Analyzing the *Special Issue* offers a glimpse of the Chinese adherents' learning after being initiated.

In the late 1920s, Lama Bai continued to foster a close relationship with the lay leaders, who provided enormous support for temple maintenance. In September 1928, when Lama Bai planned to renovate the Yonghe Temple in Beijing, Hu Zihu and other lay Buddhist leaders organized a committee to fund the project. In the announcement, which praised Yonghe Temple as "an important temple for esoteric Buddhism," the laymen insisted that the advocates of esoteric Buddhism should take the responsibility to repair the temple, given the loss of imperial patronage.[27] The committee worked out a renovation proposal, planning to paint all the walls, replace the roofs and windows, buy new musical instruments, and renew the Buddha statues by covering them with gold leaf.[28]

To raise funds for the project, as well as to pray for blessing, the laity invited Lama Bai Puren to conduct a Golden Light ceremony in Tianjin, which lasted from the eighth day to the fourteenth day of October in the lunar calendar. The event was initiated by the families of Li Yuanhong 黎元洪 and Xu Shichang 徐世昌, two former presidents of the Republic of China.[29] Li's family offered their mansion as the event venue and paid for all the food, and other society members helped with other logistics of the event. The preface of the *Special Issue* explained the origin of the ceremony.[30] The writer claimed that the collective karma from past deeds had invoked disasters but reminded readers that "the Buddha's efficacious response is also unbelievable." If the Buddhists gathered together in sincere repentance, the calamities would be dispelled.[31]

While the organizers indeed referred to the common Buddhist principle of karma and repentance as a theoretical basis of the ceremony, they primarily extolled the efficacy of esoteric rites. The organizers suggested that, among the many ritual alternatives offered by different Buddhist teachers, Lama Bai's Golden Light Ceremony was particularly efficacious in fulfilling goals. They extolled the efficacy of the Golden Light Sutra, calling it the "king of all the scriptures" and advocated the esoteric rite as the best way to enact the wisdom of scripture. "If we respect it, the protective gods of the earth (*dishen* 地神) will protect us. If we follow the scripture in accord with the exoteric teachings, the benefit is vast. If we practice in accord with the esoteric teachings, the effect is even more profound. Only Buddha can discern its excellence and profundity."[32]

To explain the distinction of the esoteric practice based on the scripture, the lay organizers proclaimed that even though the scripture was part of the Chinese Buddhist canon, simply learning and chanting the scripture, or intellectual reflection on the scripture, was insufficient. Esoteric practice—incorporating mantras, hand-signs, and visualization—would maximize the effect for individual praxis and communal benefit. To ensure the proper transmission of the esoteric teachings, they highlighted the significance of inviting a qualified master. They claimed, "Learning and cultivation mutually strengthen each other. We need transmission from a guru to learn such a profound teaching."[33]

The lay disciples' views seemed to echo Lama Bai's perspective about esoteric practice. In the preface of the *Special Issue*, the disciples proclaimed that Lama Bai had mastered both esoteric and exoteric knowledge about the Golden Light Sutra, but that he prioritized esoteric practice when instructing the disciples. And the preface claimed, "Lama Bai told us the importance of hearing, reflection, and practice (*wen si xiu* 聞思修) of the exoteric teachings. However, in the actual training, he emphasized the esoteric knowledge that he was transmitting to us, due to [its effect in] repentance and dispelling the disasters."[34]

Emphasizing the virtue of esoteric teachings, Lama Bai performed a variety of esoteric rites at the laypeople's request. In addition to performing the seven-day Golden Light Ceremony, Lama Bai conducted three fire-offering rituals to pray for blessings, and he also conferred esoteric consecration three times. On the first day, Lama Bai initiated about thirty core members of the society to the practice of Longevity Buddha (Changshoufo fa 長壽佛法).[35] The second consecration was conferred on about three hundred ordinary members affiliated with the lay society. The third rite, a connection-establishing consecration (*jieyuan guanding* 結緣灌頂), was openly given to some four hundred attendees. In addition, the lamas delivered a lecture about the merits of esoteric teachings to an audience of at least two hundred.[36]

Lama Bai's performance of the esoteric rites was a huge event for the newly founded lay Buddhist society in Tianjin to manage. Yet it was well organized, thanks to volunteers who dedicated themselves to assuming different tasks. Some arranged the offerings and altar adornments, some received the attendees, and some took charge of observing and documenting the various ritual events.

When Lama Bai initiated the disciples to an esoteric practice, he demonstrated how to chant the mantra, make the hand signs, and visualize accordingly. Based on his oral instruction, the lay assistants transcribed the mantra, described the process of making the hand signs, and specified the steps of making mental images.[37] They transcribed the Tibetan mantra into both Chinese and Roman letters to help adherents pronounce the mantra accurately. For example, the three-syllable mantra was transcribed with Chinese characters as 鄂姆-阿-吽 (*e mu a hong*) and also in Roman syllables as "om A Hoong."[38] The translators explained that, compared to the Chinese transliteration, the Romanized words would help some readers imitate the practice in a more precise way. Details like this show the organizers' meticulous efforts to communicate Lama Bai's guidance. By sponsoring and staffing ceremonies in such rich ways, the lay organizers created opportunities for ordinary Chinese Buddhists to learn esoteric techniques.

Their efforts led to the publication of the *Special Issue*, which provided supplementary background information—such as the history of the different Tibetan Buddhist lineages—so that Chinese readers could understand the historical transformation of Buddhism on Tibetan soil. The *Special Issue* also identified the Buddha statues on the esoteric altar (*mitan* 密壇), the liturgical instruments, sets of offerings, and the meanings of the ritual procedures, all of which further helped the readers to appreciate the different ritualistic expressions and implications.[39]

Based on Lama Bai's oral instruction, the lay volunteers carefully compiled manuals for his disciples; originally produced for the consecration recipients in the Tianjin lay Buddhist society, these manuals were included in the *Special Issue* and thus circulated beyond the society, accessible to other Chinese Buddhists.[40] They are some of the earliest esoteric manuals available to Chinese Buddhists, offering a glimpse of how adherents learned about esoteric practices when the manuals were first published in the *Special Issue* of the late 1920s and later through successive readings.

The *Special Issue* detailed all the practices as Lama Bai taught them during the Tianjin ceremony.[41] The manual of "Wuliangshoufo fa" 無量壽佛法 (the practice of the Infinite Life Buddha), for example, included a set of chants and visualization: the verse about taking refuge, the verse of arising a vow, the four infinite minds, the mantra of purifying karma, visualization of the Buddha giving consecration, the mantra of consecration, the mantra of heart, the one-hundred-syllable mantra, and the visualization of infinite light.[42]

Through active cooperation, the Golden Light Ceremony developed and deepened the bond between Lama Bai and the laity. The ceremony not only provided the lama with the revenue needed for temple maintenance, but also helped him to enhance his connection with the followers in Beijing and Tianjin. At the same time, while Lama Bai played a pivotal role in transmitting the esoteric practices, the disciples dedicated time, funding, and talent to facilitate their dissemination. The laypeople, by learning and circulating the obtained esoteric knowledge, also contributed greatly to the communication between Chinese and Tibetan Buddhist traditions. Their active recording, translating, and written commentary helped to expand further the influence of esoteric Buddhism among Chinese Buddhists. Such a reciprocal and productive relationship continued to facilitate the development of esoteric Buddhism in Chinese cities.

Laywomen

Women contributed to the spread of esoteric Buddhism in multiple ways in the early decades of the twentieth century. In addition to being patrons, they organized women's lay societies, debated the role of women in modern Buddhism, and built seminaries for women to advance education.[43] Some women even became esoteric teachers. Previous scholarship has outlined the endeavors of eminent nuns,[44] but Buddhist writings have hardly documented laywomen's involvement at all compared to the way that male counterparts and outstanding monks and nuns have been discussed. The stories of a few representative laywomen of this period in modern China serve to reveal some facets of the female laity.

Women accounted for a considerable proportion of Buddhists affiliated with esoteric Buddhism in modern China. There were several women's communal organizations dedicated to esoteric practice. One example is a society established in Hong Kong by Zhang Yuanming 張圓明. Zhang's husband Li Yizhen 黎乙真 was a leading layman who promoted Zhenyan Buddhism there. In 1924, when Gonda Raifu was visiting Guangdong Province, Li invited him to his home in Hong Kong to consecrate his family and other enthusiasts. Later, Li traveled to Mount Kōya to receive empowerment from Gonda to be an *ācārya*.⁴⁵ In 1925, Li founded the Zhenyan Lay Buddhist Society in Hong Kong. In 1927, Li conducted a consecration rite for the first time, which attracted forty disciples.⁴⁶ In 1930, as the number of female members increased, Zhang Yuanming established the Zhenyan Lay Buddhist Women's Society (Zhenyanzong nüjushilin 真言宗女居士林).⁴⁷ The couple contributed to the spread of esoteric Buddhism in Hong Kong and the two societies they founded are still active today.

It is clear from records of the esoteric consecration rites in the 1920s and 1930s that women actively participated. In July 1930, Wang Hongyuan held a three-day consecration rite in Chaozhou, and the recipients included a monk, twenty-five laymen, and ten laywomen.⁴⁸ The ceremony sparked a contest in the Chinese Buddhist communities (see chapter 1), and Wang's legitimacy as an *ācārya* was disputed. Ignoring the criticism, Wang continued to consecrate disciples, including monastic members. In April 1932, a six-day initiation ceremony attracted a nun, forty-one laymen, and thirty-two laywomen.⁴⁹ Wang presided over a large-scale ceremony at the Vihāra of Understanding and Practice in Guangzhou in 1932. The ceremony lasted for about a month, from July 17 to August 15, during which a series of consecration rites was conducted for men and women separately. Wang conferred the Womb Realm consecration on 105 men and 110 women; the Diamond Realm consecration on 26 men and 33 women; the connection-establishing consecration on 62 men and 151 women; and the consecration of the mantra of light (*guangming zhenyan* 光明真言) on 110 men and 110 women.⁵⁰

Here, the women who received consecration outnumbered the men. Extant records provide little information besides the recipients' names and the consecration they received. The exact reason for the fervor these women apparently had for esoteric consecration is unknown. Some of the female recipients on record were wives, daughters, and mothers of male enthusiasts. For example, in 1924, a layman invited Wang Hongyuan to Guangzhou to offer consecration to his family, and Wang performed the rites not only on the layman but also on the layman's mother, wife, and sister.⁵¹ Turning to esoteric Buddhism was a family matter; in many cases a male or female family member's conversion to esoteric Buddhism could influence their other relatives.

But some women pursued esoteric Buddhism without the support of family or friends. For example, when Wang Hongyuan conferred consecration to forty-one recipients in Chaozhou in 1930, a laywoman named Lady Cai came by herself to the ceremony from another county. At that time, severely flooded roads from Chenghai 澄海 County to Chaozhou were all blocked. Yet Lady Cai's "enthusiasm for seeking Dharma" prompted her to attend,[52] even though she had recently unbound her feet.[53] Having little experience in traveling by herself, she hired a guide and "waded through dozens of miles of flood" to reach the ritual site.[54] Lady Cai's case shows that some women were keen esoteric practitioners in this period, even though the lack of sources makes it hard to determine their motivations. The need to overcome difficult life circumstances may have provided a strong incentive for women; the esoteric Buddhist idea of reaching enlightenment in this lifetime may also have offered an attractive assurance for disciples who were seeking spiritual comfort for salvation.

Many laywomen, being more than mere recipients, took on the roles of event organizers, ritual assistants, and translators. Wang Hongyuan's youngest daughter, Wang Huilan 王慧蘭, is one such example.[55] Born to a Buddhist family, Wang Huilan was enthusiastic about Buddhism from an early age. At the age of eleven, she delivered a public speech, calling to people on the street to chant Buddha's name to save the country.[56] As a teenager, she became an active participant in the Children's Saving-Nation Association (Tongzi jiuguohui 童子救國會) in Chaozhou and occasionally gave talks on basic Buddhist doctrines, such as the emptiness of the four great elements.[57] She had a talent for painting, and two of her portraits of esoteric deities were selected to grace the front covers of Buddhist periodicals.[58] When her father promoted Zhenyan Buddhism in the 1920s and 1930s, Huilan became a capable assistant; when he conferred consecration on disciples, she often acted as an instructional preceptor (*jiaoshoushi* 教授師), teaching the recipients about the ritual procedures. She translated a booklet on the history of the Shingon school from Japanese into Chinese and published it in 1936.[59]

Other women, however, asserted their individual influence without much family assistance. In this time of change, women could obtain a degree of autonomy by distancing themselves from their fathers, husbands, or other male authority figures. Some elite women learned to read and write, gaining exposure to new ideas. This advantage often allowed them some liberty to make choices about their spiritual practice. They were freed from some of the constraints that many of their contemporaries experienced in domestic life. A few laywomen even became esoteric teachers in their own right. One such teacher was Shen Shuwen 申書文 (1903–1997), a lay female master of the Karma Kagyu lineage. Her achievement helps to show female agency in a space where male power dominated. But with very few surviving records from the Republican period, we cannot clearly trace her early career. She was not an active contributor to Buddhist periodicals either, making it difficult to investigate her early thoughts. Her later activities in Taiwan were better documented, and her disciples provided useful reports for us to gain a glimpse of this female religious teacher.[60]

Shen Shuwen, also known as Elder Gongga (Gongga Laoren 貢嘎老人), was a Dharma descendent of Gangkar Rinpoche (Gongga Hutuketu 貢噶呼圖克圖, 1893–1957), a master of the Kagyu school.[61] Born to a noble Manchu family, her background gave her an advantage in education and a degree of freedom. Unlike most of her contemporaries, Shen remained single for much of her life.[62] Shen had a chance to study Buddhism with eminent Buddhist monks, including Taixu and Xuyun 虛雲. In the late 1930s, with permission from Taixu, she studied Tibetan at the Sino-Tibetan Buddhist Institute in Chongqing. As a result of her interest in esoteric Buddhism, she went to the Kham area to study Karma Kagyu teachings and follow Gangkar Rinpoche. From 1942 to 1945, she lived in solitude for a three-year meditation retreat in Mount Gongga.[63] In the following years, she assisted her guru in conducting ceremonies.[64]

After Gangkar Rinpoche passed away in Beijing in 1957, Shen left for Taiwan and founded the Gongga Vihāra (Gongga Jingshe 貢噶精舍) in Taipei in 1959. This center was one of the earliest Tibetan Buddhist institutions in Taiwan.[65] Shen conducted consecration for male and female disciples, transmitting the Great Seal (*dashouyin* 大手印), the transfer of awareness (*powafa* 頗瓦法), and other practices.[66] In 1973, Gongga Vihāra began publishing a periodical titled *Eyes of the True Dharma* (*Zhengfayan* 正法眼), which became the first Buddhist journal dedicated to promoting Tibetan Buddhism in Taiwan.[67] After she passed away in 1997, Shen was mummified, which was seen by her disciples as evidence of her spiritual attainment. The recent research by Fabienne Jagou and Stephania Travagnin has examined her role in the spread of esoteric Buddhism in Taiwan.[68]

Another respected female adept was Fang Yu 方于 (1903–2002), a college teacher and translator working in Nanjing and Kunming. Compared to Shen, fewer studies have been done on Fang and her religious circle. Fang was born in Jiangsu and grew up in Shanghai. Her father, an editor at the Shanghai Commercial Press, provided her with a good education. At age eighteen, Fang won a government fellowship to study music at Conservatoire de Lyon in France.[69] After returning to Shanghai in 1927, she taught at the Nanjing National Music College. In 1929, Fang married Li Dan 李丹, a scholar of literature whom Fang had met during her stay in France and who just returned to China. In the next decades, they both worked as college teachers and raised two children. Fang and her husband dedicated themselves to education and translation. Their most significant work includes a translation of Victor Hugo's *Les Misérables* from French into Chinese.[70]

Fang studied esoteric Buddhism with Norlha Lama, an active Tibetan Buddhist master in the eastern coastal area during the 1920s and 1930s. When working in Nanjing in 1935, Fang attended a Dharma ceremony held by Norlha and received initiation. In the months thereafter she learned more esoteric practices and became a devoted adherent.[71] In 1936, threats of war drove many residents of the capital city into exile. Fang's family also moved to Kunming in southwest China, where she taught at the National Southwest Associated University and later at Yunnan College of Art. She kept learning esoteric praxis and received initiation from Gangkar Rinpoche and Norlha's disciple Wang Jiaqi 王家齊 (1895–1959).[72] In the 1940s, Fang grew as an important organizer of Buddhist activities in the city. In 1949, Fang and the other laypeople founded Lotus Vihāra (Lianhua jingshe 蓮華精舍) to honor the teachings of Padmasambhava (Lianhuasheng Dashi 蓮華生大士), the ancient Indian master who transmitted esoteric teachings to Tibet.[73] Lotus Vihāra had served as the major center for esoteric practitioners in Kunming until its closing in 1954. After the Cultural Revolution, Fang raised funds and initiated its rebuilding. Its reopening in 1995 provided a needed place for the esoteric practitioners in Kunming. Fang continued with spreading esoteric Buddhism until she passed away in 2002.[74]

Esoteric Buddhism provided a viable venue for female Buddhists like Shen Shuwen and Fang Yu to make a reputation for themselves as religious adepts and leaders. In conventional Chinese Buddhist communities, laywomen met with great resistance in attempting to secure religious power. They had less opportunity to occupy central positions in a lineage than monks and laymen. The methods of transmission in esoteric Buddhism, however, sometimes allowed them to trespass the socially sanctioned male dominance.

Through receiving consecration from legitimate masters, some laywomen had the opportunity to assess esoteric teachings and gain respect for their achievements. In this regard, in the transmission of esoteric Buddhism, space was carved out for laywomen to establish influence and make contributions, although their influence was still often confined to the circle of esoteric Buddhists.

Lay Translators and *The Tibetan Book of the Dead*

During the Republican period, certain Tibetan Buddhist texts were introduced to Chinese Buddhists, thanks to the efforts of lay translators. The broad participation of the laity in translation was a historic phenomenon that had hardly been seen in Chinese Buddhism to that point.[75] As the research of Gray Tuttle has shown, the laity contributed a large proportion of the translated text in the two major collections that appeared in the 1930s and 1940s—namely, *The Dharma Ocean of the Esoteric Vehicle* (*Misheng fahai* 密乘法海) and *The Secret Scriptures of Tibetan Esoteric Dharma Practices* (*Zangmi xiufa midian* 藏密修法秘典).[76] The lay translators' introductions to *The Tibetan Book of the Dead* provide a valuable resource through which to examine their understanding of the specific features of Tibetan esoteric Buddhism in relation to Chinese Buddhism.

In the early twentieth century, Europeans who encountered certain Tibetan Buddhist texts had controversially sparked fascination with Tibet in the West.[77] Among these texts, *The Tibetan Book of the Dead* was possibly best known to European readers.[78] The spread of Tibetan esoteric Buddhism in China paralleled the waves of European interest in the Orient. Some works that were a hit in Europe also drew the attention of Chinese readers. How did the Chinese Buddhists read them? The Chinese translation and interpretation of *The Tibetan Book of the Dead* shows that some Chinese Buddhists took it as a guide to assist their esoteric praxis. The Chinese rendition also manifested the Western influence on the shaping of Chinese knowledge of Tibetan Buddhism. Some Chinese advocates used the reported popularity of Tibetan Buddhism in the West to argue for the validity of Tibetan Buddhist teachings.

Liberation Through Hearing During the Intermediate State (Wylie: *Bar do thos grol*, also known as Bardo Thodol, hereafter abbreviated as *Bardo Liberation*) is a scripture in the Nyingma tradition of Tibetan Buddhism. The text, commonly attributed to the eighth-century Indian master Padmasambhava, was discovered by Karma Lingpa (1326–1386), a revealer who unearthed many hidden texts in the fourteenth century. The text identifies six types of *bardo* or intermediate states. In particular, the transitional stage between the ending of this life and the beginning of the next rebirth provides a crucial opportunity for liberation. The text gives graphic descriptions of the death process and offers relevant ritual programs for the dying and the dead. The book also has relevance for living Buddhists. If, while still alive, they had become familiar with the scenes and signs of the death process and kept their mind on the savior deities, then, as newly dead, they could grasp the chance to perceive reality in the transitional state of death.[79] The American writer Walter Evans-Wentz, after learning the text from Lama Kazi Dawa-Samdup (1868–1922), rendered an English version in 1927, known as *The Tibetan Book of the Dead*.[80] In the text, Evans-Wentz also furnished his interpretations. Although later scholarship has criticized Evans-Wentz for misunderstanding the text, his rendition stirred Westerners' imagination of Tibet.[81]

Interestingly, Han Buddhists also first learned about the teaching of liberation in the intermediate state through Evans-Wentz's English rendition. Despite their interest in esoteric practice, Han Buddhists sometimes found themselves unable to attain in-depth training directly from their Tibetan masters. Due to linguistic barriers, many Tibetan masters could not communicate teachings to their Han disciples freely and with nuance. After the disciples were conferred consecration, they were often troubled by the deficiency of textual guidance.[82] For some Han Buddhists, English and Japanese translations provided an accessible entry into Tibetan teachings.

In 1936, Zhang Miaoding 張妙定 translated *The Tibetan Book of the Dead* from English into Chinese and published *Zhongyin jiudu mifa* 中陰救度密法 (The secret teaching of bardo liberation). Some Han Buddhists came to believe that Tibetan Buddhism provides effective instruction for attaining liberation after death.[83] The political instability and threats of war of the 1920s and the 1930s were the principal impetus for Han Buddhists' concern about death. Though teachings on the afterlife were available in the Chinese Buddhist canon, some esoteric practitioners found that these teachings did not satisfactorily put their anxiety about death to rest. They felt that the Tibetan teaching of *bardo* liberation provides a set of visualization techniques upon which to rely. Zhang, the Chinese translator, highlighted the practical features of the Tibetan teaching. He wrote that the text distinctively provides a clear and detailed account of the death process, which is something rarely found in canonical Chinese Buddhist works.[84] He argued that Chan and Pure Land Buddhists could not ensure a desirable rebirth because of heavy karma. Given the impermanence of human life, it is important to learn the signs of death to better prepare oneself for the journey. The text is precisely "a guide for the journey of the intermediate state after death."[85] Furthermore, Zhang argued that Han Buddhists could find in the text "ways to a complete salvation," for it offers ritual programs to liberate the dead in the forty-nine days between the moment of death and the entry into the next rebirth.[86]

For Zhang, the Western translation of *The Tibetan Book of the Dead*, rather than other death-ritual texts from Chinese Buddhist traditions, was itself proof of the validity of the Tibetan teachings. He tried to use the English edition to dispel Han Buddhists' suspicion of Tibetan Buddhism, saying, "Western Europe is a place of non-metaphysical materialism (*xingxia weiwu zhi bang* 形下唯物之邦), and the Europeans heard about Mahāyāna Buddhism millennia later than us. Yet they accepted this precious teaching before us. Shouldn't we feel ashamed for acquiring this teaching in a roundabout way through Europe?"[87] In the preface to the Chinese translation, Zhang trumpeted the superiority of Tibetan Buddhism, claiming that it is more organized and complete than other Buddhist traditions. He claimed that its feature of systematization is most visible in the Tibetan doctrine of *lamrim*, which arranges the Buddhist teachings along the stages of the path to liberation and provides instructions to disciples of varying capacities.[88] Zhang argued that Tibetan Buddhism encompasses the esoteric teachings in their entirety, as demonstrated by the profusion of tantric programs including the teaching of *bardo* liberation. Given its systematization and its integration of advanced esoteric teachings, Zhang claimed that Tibetan Buddhism "is far superior to" the Buddhist traditions of Southeast and East Asia.[89]

Another translation of Evans-Wentz's English version is *Zhongyou wenjiao dedu mifa* 中有聞教得度密法 (The secret teaching of liberation through hearing during the intermediate state), which was rendered by Zhao Hongzhu 趙洪鑄 in 1945.[90] Zhao served as a government officer in the Northwestern Bureau of Salt Management in Lanzhou in Gansu Province. In the 1920s, Zhao worked as a translator for *The Pacific Daily* (*Taipingyang ribao* 太平洋日報) in Nanjing, the capital city which many Tibetan and Mongolian lamas visited.

ESOTERIC BUDDHISM FOR LAYPEOPLE

In 1933, Zhao received consecration from Dorje Chopa. Zhao first encountered *The Tibetan Book of the Dead* in Zhang rendition. After reading it, he considered the text to provide convenient access to Tibetan esoteric practice. Zhao purchased an English copy and spent three years retranslating it. Compared to Zhang's version, Zhao's translation is marked by its practical intention and rhythmic style. He rendered it in verses of four syllables, in order to produce a version that is easy for chanting at death-bed services. Zhao proclaimed that the text is a "rare jewel," for it guides dying persons to "realize their self-nature and immediately become liberated from the cycle of birth and death."[91] By listening to the instructions and considering the meaning, those on their deathbed would perceive reality and gain enlightenment. He also noted that living people could benefit from learning about the transitional state. In addition to *The Tibetan Book of the Dead*, Zhao translated *Tibetan Yoga and Secret Doctrines*, another English rendition by Lama Kazi Dawa-Samdup and Walter Evans-Wentz.[92] Zhao translated its twenty-eight categories of yogic precepts, which were published as "Xizang fabao guanzhu" 西藏法寶貫珠 (String of jewels in Tibetan Buddhist teachings) in 1947.[93]

Zhao's retranslation of *The Tibetan Book of the Dead* was applauded by Dai Jitao and Li Jinxi 黎錦熙. Dai was a high-ranking politician who promoted Buddhism as a link between the Nationalist government and Tibet (see chapter 2).[94] In the preface to Zhao's translation, Dai acclaimed the text for its provision of comprehensive doctrines and ritual programs. In his view, although Chinese Buddhist schools had developed thought and practices relevant to death, the Tibetan book was distinctly "nuanced and complete," and said that "such completeness has never been seen in the translations in this land."[95] The Buddhist writer Li Jinxi also emphasized the significance of exploring the theories of death and the rites of Tibet. He reminded his readers about the cruelty of war and the fragility of human life. For Li, personal spiritual cultivation was particularly necessary in chaotic times, for it not only ensured a desirable rebirth after death, it also contributed collectively to the creation of a more peaceful world in the present life.[96] Li, however, criticized Evans-Wentz's introduction and addenda that constituted about half of the length of the English version, seeing those parts as "complex and redundant."[97] Yet he recognized them as Evans-Wentz's commentary on the original Tibetan teaching.

Although *The Tibetan Book of the Dead* was stimulating interest among Han Buddhists as early as the 1930s, a Chinese translation of the original Tibetan

ESOTERIC BUDDHISM FOR LAYPEOPLE

Bar do thos grol was not available until the publication of *Zhongyou jiaoshou tingwen jietuo mifa* 中有教授聽聞解脫密法 (The secret teaching of liberation through hearing during the intermediate state) by Sun Jingfeng 孫景風 in 1960.[98] This book was a product of Sun's effort to translate Tibetan tantric manuals for Han practitioners who were often troubled by the lack of ritual manuals to assist their practice after receiving consecration from the Tibetan masters. Some enthusiasts began to train themselves in Tibetan or Sanskrit to translate texts to facilitate their spiritual cultivation.

Sun was a low-ranking government officer working in Nanjing and Shanghai. As one of the founders of the Nanjing Lay Buddhist Society (Nanjing jushilin 南京居士林), Sun studied esoteric Buddhism with Norlha Lama. Frustrated by the lack of materials to assist his practice after receiving consecration, Sun started to learn Tibetan and Sanskrit. Sun faced great difficulties when he began: he was about forty years old and did not have a Tibetan teacher who could freely communicate with him in Chinese. Sun trained himself by reading Tibetan and Chinese scriptures comparatively and taking note of the terminology. After two decades of hard work, Sun had collected more than one hundred thousand Sanskrit and Tibetan Buddhist terms, with which he compiled a Sanskrit / Tibetan / Chinese dictionary in 1951.[99]

In the 1930s and 1940s, Sun dedicated himself to the collection and translation of Tibetan tantric manuals. For Sun, translation was primarily about spiritual cultivation rather than being an intellectual endeavor. He regarded his translation as "a preparatory practice" (*jiaxing* 加行) for esoteric cultivation.[100] In a letter to a friend, he described his daily labor of translation in ritualistic language: "The desk is my mandala; ink and pen are deities sitting on the mandala. When I write a Sanskrit or Tibetan word, I visualize light emitting from the word. When I hear a disturbing noise, I imagine the sound to be the melodious chanting of the deities. Pen and ink are my ritual arena. In this way, I have been cultivating my unfailing faith, practicing the six perfections of wisdom and the way of bodhisattva."[101]

Sun moved to Henan Province in central China in the 1930s and taught at the Kaifeng Buddhist Seminary (Kaifeng foxueyuan 開封佛學院).[102] In Kaifeng, he worked on collecting Tibetan texts and translation. In the 1930s and 1940s, he had collected about one hundred Tibetan tantric manuals and he worked on translating them into Chinese.[103] To manage the circulation of the high-level Tantric manuals, he only allowed access to qualified disciples who had received relevant esoteric initiations. The more basic of the manuals—more than thirty of them—were openly published.[104] After reading Zhang's translation of *The Tibetan Book of the Dead*, Sun wrote to Zhang to request a copy of the original Tibetan text.[105] But Sun did not succeed in obtaining a copy of the Tibetan original until a manuscript was found in the legacy bequeathed to him by his Tibetan teacher Bao Khenpo (Bao Kanbu 寶堪布). After reading the Tibetan original, Sun found that it was more complete than the English version, so he decided to translate from the Tibetan original into Chinese. He also added definitions for the terminology and provided images of mandalas to assist visualization practice.[106]

Translation by the laity was primarily triggered by the actual need to assist their esoteric practice. This practical intention may explain why in this period, tantric manuals constituted a majority of the texts translated by the laity. Sun, for example, regarded translation as a way of cultivation to uphold the teachings given to him by his Tibetan masters. By 1940, he had translated more than seventy tantric manuals.[107] In the earliest history of the Chinese reception of the *Liberation Through Hearing During the Intermediate State*, it is clear that Chinese Buddhists did not necessarily obtain knowledge directly from Tibetan or Mongolian monks. The Western-language versions of Tibetan texts that had yet to be translated into Chinese provided them an alternative means of learning about Tibetan doctrines. Without an institutionalized project attempting to systematically translate the Tibetan canonical works as a whole, the Chinese Buddhists' translative effort was fruitful yet sporadic. Along with the introduction of esoteric practices by their masters, the Han practitioners translated extensive texts in this period, largely centered on manuals to assist their understanding and visualization practice. The translators' personal interest, experience, and exposure to esoteric Buddhism greatly influenced their choices of the Tibetan works to be translated.

Conclusion

The laity played a significant role in the rise of esoteric Buddhism in the first decades of twentieth-century China. As a bridge between the lamas and ordinary Buddhists, a number of lay societies expedited the foothold that esoteric Buddhism was able to gain in Chinese cities. Some lay societies were exclusively devoted to the promulgation of esoteric practice, but many integrated the patronage of esoteric Buddhism into their broad and inclusive programs. The lectures given and ceremonies conducted by esoteric teachers greatly diversified the activities in lay societies.

The teachers and the disciples mutually benefited from such interaction. While lay supporters gained access to esoteric practices, esoteric teachers also enhanced their influence in Chinese Buddhist communities. By sponsoring ceremonies, offering translation, and providing supplementary explanations through publications, the lay leaders offered many opportunities for Chinese Buddhists to gain exposure to esoteric Buddhism. Lay societies provided an important platform for the public display of esoteric Buddhism, allowing esoteric masters to articulate their teachings to a large audience.

Esoteric Buddhism influenced the ways in which the laity participated in religious affairs. With the importation of new thought and practice, the disciples had more religious options than before. Not bound to a particular monastic order, the laity were more likely than monastics to gain exposure to thought and practices outside the confines of the usual religious conventions. The laypeople actively translated texts, published periodicals, and patronized a variety of activities related to esoteric Buddhism. After receiving the necessary transmission, some laymen and laywomen exercised influence and even challenged the traditional and hierarchical monastic-laity paradigm. Chinese Buddhists continued to engage with the new ideas and practices of esoteric Buddhism, applying esoteric Buddhist teachings with respect to the established philosophical frameworks in Chinese Buddhism.

FOUR

Debates on Esoteric Buddhism

WHAT DID "ESOTERIC Buddhism" (*mijiao*) mean to Chinese Buddhists in the early twentieth century? When Taixu proposed introducing "esoteric Buddhism" in 1915, he was thinking of reestablishing the Zhenyan school, one of the eight schools of the ancient Tang dynasty. The esoteric Zhenyan tradition, as he imagined it (see chapter 1), was based on the teachings of the three Indian masters and early Chinese masters like Yixing. To reestablish the school, Taixu proposed sending fifty monks to Japan for five years of study, expecting them to bring back esoteric teachings to restore Chinese esotericism.[1] The ambition of Taixu and his supporters to revive esoteric Buddhism during the 1910s was inspired by a historical narrative declaring that a body of esoteric teachings had been transmitted from Indian teachers to Chinese teachers of the then Zhenyan school, and from there to the Japanese Shingon teachers. They therefore perceived Japanese Shingon Buddhism as an intact treasury of esoteric teachings that could be tapped to revive Chinese esoteric Buddhism.

Guided by this vision, Taixu's disciple Dayong traveled to Japan, along with a few other enthusiasts. To the same end, Taixu also encouraged Wang Hongyuan's translative projects in the late 1910s and early 1920s. But Chinese Buddhists, armed as they were with the accumulated knowledge about the doctrines and practices, diverged in how they evaluated the esoteric teachings—especially those developed in the cultural context of Japan. Enthusiasts of Tibetan Buddhism further complicated the discussion as

[95]

Tibetan and Mongolian lamas and some Han adepts began transmitting esoteric teachings in Chinese cities in the mid-1920s.

Instead of seeing the transmission as an accumulation of imported knowledge, I approach it as a nonlinear, dialectical process that was shaped by cross-cultural communication as well as local adaptation. Embedded in certain sociohistorical settings, a number of Japanese and Tibetan doctrines and practices were susceptible to scrutiny in the Chinese cultural context. To explain the divergences, Han Buddhist intellectuals actively engaged with the newly obtained teachings. Among a range of Japanese ideas, the proclaimed superiority of "esoteric Buddhism" over "exoteric Buddhism" was found by many to contradict the principles of the already established conceptual frameworks of Chinese Buddhist philosophical schools. A variety of Tibetan practices—such as ritualized sexuality and institutionalized reincarnation—also raised the question about the authenticity and compatibility of the traditions.

An analysis of the debates in the 1920s and 1930s sheds light on our understanding of the Chinese reception of esoteric Buddhism in several ways. Han Buddhists' discussions represented decades of intellectual struggle to organize bodies of Buddhist knowledge into a coherent framework. When Taixu and his followers organized an ambitious plan to seek inspiration from non-Chinese traditions, they were challenged by newly obtained esoteric doctrines. To address the doctrinal contradictions, they made interpretative decisions at controversial points. As a result of debates in which Han Buddhists reasoned, evaluated, and created new understandings, the competing discourses developed in parallel. First, Han Buddhists assessed the translated Zhenyan esoteric doctrines, examining their conflicts with Chinese doctrinal classification systems. Second, they debated the effects of Zhenyan esoteric praxis, especially the assessment of the idea about "reaching Buddhahood in this lifetime." Third, the Chinese monk Chisong attempted to ameliorate the doctrinal conflicts between Zhenyan and traditional Chinese Huayan Buddhist philosophy. And fourth, the enthusiasts' defended Tibetan esoteric Buddhism by justifying the seemingly deviant practices. The different agent groups, relying on their precedent knowledge of Chinese Buddhism and its needs and challenges, made varying interpretations about esoteric Buddhism. The debates collectively raise a more general question about the evolving reception of the newly introduced knowledge in Chinese Buddhist communities, as well as the trends that contributed to such reception.

Conflicts in Doctrinal Classification

Beginning in the late Qing period, China witnessed an increase in the pursuit of learning from Japan. The Chinese government's defeat in the 1895 Sino-Japanese War prompted Chinese intellectuals to take initiatives in learning from Japan, as reflected in the rising number of students going to Japan and the increase in translating Japanese books. The translation of Zhenyan teachings evoked fascination and curiosity among Han Buddhists, leading young intellectuals to pursue learning in Japan (see chapter 1). Thus it was that in the early 1920s, some monks traveled to Japan to receive training at Mount Kōya.[2] The most renowned among them were Dayong, Chisong, and Xianyin.[3] The lay enthusiast Wang Hongyuan also traveled to Japan to receive the highest Dharma-transmitting consecration (*chuanfa guanding* 傳法灌頂) from Gonda Raifu. In the late 1910s and early 1920s, Chinese Buddhist communities witnessed the spread of Zhenyan Buddhism in Guangdong, Shanghai, Hubei, Jiangxi, and Beijing.

Nonetheless, in light of the newly accumulated knowledge, a dispute known as "the debate over esoteric Buddhism and exoteric Buddhism" broke out among Chinese enthusiasts. The findings of scholars who have discussed this debate reveal important dimensions regarding the introduction of esoteric Buddhism from Japan and Tibet. Mei Jingxuan, for example, has analyzed four aspects of the dissension: the legitimacy of laymen becoming spiritual teachers; misunderstandings about sexual tantra; bias against esoteric artistic representations; and divisions between popular and elite beliefs.[4] Luo Tongbing has provided an in-depth analysis of Taixu's works related to esoteric Buddhism and identified Taixu's changing attitudes over time.[5]

The earliest exposure of Taixu and his disciples to Zhenyan Buddhism occurred right after Dayong and Chisong arrived in Japan; the letters exchanged between Taixu and the two monks reveal that one of the deepest disagreements among Han Buddhists concerning esoteric teachings was how they compared the relevance of their teachings to other predominant teachings in Chinese Buddhism. Shingon Buddhism developed a distinctive doctrinal classification system to highlight the uniqueness of esoteric teachings. Although the difference between "esoteric Buddhism" and "exoteric Buddhism" was central to the Shingon teachings, the traditional Chinese doctrinal classification systems lacked bibliographical counterparts to substantiate those differences. How to categorize esoteric knowledge thus posed a major intellectual challenge to Han Buddhists in their initial contacts.

From the fourth century onward, to explain the contradictions among Buddhist scriptures, Chinese Buddhist thinkers systematized the scriptures and soteriological ideas to make them into a coherent whole.[6] Modern scholars generally agree that doctrinal classification (*panjiao*) represents Chinese Buddhists' attempts to solve hermeneutical problems in the growing corpus of Buddhist scriptures. As Chinese Buddhists became more familiar with the translated scriptures, they were puzzled by a range of confusing and sometimes contradictory doctrines, resulting in their formulation of theoretical frameworks to explain the contradictions. The general assumption is that Buddha revealed the truth to different degrees to take account of the varying qualifications or abilities of each audience. Some scriptures unfold the ultimate truth more fully than others to enlighten the advanced bodhisattvas. Based on this common agreement, exegetical schools prioritized different doctrinal tenets and proposed a variety of frameworks. The scholarly tradition of doctrinal classification flourished in the Sui (581–618) and Tang dynasties.[7] The two most influential structures were the "five bibliographical categories" of the Huayan school and the Tiantai school's classification of Buddhist teachings into "five periods and eight teachings."[8] But neither the Huayan nor the Tiantai school listed "esoteric Buddhism" as a separate bibliographical category in parallel with other major teachings.

Esoteric elements such as the use of spells (*dhāraṇī*) originated very early in the Indian Mahāyāna tradition and permeated many facets of Buddhism. The esoteric beliefs and practices were gradually systemized into a new genre of literature named "tantra" sometime during the sixth to seventh centuries. When a number of tantras were transmitted to China in the Tang dynasty, the Chinese bibliographers did not differentiate these texts from the Mahāyāna literature. Prior to Kūkai, Japanese scholars followed the Chinese convention and did not distinguish esoteric components from Mahāyāna thought either. Kūkai formulated "the esoteric teachings" as an independent category that had not been seen in the works of his Indian and

Chinese predecessors.[9] In *The Catalog of Imported Items*, Kūkai promulgated the teachings translated by the three Tang esoteric masters as an "esoteric vehicle."[10] Based on the new categorization, he came up with an elaborate theory to distinguish his thought from that of his contemporaries.[11]

Kūkai differentiated the teachings based on his exposition of the Mahāyāna theory of "three bodies of Buddha (*trikāya*)."[12] He postulated that only the esoteric teaching is a direct revelation of the ultimate truth or *dharmakāya* ("truth body"); the exoteric teaching is preached by the *sambhogakāya* ("reward body") and *nirmāṇakāya* Buddhas ("body of manifestation").[13] In this definition, Kūkai conceived that since *dharmakāya* Buddha manifests his state of enlightenment only in the esoteric teachings of the three mysteries, esoteric teachings are more subtle than the exoteric teachings and apprehensible only to a small audience.[14]

Based on the taxonomical categories of esoteric teachings and exoteric teachings, Kūkai reconstructed doctrinal classification in a way different from the Chinese antecedents.[15] With the newly crafted bibliographical categories of both types of teaching, Kūkai reconsidered doctrinal classification. In the *Himitsu mandara jūjū shinron* 秘密曼荼羅十住心論 (Ten abiding stages of mind according to the secret mandalas, hereafter the *Ten Abiding Stages*), Kūkai conceptualized ten ways to divide the existing scriptures.[16] He identified the teachings of Shingon as supreme in the knowledge hierarchy and presented the exoteric teachings of the seven exegetical schools of the early Heian period (794–1185) from the fourth to the ninth stage.[17]

Kūkai's doctrinal taxonomy became prevalent in Japan beginning in the early Heian period, but in China it was barely known until its introduction in the late 1910s. Kūkai's advocacy of esoteric Buddhism over other teachings shocked many Chinese Buddhist intellectuals in the early 1920s, including some devoted practitioners like Dayong and Chisong. Trained in Tiantai and Huayan philosophies, the two monks had established themselves as promising scholar-monks before traveling to Japan.[18] Surprised by what they saw as doctrinal discrepancies, they examined Kūkai's theory and found it to differ from the major frameworks of doctrinal classification in Chinese Buddhism.[19]

In general, Dayong and Chisong disagreed with Kūkai's privileging of the esoteric teachings over the exoteric teachings. They were particularly dismayed to learn that Kūkai's classification downplays the Lotus Sutra and the Avataṃsaka Sūtra, the central scriptures of the Tiantai and Huayan schools.[20]

Using Chinese taxonomical terminology, they scrutinized Kūkai's proposition through the perspectives of Tiantai and Huayan philosophies. In a letter to Taixu in the summer of 1922, Dayong and Chisong cast doubt on Kūkai's doctrinal classification of the ten stages of teachings.[21] Using the terminology of Huayan, Chisong attempted to assign the esoteric teachings into a category within the Huayan framework of doctrinal classification. Dayong wrote:

> Chisong and I have discussed Master Kūkai's classification of the ten mental stages many times. We found it hard to believe and accept. Chisong thought that esotericism [*mizong*] should belong to the category of the common teaching of the perfect teaching [*tongyuan* 同圓], same as the Lotus Sutra; the Avataṃsaka Sūtra belongs to the category of the separate teaching of the perfect teaching [*bieyuan* 別圓]. Chisong supposed that esotericism minutely describes rituals such as worshipping the eight divisions of gods and dragons [*tianlong babu* 天龍八部], therefore it cannot compare to the Avataṃsaka Sūtra that exclusively elaborates the ways of bodhisattvas.[22]

For Chisong, then, the esoteric practices, given their ritual components of worshipping gods and deities, could not compare to the more subtle teachings of the Huayan philosophy. Likewise, Dayong also rejected Kūkai's definition. Unlike Chisong, who dismissed Shingon for its emphasis on rituals, Dayong suggested that they should not judge solely in terms of rituals.[23] Dayong denied Kūkai's doctrinal classification because he departed from the positions of the Indian and Chinese esoteric antecedents. Investigating the Indian master Nāgārjuna's *Treatise on Bodhi-Mind* and the Chinese master Yixing's *Commentary on the Mahāvairocana Sūtra*, Dayong proclaimed that neither of these two commentaries supports Kūkai's assumption that esotericism transcends the Lotus Sutra or the Avataṃsaka Sūtra.[24] He went on to contend that the Tiantai and Huayan exegetical schools' doctrinal classifications predated Yixing's composition. If Yixing really considered esotericism as superior to Tiantai and Huayan teachings, he would have stated this point clearly in his writings. Also, Yixing quoted widely from the Lotus Sutra to explicate the esoteric doctrines. Hence, Dayong regarded Kūkai's interpretation of the Mahāvairocana Sūtra to be a departure from the position of Master Yixing.

Taixu took their reports seriously and he requested that Dayong provide more details regarding Kūkai's teachings. Dayong responded with a lengthy exposition on Kūkai's theoretical discrepancies. He argued that Shingon esotericism distinguishes itself from Indian and Chinese esotericism by its theory about the fruits (guofen 果分, Skt. phala-bhāva) of Buddha's enlightenment. In Dayong's understanding, Kūkai asserted that the esoteric teachings, being a direct revelation of Buddha's enlightenment, are superior to the indirect revelations found in the exoteric teachings. Referring to Indian and Chinese canonical works, Dayong highlighted the contradiction between Kūkai's proposition and the traditional view about Buddha's enlightenment, suggesting that the ultimate enlightenment is ineffable and beyond language, as he wrote: "Neither Indian nor Chinese, neither esoteric Buddhism nor exoteric Buddhism, has preached the effable nature of fruits."[25] Hence, Dayong rejected Kūkai's claim that esoteric teachings are a direct revelation and superior to exoteric teachings.[26]

In his examination of Kūkai's theories, Dayong repeatedly affirmed the absolute exegetical authority of ancient Indian and Chinese philosophers. In particular, he suggested to Taixu that they should fully embrace Yixing's endeavors to restore esoteric Buddhism in China.[27] Despite his critiques, Dayong still believed in seeking inspiration from Japanese and Tibetan esoteric masters. He told Taixu that he was planning to pursue further training in Japanese Shingon, Japanese Tendai, and Tibetan esotericism, so that "in the future, we can selectively incorporate the special strengths of Japanese and Tibetan esotericism to build esotericism."[28]

Dayong's letters shed light on the Chinese Buddhist reformers' changing attitude to Japanese esoteric Buddhism. In 1915, seeing Kūkai as a legitimate inheritor of the Chinese esoteric masters, Taixu regarded Shingon Buddhism as a source of inspiration to recover the lost Chinese esoteric teachings.[29] A decade later, acknowledging the discrepancies, Taixu no longer considered Shingon teachings to be an intact treasure of ancient Chinese esotericism, even though he continued to promote cross-cultural religious transmission in the 1920s and 1930s.[30] Having recognized the historical development in Japan, Taixu, Dayong, Chisong, and other Buddhist scholars scrutinized a plurality of esoteric ideas and practices. The preexisting knowledge systems of Tiantai and Huayan provided important theoretical grounds in their interpretations. Several propositions related to esotericism stirred up disputes among the Chinese Buddhists. When certain doctrines, such as doctrinal classification by Kūkai, were questioned, its practices also came under attack. The divisive opinions not only reflected the interpreters' perception and judgment about the imported doctrines, but also revealed the conflicts regarding authority in Chinese Buddhist communities.

Attaining Buddhahood in This Very Body

Although Taixu was ambitious in introducing esoteric Buddhism from Japan, he was cautious about certain ideas that he found inconsistent with the Mahāyāna teachings of Chinese Buddhism. As a result, a principal idea in Japanese esoteric teachings could become controversial in a Chinese reading. Taixu and many other early advocates made judgments based on their attained knowledge of Chinese Buddhism as well as their understanding of the situations in Chinese Buddhist communities. The extent to which a new doctrine or practice was accepted often depended on the interpreter's assessment of its compatibility with the fundamental teachings of Chinese Buddhism. In this regard, the introduced ideas were transmitted intermittently and adopted selectively, influenced by the translator's interest as well as the conditions in the host context. When Taixu integrated the introduction of non-Chinese Buddhist teachings into his reformative schemes, compatibility was weighted heavily in his evaluation.

For Wang Hongyuan and many early adherents of Zhenyan Buddhism, the superiority of esoteric teachings rested not only on its doctrines, but also on its praxis. Esoteric Buddhism provided a distinct set of practices to actualize the goal shared by all the Mahāyāna Buddhist traditions—to reach the highest enlightenment for the sake of all sentient beings. In general, Mahāyāna Buddhist scriptures depict the pursuit of enlightenment as a gradual path that entails the practitioners' assiduous efforts for eons to perfect wisdom and merit.[31] By contrast, esoteric teachings proclaimed the possibility of becoming a Buddha at a faster pace.[32] A Japanese legend had it that Kūkai once manifested himself as Mahāvairocana Buddha in meditation, which was taken by some devotees as evidence of Kūkai's attainment of Buddhahood. For many Chinese believers, the concept of "attaining Buddhahood in this very body" encapsulated the essence of esoteric practices. Wang Hongyuan drew on the notion to promote Zhenyan Buddhism, highlighting the speedy achievement of Buddhahood through the esoteric techniques of the "three mysteries" of body, mind, and speech.[33] Based on that notion, Wang Hongyuan and his followers proclaimed the superiority of esotericism, which caused much contention among Han Buddhists.

In the fall of 1925, concerned about the divided opinions, Taixu criticized the Zhenyan proponents for their attachment to the notion of becoming Buddha in this body.[34] Using theories of Tiantai and Chan Buddhism, Taixu understood the notion primarily as a rhetorical device.[35] Comparing it to a Chan statement of "becoming a Buddha at once (lidi chengfo 立地成佛)," and arguing that both concepts are no more than nominal designations (jiaming yanju 假名言句) for teaching purposes, Taixu suggested that these concepts not be taken literally.[36]

Furthermore, from the standpoint of Tiantai theories, Taixu concluded that esoteric teachings do not go beyond Mahāyāna teachings in terms of doctrines or praxis.[37] For example, some Chinese Zhenyan adherents proclaimed that human beings are able to become Buddhas in this lifetime, since the human body and a Buddha's body alike are constituted by the six great elements.[38] Taixu argued that, instead of suggesting an immediate transformation from an ordinary being into a Buddha, the concepts of the six elements only reaffirms the fundamental Mahāyāna idea that all sentient beings possess Buddha nature and have an innate potential for awakening.[39] Also, Taixu negated the greater effectiveness of esoteric meditative methods. Based on the Tiantai theories, Taixu claimed that, with its techniques falling into many known meditative methods to perceive reality, the esoteric incorporation of the three mysteries does not surpass the traditional meditative means as have been enumerated in the Tiantai classics.[40] Referring to Tiantai thoughts, Taixu judged that Kūkai's legendary appearance as a Buddha only indicated his entry into a profound meditative state, rather than being evidence of his becoming a Buddha.[41] In this way, questioning the notion of "becoming a Buddha in this body," Taixu rejected the claim about the superiority of esotericism over exoteric teachings.

While the discussion occurred mainly among some Chinese Buddhist intellectuals, Dayong, Chisong, and Taixu's suspicious remarks rattled the Chinese Buddhist communities and rippled abroad. The Japanese response has rarely been discussed in previous scholarship. In 1925, when Taixu led a Chinese delegation to visit Kōyasan University in Japan, Kaneyama Bokushō, Dayong's teacher at Mount Kōya, expressed his disappointment.[42] In a speech at the reception, Kaneyama explained the historical development of Shingon Buddhism in order to "correct the wrong views of Dayong" and defend the authority of Kūkai's exposition.[43] Kaneyama believed that Kūkai realized Buddhahood while alive and used Kūkai's case to argue for the efficacy of esotericism. He claimed: "Master Kūkai followed the secret teachings and reached the state of Buddha in this very body. Such is the secret doctrine of 'reaching Buddhahood in this very body,' which cannot be matched by general Buddhist teachings (yiban fojiao 一般佛教), given their need for eons to attain enlightenment."[44]

Rather than debating the merit of esotericism, Taixu stood back from the dispute and urged all parties to adopt an ecumenical attitude. At the meeting, Taixu did not reply directly to Kaneyama's proclamation that esotericism differs from exoteric Buddhism in providing rapid ways to realize enlightenment. Taixu simply commented that they could not reach a consensus immediately. Instead, Taixu cautioned against the possible divisions created by sectarian attitudes in Buddhist communities. He warned that privileging esotericism may strengthen partisan positions and sabotage the mission to build a modern Buddhism across the globe, as he responded:

> Standing on the stage of the present-day world, instead of establishing sects and claiming Buddha's self-realization [in a specific sect's teachings], isn't [it the case] that the Buddha's self-realization embodies [the teachings in] all scriptures? [Shouldn't we] practice in our minds every Dharma-door that the Buddhas, bodhisattvas, and patriarchs have established and seize the opportunity to transcend a world of sects?[45]

The dialogue between Kaneyama and Taixu shows that the evaluation of esoteric teachings in relation to exoteric teachings remained a point of dissension in cross-cultural religious communication in the 1920s. When assessing the imported knowledge, various Buddhist groups referred to different sources of doctrinal authority, which resulted in a diversity of interpretations. While Wang Hongyuan and other proponents fully accepted Kūkai's advocation, Taixu, Dayong, and others found certain ideas incommensurate with the Chinese Buddhist philosophical frameworks. Given the conflicts, the proponents strived to explain the doctrinal disparity and accommodate the teachings to Chinese Buddhist conventions. Meanwhile, cautious about the potential threats that might split the Buddhist communities, Taixu adjusted his reformative scheme and importation plans, a move evident in his changing attitudes toward esoteric Buddhism at different phases.[46] Taixu and the critics not only scrutinized the Zhenyan esoteric doctrines but were also wary of the different practices and their impact on the Chinese Buddhist institutions.

The Role of Lay Teachers

Zhenyan Buddhism brought to the Chinese Buddhist institutions ideas and practices that were conceived as challenges, as manifested in the changing relationship between laity and monastics. Many Buddhist scriptures depict an ideal Buddhist community constituted by the four orders (sizhong 四衆) of monks, nuns, laymen, and laywomen, with monks and nuns playing a leading role in disseminating Buddha's teachings.[47] In the early twentieth century, lay Buddhists increasingly assumed roles that presumably had previously been dominated by the clergy.[48] The introduction of esoteric Buddhism provided new sources of authority outside the traditional priesthood.[49] While mutual support and collaboration assisted in rejuvenating Buddhism through the introduction of esoteric teachings in the 1920s and the 1930s, the Buddhists found themselves divided over the shifting power structure. Against convention, some Buddhists supported the legitimacy of a lay ācārya to teach and confer consecration to monks and nuns. Others asserted a hierarchical source of authority and the monastics' full leadership. An analysis of the dispute reveals the intensified tensions between laity and monastics, providing insight into the influence of esoteric Buddhism on Chinese Buddhist institutions.

In November 1923, an announcement from Wang Hongyuan disturbed many Buddhists.[50] Wang intended to receive from the Japanese master Gonda Raifu the highest Dharma-transmitting consecration, which would authorize Wang to become an ācārya.[51] Wang was roundly criticized by many Buddhists, especially by the monks who were then promoting Zhenyan Buddhism.[52] Xianyin and Manshu Jiedi 曼殊揭諦—two monks who were studying in Japan, both wrote to Wang to dissuade him from receiving the consecration as a layman.[53] Arguing that the position of an ācārya was reserved for the monastics, they urged Wang to abandon secular life and join the clergy before taking such consecration.[54]

To prove the legitimacy of being a lay *ācārya*, Wang tried to find doctrinal grounds in the Chinese Buddhist canon. On the whole, the scarcity of textual records provided little information about the lay *ācārya* in history. Wang argued that esoteric ritual manuals do not stipulate clearly that an *ācārya* must be monastic. In a Tang-dynasty Buddhist account, the *Sequence of Masters and Dharma Transmissions* (*Shizi xiangcheng chuanfa cidi* 師資相承傳法次第), Wang found precedents of a few lay recipients being present in the rite of Dharma-transmission consecration.[55]

When Wang claimed that Chinese esoteric tradition has a history of authorizing laymen to become *ācārya*, the critics castigated Wang for misapprehension.[56] Dayong asserted that although some laypersons had indeed received the consecration in the Tang dynasty, only the monastics were authorized to transmit the esoteric teachings.[57] Manshu Jiedi affirmed that without any written record of their Dharma descendants, the laypeople may only have assisted in the liturgical affairs instead of hosting Dharma-transmission consecration as *ācārya*.[58] Furthermore, the critics warned against a lack of control in conducting consecration rituals and a risk of exposing the secret teachings to underqualified candidates. They argued that *ācārya* is crucial in keeping the esoteric tradition alive, and that only monks are competent to act in that capacity for they have undergone rigid training in discipline and doctrines.[59]

Wang dismissed the objection and received consecration from Gonda in Chaozhao in June 1924.[60] Later that year, Wang traveled to Japan to receive full consecration from Gonda, which entitled him to spread the teachings as an *ācārya*. After returning to Chaozhou, Wang started to perform consecration rites. His followers were mostly lay Buddhists but also included some monks and nuns.[61] With support from the Vihāra of Understanding and Practice, a Buddhist society in Guangzhou, Wang presided over a series of ceremonies at Six Banyan-Tree Temple (Liurongsi 六榕寺) and consecrated more than five hundred attendees, including monastics in 1932.

Wang was criticized by the monastic leaders for conferring consecration on monks and nuns as a layman.[62] In defense of Wang, the organizers explained why they had invited Wang rather than a monk to host the ceremonies. For the supporters, the legitimacy of Wang depended as much on the transmission he gained from Gonda as on the distinction of esotericism. The organizers argued that Gonda's consecration had admitted Wang into the line of Kūkai, making him an authorized *ācārya*. In the defense,

Wang's followers referred to the distinction of esotericism to argue for the legitimacy of lay ācārya. They claimed that by distinguishing them from other Buddhist teachings held by the Chinese monastics, esoteric teachings could be promulgated by both laity and clergy in the same capacity.[63]

The advocates also held divergent views toward the relation between esoteric teachings and exoteric teachings. The different groups did not reach a consensus and generated a variety of opinions. On one end of the spectrum, as represented by Wang Hongyuan, esoteric teachings were distinct in all aspects: the superiority of their doctrines, the praxis actualizing rapid enlightenment, and the possibility of building a more inclusive leadership. On the other end of the spectrum, as represented by Taixu, as much as he generally aspired to introduce esoteric teachings to advance a reform agenda, he was cautious about their compatibility with the preexisting Chinese Buddhist systems of knowledge. Taixu was also cautious about the frictions and challenges that he thought might undermine the existing structure of authority. As a result, competing interpretations were generated in parallel, reflecting the varying concerns of the interpreters. While some adherents insisted on following Japanese exegetical authorities, others appropriated the Chinese Buddhist philosophical frameworks as an analytical tool through which to approach the imported knowledge. The different considerations gave rise to different judgments about the Zhenyan teachings. One case in point is the dispute between Wang Hongyuan and Chisong regarding Zhenyan and Huayan teachings, which exemplifies the Han Buddhists' active attempts to negotiate the contradictions.

Comparing the Doctrines

Wang Hongyuan and Chisong played key roles in disseminating Zhenyan esotericism, yet they differed markedly in assessing its teachings in juxtaposition with prevalent Chinese Buddhist thought—particularly the Huayan doctrines with which they were both familiar. According to his biography, Wang Hongyuan was fond of reading the Avataṃsaka Sūtra—the central scripture of Huayan tradition.[64] After learning about Zhenyan esotericism in the late 1910s, Wang favored Kūkai's teachings. Although Wang continued to exposit the Avataṃsaka Sūtra and praise its profundity, he thought Zhenyan esoteric teachings reveal the ultimate truth more subtly. This stand is evident in his exposition of the *Preface to Interlinear on the* Avataṃsaka Sūtra (*Huayan shu xu* 華嚴疏序)—an important commentary by the ninth-century Huayan philosopher Chengguan 澄觀, in which Wang adopts Kūkai's doctrinal classification to understand Huayan teachings.[65]

Wang asserted that Huayan teachings are more profound than all other nonesoteric teachings, but he insisted that esoteric teachings are superior to Huayan.[66] His view is in line with Kūkai's doctrinal categorization, in which Huayan teachings are assigned to the ninth of ten stages, and esoteric Buddhism is identified as the highest. Wang reiterated Kūkai's proposition that esoteric Buddhism offers a more thorough revelation of Buddha's ultimate achievement and a more detailed delineation of the spiritual procedures. Wang proclaimed that esoteric Buddhism is soteriologically distinct in providing ways to attain Buddhahood in this lifetime.

By contrast, Chisong challenged Kūkai's differentiation from the standpoint of the one-vehicle thought (*yishengjiao* 一乘教) of Huayan.[67] Chisong articulated the differences between Huayan and esotericism in his essay "Evaluation of the Huayan and Esoteric Teachings" (Xian mi jiao heng 賢密教衡). One of the essay's most explicit features is a systematic effort to examine Kūkai's teachings from the perspective of Huayan philosophy. He criticized some Chinese advocates for following Kūkai's teachings dogmatically, dismissing other profound scriptures, and confusing their followers.[68] Chisong seemed to be especially suspicious of Kūkai's hierarchical categorization of Buddhist knowledge, such as the differentiation between exoteric teachings and esoteric teachings as well as the ten-stage doctrinal classification. To set a solid theoretical foundation for the exegetical program, Chisong referred to the Avataṃsaka Sūtra, commentaries on the Mahāvairocana Sūtra by ancient Indian and Chinese esoteric masters, as well as the scholarship of Japanese Tendai master Annen.[69]

In Chisong's interpretation, Kūkai's differentiation of exoteric and esoteric teachings stands in contrast to the one-vehicle philosophy that emphasizes the totality of all teachings. Ancient thinkers of Huayan tradition advocated the nonduality of principle and phenomena (*lishi buer* 理事不二), seeing all phenomena as a manifestation of a principle. From this perspective, myriad phenomena arise from the cosmic realm of principle just as waves rise from the ocean. With this totalistic vision, Huayan thinkers promulgated the one-vehicle philosophy that regards the teachings of different schools as conveniences to inspire disciples of varying capacities to

Buddhahood. Based on the one-vehicle doctrine, Chisong denied Kūkai's privileging of esoteric Buddhism.[70]

Chisong used the image of the ocean and its waves (a common parable in Huayan literature) to highlight the interconnection of Buddhist teachings. The ocean is defined by the totality of waves that subsume one another. Likewise, Buddhist teachings are defined by the totality of teachings that interpenetrate. Given the interconnection of all teachings, Chisong argued that Kūkai's classification cannot apply to Huayan Buddhism, nor can it neatly assign teachings of other schools into the bifurcated categories of esoteric Buddhism and exoteric Buddhism. In addition, he claimed that Huayan Buddhism also embodies the three mysteries of body, speech, and action that mark esotericism. Chisong wrote:

> Master Fazang comments that the Avataṃsaka Sūtra is a vast source of varying scriptures, just like [an ocean with] a thousand torrents of teachings pouring in. All merit returns and [the sutra] subsumes all scriptures. To whom is it exoteric? To whom is it esoteric? ... [In this scripture,] every one of its doctrines cannot be fully expounded even over inexhaustible eons; all of its chanting are true words [dhāraṇī]; none of its actions are different from secret signs [mūdras]. If we arbitrarily differentiate them, it is like trying to differentiate the waves in an ocean, saying that this wave comes from a river, that wave comes from a stream, and that wave comes from a ditch.[71]

Here Chisong claims that the inclusiveness of Huayan Buddhism allows it to subsume all teachings, making it impossible to label Huayan teachings.[72] Chisong argued that Huayan teachings transcend the classification of esoteric teachings and exoteric teachings, writing that "the designations of esoteric Buddhism and exoteric Buddhism stand outside Huayan, so we cannot judge whether Huayan is esoteric or exoteric."[73]

Abandoning Kūkai's doctrinal schemes, Chisong proceeded to fit esotericism into the existing categories of doctrinal classification. He adopted the terminology of the Huayan school to evaluate the two major esoteric scriptures of Zhenyan Buddhism: the Mahāvairocana Sūtra and the Vajraśekhara Sūtra. Chisong regarded them as some of the most profound teachings of Buddhism—although not as profound as the Avataṃsaka Sūtra—and thus he assigned them to the category "perfect teaching" (yuanjiao 圓教). Huayan philosophers placed the most important Mahāyāna texts, such as the Lotus

Sutra and the Avataṃsaka Sūtra, in the same category. Chisong explained that the Mahāvairocana Sūtra and the Vajraśekhara Sūtra belong to this category because they have features similar to the Lotus Sutra, namely that they "start with expedient teachings to show the ultimate truth and assimilate the derivative into the original."[74] Within the category of perfect teaching, however, ancient Chinese Huayan theorists assigned the Avataṃsaka Sūtra to the highest subcategory, known as the separate teaching of the perfect teaching (*bieyuan*), because the scripture articulates the most sophisticated truth for the advanced bodhisattvas.[75] Following this logic, and comparing the two tantras to the Avataṃsaka Sūtra in terms of ten aspects, Chisong claimed that he could not classify them as *bieyuan* along with the Avataṃsaka Sūtra. Instead, he assigned them to the second subcategory, the common teaching of the perfect teaching (*tongyuan*), the same as the Lotus Sutra.[76]

While Chisong insisted on the totalistic framework of one-vehicle and denied Kūkai's classification, other Zhenyan practitioners argued that the esoteric teachings are not bound by any exoteric philosophical framework. They rejected Chisong's claim that all Buddhist teachings bear features of the three mysteries, saying that the three mysteries are unique to esoteric teachings. Among the three mysteries, they particularly advocated the distinctiveness of the body mystery (*shenmi* 身密) in esotericism. They claimed that exoteric Buddhism does not sufficiently expound on the body mystery, so its followers are not fully helped to experience the conjunction of the three mysteries through which they could gain insight into the ultimate truth. For example, Cheng Zhai'an 程宅安 maintained that although the practices of chanting scriptures and observing the mind in exoteric Buddhism bear some similarities to the esoteric mysteries of speech and mind, esotericism is superior in its elaborate guidance on experiencing the body mystery.[77] Wang Hongyuan also emphasized the significance of employing the body, arguing that the Huayan tradition does not fully reveal the three mysteries because it lacks an explanation of the body mystery.[78] Wang Hongyuan called Chisong "a slave of Huayan tradition" and charged him with betraying the esoteric teachers.[79] For Wang, the distinctiveness of esotericism lies in its collective teachings of the three mysteries that guide practitioners to achieve enlightenment faster, a distinction evident in his rejoinder: "Does Huayan school ever offer the secret teaching of becoming Buddha in this very body?"[80]

Moreover, Wang argued for the absolute authority of Kūkai's teachings and urged the followers to subject themselves to this authority. For him, reading from a perspective of the existing Chinese teachings would only result in a misapprehension of the newly acquired esoteric knowledge. Wang wrote:

> Chisong quoted voluminous treatises of the Huayan masters while suppressing and distorting the esoteric teachings. Alas! Esotericism just arrived in China, like a sprout of grass, like a newborn baby. [We should] nourish and nurture it, wary of its dying. How can we suppress and destroy it? Now suppression and destruction are coming from an ācārya who is transmitting esoteric Buddhism. Alas! Chisong's publication will make esotericism subordinate to the Huayan tradition forever. It will be weakened and probably ended.[81]

In response, Chisong argued that a sectarian attitude is itself an obstacle to a Buddhist's spiritual endeavor. Based on the one-vehicle doctrine, he asserted that the ultimate aim of Buddhism is to help all sentient beings to reach enlightenment. If the disciples stubbornly adhere to the dogmas of their schools, they can neither sustain the teachings of their school nor advance their individual spiritual progress toward enlightenment. For the sake of restoring Buddhism and for personal cultivation, Chisong proposed that Buddhists should abandon their sectarian prejudices and expose themselves to all teachings.[82]

Based on the one-vehicle thought of Huayan tradition, Chisong promulgated an open attitude toward adopting esoteric teachings. For Chisong, the universality of one-vehicle philosophy serves as a principle of assimilation, based on which it becomes necessary and possible to accommodate the introduced teachings. He asked Han Buddhists to be open to learning diverse teachings. At the same time, he said, the intellectuals should clarify the doctrinal conflicts to attune the esoteric teachings to the existing systems of knowledge. In practice, varying teachings supplement each other and jointly contribute to the practitioners' spiritual progress. Hence, in Chisong's interpretation, he appropriates the all-encompassing framework of the one-vehicle to approach the introduced teachings.

In short, debates between Wang and Chisong reveal the enthusiasts' divergent views about how to approach esoteric teachings. The interpretative differences stemmed from their varying understanding of doctrinal authority. Some practitioners proclaimed the superiority of esoteric Buddhism over exoteric Buddhism. Others saw this claim as conflicting with the one-vehicle philosophy of Huayan philosophy. Instead, they ameliorated the contradictions by subsuming esoteric Buddhism under the conventional framework of the one-vehicle philosophy. Insisting on the universality of the cosmic truth, they explained the differences between esoteric Buddhism and exoteric Buddhism through the notion of convenience.

Discussing Tibetan Esoteric Buddhism

The discussion over esotericism focused on Zhenyan Buddhism in the early 1920s but expanded more broadly to other forms of esoteric Buddhism. With its increased presence in the late 1920s and 1930s, Tibetan esotericism drew much attention. Also, its distinctive practices and customs—such as ritualized sex in the highest tantra and institutionalized incarnation—further contributed to suspicion. As in the debate about Zhenyan esotericism, so too this dispute occurred mostly among Han Buddhists. With little direct input from the Tibetan and Mongolian lamas, the defense came primarily from the Han advocates. What were their strategies in communicating Tibetan esoteric teachings in relation to the preexisting Chinese Buddhist ideas and practices? Investigating the writings of the Han monks who pursued study in Tibetan seminaries in the late 1920s offers an answer to this question. The advantage of knowing both Chinese and Tibetan Buddhist traditions enabled the monks to speak directly to the folks at home. They wrote letters and essays and gave lectures to expound their views, but previous scholarship has barely examined these materials. An analysis of their apologetics would help to explore the Chinese discussion of esoteric Buddhism, as well as the tensions that shaped such expression.

When Dayong's group traveled to Kham in the late 1920s (see chapter 1), some of them received years of rigorous training in seminaries in Lhasa. After returning to their home communities in the 1930s, they became well-known writers and translators. Fazun was one of the most famous. His writings provide much information about the early representation of Tibetan esotericism.

Fazun's experience was typical, and shared similar trajectories with several monks in his cohort. Born in a poor family in Hebei in 1902, Fazun became ordained at age eighteen in a small temple at Mount Wutai. Yearning for knowledge, he entered Wuchang Buddhist Seminary, which was founded by Taixu in Hubei in 1922 to spur monastic educational reform.[83] Fazun earnestly studied Chinese Buddhist teachings until Dayong's return from Japan in 1923. Dayong's performance of Zhenyan rituals aroused enthusiasm in many seminary students. After Dayong shifted his interest to Tibetan Buddhism, Fazun and some other monks also followed him. After graduating from Wuchang Seminary, they went to Beijing to join the newly opened Tibetan College in 1924. In spite of years of failed attempts to proceed to Lhasa, they learned with the Tibetan lamas in the border region of Kham. Thanks to Amdo Geshe's assistance, Fazun ultimately got his chance to enter Drepung Seminary in Lhasa in 1930. He studied with Amdo Geshe and other teachers, until Taixu summoned him to return to teach at the Sino-Tibetan Buddhist Institute in Chongqing in 1933.

Life was not easy for Fazun and the other Han monks at Lhasa. The monks received a great deal of support from their Tibetan masters, but they still had challenges to overcome. Under constant financial stress, they lived a very simple life on a minimum stipend provided by the home patrons.[84] Fazun recalled that he lived on barley powder and butter tea throughout the years.[85] The harsh climate and tough living conditions resulted in one monk's early death.[86] In spite of the difficulties, the Han monks cherished the hard-won opportunity to study in Lhasa, as their letters to Taixu and other supporters reveal. Depicting life and education in Tibetan seminaries, these letters circulated through the popular periodical *Voice of the Sea Tide*. The monk travelers' first-hand observation provided a window into their world for Chinese readers. Their training in Kham and later in Lhasa also exposed them deeply to Tibetan Buddhism, allowing them to delineate its systematic education, rich literature, and erudite teachers. In a letter to Taixu, the monk Chaoyi 超一 explained the curriculum of Tibetan seminaries, which entailed intense study in a wide range of subjects. He supplied testimony to disabuse the readers of prejudices about the lamas' moral behaviors, arguing that the lamas studied the disciplinary codes thoroughly and followed them rigidly.[87] In Lhasa, the Han monks were thrilled to learn discipline, logic, and commentaries from the most respected teachers like Pabongka Rinpoche and Khangsar Rinpoche. Meanwhile, they were further exposed to esoteric teachings, receiving empowerment to learn a variety of esoteric practices. For example, the monk Chaoyi claimed that he received over three hundred types of initiations, mostly from Khangsar Rinpoche.[88]

Fazun and his peers were keen about building connections between the Chinese and Tibetan Buddhist leaders. They supported Taixu, who was building the Sino-Tibetan Buddhist Institute in Chongqing to promote the study of Tibetan Buddhism. Fazun recommended his guru Amdo Geshe to Taixu, arguing that the erudite teacher could benefit the Chinese Buddhists greatly. Fazun also persuaded Amdo Geshe to visit Chongqing, and in 1933, Fazun returned to Chongqing to arrange the trip. In 1935, he went back to Lhasa in an attempt to bring Amdo Geshe to Chongqing, but unfortunately, Amdo Geshe passed away before he could make the trip. In dismay, Fazun spent his last year studying in Lhasa and returned to Chongqing in 1936, where he dedicated himself to teaching and translation at the Sino-Tibetan Buddhist Institute until its closure in 1950.[89] Like Fazun, his cohort—including Nenghai, Chaoyi, and others—also actively disseminated Tibetan teachings by translation, writing, and preaching (see chapters 5 and 6).

Nonetheless, even as Fazun and his peers became more solid in their beliefs, some other enthusiasts became disillusioned. A few former practitioners openly criticized Tibetan esoteric Buddhism for its divergence from what they understood as the norm. The tension became evident in a series of articles in Buddhist periodicals in 1934 and 1935. The monk Huiding 慧定 wrote in response to dozens of questions about Tibetan esotericism, which further prompted suspicion among some Han Buddhist intellectuals.[90] Huiding was a layman from Sichuan who had spent over a decade practicing Pure Land Buddhism. After becoming fascinated by Tibetan Buddhism, he traveled to Kangding in 1934 to be ordained in a Tibetan temple. After a few months, disappointed by what he had witnessed, Huiding returned to Sichuan and criticized Tibetan Buddhism.[91] Huiding identified what he considered the issues of Tibetan esotericism, such as meat eating, transgressive behaviors in rituals, and its system of reincarnation. Arguing that all these practices contradicted the values and conventions of Chinese Buddhism, Huiding advised the common believers to continue embracing the predominant praxis of Chinese Buddhism. In particular—and by enumerating the advantages—he promoted Pure Land Buddhism as an easy path to salvation.

In response, the advocates of Tibetan Buddhism rebuked Huiding's critique. Fazun claimed that Huiding's observations would not withstand scrutiny, for his stay at the border region was too brief to allow for an in-depth perception of Tibetan Buddhism. Questioning his credibility, Fazun pointed out the errors in Huiding's description of central Tibet's culture and geography.[92] In general, the defenders acknowledged the points of controversy, but instead of seeing them as fundamental conflicts, they explained the divergences as methodological devices or adaptions for different cultural contexts. For example, Huiding quoted the Laṅkāvatāra Sūtra (Leng qie jing 楞伽經)—an important scripture in the Chinese Buddhist canon—to disapprove Tibetan lamas' eating meat. He advocated vegetarianism not only for ritualistic purity, but also for its soteriological significance in the present age.[93] Citing the doctrine of karma, Huiding highlighted the relevance of vegetarianism in an already turbulent world, warning that slaughtering animals would increase and promulgate violence. Against the background of battles raging in the world, he condemned eating meat as unethical, and as evidencing a lack of compassion and self-discipline.

Nonetheless, the adherents did not see meat eating as an issue. They argued that vegetarianism was a regional custom that emerged late in Buddhist history, and that it should therefore not be held as a universal criterion for moral judgment. Tracing the history of dietary practices, Fazun argued that vegetarianism was an exceptional result of Buddhism's evolution in Chinese culture. More broadly, Indian, Tibetan, and other Buddhist traditions did not forbid eating meat. Echoing Fazun, another writer named Yuanfang 圓方 argued that the Tibetan Buddhists were simply following the predecessor of Sakyamuni Buddha, whose order lived on alms and couldn't demand vegetarianism of its followers.[94]

Also contentious was the described use of sexuality in the consecration rites of high tantra, such as the sexual symbols integrated with the consecration rites of Supreme Yoga tantras.[95] Huiding and other critics dismissed this type of sex yoga (shuangshenfa 雙身法) as an admixture of non-Buddhist traditions, and thus as evidence of Buddhism's decadence in its last days in India. Seen as defiling and deviant, such sex rites contrasted sharply with the monastic rules. Any monk performing sex under the guise of the ritual was breaching the vow of celibacy, they said.[96] In response, Fazun argued that Huiding's imagination bore little relation to Tibetan reality. Referring to what he witnessed in Lhasa, Fazun argued that the Tibetan monks of the Gelug lineage strictly adhered to the disciplinary codes. Also, criticizing sex yoga as a disguised form of fulfilling sensual desire was to pervert its symbolic meanings, Fazun said. Being beyond ordinary comprehension, this technique demanded strict secrecy and authorization, performed only by a small number of qualified adepts to facilitate their practice. Fazun concluded that Huiding's critique was unwarranted and only exposed his ignorance about esoteric Buddhism.[97]

Another controversial point was the institution of reincarnation in Tibet. The first line of successive reincarnation emerged in the Kagyu order in the thirteenth century, after which reincarnation of the eminent teachers became common in all Tibetan orders.[98] Revered by the devotees, many reincarnate lamas—including the Dalai Lama and the Panchen Lama—acted as important religious and political leaders in Tibet. It was believed that a highly realized lama, instead of being individually liberated from the cycles of life and death, would out of compassion voluntarily choose to be reborn in the worldly existence. Hence, after a preeminent guru passed away, his disciples would seek his incarnation. Having been officially recognized, a reincarnate lama (*tulku*) would go through educational training before he was sufficiently mature to uphold the lineage.

Faith in the reincarnate lamas deeply influenced the Tibetans' beliefs and praxis. When studying in Kangding in the late 1920s, Dayong and his peers also accepted the custom. They trusted its rationale, that a guru was capable of directing his rebirth in worldly circumstances in order to benefit suffering beings. This conviction culminated in Dayong's purported reincarnation. After Dayong passed away in 1929, Dayong's cohort sought his reincarnation under the auspices of his teacher Lama Jampa. In 1932, a two-year-old boy from Kangding was recognized as Dayong's reincarnation. Several Chinese reports detailed the boy's exceptional intellect and faith in Buddhism. As in other accounts of reincarnation in Tibet, the discovery and recognition of Dayong were filled with miraculous details. One biography said that before being recognized, and without knowing the identity of the guests, the boy rejoiced at the visit of Dayong's disciples to his home and wept when they left. The boy studied with Lama Jampa until 1940, when Dayong's disciples brought him to Lhasa under the patronage of lay supporters. Because Dayong had yearned for formal education in Lhasa but was never able to achieve this during his life, Dayong's disciples cheered the boy's arrival at Lhasa and his entry to Drepung Seminary as an accomplishment of Dayong's unfulfilled aspiration.[99]

Nonetheless, some Chinese Buddhists felt dubious about the institutionalized reincarnation, finding it to conflict with the teachings of Pure Land

Buddhism. The central concern of Pure Land Buddhists is to build faith in Amitābha Buddha in hopes of being reborn in his paradisiacal land of bliss at the time of death. For those who doubt that it is possible for practitioners to be liberated through their struggle at an age of degeneration, the easy way to attain salvation is to rely on Amitābha Buddha's power and be reborn in the land of bliss. In contrast to our mundane world, Amitābha's world has no suffering, providing a shelter where the practitioners could focus on spiritual cultivation. Those who are reborn there could expect to receive Amitābha Buddha's direct instruction and make constant progress toward full enlightenment. Building faith in Amitābha Buddha and hoping for rebirth in his land are therefore essential. After its promotion by the fifth-century master Huiyuan 慧遠, chanting the name of Amitābha Buddha became a prevalent practice for Chinese Buddhists.[100]

Based on the theories of Pure Land Buddhism, when exposed to the Tibetan conceptualization of reincarnation some Buddhists expressed concern about its implication. Given the dissatisfaction in the cyclic existence, it seemed absurd to hope to extend one's life into the next worldly existence rather than to attain rebirth in the land of bliss. When staying in Kangding, Huiding encountered several groups of Tibetan lamas who were searching for their incarnate gurus. He despised the practice and scorned its practitioners as "prisoners who long for the jails."[101] Huiding asserted that being reborn in samsāra is not desirable, otherwise Amitābha Buddha would not have proclaimed the merits of the land of bliss. Likewise, in a series of essays comparing esoteric Buddhism with Pure Land Buddhism, the writer Rongkong 融空 questioned the power of the deceased lamas in orienting their rebirths. He cited ancient Chinese accounts of several adepts who were said to have failed to retain the intellectual attainments of their past lives after being reborn as humans.[102] Hence, the critics claimed that the desire to continue living in samsāra is disorienting. The Tibetan institution of reincarnation would only distract the practitioners' attention from the aim of being reborn in the land of bliss.

Taixu criticized Huiding's and Rongkong's arbitrary judgment for seeing a rebirth in pure land as the sole motive for a diverse range of Buddhists. Taixu asserted that the adepts' spiritual attainment and aspiration allow them to opt for various means to benefit the suffering beings, including reincarnating as a human guru.[103] Following Taixu, Fazun went further in rebuking the critics' disparagement. Fazun argued that the Tibetan system of incarnation is in no way contradictory to the doctrines in Pure Land Buddhism. In fact, Tibetan Buddhism offers a variety of ideas and methods to facilitate a good rebirth in pure lands—including in Amitābha Buddha's land of bliss. But unlike ordinary beings who are chained to the cyclic existence of death and birth by their ignorance and craving, the eminent lamas' rebirth is driven by compassion. An altruistic guru continually and voluntarily returns to the world to guide others toward liberation.[104] Also, he claimed that Tibetan esoteric Buddhism provides a treasury of knowledge related to death and rebirth, enabling the adepts to have control over their destinies. Therefore, their reincarnation only reveals their profound compassion, as well as the high spiritual achievement necessary to go beyond the constraints of life and death.

The debate about reincarnation reflected the different possible ways to anticipate the destinies of the high achievers after passing away. For the believers of Pure Land Buddhism, the teachers delivered the message to nurture and strengthen the disciples' faith in Amitābha Buddha. The historical patriarchs—such as Master Huiyuan—shared the same aspiration to be reborn in the land of bliss. The tradition also circulated numerous accounts of exemplary adherents who were believed to have kept their minds on the Amitābha Buddha till the last moment to attain rebirth.[105] Being reborn in the land of bliss, rather than in this world of impurity, was expected by the masters and disciples in Pure Land Buddhism. But the Tibetans commonly held that a high achiever, instead of seeking a personal liberation from the cyclic existence, could also willingly be reborn into this worldly existence.[106] With wisdom and compassion, the incarnate teachers were trusted to guide the disciples effectively. Embodying the historical masters in India and Tibet, their living presence enabled the devotees to accumulate merit by paying reverence.[107] For centuries, this faith generated and sustained various lines across Tibetan traditions. But when introduced to a circumstance in which such culture did not preexist, the practice entailed exposition, especially when it contradicted the predominant beliefs.

The different voices reflected the divisive views regarding the compatibility of Tibetan esoteric Buddhism in the Chinese cultural milieu. In the 1930s and 1940s, Taixu and Fazun expanded cross-cultural education at the Sino-Tibetan Buddhist Institute in Chongqing. But even though they attempted to clarify the seemingly different and transgressive practices, the Chinese critics remained suspicious. Questions about meat eating, ritualized sex, reincarnation, and other practices did not diminish. In 1937, Huiding's supporters collated his essays and published them in book form to alert the readers to meat eating and other "fallacies" of esoteric Buddhism. The editors wrote that given the potential for catastrophic violence and war, Buddhists should continue to abide by vegetarianism.[108] Huiding also reasserted that at a decadent age, Chinese Buddhists needed to strengthen their faith in Amitābha Buddha. Aware of the skepticism, the advocates sought a strategic accommodation of esoteric Buddhism. Additional Chinese Buddhist discussions regarding the divergences reveal how the returning monks promoted esoteric Buddhism by drawing on predominant beliefs (see chapter 6). In their interpretations, the Tibetan Buddhist teachings were presented as taking on new significance when combined with the Chinese Buddhists' concerns of study and praxis.

Conclusion

The transmission of esotericism in the 1920s and 1930s was conditioned by several dynamics in the Buddhist communities, including the reformative trend to restore Chinese Buddhism, communication with non-Chinese Buddhist traditions, and the rise of the laity in religious affairs. The cross-cultural transmission was not a mere replication of knowledge but involved the reconstruction of meanings in the host context. In the process, no individual or organization exercised unchallenged authority in defining esoteric Buddhism at large; competing discourses occurred, giving rise to a variety of interpretations and articulations. The debates among Han Buddhists also reflected an effort toward redefining esoteric teachings in connection to the preexisting Chinese Buddhist structures of knowledge. After the Tang dynasty, such detailed attention to esoteric teachings was in itself an unusual phenomenon in the Chinese Buddhist intellectual tradition.

In general, Taixu, Dayong, Chisong, and other Buddhist intellectuals showed an open but critical attitude toward the esoteric teachings. They emphasized the significance of introducing esoteric teachings from non-Chinese Buddhist traditions to revive Chinese esotericism. Recognizing the doctrinal divergences, they strived to integrate the esoteric concepts into the Chinese Buddhist structures of knowledge. In particular, they often appropriated a perspective of inclusiveness—such as the one-vehicle doctrine of Huayan—to account for the doctrinal divergences of esoteric Buddhism. At the same time, they remained suspicious of certain esoteric doctrines that they regarded as incompatible with the doctrinal structures of Chinese Buddhism. To overcome doubts, the advocates actively found ways to explain the conflicts.

The introduction of esoteric Buddhism also resulted in unexpected effects on Buddhist institutions. Even when the monastic advocates tried to deny laypersons a full access to roles of leadership, some lay teachers like Wang Hongyuan established themselves as *ācārya* and attracted a following. The competing voices about esoteric Buddhism reflected the doctrinal discrepancies between the different Buddhist traditions as well the varied interpretations of Han Buddhists about the introduced knowledge.

FIVE

The Path to Enlightenment

CHINESE BUDDHISTS' DEBATES regarding esoteric Buddhist philosophy and praxis in the 1920s and 1930s focused on doctrinal classification, the authority of lay teachers, transgressive practices, and the legitimacy of reincarnation.[1] Although the Chinese primarily found esoteric practice appealing, scholarly richness also drew their attention.[2] The exoteric components were an important part of the imported knowledge, with some principal Tibetan philosophical works—such as Tsongkhapa's *Lamrim Chenmo*, being translated into Chinese for the first time. Compared to tantras that required special authorization to access them, the philosophical texts reached a wide audience ranging from scholars to ordinary practitioners. Through the mid-1920s and after, Han Buddhist intellectuals added Tibetan commentaries to their translation and interpretation agenda, bringing a broad spectrum of texts and doctrines to public attention. As Han Buddhists discussed *lamrim* teaching, a defining and characteristic philosophy of the Tibetan Gelug lineage, they expressed considerable concern about the instrumental use of Tibetan doctrines, as well as their conformity with Chinese Buddhist thought and praxis. Emphasizing that *lamrim* could supply a constructive framework to integrate Buddhist ideas and reveal their practical aspects, Taixu, Dayong, Fazun, Nenghai, Chaoyi, and other advocates presented it as a teaching of special significance to Han Buddhists.

Lamrim: The Path to Enlightenment

Lamrim, meaning "stages of the path" or "graduated path," is a textual tradition concerning the path to enlightenment. The path or *mārga* constitutes the core of Buddha's teachings as one of the four noble truths. Different Buddhist traditions have formulated different theories to illustrate the path toward the cessation of suffering.[3] Originating from Nāgārjuna and Asaṅga, two prominent Indian philosophers, Atiśa further elaborated the *lamrim* teaching in *Bodhipathapradīpa* (Lamp for the path to enlightenment; Ch. *Puti dao deng lun* 菩提道燈論) in the eleventh century.[4] It divides the spiritual path from being a beginner to becoming enlightened into three main stages. Instructions are taught in accordance with the practitioners' levels of motivation: for persons of low capacity (*xiashi* 下士) to pursue a desirable rebirth; for persons of medium capacity (*zhongshi* 中士) to renounce the cycles of birth and death; and for persons of the highest capacity (*shangshi* 上士) to reach awakening for the sake of benefiting all sentient beings.

The *lamrim* teaching has found its way into many Tibetan Buddhist orders and launched a genre of literature. One of the most important writings is *Lamrim Chenmo* (The great treatise on the stages of the path to enlightenment; *Puti dao cidi guanglun*) by Tsongkhapa—the founder of Gelug lineage in the early fifteenth century.[5] Tsongkhapa composed *Lamrim Dordu* (Brief treatise of the stages of the path; Wylie: *Lamrim mdor bsdus*; Ch. *Puti dao cidi luelun* 菩提道次第略論)—also known as a condensed version of *Lamrim Chenmo*. Tsongkhapa also wrote a separate work on esoteric practices in light of *lamrim*, namely, *Ngagrim Chenmo* (The great treatise on the stages of the esoteric path; Wylie: *Sngags rim chen mo*; Ch. *Mizong daocidi guanglun* 密宗道次第廣論). But Tsongkhapa's *lamrim* teaching was barely known among Chinese Buddhists until modern times. The monks traveling to Tibet in the late 1920s—especially Dayong, Fazun, Nenghai, and Chaoyi, played an important role in introducing *lamrim* literature to Chinese Buddhists. A common tendency in their promotion of the *lamrim* teaching was an emphasis on *Lamrim Chenmo* and *Lamrim Dordu* (hereafter the *Brief Treatise*)—the comprehensive and the succinct versions of *lamrim* teaching that generally elucidate the way to realize enlightenment, rather than on *Ngagrim Chenmo*—the version focusing on the esoteric practices. Also, their public discussions of *Lamrim Chenmo* emphasized specific contents that illuminate the more general exoteric Buddhist teachings, overlooking aspects related to esoteric teachings.

Why did they highlight the *lamrim* teaching and how did they interpret it? The following discussion examines their interpretation and the motivations behind it.

Some Zhenyan adherents turned to Tibetan Buddhism in the 1920s (see chapter 4). Regarding Tibetan esotericism as completer and more systematic than Japanese esotericism, Dayong resolved to bring such teachings to China from Tibet. In 1925, he led a group of Buddhists toward Lhasa but was blocked at the border region for years (see chapter 1); they studied with the local Tibetan lamas in the meantime. Among the many Tibetan doctrines they studied, the *lamrim* teaching had a special appeal. In 1927, Dayong started to translate the *Brief Treatise* into Chinese, but he unfortunately passed away in 1929 after completing only five chapters.[6] Before his death, Dayong entrusted the unfinished project to Fazun, who continued to immerse himself in the study of *lamrim* after he arrived at Lhasa.[7] In 1931, Taixu established the Sino-Tibetan Buddhist Institute in Chongqing to promote monastic education in Tibetan Buddhism.[8] At Taixu's invitation, Fazun returned to head the institute in 1934, where he finished translating the full text of *Lamrim Chenmo*, in twenty-four chapters.[9] Fazun resumed Dayong's unfinished work and completed the translation of the *Brief Treatise* in 1942.[10] The publication created a sensation among Chinese Buddhist intellectuals. Two thousand copies of *Lamrim Chenmo* were reportedly sold almost immediately after being published in Wuhan. According to Fazun, the Buddhist intellectuals were completely fascinated by *lamrim*; as Fazun described it, "their exhilaration is beyond words."[11]

Before the publication, Dayong, Fazun, and many other advocates had already presented *lamrim* as a special Tibetan inspiration to Han Buddhists. On his deathbed, Dayong asked Fazun to transmit *Lamrim Chenmo* at any cost, saying, "If you could bring it back to the home folks, then the lay patrons' funds supporting our group of thirty-plus members would have been used wisely rather than have gone to waste."[12] In a memoir about their trip to Lhasa, Fazun explained why they valued the *lamrim* doctrine so much when studying with teachers in Kham and Lhasa. In the early 1920s, said Fazun, while the Panchen Lama, Lama Bai Puren, and other lamas' esoteric rituals sparked Han Buddhists' interest in esoteric Buddhism, they did not mention much about Tibetan scholarly traditions.[13] When leaving Beijing in 1925, Dayong's cohort was primarily motivated to introduce esoteric teachings. But after studying more systematically with the Buddhist masters in Kham, and as their knowledge increased, they were amazed by the highly developed Tibetan scholasticism. Fazun recalled that when he was exposed to Tibetan commentaries, he found their philosophical breadth was far beyond what he could have anticipated in his home communities.[14] Esoteric praxis did not lose its appeal, but the unexpected richness of the philosophical content further intensified their faith in Tibetan Buddhism.

For Dayong and his cohort, *Lamrim Chenmo* is the consummate work of Tsongkhapa, fully embodying the systematic aspect of the Tibetan scholarly tradition. They therefore prioritized its translation, seeing it as a valuable inspiration to offer to the Chinese Buddhists. Their promotion of *Lamrim Chenmo* was also out of practical consideration. In Fazun's view, its special importance rests on its graduated organization of all Buddhist teachings and practical orientation.[15] "Except [for] *Lamrim Chenmo*," he said, "no other book can organize all Buddhist teachings into a guide to the sentient beings for their practice."[16] Compared to many Chinese Buddhist treatises, *Lamrim Chenmo* organizes Buddhist teachings in a remarkably systematic way, which helps the practitioners to absorb and apply the knowledge. Fazun explained the significance of *lamrim*:

> The Buddha preached many methods of practice; none of them is not essential to the attainment of enlightenment. So to become an enlightened one, one has to master all the practices. The problem is, there are so many practices and they are all important. In reality, which one shall be practiced first, and which one can be practiced later? They shall be practiced in a sequential and meaningful order. To follow the path of bodhisattva, all of the Buddha's teachings—regardless of the vastness—must be learned without missing one. A plentitude of teachings needs to be arranged along a path without missing any step. Such a complete and graduated path is a path of completeness and perfection, such is the meaning of *lamrim*.[17]

Fazun claimed that the graduated teachings enable disciples to start with the practices that best accord with their capacities. In an article to explain the different Tibetan schools in comparison to the Chinese Buddhist schools, Fazun presented *lamrim* as a useful inspiration to restore Chinese Buddhism. He criticized some Chinese scholarly traditions for lacking guidance relevant to meditative practice. He took the Chengshi 成實 and the Sanlun 三論 schools of the Tang dynasty as an example, arguing that while the philosophers generated theories, they did not elucidate the ways in which the adherents could rely on these philosophical works in practice.[18]

Fazun claimed that, in addition to its focus on practicability, the *lamrim* teaching excels in supplying a more inclusive means to encompass all Buddhist teachings. He criticized the Chinese Tiantai and Huayan schools, for they highlight certain scriptures and deemphasize others, leading to the disciples' negligence of some Buddhist teachings.[19] As a result, in Fazun's view, many Han Buddhists were proclaiming themselves to be Mahāyāna Buddhists, yet were ignoring the early teachings such as those in the Āgama (*A han jing* 阿含經). Such intellectual negligence was harming the individual practitioners' spiritual growth and undermining any effort to advance Buddhist scholasticism in China, he said.[20]

By contrast, Fazun claimed that the *lamrim* teaching stands out for its comprehensiveness and practicality. By depicting the various Buddhist teachings as essential at different steps along the path to Buddhahood, it supplies its practitioners with an inclusive framework of formation. It also helps practitioners avoid the pitfalls of neglecting any particular teaching.[21] Hence, distinct from Dayong and Chisong in their evaluation of Zhenyan esotericism, Fazun didn't attempt to use the terminology of Tiantan or Huayan doctrinal classification to approach esoteric Buddhism. Instead, he tried to use the Tibetan *lamrim* as the theoretical underpinning by which to assess all Buddhist teachings, including the Tibetan esoteric teachings. Following Atiśa and Tsongkhapa, Fazun explained esoteric teachings as the advanced steps for certain practitioners on the path of bodhisattva. He claimed that the esoteric practitioners were also driven by the altruistic intention to save all sentient beings. Yearning for the rapid achievement of Buddhahood, they proceeded to the stage of esotericism to perfect their wisdom and merits swiftly.[22] For Fazun, *lamrim* not only provides a principle to subsume all Buddha's teachings, but also helps the disciples to understand a particular practice by referencing its position on the path.

Likewise, Taixu applauded *lamrim* teaching for its systematic doctrinal organization and effective instructions to the devotees. In a preface to Fazun's translation of *Lamrim Chenmo*, Taixu praised it as "incomparable" by virtue of its interconnected perspective of various theories and practices. For him, an incredible feature of *lamrim* is its inherent assumption that advanced practice necessarily depends on the more fundamental ones, such as ethical conduct. Also, emphasizing the interconnection between different teachings, the staged path weaves all teachings into an integral whole without generating conflicts. For Taixu, such a perspective spoke to his vision of Buddhism as a complete and coherent unity. He considered that many contemporary Chinese and Japanese Buddhist schools tended to harbor prejudiced views, and they privileged certain Buddhist teachings over others, writing that "Japanese Buddhism, after the Meiji restoration, is still divided by sectarian schools rather than standing as a unified and complete Buddhist body."[23] He warned that prejudiced attitudes would hinder the overall restoration of Buddhism.[24]

Taixu praised the Tibetan *lamrim* system as an inspiration for the restoration of Chinese Buddhist scholarly traditions. In the preface to Fazun's translation of *Lamrim Chenmo*, contrasting the Chinese Buddhist scholasticism to the Gelug scholarly tradition, Taixu ascribed the prosperity of Gelug scholasticism to the organizing capacity of the *lamrim* framework. Stressing the interconnection between different teachings, he observed that *lamrim* organizes a diversity of teachings in a meaningful sequence leading to the goal of enlightenment. Such an arrangement of the teachings along a graded path also provided entry points for Buddhists of varying capacities, allowing them to apply teachings useful to them. In contrast, he attributed the decline of Chinese Buddhist scholasticism to the neglect of doctrinal learning. According to his description, the majority of Chinese Buddhists were interested only in devotional or meditative practices. Meanwhile, Buddhist scholars' narrow focus on a small fraction of the Chinese canonical literature also profoundly limited their discussion.[25] Hence, Taixu seems to suggest that *lamrim* teaching could contribute to the intellectual domain, by encouraging the general Buddhist emphasis on reading and learning doctrines, and by inspiring scholars to go beyond adherence to certain teachings and to construe the scholasticism broadly.

Dayong's cohort played an important role in the promotion of the *lamrim* teaching. Sharing the same appreciation, the monks Chaoyi and Nenghai also preached on *lamrim*. Chaoyi had a similar life trajectory as Fazun. Before the trip, they had both studied at the Wuchang Buddhist Institute and the Tibetan College in Beijing. After studying in Lhasa, Chaoyi was also invited by Taixu to teach Tibetan Buddhism at the Sino-Tibetan Buddhist Institute in Chongqing. Upon his return, Chaoyi translated some verses of *Lamrim Chenmo* in 1933.[26] Chaoyi and Fazun both preached in temples and lay societies in Sichuan, Jiangsu, Beijing, and Qinghai.[27]

Though Fazun taught *Lamrim Chenmo* to the students at the Sino-Tibetan Institute, little record of his lectures remains. The extant record of an elaborate discussion of *Lamrim Chenmo* is one by Nenghai, another monk traveler who joined Dayong in presenting *lamrim* as a special inspiration to Chinese Buddhists. After returning from Lhasa, *lamrim* became a frequent theme in Nenghai's lectures and writings from the 1930s to the 1960s. The following section explores Nenghai's philosophy as expressed in his interpretation. An examination of his lecture notes reveals that, while Nenghai generally accepted Tsongkhapa's exposition of *lamrim*, he actively engaged with thoughts and practices that were prevalent in Chinese Buddhist communities. Using the *lamrim* framework, he attempted to ameliorate the tension between doctrinal study and praxis, as well as conflicts between Gelug and Chan teachings regarding sudden enlightenment.

Nenghai's Interpretation of *Lamrim*

The monk Nenghai is remembered as the founder of a Gelug lineage in Chengdu in the 1930s (for more on his lineage see chapter 6). Unlike Fazun and Chaoyi, Nenghai had no seminary experience before going to Lhasa. Nor did he join the faculty at the Sino-Tibetan Institute in Chongqing after returning. Yet Nenghai showed sustained interest in Tibetan esoteric praxis, and such praxis likewise characterized the lineage that he built. But like Fazun and Chaoyi, Nenghai presented the *lamrim* doctrine as a specific inspiration, and he elaborated on how it could serve as a guide for practice.

It appears that when preaching *lamrim*, Nenghai was at the same time proposing a holistic view of Buddhist knowledge and practice. This holistic view is manifested by his integration of various scriptures, deconstruction of established categories, and accounting for doctrinal divergences. This view is possibly oriented by two considerations: first, to present *lamrim* as a hermeneutical device in integrating doctrinal learning and practice; and, second, to respond to Han Buddhist intellectuals' suspicion about esoteric Buddhism. As a result, Nenghai's interpretation shows syncretism from both Tibetan and Chinese traditions, as well as an eclectic tendency to reconcile doctrinal conflicts.

Instead of addressing a small coterie of esoteric enthusiasts, Nenghai promoted *lamrim* as an inspiration for all Chinese Buddhists. Unlike esoteric

FIGURE 5.1 A black-and-white photo of Nenghai is circulated and worshiped by the disciples.

teachings exclusively reserved for the qualified adepts, he proclaimed, the *lamrim* doctrine provides general outlines that all Buddhists, regardless of their praxis choices, could benefit from learning. Nenghai appropriated *lamrim* to emphasize doctrinal knowledge as an essential foundation for practice. Following the standard Gelug explanation, Nenghai proceeded to explain the three principal stages of *lamrim*, claiming that such organization of knowledge helps practitioners of different motivations to reach three graduated but interconnected goals: to attain a desirable rebirth by behaving ethically and refraining from evil conduct; to renounce the cyclic existence after realizing its impermanence and suffering in the six destinies; and to develop bodhicitta (*putixin* 菩提心)—an enlightened mind to strive for the spiritual liberation of all sentient beings from the cycle of birth and death.[28] In the lecture notes, Nenghai defined *lamrim*:

> *Lamrim* covers the thirty-seven practices that lead to enlightenment. It is a tool for guiding practice: it doesn't help if it only explains the terminology. Also, the Tibetans praise *lamrim* and call it "complete stages." [It is] complete because it incorporates both esoteric and exoteric [teachings]. [It is] graduated because [the constituents] are arranged skillfully. Only practitioners realize how amazing *lamrim* is. It is as intricate as a machine: when the first wheel turns, other wheels turn simultaneously.[29]

Here, emphasizing the instructional function of *lamrim*, Nenghai praised its complete and orderly organization of Buddhist knowledge. In his interpretation, its arrangement of the teachings is inclusive, covering all the knowledge needed by Buddhists at different stages along the path to enlightenment.

Nenghai played an active role in promoting the *lamrim* teaching, and his lectures attracted large numbers of monks, nuns, and laity. For example, in 1935, Nenghai was invited to teach *lamrim* at Guangji Monastery in Beijing. It was reported that approximately five hundred monastics and three hundred lay members came to his sermons.[30] A few months later, he was invited to give lectures on *lamrim* in Nanjing, which also attracted about five hundred attendees.[31] He composed a text titled *Puti dao cidi kesong* 菩提道次第科頌 (Compendium of *lamrim*, hereafter abbreviated as the *Compendium*), in which he explained the key verses of *Lamrim Chenmo*. On more than ten occasions before his death in 1967, he delivered lectures based on this text to laity and clergy in Shanghai, Wuhan, Chongqing, and other cities.³² According to biographies by his disciples, Nenghai used *lamrim* to instruct their practice, collating verses from *Lamrim Chenmo* for them to recite, and translating a ritual manual to guide their meditation based on its contents.³³ Nenghai's view of *lamrim* is expressed most fully in a series of lectures published as *Puti dao cidi kesong jiangji* 菩提道次第科頌講記 (Lecture Notes on the Compendium of Lamrim).³⁴ These lecture notes unfold the ways in which he presented *lamrim* to his disciples, many of whom had prior knowledge of Buddhism. In the following discussion I investigate the thoughts and interpretative strategies of his notes.

Nenghai's interpretation was more than a transliteration of *Lamrim Chenmo* in the sense that he actively engaged with texts and theories from the Chinese Buddhist traditions to explicate his points. In general, he quoted Tsongkhapa and accepted the Gelug founder's stance on most issues. Yet, like other commentators, Nenghai went beyond merely glossing the terminology and explaining the root text. In his exposition, Nenghai consulted Chinese canonical classics extensively to substantiate the points. Frequently cited sources included Mahāyāna classics such as the Lotus Sutra and the Avataṃsaka Sūtra, scriptures on the perfection of wisdom, Chan *gong'an*, the Āgama, and works of Chinese philosophers.

In presenting *lamrim* as a complete and orderly framework, Nenghai was at the same time suggesting a holistic view of Buddhist knowledge. A theme running throughout his lectures is the significance of *lamrim* in the study and practice of Buddhism. In his interpretation, an important inspiration of *lamrim* is its stage-by-stage categorization of Buddhist teachings. By organizing Buddhist knowledge and practices along the spiritual path of cultivation, *lamrim* serves to bring about what is implicit in the diverse Buddhist teachings, underscore their common ground, and organize them in a way oriented by the bodhisattva ideal and leading to universal liberation.

In his elaboration, the *lamrim* doctrine coherently integrates the three vehicles of Hīnayāna, Mahāyāna, and Tantrayāna (*misheng* 密乘). To Nenghai, the sequential arrangement of various teachings along the path does not suggest an escalation in significance. He insisted: "The teachings do not vary in their significance, rather, the practitioners vary in [their] capacities."³⁵ The diverse Buddhist doctrines are mutually related and compatible. Nenghai claimed that from the perspective of *lamrim*, "The teachings of three persons do not stand discretely, nor are they disconnected."³⁶ No teaching should be regarded as less valuable than another; they all constitute part of the path to enlightenment.

Nenghai's holistic view can be further exemplified by his critique of two hierarchical tropes about Buddhist knowledge: the superiority of Mahāyāna over Hīnayāna, and of Tantrayāna over Mahāyāna. In his interpretation these imbalanced views result from an ignorance of the interconnections between the diverse teachings, and as such they hinder the Buddhists' study and practice. For example, Nenghai claimed that the so-called Hīnayāna teachings had been unfairly underestimated by many Han Buddhists. In history, Mahāyāna Buddhism or the Great Vehicle (*dasheng* 大乘), with its bodhisattva ideal that emphasizes universal salvation, dominated Chinese Buddhism. Some prevalent Mahāyāna scriptures, such as the Lotus Sutra, promote the bodhisattva ideal and dismiss the Hīnayāna or the Small Vehicle (*xiaosheng* 小乘).

Building on the *lamrim* framework, Nenghai was drawing Han Buddhists' attention to the teachings that are conventionally associated with Hīnayāna. He argued that these teachings form an indispensable moral foundation by which all practitioners could eliminate their afflictions. In his view, by neglecting these basic teachings many Han Buddhists were embracing a lofty ideal of bodhisattva. He lambasted such practitioners for "only talking about the bodhisattva path but failing to practice the bodhisattva path."[37] Using the *lamrim* terminology, he claimed that adherents of great capacity who are motivated by the bodhisattva ideal cannot accomplish the desired achievements without mastering the preliminary training in morality.[38] Unless they fully understand persons of inferior and medium capacities, the persons of great capacity are unable to guide all sentient beings effectively toward enlightenment—and thus would undermine their endeavor of universal salvation.[39] He argued that they should integrate knowledge of all kinds and pay special attention to morality. For example, he asserted that if practitioners develop faith in karmic theory (a topic in the first category of persons of inferior capacity) and perceive the principle of conditioning (a topic in the category of persons of medium capacity), their wisdom would grow considerably. With proficiency in the fundamental teachings of ethics and doctrines, the aspirants could readily enter the bodhisattva path and develop insights into reality.[40] Therefore, Nenghai considered it "a huge mistake" to endorse Mahāyāna teachings exclusively while ignoring Hīnayāna teachings, a position he observed among Han Buddhists.[41]

Questioning the conventional systems of doctrinal classification in Chinese Buddhism, Nenghai approached the Chinese Buddhist canonical works through the new lens of *lamrim*. In particular, Nenghai envisioned the Āgama scriptures as a rich but long-forgotten source of inspiration for scholarly learning and meditative practice. In Chinese traditional systems of doctrinal classification, these early Buddhist scriptures are assigned to the category of Hīnayāna. As a result, Han Buddhists rarely devoted themselves to the scholarly learning of the Āgama, let alone based their practice on them. Nenghai emphasized the significance of the Āgama for providing fundamental teachings. As he saw it, Tibetan scholarly flourishing had much to do with its integration of all the Buddhist teachings—including studying the so-called Hīnayāna teachings. In his view, to develop scholasticism and to guide individual practice, Han Buddhists should also cultivate a proper understanding of the basic teachings by paying attention to the Āgama.

For the same reason, and from a holistic perspective, Nenghai was critical of the idea that privileged Tantrayāna over Mahāyāna, the relationship between esotericism and exoteric Buddhism that emerged as a focal point of debate among Chinese Buddhists in the 1920s and 1930s (see chapter 4). Disagreements persisted between some Zhenyan practitioners who regarded esotericism as the culmination of Buddhist teachings and those who, by contrast, remained suspicious of the authority and authenticity of esoteric teachings. While promoting Tibetan esotericism, Nenghai appeared to be less polemical than many of his contemporary esoteric advocates. Cautious about the implication of esoteric superiority, he tended to ameliorate the splitting views.

For example, a hotly debated issue concerned the possibility of achieving Buddhahood in this very life through esoteric practices. While the Zhenyan advocate Wang Hongyuan upheld the idea of claiming esoteric superiority, Taixu and other critics generally persisted in the conventional Mahāyāna view that the attainment of Buddhahood entails a long and gradual process of cultivation.[42] Nenghai seemed to avoid endorsing either side in the dispute deliberately. Instead, he gave an eclectic explanation, saying that "the time taken to become a Buddha is uncertain."[43] For him, both views are provisional tools to teach disciples of different dispositions: the notion of taking eons to reach Buddhahood serves to humble the arrogant ones, while the notion of reaching Buddhahood in this lifetime invigorates the timid.[44] Time, as a provisional phenomenon, could not be grasped as a definitive parameter to indicate one's spiritual progress accurately. In other words, becoming a Buddha does not depend on the duration of spiritual cultivation, but on the extent to which one eradicates all afflictions.[45]

Moreover, taking a holistic view, Nenghai constructed "esotericism" in connection with, rather than in contrast to, exoteric Buddhism. Quoting Tsongkhapa, Nenghai argued that the esoteric teachings and the exoteric teachings share common ground, as embodied in the graduated teachings of the three persons (*sanshi dao* 三士道). He explained esoteric teachings as an optional choice for some advanced practitioners. Yet he noted that esoteric practitioners nonetheless have to master exoteric teachings as a prerequisite, and he wrote:

> When one practices esotericism, it is indispensable to practice the teachings of the three persons in exoteric Buddhism. [This is because] the paths of the three persons are the foundation of cultivation, without a foundation, there will be no achievement. Before Tsongkhapa, some adepts entered the esotericism directly without practicing in the preliminary paths of three persons. After Tsongkhapa raised the Dharma-banner, the preliminary teachings become indispensable.[46]

Hence, following Tsongkhapa's stand, Nenghai highlighted the interconnection between esoteric and exoteric teachings. He defined esotericism in relation to exoteric Buddhism when he wrote: "Esotericism is special teaching [that furthers] the general teachings of the three persons."[47] In his view, if one lacks a solid basis in the exoteric teachings—such as those relevant to Buddhist ethics—then the exclusive practice of esoteric teachings is "rapid but unsafe." So for those who showed interest in esotericism, Nenghai reminded them to incorporate both exoteric and esoteric practices to ensure "safe and rapid" progress along the path to enlightenment.[48]

By regarding the exoteric teachings as an essential foundation, Nenghai's definition reflected an attempt to address the conflicts between esotericism and exoteric Buddhism as perceived by some Han Buddhists at his time. Unlike Wang Hongyuan, esoteric teachings for Nenghai do not surpass the exoteric teachings in revealing more of the ultimate truth. With *lamrim* as a hermeneutical device, Nenghai envisioned a harmonious and compatible form of Buddhism that integrates diverse teachings and practices into a coherent whole. Although he continued to use categories to refer to Buddhism—like Hīnayāna, Mahāyāna, and Tantrayāna, as well as esoteric and exoteric—he was cautious about showing partiality. A teaching was interpreted as a part of a body of Buddha's teachings and inherently interconnected with all others. Drawing on *lamrim*, he seems to argue that the varied forms of Buddhist knowledge cross-pollinate each other: they are complementary to and interdependent on each other.

Integration of Doctrinal Learning and Meditative Praxis

Resonating with Dayong, Taixu, and Fazun, Nenghai highlighted the practical use of *lamrim*. In his writings, Nenghai explained why *lamrim* could be an inspiration to reappraise doctrinal inquiry and meditative practice. Such representation reflects a common concern shared by many Chinese Buddhist intellectuals in the late nineteenth and early twentieth centuries, when the proper relation between textual learning and meditation became a subject of dispute. The Chan tradition, a dominant form of Chinese Buddhism, suggests the ultimate irrelevance of reasoning to the experience of awakening. Compared to the more scholastically inclined schools that promote the analytical study of canonical texts as a means to dispel ignorance, the Chan tradition emphasizes the primacy of intuitive experience. Its rhetoric of immediacy advocates that awakening comes through direct insight rather than from conceptual knowledge.

In the late nineteenth and early twentieth centuries, when modern higher education was taking shape and religious studies became an academic discipline in China, Buddhists were challenged to reconsider the relevance of scholarly learning to their spiritual and intellectual life.[49] Some Buddhist scholars regarded the decline of scholarship in the past centuries as a sign of Buddhism's decadence. They attempted to revive Buddhist scholarship through reformative initiatives, including reprinting canonical scriptures, opening seminaries and colleges, and publishing newspapers and periodicals.

With the increased attention to scholasticism, the proper relationship between textual learning and meditative praxis became a subject of dispute. In his research on modern Chinese Buddhism, Holmes Welch regards the balance between study and practice as the most basic and pervasive issue that divided the Buddhist community.[50] In Buddhist journals and newspapers in the Republican period, we can find many articles debating the issue. Some

FIGURE 5.2 The disciples also built statues of Nenghai for worshipping in the temples. A statue of Nenghai inside the Memorial Hall, Mount Wutai.

FIGURE 5.3 A statue of Nenghai in Jinci Monastery.

writers criticized Chinese Buddhist traditions, arguing that the general emphasis on intuition had hindered the advancement of scholarly learning. In 1922, Ouyang Jingwu 歐陽竟無, a famous lay Buddhist scholar, criticized Chan practitioners for overlooking textual study. He asserted that their overemphasis on an intuitive approach and their neglect of doctrinal study would result in the ultimate vanishing of Buddhist teachings.[51] On the other hand, other Buddhist leaders feared that philosophical inquiry would distract disciples from spiritual cultivation. Since very few intellectuals went so far as to negate the value of meditation completely, and since most Buddhist adepts acknowledged the merit of scriptural knowledge, the two positions were not totally at loggerheads. The focus of contention was rather the appropriate relationship between study and practice.

Against this background, Nenghai's interpretation of *lamrim* could be understood as an attempt to balance the study and practice of Buddhist teachings. Certainly, Nenghai advocated scholarly learning of Buddhist teachings, and he devoted himself to translation and exposition. He was aware of the formation of new approaches to Buddhist philosophy in academic and religious settings. For example, according to biographies written by his close disciples, when Nenghai was a layman, he showed interest in Buddhist philosophy. He learned about the emergence of scholarly interest in mind-only thought among Buddhist intellectuals. When serving in the Sichuan army and deployed to Beijing in 1915, he attended classes on Buddhist philosophy given by a scholar named Zhang Kecheng 張克誠 at Peking University.[52] Nenghai greatly appreciated Zhang and learned mind-only thought with him.[53] Nonetheless, unlike for those who firmly believed in the scholarly inquiry/religious cultivation dichotomy, intellectual quest carried practical significance for Nenghai. Nenghai criticized some Buddhist scholars who studied Buddhist doctrines but ignored their relevance to meditation. For him these scholars were too "attached to words and letters," and they "gained wisdom solely from hearing but lacked insights from contemplation and meditation."[54] Nenghai held that doctrinal study must be oriented toward soteriological liberation and be accompanied by meditative experience. In his writings and lectures, Nenghai was particularly concerned with the practical significance of doctrinal study, which he wished to commend, and he singled out *Lamrim Chenmo* as an exemplary work that balances a pragmatic consideration for guiding meditation and an appreciation for theoretical sophistication.

Nenghai promoted the *lamrim* teaching for it provides easy access to Buddhist teachings and does so in a systematic and practical manner. In his understanding the Buddhist scriptures lay out a wide range of meditative contents, and *Lamrim Chenmo* systematically summarizes them.[55] It not only equips adherents with a complete vision of the path to liberation, but also provides practical instructions at every stage. By studying *Lamrim Chenmo* to become familiar with the doctrinal contents, adherents could rely on the acquired intellectual knowledge as a basis for meditation.[56] In this regard, by introducing the *lamrim* teaching, Nenghai was supplying a methodological model to ease the tension between doctrinal learning and meditative praxis.

Nenghai's advocacy of combining study and praxis resonates with Tsongkhapa's view that cultivation is a triad of hearing, thinking, and meditating (*wen si xiu*).[57] This paradigm regards doctrinal study as essential for meditation. Buddhist traditions have developed various meditative techniques.[58] Generally, Buddhist meditation practices include elements of calm abiding (*śamatha*) and insight (*vipaśyanā*).[59] Calm abiding is a mental state in which the mind becomes very settled and focused. Conjoined with calm abiding, meditators keep contemplating on the mind-objects, based on which the perception of reality arises.[60] A major controversy concerns the extent and ways in which intellectual exercise could be harnessed for meditative praxis. Rejecting the views that consider reasoning to be an obstacle to meditation, Tsongkhapa acknowledged the role of conceptual cognition in meditation.[61] For Tsongkhapa, intellectual comprehension is essential for the development of insight, which facilitates the rise of a direct perception into the ultimate truth.[62]

Following Tsongkhapa, Nenghai considered logic and reasoning beneficial rather than distracting in meditative training. By hearing and reciting the fundamental theories, the disciples could eliminate misconceptions, thereby developing conviction in the meditative contents. Upholding a triad of hearing, thinking, and meditative practice, Nenghai was in favor of the analytical meditative approach promoted by Tsongkhapa, rather than the intuitive approach advocated in Chan tradition. Nenghai claimed that intellectual and experiential approaches ultimately converge upon the same realization. He adopted analytical meditation as the major praxis in his lineage, and he declared, "The cultivation in our temple starts from apprehension and analysis (*jueguan* 覺觀)."[63]

THE PATH TO ENLIGHTENMENT

Following Tsongkhapa, Nenghai emphasized a systematic study of Buddhist doctrines as a prerequisite for meditative praxis. In a lecture on meditation, Nenghai used "suffering" (the first of the four noble truths) as an example to explain how analytical learning works in meditation.[64] The practitioners should first learn about the four attributes of the first truth, namely impermanence, misery, emptiness, and no-self. Through recitation and reflection, the cognitive knowledge matures into certainty. Such reflection is a transformative process, in which doubts and coarse defilements become diminished. With defilements reduced, the stream of consciousness calms down.[65] With the increased concentration of the mind, conceptual analysis becomes more stable and a direct insight may occur. In this way, Nenghai suggested that intellectual learning of the four noble truths provides a convenient way to cultivate a direct insight into them.[66] Hence, following Tsongkhapa, Nenghai considered philosophical learning as essential to analytical meditative training. This emphasis greatly influenced Nenghai's conception of monastic education and shaped the lineage's institutional building. Nenghai created a graduated training system to integrate doctrinal study and meditation (see chapter 6). His disciples were expected to memorize and contemplate the doctrines in the preliminary training as a preparation for their meditative practice.[67]

Furthermore, Nenghai attempted to proclaim this perspective to a broad spectrum of Han Buddhists. He held that doctrinal learning is not only essential for analytical meditation, but also valuable to intuitive meditation. It helps to validate what one attains through all forms of meditative praxis. In Nenghai's view, many Chan practitioners emphasized intuitive experience without seeking intellectual substantiation. For that reason, he thought that such intuition risks gaining a flawed or incorrect view of reality. Instead of perceiving the ultimate truth in its totality, a self-recognized awakening experience could be nothing more than a glance into a specific aspect of reality.[68] Therefore, Nenghai argued, meditative perception, if derived solely from intuition, requires intellectual justification to ensure its validity. When theoretical verification is precluded, meditators cannot acknowledge the pitfalls.[69] For example, in Nenghai's description, some Chan meditators claimed to have realized the doctrine of the middle way. But a careful examination disclosed that their views still adhered to extreme positions of nihilism or externalism, thereby contradicting the middle way doctrine that the Buddha revealed in the Mahāprajñāpāramitā Sūtra.[70] While Nenghai was not denying the approach of Chan meditation, he was trying to prove the value of doctrinal learning for the meditators. That is, conceptual knowledge derived from hearing and thinking helps to interpret and justify the knowledge gained through intuitive meditation.

A Reflection on Chan Meditation

While Nenghai adopted the meditative theories and methods proposed by Tsongkhapa, he tried to reconcile the divergent views held by Chinese Chan and Tibetan philosophers. Unlike the ancient Tibetan scholars who completely rejected the validity of Chan meditation, Nenghai promoted analytical meditation in his lineage and he simultaneously affirmed the possibility of an intuitive approach to enlightenment. He extended the *lamrim* framework to explain an array of Chinese doctrines and practices, including those that the Tibetan masters had negated, thereby presenting a holistic view of Buddhist teachings.

Nenghai faced a major challenge in how to address the conflict between the sudden enlightenment teaching of Chan Buddhism and the position of gradual enlightenment that dominated in Tibetan Buddhism. Tibetan historical evidence suggests that the earliest contact of the northern Chan school with Tibetans could be traced to the middle of the eighth century.[71] The Tibetan historical book the *Testament of Ba* documents five Tibetan envoys' reception of teaching from a Chan master named Kim Hwa-shang (Ch. Jin Heshang 金和尚).[72] Except for the *Testament of Ba* and fragmentary Chan documents discovered in Dunhuang, Master Kim's tale remained relatively obscure in Tibetan histories and left few traces in Tibetan written history.[73]

Another more well-recorded and discussed event was the Samye debate in the latter decades of the eighth century. This was a pivotal event in Tibetan Buddhist history, after which Chan teaching was prohibited by royal decree.[74] The debate was between Kamalaśīla, the Indian scholar who represented the gradual position, and the Chan monk Moheyan 摩訶衍 who expounded a radical and rather sudden enlightenment stand. They differed in how they viewed the problems of the relationship of relative and absolute truths, sudden and gradual enlightenment, and the role of learning and intuitive practice. According to Tibetan sources, the decision was in favor of the gradual enlightenment teaching: Moheyan was expelled from central Tibet, and Chan literature was subsequently banned from circulation in Tibet.[75]

Historically, the Gelug tradition rejected the sudden enlightenment position held by Moheyan and endorsed gradual enlightenment. Nenghai was aware of the historical debate and the Gelug position. Nonetheless, while adopting most of Tsongkhapa's stands, Nenghai did not follow him to dismiss Chan teachings. Instead, Nenghai tried to downplay certain doctrinal disagreements between the two traditions and highlight what they had in common.

Nenghai conceived of *lamrim* as an inclusive framework to embrace diverse Buddhist teachings, including views that were conventionally considered to oppose each other. He explained the disparate doctrines as teaching conveniences at different stages. In general, Nenghai inherited the Gelug perspective that the attainment of Buddhahood entails a gradual process of practices, along the stages elaborated in the *lamrim* teaching. He also agreed that, in addition to the meditative techniques, disciples should acquaint themselves with Buddhist ethics and philosophy.

Unlike the Tibetan predecessors, Nengai needed to address the concerns of his Chinese audience. Like Nenghai, most of his disciples received ordination in the Chan tradition and had some prior knowledge and experience of Chan.[76] They may have had many doubts about the Gelug critique of Chan. As a result, he often discussed Chan and Gelug perspectives in juxtaposition and provided analysis.

In his lectures, Nenghai actively engaged with the Chan teachings and evaluated them through the lens of *lamrim* in an attempt to account for the conflicts between Gelug and Chan teachings. For example, Nenghai explained the function of *gong'an*, or paradoxical phrases that are used as teaching tools in the Chan tradition. Nenghai argued that *gong'an* serves as a convenient device to instruct devotees of certain capacities in specific contexts, but insisted that their implications should not be applied unconditionally.[77] For example, as one *gong'an* states, "Put down the butcher's knife, become enlightened at once."[78] Based on the *lamrim* framework, Nenghai disproved this view of sudden awakening, saying: "Putting down the knife is an incipient step on the path toward Buddhahood. If [the butcher] puts down his knife, then takes it up again, is it different from not putting it down? The last moment when the butcher decides not to take up the knife again, is the real putting down. This [last moment] is a result of numerous moments of

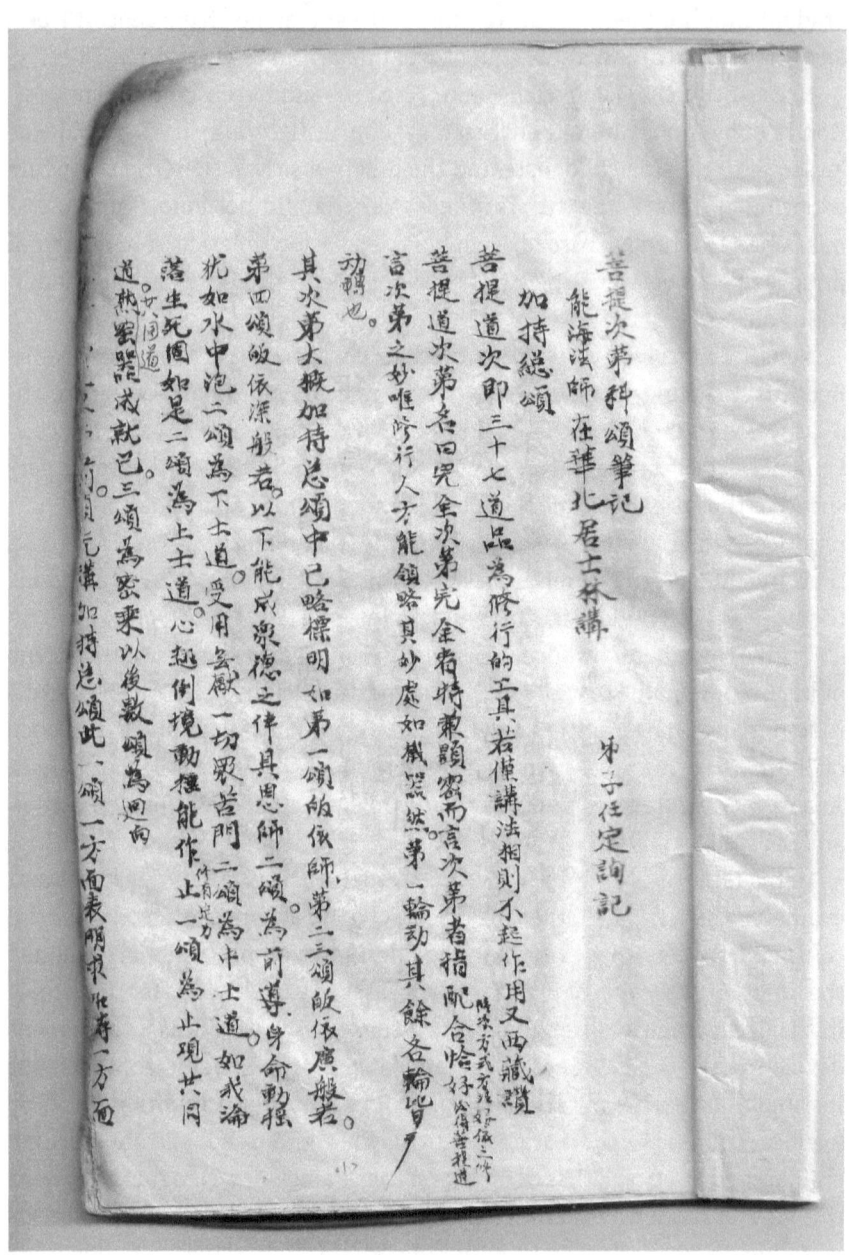

FIGURE 5.4 Lecture notes on *Lamrim Chenmo*, given by Nenghai in Beijing Lay Buddhist Society, recorded by Ren Dingxun in 1935.

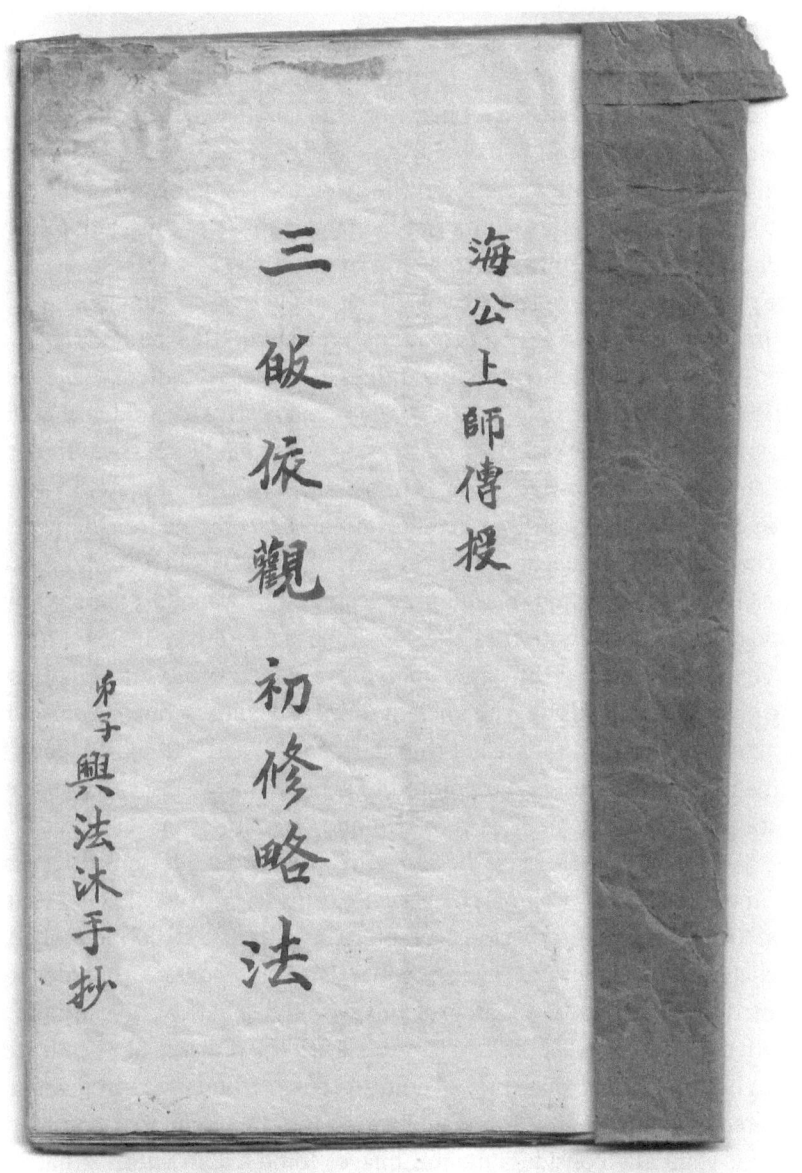

FIGURE 5.5 *The Guide to Visualize the Three Refuges,* instructed by Nenghai, recorded by Disciple Xingfa 興法 (not dated, possibly in the early 1940s).

practice."⁷⁹ What Nenghai attempted to stress is that sudden awakening, or the moment of getting a glimpse of the ultimate reality, is an intermediary stage on the path toward enlightenment. This moment signals a milestone on the path. But if the disciples make no further efforts, they may lapse into their habitual modes of behavior. Here Nenghai also suggested the importance of having a complete view of the graduated path. Aware of the different stages, the disciples would not become complacent after obtaining a glimpse of reality. A full vision of the gradual path would, therefore, encourage practitioners to continue their efforts along the spiritual journey.[80]

In other cases, he also had to explain some meditative methods that were more common in Tibetan Buddhism than in Chinese Buddhism, such as the efficacy of visualization. Visualization is a meditative technique that characteristically defines esoteric practices, in which meditators generate mental images of divine figures or other objects to contemplate.[81] Nenghai preached on a variety of Tibetan esoteric manuals, ranging from daily prayer to the high tantra such as Yamāntaka rituals.[82] He extolled Tsongkhapa for enriching esoteric thought and practices, and he warned against viewing Tsongkhapa's contribution as alien to Chinese Buddhism. Instead, he tried to connect the newly translated doctrines and practices with the preexisting ones. He claimed that the ancient Chinese Tiantai school also provided oral teaching on meditation, but that the transmission line had not been sustained.[83] Moreover, Nenghai pointed to some Chinese scriptures that enumerate a variety of meditative techniques, arguing that *Zuo chan sanmei jing* 坐禪三昧經 (The Sūtra on the Samādhi of Sitting Meditation) also touches upon visualization.[84] Compared to these extant scriptures, Nenghai claimed that Tsongkhapa's instruction on esoteric meditation is distinctively comprehensive and elaborate. Tibetan esotericism could provide a broader scope of meditative knowledge than previously available in the Chinese canon.[85]

After using canonical references to justify the practice of visualization, Nenghai proceeded to explain the different methods when he was confronted by Chan meditators. Visualization is not common in Chan meditation; it generally considers mental images to be a distraction, an attitude reflected in the following *gong'an*: "If you meet a Buddha, kill the Buddha. If you meet a patriarch, kill the patriarch."[86] In Chan Buddhism, the *gong'an* is usually understood as a warning to the disciples about attachment to any appearances. If an image of Buddha emerges in meditation, the meditators should not attach importance to it or grasp it as real.[87] But guru yoga—a common practice in Tibetan tantric Buddhism—involves visualizing one's guru or spiritual teacher as an enlightened one. It seems that Nenghai's students might have asked him about the different attitudes as reflected in the *gong'an* and guru yoga. In a lecture, he explained how the *gong'an* represents a profound insight that any conditioned appearance is ultimately empty of inherent substance.[88] Yet, guru yoga is especially useful for beginners in the initial phase. Meeting the Buddha in visualization and receiving blessings helps to empower beginners to enter the path.[89] Here again, Nenghai tried to solve the confusion caused by methodical disparities. In his exposition, the divergent statements on appearances serve different functions and are intended for practitioners at different stages.

Based on the *lamrim* framework, Nenghai actively engaged with doctrines from the different traditions to assimilate them into a whole. This attempt is obvious in his efforts to explain the contradiction between analytical meditation, which is commonly upheld by the Gelug teachers, and intuitive meditation, which is prevalent in the Chan tradition. While promoting analytical meditation, unlike the Gelug patriarchs, Nenghai did not deny the efficacy of the intuitive approach. Nenghai claimed that, while the analytical approach works well for most practitioners, the intuitive approach is efficient for some practitioners with specific qualities. He praised the Indian patriarch Bodhidharma for transmitting Chan teaching to China, saying that many Chan masters reached awakening experience through intuition-oriented meditation. Nonetheless, Nenghai regarded Chan teaching as a convenience employed by the Bodhidharma.[90] Nenghai claimed that, when Bodhidharma came to China, after finding many Chinese Buddhists obsessed by philosophy, he taught them intuitive meditation to deal with the situation. Yet Nenghai asserted that the method, taught by Bodhidharma for ancient practitioners who were preoccupied with philosophy, no longer worked as well for the modern Han Buddhists, who lacked the same sort of philosophical training.[91]

Seeing the intuitive approach as a convenient device for devotees of specific dispositions, Nenghai highlighted the gradual approach as widely suitable for Buddhists. But unlike the Tibetan philosophers, Nenghai shifted the focus from the contradiction between the sudden and gradual approaches to a focus on recognizing their common ground. He appropriated the *lamrim* framework to argue that the two seemingly conflicting positions do not suggest an absolute contradiction. He first emphasized the shared goal of the two methods, claiming that all forms of Buddhist meditative practices are oriented toward liberation. Moreover, he explained the methodical variations from the perspective of stages of the path. The sudden approach could still fit into the procedure outlined by the gradual approach: it skips some steps but still follows the overall orientation toward liberation.

A major difference between the two approaches lies in the mental activity of investigation in meditation: while analytical meditation integrates contemplation, Chan meditation regards cognitive reasoning mainly as a distraction. How could the two apparently conflicting approaches both lead to a direct insight into reality? In a lecture, Nenghai claimed that the two methods assist disciples in entering different states of concentration. One way to describe Buddhist meditative experience is through the four levels of concentration, which are accompanied by varying degrees of mental activity. An investigation is indispensable in the first concentration (*chuchan* 初禪), but no longer exists in the second concentration (*erchan* 二禪) and above. Nenghai argued that analytical meditation follows a path of progressive development, in which meditators first enter the first concentration by contemplating the contents of meditation. After their minds have become more stable, they withdraw from the investigative activity to enter deeper meditation at the next stage, in which the investigation activity is no longer visible. The intuitive meditation of Chan, however, deliberately skips the first stages and perceives reality directly.[92] Nenghai argued that the two methods are both valid but each suits disciples of different capacities. While the intuitive approach works for certain disciples, the gradual approach is more reliable for the majority of Buddhists. For that reason, while Nenghai acknowledged the merit of intuitive meditation, he considered the Gelug training paradigm of specific value to Han Buddhists. Embracing the graduate approach, he promoted Gelug school's sequential development of hearing, thinking, and meditating. The institutional invention at his temple in Chengdu also embodied his understanding of *lamrim*, emphasizing ethical and intellectual training for the monastics.

When preaching on *lamrim*, Nenghai paid special attention to two sets of tensions: the proper relationship between doctrinal inquiry and praxis, and the doctrinal conflicts between the sudden and gradual approaches to enlightenment. Nenghai seems to have been promoting the *lamrim* framework to ease these tensions. He especially used *lamrim* to elaborate an exemplary mode for combining doctrinal study and meditative practice, which incorporates ethical and intellectual training as necessary requisites for meditation. Also, Nenghai appropriated the *lamrim* framework to account for the disparities. In his explanation, some Tibetan masters' assertions might, at least superficially, disagree with the established understanding in Chinese Buddhism. Yet the different teachings are essentially complementary and compatible. In this way, Nenghai employed the *lamrim* framework to ameliorate the tension between textual learning and practice, as well as to explain away doctrinal conflicts.

Conclusion

In a dialectical process of translation and interpretation, Han Buddhist intellectuals highlighted certain doctrines as special inspirations. The *lamrim* doctrine received considerable attention in this regard. Dayong, Fazun, Taixu, Chaoyi, and Nenghai generated varied meanings for the *lamrim* teaching, meanings that were often preconditioned by their prior Buddhist knowledge and understanding of the immediate challenges Han Buddhists faced.

Dayong, Fazun, Taixu, Chaoyi, and Nenghai were commonly concerned about the practical dimension of *lamrim* framework, as well as its conformity with Chinese Buddhist thought and practices. In their elaboration, *lamrim* arranges scriptural knowledge along the stages of the path to enlightenment in an orderly way, thereby providing a practical perspective that many Chinese philosophical works lack. Based on the *lamrim* framework, Nenghai advocated a gradual approach and highlighted the significance of philosophical learning for meditative cultivation. While Nenghai followed the Tibetan scholars in many propositions, he made an apparent effort to ameliorate the conflicts between Gelug and Chan teachings. Emphasizing the common ground and the shared goal of liberation, Nenghai appropriated the *lamrim* framework to argue for compatibility between the varied teachings. In his interpretation, the contradictory positions do not entirely contradict one another but are a convenience for instructing disciples. Promoting the *lamrim* framework, Nenghai seems to propose an inclusive view of Buddhist teachings, in which the divergent doctrines are conceived as complementary constituents in a coherent body.

SIX

Tibetan Buddhism Among Han Chinese

IN BOTH CHINESE and Tibetan Buddhist traditions, Mount Wutai, located in Shanxi Province three hundred miles southwest of Beijing, was believed to be the earthly abode of Bodhisattva Mañjuśrī.[1] In the Qing dynasty, more than a hundred Chinese and Tibetan temples were scattered over its five peaks. In summer, thousands of Buddhist pilgrims—from Mongolia and the Tibetan plateau, from Beijing and as far as the coastal cities in the south—flocked to the sacred mountain to pay homage.[2] Experienced pilgrims differentiated the Tibetan Buddhist temples from the Chinese ones by the clothing of the clergy. Lamas were referred to as "yellow-robe monks" because most of them belonged to the Gelug tradition—the "Yellow-Hat Lineage." Chinese monks were called "cyan-robe monks" because they wore cyan-colored clothes. Respectively, their residential temples were known as yellow temples (*huangmiao* 黃廟) and cyan temples (*qingmiao* 青廟). This simple differentiation worked well for many temples but not for the Vinaya Monastery of Auspice (Jixiang lüyuan 吉祥律院), which was located on the western peak. Ethnically, the resident monks were Han Chinese; religiously, they practiced Tibetan Gelug teachings. They were Han monks in yellow robes.

Nenghai presided over this temple and used it to disseminate Tibetan Buddhist teachings among Chinese Buddhists. Of the Han Buddhists who traveled to Tibet in the late 1920s and 1930s, Nenghai was among the most famous. After his return in 1932, Nenghai developed seven branches in Sichuan, Shanghai, and Mount Wutai, a rare case of the interaction between

Chinese and Tibetan traditions at the institutional level. After Holmes Welch described the founding of his core temple in Chengdu as "a partial tantrification of Buddhism in China," later scholars continued to emphasize Nenghai's promulgation of Tibetan esoteric Buddhism.[3] The characterization of his lineage as being solely Tibetan esoteric describes its definitive features, but it dismisses Nenghai's efforts to incorporate various elements into his lineage. Examining how his lineage emerged—and focusing on its institutional structure as well as its interaction with other Buddhist circles—reveals how Nenghai promoted esoteric teachings: he actively emphasized the *lamrim* doctrine as his basis, on which he crafted a graduated program, a five-hall system to train disciples of different capacities in doctrinal and disciplinary learning to prepare them for advanced esoteric praxis. While promoting esoteric Buddhist teachings, Nenghai and his disciples perpetuated many Chinese Buddhist practices as a way of complying and fitting in with the established norms and values. In that vein, he also cooperated with the local Han Buddhist leaders to advance social welfare in Sichuan, such as organizing ceremonies advocating peace, rebuilding the historic Buddhist sites, and providing educational opportunities to the monks.

I begin this chapter with a review of Nenghai's secular life and early monastic career. Then I explore Nenghai's first attempt to promote esoteric Buddhism in a monastery at Mount Wutai in the early 1930s and trace the history of his founding of Jinci Monastery in Chengdu in the late 1930s. As I demonstrate, the growth of Nenghai's lineage was contingent on many social and religious factors. In addition to the new knowledge and praxis that he introduced, his strategy to assimilate elements was also important for its development. His creation of a graduated training system enabled the lineage to preserve what its members saw as the distinctive features of Gelug teachings, while at the same time facilitating its acceptance by the local Buddhist communities.

From Military Man to Monk

Nenghai, whose secular name was Gong Jixi 龔緝熙, was born in Mianzhu County of Sichuan Province in 1886. His father ran a small grocery store in town. After his parents' death when he was only ten years old, his older sister raised him.[4] At age fourteen he became an apprentice at a silk shop owned by the Zhong family in Chengdu. Thanks to his good relationship with the Zhong family, Nenghai also received a private education along with the owner's sons.[5] After the Qing government abolished the imperial civil service exam in 1905, a military career became attractive to the ambitious youngster. In Chengdu, several military schools had recently opened to supply the armies with new blood. Encouraged by the shop owner, Nenghai and the Zhong brothers decided to pursue military careers. Nenghai entered the lower-ranking officer unit (*bianmudui* 弁目隊) in 1906 and later transferred to an intensive program at the Military School of the Land Force (Lujun suchengxuetang 陸軍速成學堂).[6] The training opened the door to a military career, especially as the schools were recruiting candidates to become commanding officers. These military schools produced the first generation of warlords in Sichuan, who were most active between the 1911 Revolution and the Northern Expedition in 1927.[7] According to Robert Kapp's study, the first generation of Sichuan warlords had in common a meteoric rise followed by a similarly sudden fall at a relatively young age. Though hundreds of new graduates assumed military positions to fill the power vacuum left by the 1911 Revolution, most of them had lost power by 1927 when newly emerging forces took the political stage.[8]

Nenghai's military career followed a similar trajectory. At a time of tumultuous changes, the fragmentation of political authority gave rise to new powers in the region. After graduating in 1909, Nenghai served as an instructor at the Yunnan Military School (Yunnan jiangwutang 雲南講武堂). When the 1911 Revolution broke out, he followed his supervisor Liu Cunhou 劉存厚 to join the uprising led by Cai E 蔡鍔—a Yunnan military reformer known for his advocacy of democracy. When Liu returned to Chengdu in November 1911, and after the establishment of the Sichuan military government, Nenghai took on the position of battalion commander. In October 1913, Yuan Shikai, the president of the republic, attempted to break the revolutionary power associated with the Nationalist Party. After battles broke out between pro-Yuan and anti-Yuan forces, Sichuan endured years of instability. According to a source, as early as 1905 Nenghai and his colleagues joined the Chinese United League (Tongmenghui 同盟會), an underground revolutionary coalition founded by the Nationalist leader Sun Yat-sen. After 1913, as pro-Yuan warlords suppressed the pro-revolutionary power in Sichuan, some of Nenghai's friends were persecuted and killed. In addition to this loss and the ongoing factional conflicts, his misfortune continued.[9] Nenghai married a young woman from the Zhuang family; they enjoyed a happy marriage for a time, but his wife fell ill and died not long after giving birth to their daughter.[10] The combination of a career setback and sorrow over the loss of his wife changed his life trajectory. Coming to the realization that any "political prospect is dreamlike and life is impermanent," Nenghai became interested in Buddhism.[11] After 1914, his religious zeal apparently surpassed his political ambition and he became a devoted Buddhist.

Nenghai's enthusiasm for Buddhism was sparked by Foyuan 佛源 (1853–1926), a Chan master from the Monastery of Heavenly Jewel (Tianbaosi 天寶寺) of Chongqing. One day, when Nenghai was leading a street patrol, he passed by the Temple of the Three Righteousness (Sanyimiao 三義廟) where Foyuan was giving a Dharma talk.[12] Out of curiosity, Nenghai stood at the gate to listen for a while. Captivated by the master's message, he entered the building to listen more attentively and was impressed by Foyuan's knowledge. Not long after that, Nenghai took refuge in Buddhism and became a disciple of Foyuan. Later that year, Nenghai was deployed by the Sichuan government to Beijing. He occasionally attended lectures delivered by the Buddhist scholar Zhang Kecheng at Peking University, and this further intensified his enthusiasm for Buddhist philosophy.[13]

After returning to Chengdu, Nenghai expressed his wish to forsake secular life. Disappointed by this desire, his sister asked him to father a male offspring before leaving the family. Nenghai married his second wife from the Zhang family, and when she did not bear any children, he took another wife, the younger sister of his first wife from the Zhuang family.[14] Meanwhile, Nenghai became an active lay Buddhist leader in Chengdu. Like many other places where the Chan tradition dominated monastic Buddhism, the five public temples in Chengdu were all associated with Chan.[15] Nenghai built a close relationship with the local Buddhist leaders, especially with the Chan masters. In 1916, Nenghai and a few patrons invited Foyuan to give sermons at the Temple of the Three Righteousness. The event became a sensation in the city. Through those sermons, Foyuan converted more than three hundred attendees to Buddhism. To meet their needs, Nenghai and other organizers founded a lay Buddhist society that later grew into the largest lay Buddhist organization in Chengdu.[16] Under the patronage of the warlord Liu Yujiu 劉禹九, the society settled in Shaocheng Park, resulting in it being called the Shaocheng Buddhist Society (Shaocheng foxueshe 少城佛學社). The society served as a circulation center for Buddhist books as well as the venue for Dharma talks. Nenghai regularly invited monks and scholars from Chengdu and Chongqing to deliver talks there.[17] Given his social status and leadership in the lay society, Nenghai came to know the Buddhist figures in Sichuan very well. These connections would be advantageous to the expansion of his lineage in Chengdu.

In 1921, Nenghai finally resigned from all military posts to devote himself to Buddhist practice. His third wife gave birth to a daughter, and finally to a son in 1924. With his elder sister caring for the children, Nenghai was able to abandon secular life.[18] His wives followed him into monastic orders: Lady Zhang received ordination from Foyuan, Nenghai's trusted teacher, and Lady Zhuang became a nun at the Hall of Aidao (Aidaotang 愛道堂), a major nunnery of Chengdu.[19] Nenghai was tonsured at Mañjuśrī Monastery (Wenshuyuan 文殊院), one of the largest temples in Chengdu in 1924. A year later, he was fully ordained at the Monastery of Jewel Light (Baoguangsi 寶光寺)—another large Chan monastery in Xindu 新都—after which he studied Buddhist ethics with Master Guanyi 貫一 for several months. The leaders of the two public temples wholeheartedly supported Nenghai's monastic career. Only a few months after being ordained in 1924, Nenghai left Chengdu for Lhasa.

Nenghai's enthusiasm for Tibetan Buddhism may have originated during his time stationed at Chengdu as a battalion commander in the late 1910s when Nenghai was occasionally deployed to the Kham region where Tibetan culture prevailed. Yet little in the extant records suggests that these trips sparked such curiosity.[20] It seems more likely that Nenghai's interest in Tibetan Buddhism was associated with his penchant for philosophical inquiry. The best information we have comes from a lecture given to his disciples in 1942, in which Nenghai explained his motivation to pursue study in Tibet.[21] Unlike Dayong, who turned to Tibetan teachings as a result of his dissatisfaction with Japanese esoteric Buddhism, Nenghai showed little interest in Japanese esoteric Buddhism despite having visited Japan on business for half a year in 1915.[22]

In the lecture, Nenghai recalled that his interest was triggered by scholarly works in Tibetan Buddhism produced as part of the rising interest in the academic study of Buddhism in early twentieth-century China.[23] In the 1920s, with the thriving of religious publishing and print culture, and with the opening of language courses in universities, Chinese Buddhist scholars extended their research to encompass Sanskrit and Tibetan texts.[24] Nenghai said he came to learn about the richness of Tibetan Buddhism through recently published works produced by scholars.[25] He was especially impressed by a catalog of the Tibetan Buddhist canon composed by Huang Shuyin 黃樹因, a young scholar studying under Ouyang Jingwu at Jinling Buddhist Scriptural Press (Jinling kejingchu 金陵刻經處).[26] Huang had learned Sanskrit and Pali with the German scholar Ferdinand Lessing who was then teaching in Jinan, Shandong Province. Subsequently, from 1920 to 1923, Huang Shuyin received training in Tibetan and Sanskrit from Alexander von Stael-Holstein, an exiled Russian professor teaching at Peking University, while also studying Tibetan with lamas from Yonghe Temple in Beijing.[27] After surveying the Tibetan Buddhist canon preserved in the temple, Huang compiled a catalog of the scriptures and commentaries that were not available in the Chinese Buddhist canon. The catalog was circulated in Chengdu where Nenghai was newly ordained. Amazed by the richness of Tibetan Buddhist literacy enumerated in the catalog, Nenghai immediately decided to travel to Tibet to learn Dharma. His ambition was shared by four other monks who had just been ordained with him in the same precept-giving ceremony. Together they left Chengdu.[28] Their aspiration was contingent on the development of the academic study of Buddhism in modern China. According to Nenghai's explanation, a major reason for his pursuit of Tibetan Buddhism was his conviction of its richness, a conviction he had gained from having read works produced by Buddhist intellectuals such as Huang Shuyin. In this way, academic development also served as a source of information to Buddhist practitioners in the first decades of the twentieth century. The Chinese scholars' adoption of the modern research approach to Buddhism, as well as the establishment of religious studies as a discipline in secular universities, produced an unintended effect on Han Buddhists like Nenghai and his colleagues: their increased interest in Tibetan Buddhism.

The next year, Nenghai and the four friends joined Dayong's team in Kangding. As with the cohort of Dayong, Nenghai studied with Lama Jampa while living in his temple. Being at the temple helped the Han monks to learn the Tibetan language and other basic teachings of Tibetan Buddhism. In 1927, Nenghai went to Litang to learn esoteric rituals with the Gelug master Jamyang Chompel. With help from the lama, Nenghai and three other monks went to Lhasa in 1928, and there studied Gelug teachings until 1932 with the renowned Khangsar Rinpoche at Drepung Monastery.[29] His teachers consecrated Nenghai to receive many tantras, among which Yamāntaka tantra was central to his praxis.³⁰ The learning experience also exposed him to doctrines and scriptures that constituted the cornerstones of Tibetan monastic scholasticism. During his stay in Kham and Lhasa, Nenghai studied Abhisamayālaṅkāra (*Xianzheng zhuangyan lun* 現證莊嚴論; the *Ornament of Realization*, abbreviated as the *Ornament*), Madhyamakāvatāra (*Ruzhong lun* 入中論), Abhidharmakośa (*Jushe lun* 俱舍論), Sarvāstivāda Vinaya, and other subjects.³¹ Nenghai's prior knowledge of Buddhism helped him to identify and bring back texts hitherto unavailable in Chinese.

In addition to tantras, Nenghai promoted commentaries that he considered important for Han Buddhists to understand Buddha's teachings, among them the *Ornament of Realization*, a treatise elucidating the Prajñāpāramitā, or perfection of wisdom teachings.³² In ancient India, generations of Buddhist philosophers produced a large number of exegetic works on the Prajñāpāramitā literature. Traditionally attributed to Maitreya, who revealed it in fourth-century India, the *Ornament* systematically outlines the teachings in the voluminous Prajñāpāramitā sutras.³³ In the Tibetan Gelug seminaries, the *Ornament*, as well as its exegeses composed by Indian and Tibetan scholars, constituted an important part of the core monastic curriculum. Among the commentaries on the *Ornament*, Tsongkhapa endorsed the positions of the *Clear Meaning Commentary* (*Xianguan zhuangyan lun xianming yishu* 現觀莊嚴論顯明義疏, Wylie: 'grel pa don gsal) by the eighth-century Indian exegete Haribhadra. But in spite of the significance in Tibetan scholarship, neither the *Ornament* nor the *Clear Meaning Commentary* was translated into Chinese until modern times.³⁴ After returning, Nenghai translated the *Clear Meaning Commentary* and preached on it to the disciples.³⁵ In one such sermon, Nenghai argued that the Tibetan commentaries help to reveal the practical intentions in the Mahāprajñāpāramitā Sūtra, a lengthy scripture in the Chinese Buddhist canon.³⁶ In his view, the Mahāprajñāpāramitā Sūtra, translated by Xuanzang in the seventh century, is important in revealing the Buddha's teachings of perfect wisdom. But its voluminosity poses a great challenge to the Chinese Buddhists, with its many themes buried in its six hundred fascicles. The *Ornament*, by organizing its teachings into eight divisions and seventy subjects, makes its contents explicit. By translating and giving sermons, Nenghai promoted the *Ornament* and the *Clear Meaning Commentary* to Chinese Buddhists.³⁷

Furthermore, Nenghai regarded the *lamrim* teaching as a special inspiration to the Chinese Buddhists (see chapter 5). We know that while staying in the Kham region, Nenghai started to translate some verses of *Lamrim Chenmo*, Tsongkhapa's major work on the *lamrim* doctrine. Slowly he was becoming an important interpreter of the work. In the winter of 1927, he temporarily returned to Chongqing to give a one-week lecture series, the earliest record of his public talks on the *lamrim* doctrine.[38] Nenghai's lecture excited the audience; in response, ten monks followed him and traveled to Kangding to study Tibetan Buddhism.[39]

Lamrim became central to his instruction after his return from Lhasa in 1932. Nenghai extracted the main verses from *Lamrim Chenmo* and collated them into a short piece titled "Puti dao cidi kesong" 菩提道次第科頌 (Synopsis of *Lamrim Chenmo*). There, he also charted all the steps to enlightenment. It later became part of the curriculum for his disciples. As a required text for all the monks to learn and recite, it was reprinted over fifteen times at Jinci Monastery. As Nenghai was attracting more and more disciples and as demand for the text was increasing, Mañjuśrī Monastery—a major public temple in Chengdu—printed it for wider circulation.[40] In 1957, Nenghai extracted more excerpts from *Lamrim Chenmo* and collated them as "Puti dao cidi xinlun" 菩提道次第心論 (Core of *Lamrim Chenmo*).[41] Both the "Synopsis" and the "Core" were to assist his disciples' learning, especially the beginners, who found it difficult to comprehend the full text of *Lamrim Chenmo*.[42]

The *lamrim* teaching spoke of a graduated vision of the path to liberation. By interpreting the *lamrim*, Nenghai was promoting this graduated path for Han Buddhists. While he did not completely reject Chan teaching as the ancient Tibetan masters did, he was cautious about its weakness in neglecting some training that the Gelug school considered both fundamental and essential. But this weakness could be remedied by a graduated perspective of *lamrim*. When studying in Kangding in 1928, in a letter to the Chan master Guanyi, his teacher in Chengdu, Nenghai evaluated Chan teaching in comparison to esoteric Buddhism. From that letter we learn that he regarded Chan as specialized teaching that could result in sudden awakening—an experience similar to that achieved through the practice of the high tantra. Nenghai claimed that the Chan tradition did not do an adequate job in explaining the preparatory steps leading to the awakening, however, and that this compromised the benefits of the practice for ordinary practitioners. He also suggested that Chan practitioners need to put more emphasis on disciplines and doctrinal learning.[43] But *lamrim* was not merely a doctrine for learning; it was also a leading principle for the praxis in Nenghai's lineage. Nenghai not only taught about *lamrim*, but he also tried to establish a graduated system based on the ideas of *lamrim* to train the disciples.

Nenghai's Reform at Mount Wutai

In 1932, Nenghai took the sea route to Shanghai, leaving Lhasa by way of India. In 1938, he founded Jinci Monastery in Chengdu, which later became the core temple of his lineage. In previous scholarship about Nenghai's lineage, insufficient attention has been paid to its interaction with the local Buddhist communities even though this interaction was important for the lineage's creation and development. Before building Jinci Monastery, Nenghai failed to institutionalize esoteric practice in a Chan-dominant public temple at Mount Wutai in 1936. The frustration led him to seek institutional autonomy while still maintaining close affiliation with the local Buddhist

FIGURE 6.1 The entrance to Old Jinci Monastery 古近慈寺 in Chengdu. Nenghai's base temple was destroyed in the 1960s. His disciples constructed a small temple near the original site in 1982 and named it Old Jinci Monastery.

community. By contextualizing the rise of the lineage, the section explores Nenghai's early encounters with other Buddhist groups, and how those encounters shaped his strategies in dealing with the subsequent conflicts.

In the spring of 1933, Nenghai's return to Sichuan elicited considerable sensation. A typical celebratory response was for local Buddhist leaders to invite him to deliver sermons. For example, on invitation from the Monastery of Great Compassion, a large public monastery in Chengdu, Nenghai preached on the Sutra of Humane Kings. Attracting over 1,500 persons, the event was reported to be of unprecedented scale in the city.[44] His fame spread beyond Sichuan, and as a result Nenghai was invited to host ceremonies with masters of national reputation. For example, in 1936 Nenghai was invited to Shanghai to perform Yamāntaka rituals in the calamity-pacifying Dharma assembly with five other famous Tibetan and Chinese masters. This three-month assembly was cross-regional, jointly organized by over twenty major temples and lay Buddhist organizations from Beijing, Shanghai, and Tianjin. The event organizers advertised Nenghai by boasting of his excellence in "both esoteric and exoteric teachings."[45] The widely reported ceremony greatly enhanced Nenghai's fame.

Nenghai started to teach esoteric praxis to monks, beginning the instruction at the Guangji Monastery (Guangjimaopeng) at Mount Wutai.[46] This temple held an important position for Chinese Buddhism at Mount Wutai and even in north China. In the late Qing period, since the Chinese temples at the sacred mountain were privately owned, many pilgrims suffered as a result of the shortage of accommodations. In 1907, two monks named Hengxiu 恆修 and Chengcan 乘參, grieving for two pilgrims frozen to death, vowed to build a public temple to house the pilgrims. In 1915, they succeeded in raising funds to build the temple.[47] What began as a small shack offering free tea and two daily meals of porridge to the pilgrims eventually grew to be the largest temple of Chinese Buddhism at Mount Wutai. In summer, when pilgrims flocked to the mountain, the temple typically accommodated six to seven hundred visitors. In other seasons, it housed over one hundred resident monks. It followed the Chinese Buddhist convention with the regular daily practice of Chan meditation.[48] It also organized an annual summer retreat and intense Chan meditation programs in winter.[49]

Nenghai attracted his first batch of monastic followers at this public temple. In the 1930s, the temple's revenue depended on funds from the lay people in Beijing and Shanghai. Recommended by the leaders of the Lay

TIBETAN BUDDHISM AMONG HAN CHINESE

FIGURES 6.2, 6.3, AND 6.4 Mount Wutai is the home of Jixiang Vinaya Monastery (figure 6.2), the temple where Nenghai spent his last years in 1950s and 1960s; when I visited there in 2013, it was under construction (there is a crane behind the temple). On the sacred mountain, the disciples also established stūpas for Nenghai (figure 6.3) and his guru Khangsar Rinpoche (figure 6.4).

Buddhist Society in Beijing, the abbot invited Nenghai to teach Vinaya at Guangji Monastery in the summer retreat of 1934.[50] In the summer of 1936, by which time Nenghai had lived and taught in the temple for three years, the monks elected him to be their abbot. After translating the Thirteen Deities of Yamāntaka Tantra (Daweide shisan zun yigui 大威德十三尊儀軌), Nenghai began to instruct the practice.[51] He guided some forty monks into the esoteric meditative praxis, and on this basis his lineage began to take shape.[52] Some devotees hadn't planned to practice esoteric Buddhism before coming to the temple for the summer retreat, but having heard Nenghai's lectures they decided to follow him. For example, the monk Qingfo 請佛, who was ordained in a small temple in Shanxi, came to Guangji Monastery to learn about monastic disciplines. After listening to Nenghai's speech, he

FIGURES 6.2, 6.3, AND 6.4 Continued

FIGURES 6.2, 6.3, AND 6.4 Continued

developed an interest in esoteric Buddhism.[53] A few other monks came to the temple specifically to study with Nenghai. The monk Zhaotong 昭通, for example, grew up in Hubei Province and had just graduated from a four-year seminary in Fujian when he learned that Nenghai was transmitting esoteric teachings. He traveled to Mount Wutai to meet Nenghai, whom he then followed faithfully for the next thirty years.[54]

As the number of followers increased, Nenghai refashioned the institutional structure at the Guangji Monastery in order to reduce friction with the Chan meditators. He separated the monks into two groups and placed them in different halls. Those who were interested in Chan meditation continued to practice in the Chan Hall, while the esoteric practitioners were placed in the Recitation Hall (Niansongtang 念誦堂).[55] In the latter, Nenghai guided his disciples in chanting mantras and practicing visualization. Though separated during the hours of meditation, the two groups did all other activities together. During the retreat, all the monks attended Nenghai's daily lectures on Vinaya, which Nenghai emphasized as a common foundation for all monastics, regardless of their different meditation methods.⁵⁶

At the temple, Nenghai instructed the followers in Yamāntaka tantra. He invited Jasagh Lama (Zhasake Lama 札薩克喇嘛), the head lama administrating the Tibetan Buddhist monasteries on Mount Wutai, to confer consecration to his disciples. Nenghai established a bronze statue depicting Yamāntaka, the wrathful expression of Bodhisattva Mañjuśrī, at the temple for ritual use. The statue was in the style of two bodies (*shuangshen* 雙身), depicting the male deity in sexual union with his female consort. Nenghai invited the lama to preside over the eye-opening ceremony for the statue, after which the two of them conducted a fire offering to evoke divine blessing.⁵⁷

The more Nenghai promoted esoteric Buddhism, the more suspicious nonbelievers became. A split became evident in the winter of 1936. Nenghai's disciple Zhaotong implied that the conflict was related to financial issues, since some patrons donated directly to the Jasagh Lama rather than to the temple at the ceremony.⁵⁸ It also seems possible that some Chan monks disagreed with Nenghai's worshipping of the Yamāntaka statue. Because of these increasing tensions, Nenghai's attempt to teach esoteric praxis at Guangji Monastery was unsuccessful, even though he secured support from the former abbot and the lay patrons.⁵⁹ Given the resistance from the majority of monks, Nenghai gave up the attempt to create a space for esotericism in the Chan-dominated public temple. A few months later, in February 1937, Nenghai and his disciples moved out. With support from the Jasagh Lama, they moved to the lama's private temple, the Sudhana Cave (Shancaidong 善財洞), to continue with esoteric praxis at Mount Wutai.⁶⁰

The moving-out event marked a significant transformation in Nenghai's strategies in the building of his lineage. The event signaled a growing sense of sectarian consciousness in him and his disciples. They had faith in the Gelug teachings and praxis, but this faith was not shared by other monks. According to Zhaotong's memoir, they recognized that "the Tibetan teachings cannot fit neatly with Chinese Buddhist monasticism; there exists some conflict."⁶¹ The experience convinced Nenghai of the need to build their temple. He began to seek autonomy in administrative management and operation in order to fulfill his plan of training disciples in the Gelug teachings. The following discussion examines the founding history of Jinci Monastery in Chengdu, as well as its distinct features and principles. As the years passed,

Nenghai worked toward creating an institution to promote esotericism while accommodating to the Chinese Buddhist conventions. Not only did he establish a system to oblige disciples of different capacities, but he also used the *lamrim* teaching as the theoretical foundation for this institutional creation.

The Building of a Tibetan Lineage

The Marco Polo Bridge Incident of July 7, 1937, marked the onset of open warfare between Japan and China; afterward, the political situation in north China rapidly worsened. Only about three hundred miles southwest of Beijing, Mount Wutai was under direct threat as the Japanese troops pushed south. Many Chinese considered Chengdu, located in the Sichuan basins surrounded by a natural barrier of mountain ranges, as a sanctuary during wartime. In the fall of 1937, Nenghai and his disciples retreated to Chengdu. After the building of Jinci Monastery on the outskirts of Chengdu in 1938,

FIGURE 6.5 Iron Statue Nunnery, the nunnery of Nenghai's lineage, in Chengdu.

TIBETAN BUDDHISM AMONG HAN CHINESE

FIGURE 6.6 Inside Tsongkhapa Hall, Iron Statue Nunnery.

Nenghai's lineage expanded with branches in Sichuan, Shanghai, and Mount Wutai. As Ester Bianchi's research about the Iron Statue Nunnery (Tiexiangsi 鐵像寺) in contemporary Chengdu shows, Nenghai's lineage was known for the synthesis of Chinese and Tibetan practices.[62] Yet few studies have examined Nenghai's strategies to create an institutional system to disseminate Tibetan teachings or the interaction between his lineage and other Buddhist circles in the initial stage of formation. This section examines the founding history of Jinci Monastery to contextualize the rise of the lineage in Chengdu.

Upon his return to Chengdu in 1937, Nenghai was warmly welcomed by the Buddhists.[63] When he was a lay leader, Nenghai had cultivated close contacts with the eminent monks in Sichuan. He maintained a close connection with the abbots of Mañjuśrī Monastery and the Monastery of Jewel Light, where he was ordained and received the full precepts. He had substantial help in getting settled from Faguang 法光, the retired abbot of Mañjuśrī

Monastery, and Changyuan 昌圓, the president of Sichuan Buddhist Association (Sichuan fojiaohui 四川佛教會). On Faguang's invitation, Nenghai and over forty of his disciples resided at Mañjuśrī Monastery in 1938. As a large public temple, the monastery was capable of housing two- to three-hundred persons.[64] Although Faguang offered them long-term residency, Nenghai nevertheless declined because of the "lack of autonomy."[65] After the failed experiment at Guangji Monastery at Mount Wutai, Nenghai was determined to build a new institution to materialize his visions. To this end, Faguang offered Nenghai Jinci Temple for his use, one of Mañjuśrī Temple's six subtemples (xiayuan 下院).[66] Located on the outskirts of Chengdu, the Jinci Monastery was then a small, dilapidated temple that urgently needed to be renovated.[67] Since Nenghai was under financial pressure to support his disciples, the monk Changyuan helped to raise funds to renovate the temple.[68]

With support from the local Buddhists, Nenghai moved into Jinci in the spring of 1938.[69] Inspired by the Gelug seminary curriculum, Nenghai envisioned the temple as "a place to uphold and disseminate the teachings of Tsongkhapa"; as a result he expanded the Jinci buildings.[70] In addition to building a Dharma Hall and a library that were common in Chinese temples, Nenghai also built halls and statues marked with distinct Tibetan elements. In the next few years, Yamāntaka Hall, Tsongkhapa Hall, and an altar for fire offerings were constructed. In 1945, Nenghai opened a translation center, staffed by his disciples conversant with the Tibetan language.[71]

A distinct feature of Jinci Monastery was the five-hall system, a program that Nenghai created to embody understanding and application of the Tibetan teaching of *lamrim*. Because Nenghai understood the *lamrim* system to accommodate the Buddha's teachings for disciples at varying stages on the journey to enlightenment (see chapter 5), the monks were grouped based on their ages and abilities into five different halls, each hall providing a different educational focus. The first, the Hall of Novice Monks (Shamitang 沙彌堂), was for the junior members.[72] Before being fully ordained at twenty, the young monks learned the basic ethics, mantras, and also studied the Tibetan language with a senior monk named Ciqin 慈親, who had returned from Lhasa.[73] The second, the Hall of Learning Skills (Xueshitang 學事堂), was for guest monks who would spend a year learning about the routines at Jinci. After the probationary periods in either of the first two halls, a fully ordained monk could then enter the third, the Hall of Precept Learning (Xuejietang

學戒堂) to study Vinaya (the monastic disciplinary codes) and doctrines for five years. Monks in this hall undertook most of the daily duties around the monastery, such as cooking and working in the administrative offices.[74] An instructor (*tangzhu* 堂主)—usually a senior disciple of Nenghai—managed each hall and would oversee the oral examinations for monks who completed five years of training. After demonstrating a satisfactory level of disciplinary and doctrinal knowledge, the monks became qualified to proceed to the last two halls, which were associated with esoteric praxis and were under Nenghai's direct instruction.

In the fourth, the Hall of Preparatory Practice (Jiaxingtang 加行堂), Nenghai initiated the monks into the practice of advanced tantra.[75] The monks learned mantra and visualization, practicing the rising stage of the Yamāntaka tantra. When the senior members had mastered these techniques, and with Nenghai's approval, they would enter the highest and fifth level of the system—the Vajra Hall (Jingangtang 金剛堂). In the early 1940s, the resident meditators of this hall, many of whom were among the

FIGURE 6.7 The entrance to Yunwu Temple, in Mianzhu, Sichuan; it used to be the retreat center for Nenghai's lineage.

FIGURE 6.8 Guanyin Hall in Yunwu Temple, Mianzhu, Sichuan.

first batch of disciples who had followed Nenghai from Mount Wutai, focused on practicing the completion stage of Yamāntaka tantra. In 1943, to facilitate their meditative practice, Nenghai built the Temple of Cloudy Fog (Yunwusi 雲霧寺) in his birthplace in Mianzhu County. Thereafter the members of the Vajra Hall moved to the subtemple. Sitting on top of a scenic mountain, the temple provided a conducive environment for meditation. Without the distraction of worldly affairs, the senior monks could devote their entire time to meditation.[76]

The five-hall system, as well as the affiliated constructions, led to the praxis of tantra, which Nenghai and his disciples believed could result in a swift transformation and facilitate deep insight into reality. Nonetheless, inspired by a graduated vision of the journey to liberation, Nenghai and his disciples agreed that such advanced praxis demanded the disciples' full preparation in disciplinary conduct and doctrinal knowledge. Following Tsongkhapa's stand, Nenghai claimed that the esoteric practice should be based on ethics and nonesoteric teachings.⁷⁷ The candidates for esoteric praxis should be disciplined and learned, well developed in the goal of learning tantra in ways that were rooted in the bodhisattva ideal of universal salvation. So when organizing the monastic training along the steps described by *lamrim*, he emphasized the Vinaya and doctrinal study. By crafting the five-hall system, Nenghai attempted to build a monastic education aligned with the Buddha's prescription of the three learnings: ethics, meditation, wisdom. Nenghai argued the tendency by some Han Buddhists to prefer meditation over learning Vinaya and doctrines was undermining Buddhism. He wanted to repair such perceived weakness with Tibetan Buddhist strength, borrowing for monastic training the elements from the Gelug school, specifically its focus on Vinaya and doctrinal learning. He anticipated that the five-hall system would provide the monastics with a solid intellectual and disciplinary foundation, and better prepare them for the meditative praxis.

The five-hall system also allowed Nenghai to control the esoteric transmission, for it gave him sufficient time to become familiar with the candidates' capacities. An enthusiast, even with an earnest interest in advanced tantra, would have to go through at least five years of training. Before being admitted to the highest halls to learn the high tantra, the candidates needed to demonstrate their understanding of Buddhist theories and moral rules.⁷⁸ In spite of its rigidity, the temple attracted many practitioners who shared Nenghai's convictions. Within a decade, Jinci Monastery grew to over 250 monks and about 70 novice monks.⁷⁹ When Nenghai gave lectures or conducted the precept-giving ceremony, the temple often drew about five hundred people.⁸⁰ By the early 1940s, the whole system was ready to produce a learned and disciplined clergy. As the next section shows, while maintaining its Gelug distinctions, the temple adopted certain elements of Chinese Buddhism, which sustained its connection with the other Han Buddhist circles and facilitated its rapid development.

A Confluence of Chinese and Tibetan Buddhism

In addition to its training system, Jinci Monastery's Gelug affiliation was constantly expressed and reaffirmed in daily routines, such as the disciples' practice of guru yoga. In esoteric Buddhism, since the practitioners need to rely on their guru to have access to the secret teachings, the guru is of paramount importance. Guru yoga is a set of devotional practices in which the practitioners learn to visualize the guru as an enlightened one. After the fourth Panchen Lama Lobsang Gyaltsen standardized the liturgical practice in *Lama Chöpa* (Wylie: Bla ma mchod pa; Ch. *Shangshi gongyangfa* 上師供養法) in the seventeenth century, it became one of the most popular practices among the Gelug devotees.[81] Central to the praxis is faith in the guru, who is respected not merely as the one who transmits knowledge, but also as the embodiment of all the knowledge and merit that one wishes to cultivate. By contemplating the guru's wisdom and merits, the aspirants cultivate, sustain, and strengthen faith. Faith in the guru connects to the cosmic Buddhas and the past Gelug masters. Hence, the idea that guru yoga helps to generate an enormous amount of merit to facilitate a swift transformation makes it a popular practice among the esoteric practitioners.[82]

FIGURE 6.9 Tsongkhapa Hall in Jinci Monastery, the new base temple (also known as Jinci Vihāra) was constructed by Nenghai's disciples in 2006, adjacent to the Old Jinci Monastery.

TIBETAN BUDDHISM AMONG HAN CHINESE

FIGURE 6.10 The inside of Tsongkhapa Hall, Jinci Monastery.

After Nenghai built Jinci Monastery in Chengdu, he highlighted guru yoga to nurture faith among his disciples. The daily practice also sustained and reinforced the connection with the Tibetan Gelug lineage. In 1938, Nenghai translated *Lama Chöpa* into *Shangshi wushang gong guan xing fa* 上師無上供觀行法 (Practice of visualization of the ultimate offering to the guru). Nenghai prescribed the practice to all disciples. Every morning, the monks gathered in the Yamāntaka Hall to chant together. By reciting together, they paid homage to the Gelug masters and strengthened their shared beliefs. After the chanting, the monks went back, each to his own hall, to concentrate on their specialized practice: the senior monks practiced the Yamāntaka mantra separately, while other monks chanted the Mañjuśrī mantra and other required manuals.[83]

Centering itself on practices like guru yoga, Jinci Monastery operated as a Gelug temple in Chengdu. More significantly, unlike other temples in its vicinity, faith in their guru carried practical significance and created sectarian identity among Nenghai's disciples.[84] The lineage was united not only by its commitment to the Gelug teachings but also by a shared trust in a line of masters. As Nenghai's disciples highlighted in their memoirs, he had received the teachings from his guru Khangsar Rinpoche, whose empowerment was important for Nenghai to claim legitimacy in transmitting the teachings further. Given the centrality of the guru in the transmission narrative of esoteric Buddhism, nurturing and sustaining the same faith became crucial for continuing the line through the generations.

Nenghai set an example for his followers in terms of respecting the guru. In their memoirs, the disciples recalled Nenghai's deep admiration of Khangsar Rinpoche. After Nenghai founded Jinci Monastery in 1938, he journeyed to Lhasa for a second time in 1940, hoping to invite Khangsar Rinpoche to Chengdu to guide his devotees directly. Several monks accompanying him to Lhasa provided many details about Nenghai's unshakable faith in Khangsar Rinpoche. They witnessed Nenghai showing the utmost reverence and

FIGURE 6.11 Tsongkhapa Hall, Shijing Temple 石經寺, in Chengdu.

FIGURE 6.12 Stūpa of Nenghai, in front of Tsongkhapa Hall, Shijing Temple; the others are stūpas of his disciples Yongguang and Zhenyi 貞意.

piety on the journey. For example, crossing mountains and rivers as they trudged for four months to Lhasa, whatever difficulty they encountered, be it a blizzard, a flood, or a band of robbers, Nenghai would remind the disciples to recall the merits of Khangsar Rinpoche and to evoke blessings from the divine protectors.[85]

After arriving in Lhasa in September of 1940, Nenghai continued to show the deepest reverence to Khangsar Rinpoche. Every morning, afternoon, and evening he went to pay homage to the guru, bowing to him and asking for his instruction. During the eight-month stay in Lhasa, Nenghai repeated the visits almost every day, regardless of the weather. When Khangsar Rinpoche traveled to another place to give sermons, Nenghai followed him serving as an assistant and accommodating his needs. Also, when Nenghai and his disciples attended the grand celebration at Jokhang Monastery (Dazhaosi 大昭寺), like other monastics, they received some money from the donors. As a sign of deference, Nenghai immediately offered the money to the guru.[86]

Khangsar Rinpoche was kind to Nenghai and his disciples, transmitting many types of esoteric practices to them.[87] From the trip to Lhasa, Nenghai brought back a number of printed works by the Tibetan masters, including the corpora of Tsongkhapa and his two disciples, which facilitated his study and translation from the 1940s to the 1960s. Unfortunately, Khangsar Rinpoche passed away in 1941 and was never able to visit Chengdu. Before Nenghai's return in 1941, Khangsar Rinpoche encouraged him to promote esoteric Buddhism and gave him precious gifts—including his hair, gowns, bowl, boots, conch, and other personal items, all of which Nenghai and his disciples considered sacred. The disciples interpreted the lama's bequest as a sign of his appreciation of Nenghai.[88] After returning, they continued to pay homage to Khangsar Rinpoche by practicing guru yoga every day. Nenghai's apparent confidence in Khangsar Rinpoche not only helped to boost his own legitimacy as an esoteric teacher, but also set an example for his disciples to follow. Their shared faith consolidated the formation and development of the lineage.

Jinci Monastery was also noted for its distinct rites and festivals. For decades, Nenghai and the disciples faithfully and consistently conducted fire offerings. From 1938 to the end of the war in 1945, to evoke divine blessing and bring peace, they conducted fire offering every day during the first half of each month. As in other temples in Lhasa, Tsongkhapa's Day (on the twenty-fifth of the tenth lunar month of the Tibetan calendar) was a grand festival at Jinci. At the celebration in which they offered thousands of lights, the monastic and lay disciples united to affirm their faith in the Gelug founder.[89] They also commemorated the birthday of Khangsar Rinpoche on the fifth day of the fifth lunar month.[90] The festivals and rites drew many laypeople to the temple to receive blessings.

The building of Jinci Monastery signaled a change in Nenghai's tactics, one as an outcome of his previous frustration at Mount Wutai and the followers' demand for greater autonomy. In Chengdu, he consciously avoided isolating the lineage from other Buddhist circles that did not share the esoteric praxis. In general, his lineage followed the established conventions—such as vegetarianism—and tried to find common ground in doctrinal and disciplinary learning. A prominent example was Nenghai's continuous promotion of the Four-Part Vinaya or monastic codes, which were central to the monastic identity and disciplined their behaviors. The Chinese monks traditionally followed a set of monastic rules in the Four-Part Vinaya, and the Tibetans followed those prescribed in the Sarvāstivādin Vinaya. The two sets of disciplinary codes differed in numbers and some minor aspects. When turning to Tibetan Buddhism, some of Nenghai's peers abandoned the precepts of the Four-Part Vinaya and were reordained by receiving the Sarvāstivādin Vinaya. But Nenghai continued to practice and preach the Four-Part Vinaya. As Nenghai claimed, he had studied Sarvāstivādin Vinaya in Tibet, but he decided to abide by the same set of rules practiced by the majority of the Chinese monastics.[91] Nenghai's insistence helped his ideas about Vinaya reach a broad audience.

In addition to being an eminent master of esoteric Buddhism, Nenghai became known for his knowledge of Vinaya, which helped to expand his influence to other non-esoteric Buddhist circles in the 1930s. While emphasizing the disciplinary training in his lineage, Nenghai brought the same focus into the monastic circles in Sichuan, Beijing, Mount Wutai, and beyond. After returning from Lhasa in 1932, Nenghai was often invited to deliver lectures on monastic morality in other temples. For example, the Monastery of Vast Salvation (Guangjisi 廣濟寺), one of the largest temples in Beijing, invited Nenghai to preach on Vinaya in September 1935. These sermons were warmly welcomed by the monastic members, attracting hundreds of them from various temples in Beijing.[92] Likewise, more than a thousand monastics attended his lecture on Vinaya at the Shanxi Provincial Buddhist Association (Shanxi fojiaohui 山西佛教會) in Taiyuan in 1935.[93] Nenghai's reputation grew after his return to Sichuan. Many monks and nuns of local temples, including the Buddhist leaders, assembled at Jinci Monastery when he delivered lectures.

In Sichuan, Nenghai cooperated closely with Buddhist leaders like Faguang, Changyuan, Daowu 道悟, Kuanlin 寬霖—all of them were influential monks associated with the large public temples like Mañjuśrī Monastery and Jewel Light Monastery.[94] For instance, the monk Changyuan, resonating with Taixu's reformative ideas, after becoming the president of the Sichuan Buddhist Association in 1935 and the principal of the Sichuan Buddhist Seminary (Sichun foxueyuan 四川佛學院) in 1936, took the lead in many Buddhist reform initiatives, including building Buddhist schools, advancing monastic education, and protecting Buddhist temple properties.[95] On Changyuan's invitation, Nenghai provided education to the nuns of the Aidao Nunnery, the biggest nunnery in Chengdu. He allowed the nuns to attend his lectures at Jinci Monastery, supported the nuns' precept-giving ceremony, and transmitted esoteric teachings to some of them.[96] Changyuan and Nenghai cooperated in producing some learned monks and nuns in Sichuan. For example, the nun Longlian, after being ordained in 1941, studied with Changyuan at the Aidao Nunnery. She also received esoteric teachings from Nenghai and became a respected leader in Nenghai's lineage. Fluent in Tibetan, she assisted Nenghai in disseminating Tibetan Buddhism by taking notes, undertaking translation, and educating the nun disciples.[97]

Nenghai's expertise in Tibetan Buddhism, knowledge in Vinaya, and engagement in local Buddhist affairs together advanced his reputation. Based on translated texts, esoteric rituals such as fire offering were performed regularly in the monasteries. Nenghai gave empowerments, particularly those belonging to Yamāntaka, to his disciples. He attracted a large number of monastic and lay followers, including military and political leaders like Pan Wenhua 潘文華, Deng Xihou 鄧錫侯, and Liu Wenhui 劉文輝.[98] With their support, Nenghai dedicated himself to improving the welfare of the Buddhist communities in Sichuan, ranging from rebuilding the collapsed monuments (stūpas), renovating the dilapidated temples, and educating the monastics. He raised funds to rebuild two important Buddhist historical sites—the Stūpa of the Efficacy of Piety (Xiaoganta 孝感塔) in Deyang 德陽 and the Stūpa of the Rising Dragon (Longxingta 龍興塔) in Pengzhou 彭州, both of which were believed to contain Buddha's sacred relics. According to the Buddhist account, the Indian King Aśoka (third century BCE) collected Buddha's relics and divided them into 84,000 parts. After the Indian Buddhist missionaries brought some parts to China, seventeen stūpas were built to contain them for worshipping, with four in Sichuan. Unfortunately, the two stūpas were becoming dilapidated with age.[99] In the late 1930s and 1940s, Nenghai led the initiative to renovate these two sacred sites, an act praised and supported by the local Buddhists.

These activities expanded the influence of his lineage in Sichuan. Nenghai strengthened the alliance with the local leaders and established auxiliary branches for the lineage. For example, right after his return to Sichuan in the fall of 1937, Nenghai conducted rites to pray for peace at Mount E'mei (E'meishan 峨嵋山)—a sacred mountain and major Buddhist center in Sichuan. He stayed at a temple named Hall of Vairocana (Piludian 毗盧殿), where he lectured on monastic rules, drawing audiences three hundred strong.

FIGURE 6.13 Longxing Stūpa in Longxing Temple, Peng County, Sichuan; a project initiated by Nenghai in 1948 and completed by his disciples in 1997.

Impressed by Nenghai's knowledge, the monks of the temple invited Nenghai to be their abbot. On Nenghai's agreement, the temple became the first recorded sub-branch of Jinci Monastery and thereafter served as a residence for meditative retreats for his disciples.[100]

Beginning in 1938, Nenghai's lineage significantly expanded its networks, with the affiliation of six branches in Sichuan, Shanghai, and Mount Wutai. In addition to the Vairocana Hall at Mount E'mei, the lineage affiliated with two other temples in Sichuan, namely the Temple of Cloudy Fog in Mianzhu and the Hermitage of Compassionate Saint (Cisheng'an 慈聖庵) at Mount E'mei.[101] The connections were established in a similar way: during wartime, many small temples lacked resources such as funding and manpower, and some temples were even abandoned by the monks. At the request of the remaining monks, Nenghai brought in funds to renovate the dilapidated temples, and he helped the resident monks. He also empowered his head disciples to act in the branches in his absence.

In the same way, Nenghai developed the Vinaya Monastery of Auspice at Mount Wutai in 1953.[102] For Nenghai, Mount Wutai had a special significance. Recall that Nenghai and his disciples practiced Yamāntaka tantra, in which Yamāntaka was worshipped as the main deity. Mount Wutai was traditionally associated with Mañjuśrī, so Nenghai believed that the mountain was auspicious for their practice. Leading over one hundred monks, Nenghai moved to Mount Wutai and lived in the Vinaya Monastery of Auspice until he passed away in 1967.[103]

In addition to these temples in the mountains, the lineage also developed the Iron Statue Nunnery in Chengdu. Located a few miles from Jinci Monastery, it housed the nun disciples and was led by the nun Longlian. During the day time, the nuns would walk to Jinci Monastery to listen to Nenghai's Dharma talks and return to the nunnery by nightfall. Two more branches opened in two major cities: the Vajra Place of Practice (Jingangdaochang 金剛道場) in Chongqing and the Vajra Place of Practice in Shanghai. Nenghai's lay supporters played an important role in building the two branches. For example, after listening to Nenghai's lectures, the Chongqing lay followers became enthusiastic about esoteric Buddhism and wished for a permanent site where they could accommodate the monks and learn from them. In 1944, after a wealthy layman donated his mansion as a sub-branch, Nenghai sent several monks to reside there and instruct the lay followers.[104] Similarly, enthusiasts invited Nenghai's head disciple Qingding 清定 to stay in the

Garden of Enlightenment (Jueyuan 覺園), a large Buddhist center in Shanghai, after he had lectured on *lamrim* in the Temple of Dharma Treasure (Fazangsi 法藏寺) in 1947. In the winter of 1948, Qingding and four other monks conducted esoteric rites at a large calamity-pacifying Dharma ceremony, which further elevated the lineage's presence in Shanghai. In 1949, on the laypeople's invitation, Qingding and twenty monks from Jinci resided separately in a yard in the Garden of Enlightenment, which was named the Vajra Place of Practice.[105] The two subbranches were important for Nenghai to spread esoteric Buddhism in Chongqing and Shanghai.

After the founding of the People's Republic of China in 1949, the religious landscape changed and the Buddhists faced great challenges. In the early 1950s Nenghai was still able to continue translating, lecturing, and instructing others in the praxis. For example, in 1951 Nenghai visited Shanghai to bestow Yamāntaka empowerment to three hundred enthusiasts.[106] Starting in the mid-1950s, however, the state tightened control over religion, which deeply influenced the lineage. In 1955, Nenghai's head disciple Qingding was arrested on "antirevolutionary" charges and imprisoned, which ultimately led to the closure of the Shanghai branch. During the Cultural Revolution (1966–1976), when all forms of religious activities were under assault, Nenghai's lineage suffered a great loss. In the summer of 1966, the Red Guards attacked the Vinaya Monastery of Auspice, where Nenghai resided. They tore down the Buddha statues, burned the scriptures, and confiscated all the property. They expelled Nenghai and his disciples from the temple and put them in custody with other monks in the Guangji Monastery. During interrogation, Nenghai's disciples were beaten brutally, resulting in one monk's death and the serious injury of several others. In December 1966, the Red Guards announced the closure of all the temples at Mount Wutai. On the night of December 31, Nenghai indicated to a disciple that he was "leaving." Early the next morning, the monks found he had passed away peacefully in a sitting meditation position. For the followers, Nenghai's prophetic words correctly predicted his death, as well as the extraordinary calmness he manifested, signaled that he had attained the high achievement of being able to free himself from death and life at will.[107]

After Nenghai's passing, his clergy disbanded, though Nenghai's disciples gradually revived the lineage at the end of the Cultural Revolution. After being imprisoned for twenty years, Qingding was released in 1975. He served as a doctor in his hometown in Sanmen 三門 County in Zhejiang for a few

FIGURES 6.14 AND 6.15 Green Tara and Tibetan-style turning wheels in Duobao Temple in Sanmen County, Zhejiang Province. This is a large temple in eastern China, held by Nenghai's disciple Zhimin.

years, then returned to Chengdu to lead the restoration of the lineage in the 1980s. Nenghai's other disciples contributed to the revival and development of the lineage.[108] In addition to building temples, they became eminent Buddhist teachers and translators. For example, the nun Longlian built the Sichuan Nun Seminary (Sichuan nizhong foxueyuan 四川尼眾佛學院) in Chengdu in 1983, and offered education to the nuns there. The monk Zhimin 智敏 built the Temple of Numerous Jewels (Duobaojiangsi 多寶講寺) in Sanmen in Zhejiang in 1992, and developed it into a major locus for esoteric Buddhism in eastern China. Though some former monks didn't return to the clergy, they nonetheless lived up to Nenghai's wishes in various ways. Liu Mingyuan 劉明淵 and Ren Jie, who began learning the Tibetan language in Jinci Monastery in the 1940s, dedicated themselves to the translation of Tibetan Buddhism.[109]

Passing down their knowledge to the younger generations, Nenghai's disciples continued to dedicate themselves to fulfilling Nenghai's aspirations. The project of renovating the Stūpa of the Rising Dragon in Pengzhou, initiated by Nenghai in 1948 but suspended amid the political turmoil, was finally completed by his disciples in 1997. The magnificent stūpa, 81 meters tall and overlooking the city, symbolizes efforts started by Nenghai about a century ago. Inspired by the teaching of the path to enlightenment, Nenghai's disciples are continuing to advance his vision of spreading Tsongkhapa's teachings.

Conclusion

Jinci Monastery provides a case for us to observe the interaction between a newly formed esoteric Buddhist lineage and the surrounding existing Buddhist circles. Its infrastructure reflected what Nenghai had been offered in Tibet and the modifications he had made for the Chinese aspirants. The five-hall system embodied the principles derived from the *lamrim* teaching, which promoted a graduated path toward liberation. The perspective oriented the organization of the temple, its curriculum, and its daily praxis. With its emphasis on transmission and the authority of teachers in upholding such transmission, esoteric Buddhist praxis markedly characterized his lineage. Meanwhile, by sharing the common ground of doctrinal learning and disciplines, and by cooperating with the other Buddhist groups in education and protecting temple properties, Nenghai broadened the network of the lineage in Sichuan, Chongqing, Shanghai, Mount Wutai, and beyond. The growing influence of the lineage distinguished it as the single most prominent lineage for producing a trained clergy from the 1930s to the 1960s. The building of Jinci Monastery and the development of the lineage exemplified Nenghai's efforts to forge an institutional model to transmit esoteric Buddhism among Han Buddhists.

Conclusion

CHINESE BUDDHISM IN the first half of the twentieth century witnessed many notable transitions. In particular, various dynamics in Chinese society and beyond shaped the Han Buddhists' interpretation of esoteric Buddhism. These currents included the founding of the republic; the growing cultural communications among the different regions; the emergence of modern education, journalism, and the printing industry; the expansion of the public sphere; and other shifts that challenged Buddhists to articulate the role of Buddhism in a rapidly changing society. Buddhists took a series of initiatives, such as protesting against the government's confiscation of temple property, promoting monastic education, building lay Buddhist societies, advancing Buddhist journalism, and engaging in scholarly discussion. All these factors greatly conditioned the introduction of esoteric Buddhism in modern China.

By tracing the process in this book, I show how Chinese Buddhists drew on a repertoire of resources available to them to interpret esoteric Buddhism. Their engagements with the newly imported texts, ideas, and practices were conditioned by their prior Buddhist knowledge and the understanding of the rapidly changing social realities, as well as the challenges faced by Chinese Buddhism. The various expectations and understandings resulted in a plurality of interpretations. While the reformer Taixu's narrative of Buddhist revival provided a strong rationale to introduce esoteric Buddhist teachings,

CONCLUSION

it alone could not account for the multitude of interpretations. Various actors generated a multitude of discourses, and of course some of these conflicted with, supplemented, and reinforced the other. In a series of disputes in the 1920s and 1930s, for example, the Buddhists often studied esoteric Buddhist teachings in juxtaposition with the more familiar ideas from Chinese Buddhism. Seeing certain Tibetan or Japanese doctrines and practices as special inspiration, Han Buddhists endowed them with new meanings that were contingent on Chinese conditions. Taixu, Dayong, Fazun, and Nenghai also applauded Tibetan scholasticism for its integration of philosophical sophistication and practical instruction. This feature is best embodied in its highly developed commentary tradition, especially in the *lamrim* teaching given its systematization of stages of Buddhist knowledge along the path to enlightenment.

In *Esoteric Buddhism in China* I demonstrate that no one factor alone, be it religious, social, or political, can explain the plurality of interpretations. Instead, multiple factors conditioned the Chinese Buddhists' reception of esoteric Buddhism, as embodied by the controversy over the esoteric rituals in public assemblies from the 1920s to the 1940s. With support from political and Buddhist patrons, Tibetan and Japanese Buddhist masters were invited to perform many large-scale Dharma ceremonies in Chinese cities. While some non-Buddhist elites accused these rites of being mere superstition and a waste of resources, supporters advocated their efficacy of nation protection and other this-worldly profits. By attracting a large number of attendees, these assemblies greatly elevated the presence of esoteric Buddhism in Chinese social circumstances. The thriving lay Buddhist societies served as a platform for spreading esoteric Buddhism. They patronized Buddhist events, supported publication and monastic education, and facilitated communications among the different Buddhist groups. The emerging journalism also offered an unprecedented level of visibility of esoteric Buddhism to the general Chinese audience.

The study has explored the Chinese Buddhists' narratives over the doctrines of esoteric Buddhism. One hotly debated issue was the assessment of the newly imported ideas in relation to established Chinese Buddhist doctrines. The claims of Wang Hongyuan and other enthusiasts about the superiority of esoteric Buddhism over exoteric Buddhism in the late 1920s inflamed this debate.

CONCLUSION

Some Chinese Buddhists attempted to account for the conflicts of Buddhist teachings, and in so doing their discussions fostered intellectual creation. While the modern concept of global Buddhism lent support to Taixu's proposal, the principle of doctrinal inclusiveness—a prevalent Chinese Buddhist philosophy that conceives the multiple doctrines as varying manifestations of the ultimate truth—was central to many advocates' propositions about the compatibility of the various Buddhist ideas. But when they invariably strived to argue for consistency, the Buddhist writers chose different theoretical references. Dayong and Chisong respectively relied on the Chinese Tiantai and Huayan doctrines to argue for congruence in all Buddhist teachings. By contrast, Fazun and Nenghai employed the Gelug teaching of *lamrim* to explain the different doctrines and practices, conceiving the seemingly contradictory teachings as convenient instructions to guide disciples of varied capacities. In so doing, Nenghai downplayed the contradictions between the gradual teaching of Gelug training and the sudden enlightenment teaching of Chan Buddhism that prevailed in China.

In this study I highlight the Chinese Buddhists' reception of Tibetan commentaries and examine why their interpretations were confined by expectations and aspirations. While tantras appealed to certain groups of Han Buddhists, they constituted only part of the texts being translated and studied. Some skeptics of esoteric teachings found certain Tibetan commentaries philosophically profound and worthy of learning. Compared to tantras that one had to be initiated to access, Tibetan commentaries lacked such barriers to access and thus reached a wider audience. The promotion of *Lamrim Chenmo* by Taixu, Dayong, Fazun, and Nenghai is a case in point. As they interpreted it, the Tibetan *lamrim* doctrine is inspiring for its systematization of Buddhist knowledge along the stages of the path to enlightenment. Nenghai also appropriated the *lamrim* doctrine as a theoretical framework to balance textual learning and meditative practice, based on which he created a program to train the monastics in his lineage.

Many of the religious currents in present-day China manifested a continuity of the dynamics that took shape in the early twentieth century. In spite of its atheist ideology, the Communist government adopted many of the religious policies formulated in the Republican era, including using Buddhism to strengthen its connection with the Tibetans.[1] With the ending of the Cultural Revolution in 1976, many Chinese Buddhists grew interested in Tibetan

Buddhism. Some of them traveled to Amdo and Kham to study with Tibetan masters, just as Dayong and his cohorts had done over half a century before them. The Larung Gar Academy, founded by Khenpo Jigme Phuntsok in Serta County in the Kham region, attracted a large number of Han disciples.[2] Meanwhile, for better or worse, the advertisement of Tibetan culture stimulated the imagination of Tibet among Han audiences, making the Tibetan plateau and neighboring cultural regions a destination for many tourists and pilgrims.[3] New forms of participation and expression emerged in religious life. Particularly pervasive has been the influence of media and technology in contemporary Chinese society.[4] For example, social media allowed Tibetan Buddhist teachers to transcend geographical barriers and communicate with their Han disciples.[5] The influence of these factors on the dissemination of esoteric Buddhism has yet to be studied.

The introduction of Tibetan Buddhism has persisted, with translation and interpretation continuing in the Chinese Buddhist communities. Tibetan commentaries, especially those related to the teaching of *lamrim*, have entered the curriculum of many Buddhist seminaries.[6] More Tibetan subcommentaries on *Lamrim Chenmo* are being introduced to Han Buddhist readers. One of the most popular is *Liberation in the Palm of Your Hand* (Ch. *Zhangzhong jietuo* 掌中解脫) by Pabongkha Rinpoche, an eminent Gelug lama of the early twentieth century.[7] Some Han Buddhist teachers valued the *lamrim* teaching for its systematization of the common Buddhist doctrines that they have previously learned from Chinese Buddhist traditions. They selected specific components and perspectives that they considered inspiring and preached to their disciples.[8] The spike of interest in *lamrim* teaching shows that some Tibetan Buddhist teachings have gone beyond the circles of esoteric enthusiasts and penetrated the larger Chinese Buddhist communities. The ways of interpretation also vary in the process. The contemporary learning groups continue to draw on a repertoire of elements from Chinese religious traditions to approach the translated texts.[9] The meanings generated not only depend on their prior Buddhist knowledge, but also reflect the needs in their particular context. To explore the Chinese introduction of esoteric Buddhism as a dynamic history means positioning the choices, interpretations, and behaviors in a specific context. It means considering how the Buddhists understand the introduced knowledge, shared beliefs, and proper behavior in particular circumstances, during which their experiences are interwoven through processes of dispute, cooperation, and negotiation. It

CONCLUSION

suggests considering the interpretations and tactics to adjust to these conditions and to negotiate the conflicts, as well as the historical contingencies that have conditioned these interpretations. In this regard, *Esoteric Buddhism in China* is not only an account of an aspect of modern Chinese Buddhism but also a narrative about the continuing human quest for knowledge at a time of increasing cross-cultural communications.

APPENDIX 1

List of Chinese Characters

Aidaotang 愛道堂
a she li 阿闍黎
Bai Puren 白普仁
Bailin jaoliyuan 柏林教理院
Bailinsi 柏林寺
Baisangai 白傘蓋
Bao Kanbu 寶堪布
Baoguangsi 寶光寺
Baohuashan 寶華山
Baotongsi 寶通寺
beichuan fojiao 北傳佛教
Beiping huabei jushilin 北平華北居士林
bianmudui 弁目隊
bieyuan 別圓
biji 筆記
Bishansi 碧山寺
Bukong 不空
Cai E 蔡鍔
Cao Kun 曹錕
Caotangsi 草堂寺
Changdu 昌都
Changguang 常光

Changshoufo fa 長壽佛法
Changxing 常惺
Changyuan 昌圓
Chaozhou 潮州
Chaoyi 超一
Chen Lansheng 陳瀾生
Chen Taoyi 陳陶遺
Cheng Zhai'an 程宅安
Chengcan 乘參
Chengdu 成都
Chengdu foxueshe 成都佛學社
Chenghai 澄海
chengjiu 成就
Chengshi 成實
Chisong 持松
Chong Baolin 充寶琳
Chong Zhenru 充珍儒
Chongqing foxueshe 重慶佛學社
chuanfa guanding 傳法灌頂
Chuanpin 傳品
chuchan 初禪
Cui Yunzhai 崔雲斋
chunan 除難
Ciqin 慈親
Cisheng'an 慈聖庵
Ciyinsi 慈因寺
Cizhou 慈舟
Daborezong 大般若宗
Dacisi 大慈寺
Dafosi 大佛寺
Dashouyin 大手印
Dai Jitao 戴季陶
Daojie 道階
Daosheng 道生
Daowu 道悟
Daoxing 道興
dasheng 大乘

Dasheng fojiao honghuayuan 大乘佛教弘化院
dasheng shijiao 大乘始教
dasheng zhongjiao 大乘終教
Dayong 大勇
Daweide Jingang 大威德金剛
Dazhaosi 大昭寺
Deng Xihou 鄧錫侯
Deyang 德陽
dishen 地神
Ding Xuqiu 丁漵秋
Dixian 諦閑
Dongmi 東密
Dongya fojiao dahui 東亞佛教大會
Duan Qirui 段祺瑞
duban 督辦
dunjiao 頓教
Duobaojiangsi 多寶講寺
Duojie Jueba 多傑覺拔
Dushun 杜順
E'meishan 峨嵋山
erchan 二禪
Faguang 法光
fahui 法會
fan 凡
fangyankou 放焰口
Fang Yu 方于
Fayusi 法雨寺
Fazang 法藏
Fazangsi 法藏寺
Fazun 法尊
Feng Yuxiang 馮玉祥
Fengcheng mizong jushilin 豐城密宗居士林
Fengxi 奉系
fenzheng ji 分證即
fo 佛
fojiao jiguan 佛教機關
Fojiao weichihui 佛教維持會

fojing liutongchu 佛經流通處
foxuehui 佛學會
foxue yanjiuhui 佛學研究會
Foyuan 佛源
Ganzi 甘孜
gong'an 公案
Gong Jixi 龔緝熙
Gongga Hutuketu 貢噶呼圖克圖
Gongga jingshe 貢噶精舍
Gongga Laoren 貢嘎老人
gongye 共業
guan 觀
guanding 灌頂
guanxing ji 觀行即
Guanzong xueshe 觀宗學社
Guanyi 貫一
Guanghan 廣漢
Guanghui 廣慧
Guangji maopeng 廣濟茅蓬
Guangjisi 廣濟寺
guangming zhenyan 光明真言
Gui Bohua 桂伯華
guofen 果分
guomin huiyi 國民會議
Guoyao 果瑤
Guoyu 果玉
Fajie xueshe 法界學社
Hanchuan fojiao 漢傳佛教
Hankou fojiao zhengxinhui 漢口佛教正信會
Hanren 漢人
Hanzang jiaoliyuan 漢藏教理院
Hanzang xueyuan 漢藏學院
Henan fojiaohui 河南佛教會
Hengliang 恒亮
Hengxiu 恆修
Hu Zihu 胡子笏
Huabei cishan lianhehui 華北慈善聯合會

LIST OF CHINESE CHARACTERS

Huabei jushilin 華北居士林
Huang Chanhua 黃懺華
Huang Shuyin 黃樹因
Huang Sufang 黃肅方
huangmiao 黃廟
Huayan daxue 華嚴大學
huguo 護國
huguo xizai fahui 護國息災法會
Huiding 慧定
Huiguan 慧觀
Huiguo 惠果
Huishen 慧深
Huiyuan 慧遠
ji 記
Jishenghui 濟生會
jiaxing 加行
jianjiao 建醮
jiangji 講記
jiaoshou shi 教授師
jiaming yanju 假名言句
jiaming yanxiang 假名言相
Jiangjin 江津
Jiangwutang 講武堂
jiao 教
Jiaxing 嘉興
Jiaxingtang 加行堂
Jiexing jingshe 解行精舍
jieyuan guanding 結緣灌頂
Jin Heshang 金和尚
Jincisi 近慈寺
Jingangdaochang 金剛道場
jingangjie 金剛界
Jingangtang 金剛堂
Jingangzhi 金剛智
Jinguangming fahui 金光明法會
jinguangmingfa 金光明法
Jinling kejingchu 金陵刻經處

Jinsheng tuoluoni 金勝陀羅尼
Jingan 敬安
Jingansi 靜安寺
jingchan 經懺
Jingyansi 精嚴寺
jingye she 淨業社
jingzhou jiuguo 經咒救國
jiujing ji 究竟即
Jixiang Lüyuan 吉祥律院
jue 覺
jueguan 覺觀
Jueyuan 覺園
Jueyuan 覺苑
jushilin 居士林
Kaifeng foxueyuan 開封佛學院
Kaifusi 開福寺
Kaiyuansi 開元寺
Kaiyuanzong 開元宗
Kangding 康定
Kuanlin 寬霖
lama jiao 喇嘛教
Langchan 朗禪
li 理
Li Ciwu 李次武
Li Dan 李丹
Li Dingkui 李定魁
li ji 理即
Li Jinxi 黎錦熙
Li Shaoji 黎紹基
Li Yizhen 黎乙真
Li Yuanhong 黎元洪
Lianhua jingshe 蓮華精舍
Lianhuasheng Dashi 蓮華生大士
lianshe 蓮社
Lianyi shanhui 聯義善會
Liang Qichao 梁啟超
lidi chengfo 立地成佛

Linggusi 靈谷寺
Lingyinsi 靈隱寺
lishi buer 理事不二
Litang 理塘
Liu Cunhou 劉存厚
liu ji 六即
Liu Mingyuan 劉明淵
Liu Xiang 劉湘
Liu Wenhui 劉文輝
Liu Yujiu 劉禹九
Liu Zhuyuan 劉洙源
Liurongsi 六榕寺
Longlian 隆蓮
Longshou 隆壽
Longxingta 龍興塔
Lu Xun 魯迅
Lujun suchengxuetang 陸軍速成學堂
Manshu Jiedi 曼殊揭諦
Mengzangyuan 蒙藏院
miaochan xingxue 廟產興學
mijiao 密教
mimijiao 秘密教
mingzi ji 名字即
misheng 密乘
misheng xiufa 密乘修法
mitan 密壇
mixin 迷信
mixin juan 迷信捐
mizong 密宗
Moheyan 摩訶衍
Nanjing jushilin 南京居士林
Neiwubu 內務部
Nenghai 能海
Nengxing 能興
nianfo sanmei 念佛三昧
nianfo tang 念佛堂
Niansongtang 念誦堂

nüzi foxueyuan 女子佛學院
Ouyang Jingwu 歐陽竟無
Pan Wenhua 潘文華
panjiao 判教
Pengzhou 彭州
Pi Huaibai 皮懷白
Piludian 毗盧殿
Pilusi 毗盧寺
powafa 頗瓦法
Pusading 菩薩頂
putixin 菩提心
Putuoshan 普陀山
qianseng zhai 千僧齋
Qingding 清定
Qingfo 請佛
Qinghai 清海
qingmiao 青廟
Ren Dingxun 任定詢
Rimi 日密
Rongkong 融空
san da a seng qi jie 三大阿僧祇劫
Sanlun 三論
Sanmen 三門
sanmi xiangying 三密相應
sanshi dao 三士道
Sanyimiao 三義廟
Shamitang 沙彌堂
Shancaidong 善財洞
Shantou mijiao chongxinghui 汕頭密教重興會
Shanwuwei 善無畏
Shanxi fojiaohui 山西佛教會
Shanyuanan 善緣庵
Shao Mingshu 邵明叔
Shaocheng foxueshe 少城佛學社
Shanghai fojiao jushilin 上海佛教居士林
shangshi 上士
Shangshi gongyangfa 上師供養法

LIST OF CHINESE CHARACTERS

Shangxiantang 尚賢堂
Shen Shuwen 申書文
shenbian 神變
shenmi 身密
sheng 聖
Shengxiansi 聖仙寺
shicheng 師承
Shijie foxueyuan 世界佛學苑
Shilun jingang fahui 時輪金剛法會
Shishi xinbao 時事新報
shixiang 事相
shixinwei 十信位
shuangshen 雙身
shuangshenfa 雙身法
shuilu fahui 水陸法會
shuilu fashi 水陸法事
Sichuansheng fojiaohui 四川省佛教會
Sichuan foxuehui 四川佛學會
Sichun foxueyuan 四川佛學院
Sichuan nizhong foxueyuan 四川尼眾佛學院
Sifenlü 四分律
sihuayi 四化儀
sizhong 四眾
songjing fahui 誦經法會
Sun Chuangfang 孫傳芳
Sun Jingfeng 孫景風
Taihedian 太和殿
Taixu 太虛
taizangjie 胎藏界
Tanxu 倓虛
Tangmi 唐密
tangzhu 堂主
Tianbaosi 天寶寺
Tianjin fojiao jushilin 天津佛教居士林
tianlong babu 天龍八部
Tianran 天然
Tiexiangsi 鐵像寺

[195]

LIST OF CHINESE CHARACTERS

tonghua 同化
Tongmenghui 同盟會
tongyuan 同圓
Tongzi jiuguohui 童子救國會
Wang Hongyuan 王弘願
Wang Huilan 王慧蘭
Wang Jiaqi 王家齊
Wang Yuji 王與楫
wen si xiu 聞思修
Wenshuyuan 文殊院
Wu Jingjun 吳敬君
Wu Peifu 吳佩孚
Wuliangshoufo fa 無量壽佛法
Wutaishan 五臺山
Wuyi 悟一
Xia Chao 夏超
xian 賢
xianjiao 顯教
Xianshou 賢首
Xianshouzong 賢首宗
Xiantongsi 顯通寺
Xianyin 顯蔭
xiang 相
xianghao 相好
xiangsi ji 相似即
Xiaoganta 孝感塔
xiaosheng 小乘
xiaosheng jiao 小乘教
xiashi 下士
xiayuan 下院
Xichui Xuanhuashi 西陲宣化使
Xikang 西康
Xikang Xuanweishi 西康宣慰使
Xinan heping fahui 西南和平法會
Xindu 新都
Xiong Xiling 熊希齡
xiu mifa 修密法

LIST OF CHINESE CHARACTERS

xizai 息災
Xu Shichang 徐世昌
Xu Shiguang 徐世光
Xuyun 虛雲
Xuanzang 玄奘
Xuejietang 學戒堂
Xueshitang 學事堂
xunsi 尋伺
Yang Mingchen 楊明塵
Yang Wenhui 楊文會
Yaochadajiangfa 藥叉大將法
Yaoguangsi 堯光寺
Yaoshifofa 藥師佛法
yiban fojiao 一般佛教
yijing yuan 譯經院
yishengjiao 一乘教
Yixing 一行
Yizhou 益州
Yingtai 瀛臺
Yongleng 永楞
Yongyan 永嚴
yuanjiao 圓教
Yu Shayuan 余沙園
Yuchunyuan 毓春園
Yuan Shikai 袁世凱
Yuanfang 圓方
yuanjiao liu ji 圓教六即
Yuexia 月霞
Yunnan jiangwutang 雲南講武堂
Yunwusi 雲霧寺
Yunwusi 雲悟寺
yuqie 瑜伽
Yinguang 印光
Yinshun 印順
yong 用
Yongguang 永光
Yonghegong 雍和宮

[197]

yuanjiao 圓教
yuelansuo 閱覽所
yuejingchu 閱經處
Zangmi 藏密
Zangwen xueyuan 藏文學院
Zeng Ziyu 曾子玉
zengyi jishen 增益己身
Zhajiasi 札迦寺
Zhang Binglin 章炳麟
Zhang Kecheng 張克誠
Zhang Xueliang 張學良
Zhang Yuanming 張圓明
zhangcheng 章程
Zhangjia Hutuketu 章嘉呼圖克圖
Zhang Xinruo 張心若
Zhao Hengti 趙恒惕
Zhao Hongzhu 趙洪鑄
Zhao Jianji 趙見幾
Zhaojuesi 昭覺寺
Zhaotong 昭通
Zhaoxiansi 招賢寺
Zhasake Lama 札薩克喇嘛
Zhendan fojiao 震旦佛教
Zhendan mijiao chongxinghui 震旦密教重興會
Zhengguo 正果
zhengxin 正信
Zhenyanzong 真言宗
Zhenyanzong jushilin 真言宗居士林
Zhenyanzong nüjushilin 真言宗女居士林
Zhili 直隸
Zhimin 智敏
Zhipan 志磐
Zhixi 直系
Zhiyan 智儼
Zhiyi 智顗
zisun miao 子孫廟
Zhongguoren 中國人

LIST OF CHINESE CHARACTERS

Zhonghua fojiao zonghui 中華佛教總會
Zhongmi 中密
Zhongnanhai 中南海
zhongshi 中士
zongjiao 宗教

APPENDIX 2

Wylie Transliteration

PHONETIC SPELLING	WYLIE TRANSLITERATION
Amdo Geshe Jampel Rolpai Lodro	A mdo dge bshes 'Jam dpal rol pa'i blo gros
Bardo	Bar do
Bardo Thodol	Bar do thos grol
Chamdo	Chab mdo
Changkya	Lcang skya
Dartsedo	Dar rtse mdo
Dorje Chopa	Rdo rje gcod pa
Drakkar	Brag dkar
Drepung	'Bras spungs
Gelug	Dge lugs
Gangkar	Gangs dkar
Jampa	Byams pa
Jamyang Chopel	'Jam dbyangs chos 'phel
Jigme Phuntsok	'Jigs med phun tshogs
Jokhang	Jo khang
Kagyu	Bka' brgyud
Kangyur	Bka' 'gyur
Kardze	Dkar mdzes
Khangsar	Khang gsar
Khenpo	Mkhan po
Lama Chöpa	Bla ma mchod pa
Lamrim	Lam rim
Lamrim Chenmo	Lam rim chen mo
Lamrim Dordu	Lam rim mdor bsdus
Larung Gar	Bla rung sgar

WYLIE TRANSLITERATION

PHONETIC SPELLING	WYLIE TRANSLITERATION
Lhasa	Lha sa
Litang	Li thang
Lozang Gyaltsen	Blo bzang rgyal mtshan
Nyingma	Rnying ma
Norlha	Nor lha
Pabongkha	Pha bong kha
Serta	Gser rta/Gser thar
Ngagrim Chenmo	Sngags rim chen mo
Dzogchen	Rdzogs chen
Tengyur	Bstan 'gyur
Thubden	Thub bstan
Thubten Choekyi Nyima	Thub bstan chos kyi nyi ma
Tsongkhapa	Tsong kha pa
tulku	sprul sku
Wangdu	Dbang 'dus

Notes

Introduction

1. I use "China proper" to differentiate the territory dominated by Han Chinese from the frontier regions of ethnic minorities. During the Republican regime, the term "China proper" equated roughly to the "Eighteen Provinces" of the Qing dynasty (1664–1911), although there had never been a clearly demarcated geographical boundary.
2. See Holmes Welch, *The Buddhist Revival in China* (Cambridge, MA: Harvard University Press, 1968), 194–201.
3. See Dongchu 東初, *Zhongguo fojiao jindai shi* 中國佛教近代史 (The modern history of Chinese Buddhism) (1974; repr., Taipei: Dongchu chubanshe, 1987), 407–457; Chen Bing 陳兵 and Deng Zimei 鄧子美, *Ershi shiji Zhongguo fojiao* 二十世紀中國佛教 (Chinese Buddhism in twentieth-century China) (Beijing: Minzu chubanshe, 2000), 347–381; Mei Jingxuan 梅靜軒, "Minguo yilai de hanzang fojiao guanxi" 民國以來的漢藏佛教關係 (1912–1949) (Relationship between Chinese and Tibetan Buddhism in the Republican period, 1912–1949), *Chung-Hwa Buddhist Studies* 2 (March 1998): 251–288.
4. For historical communication between Chinese and Tibetan Buddhism, see: Ester Bianchi and Weirong Shen, eds., *Sino-Tibetan Budhism Across the Ages* (Leiden: Brill, 2021); Wen-Shing Lucia Chou, *Mount Wutai: Visions of a Sacred Buddhist Mountain* (Princeton, NJ: Princeton University Press, 2018); Gray Tuttle and Johan Elverskog, eds., "Wutai Shan and Qing Culture," Special Issue, *Journal of the International Association of Tibetan Studies* (December 2011); Robert Gimello and Peter Gregory, eds., *Studies in Ch'an and Hua-yen* (Honolulu: University of Hawai'i Press, 1983); Matthew Kapstein, ed., *Buddhism Between Tibet and China* (Boston: Wisdom, 2009); Marsha Weidner, ed., *Cultural Intersections in Later Chinese Buddhism*

(Honolulu: University of Hawai'i Press, 2001); Alfredo Cadonna and Ester Bianchi, eds., *Facets of Tibetan Religious Tradition and Contacts with Neighbouring Cultural Areas* (Firenze: Oslchki, 2002); Meir Shahar and Yael Bentor, eds., *Chinese and Tibetan Esoteric Buddhism* (Leiden: Brill, 2017).

5. See Fabienne Jagou, ed., *The Hybridity of Buddhism: Contemporary Encounters Between Tibetan and Chinese Traditions in Taiwan and the Mainland* Études thématiques 29 (Paris: École française d'Extrême-Orient, 2018). See also Joshua Esler, *Tibetan Buddhism Among Han Chinese: Mediation and Superscription of the Tibetan Tradition in Contemporary Chinese Society* (Lanham, MD: Lexington Press, 2020).

6. See Ann Swidler, "Culture in Action: Symbols and Strategies," *American Sociological Review* 51, no. 2 (April 1986): 273.

7. See Ann Swidler, *Talk of Love: How Cultures Matters* (Chicago: University of Chicago Press, 2013), 15, 35.

8. Regarding the development of the syncretism framework, see Ross Kane, *The Syncretism of Tradition: Reappraising Cultural Mixture in Christianity* (New York: Oxford University Press, 2020), 97–105.

9. Stephen Bevans, for instance, categorizes six types of models in contextual theology: anthropological, transcendental, praxis, synthetic, translation, and countercultural. The six models vary along a continuum, one pole of that continuum highlighting "the experience of the present" and "the experience of the past." Some approaches focus more on the social context, while others tend to be more historical and scriptural. See Stephen B. Bevans, *Models of Contextual Theology* (Maryknoll, NY: Orbis, 1996), 88, 141–144.

10. See Donald K. McKim, *The Westminster Dictionary Theological Terms* (Louisville, KY: Westminster John Knox Press, 2014), 162.

11. See Choki Coe, "Contextualizing Theology," in *Mission Trends No. 3: Third World Theologies*, ed. Gerald H. Anderson and Thomas F. Stransky (New York: Paulist Press, 1976), 20.

12. See Aylward Shorter, *Toward a Theology of Inculturation* (Eugene, OR: Wipf and Stock, 1999), 10–11.

13. Mbiti rejected the idea of the indigenization of Christianity in Africa, arguing that "theology is always indigenous." For Mbiti, the church was a result of the encounter of the God-given, eternal Gospel and "any local or regional community." On Mbiti's theology, see Kwame Bediako, "A Variety of African Responses (2): John Mbiti, or Christ as the Redeemer of the African heritage," in *Theology and Identity: The Impact of Culture upon Christian Thought in the Secondary Century and in Modern Africa* (Carlisle, CA: Regnum Books, 1992), 303–346, especially 305–306.

14. See Kwame Bediako, *Christianity in Africa: The Renewal of a Non-Western Religion* (Edinburgh, UK: Edinburgh University Press, 1995), 118–119, 123.

15. See Andrew Walls, *The Missionary Movement in Christian History: Studies in the Transmission of Faith* (Maryknoll, NY: Orbis, 1996), 7–9, 23–24.

16. See Kathryn Tanner, *Theories of Culture: A New Agenda for Theology* (Minneapolis, MN: Fortress Press, 1997), 54, 114–115.

17. See Tanner, *Theories of Culture*, 114–115.

INTRODUCTION

18. See Robert Ford Campany, "Religious Repertoires and Contestation: A Case Study Based on Buddhist Miracle Tales," *History of Religions* 52, no. 2 (November 2012): 102–103.
19. Charles Orzech defines "culture" as a metaphorical system of many layers, in which interactions between two cultures occurred in different layers and to varying degrees. In addition to the repertoire model, I rely on Nicolas Standaert's textile model in his study of cultural interaction. This model conceives the interaction as a weaving process, in which new threads or elements are added to the fabric of a culture. See Charles Orzech, "Fang Yankou and Pudu: Translation, Metaphor, and Religious Identity," in *Daoist Identity: History, Lineage, and Ritual*, ed. Livia Kohn and Harold David Roth (Honolulu: University of Hawai'i Press, 2002), 213–234; Nicolas Standaert, "Christianity in Late Ming and Early Qing China as a Case of Cultural Transmission," in *China and Christianity*, ed. Stephen Uhalley and Xiaomin Wu (Armonk, NY: M. E. Sharpe, 2000), 81–116.
20. See Ann Swidler, "Culture in Action: Symbols and Strategies," 273. See also Ann Swidler, *Talk of Love*, 16, 86–89.
21. See Ann Swidler, *Talk of Love*, 99–100.
22. See Bevans, *Models of Contextual Theology*, xvi, 4. Bevans suggests that alongside scripture and tradition, culture, history, and contemporary thought forms should also be reconsidered as valid sources for religious expression.
23. According to Bevans, a context encompasses personal and communal experiences, including those from one's life as well as those from the contemporary world. It is influenced by secular or religious culture, social locations, and social change, all of which can influence a person's experience and understanding. See Bevans, *Models of Contextual Theology*, 6–7.
24. Bruce Lawrence defines "modernity" as the "emergence of a new index of human life that was shaped by bureaucratization and rationalization as well as technical capacities and global exchange unthinkable in the pre-modern era." And "modernism" connotes "the contingent ideological reshaping of human experience in response to the modern world." See Bruce Lawrence, *Defenders of God: The Fundamentalist Revolt Against the Modern Age* (San Francisco: Harper and Row, 1989), 17, 27.
25. Like many other Asian religious traditions, Chinese Buddhism experienced changing political trends and cultural forces that accompanied modernity. For Buddhist modernism, see Steven Heine and Charles S. Prebish, eds., *Buddhism in the Modern World: Adaptations of an Ancient Tradition* (New York: Oxford University Press, 2003), 4. For Protestant Buddhism in Sri Lanka, see Richard Gombrich, *Theravada Buddhism: A Social History from Ancient Benares to Modern Colombo* (New York: Routledge & Kegan Paul, 1998); Richard Gombrich and Gananath Obeyesekere, *Buddhism Transformed: Religious Changes in Sri Lanka* (Princeton, NJ: Princeton University Press, 1988). For Engaged Buddhism, see Sallie King, *Socially Engaged Buddhism* (Honolulu: University of Hawai'i Press, 2009); Christopher Queen, Damien Keown, and Charles S. Prebish, *Action Dharma: New Studies in Engaged Buddhism* (New York: RoutledgeCurzon, 2003); Christopher Queen and Sallie King, ed., *Engaged Buddhism: Buddhist Liberation Movements in Asia* (Albany:

INTRODUCTION

State University of New York Press, 1996). For modern Japanese Buddhism, see Stephen Covell, *Japanese Temple Buddhism: Worldliness in a Religion of Renunciation* (Honolulu: University of Hawai'i Press, 2005). For Humane Buddhism in Taiwan, see Stuart Chandler, *Establishing a Pure Land on Earth: The Foguang Buddhist Perspective on Modernization and Globalization* (Honolulu: University of Hawai'i Press, 2004); André Laliberté, *Politics of Buddhist Organizations in Taiwan* (New York: Routledge-Curzon, 2004); Richard Madsen, *Democracy's Dharma: Religious Renaissance and Political Development in Taiwan* (Berkeley: University of California Press, 2007).

26. In the 1898 reform, the imperial court issued a decree to order a transformation of temples into schools (*miaochan xingxue* 廟產興學). In 1914 and 1918, the Ministry of the Interior (Neiwu bu 內務部) of the early Republican regime formulated policies to tighten control over monastic economy and association management. In the first decades of the twentieth century, many monasteries lost their economic privileges and had properties appropriated by local governments throughout the country. See Chen Bing and Deng Zimei, *Ershi shiji Zhongguo fojiao*, 39; Welch, *The Buddhist Revival in China*, 11–12; Makita Tairyō 牧田諦亮, *Chūgoku kinsei Bukkyō shi no kenkyū* 中國近世佛教史の研究 (Studies in the modern history of Chinese Buddhism) (Kyoto: Heirakuji Shoten, 1957), 261–262; Prasenjit Duara, *Rescuing History from the Nation: Questioning Narratives of Modern China* (Chicago: University of Chicago Press, 1995), 85–114.
27. See Taixu, "Zhengli sengqie zhidu lun" 整理僧伽制度論 (The reorganization of the sangha system), vol. 9 in *Taixu dashi quanshu* (Collected Works of Venerable Master Taixu) (1915; repr., Taipei: Miaoyun ji wenjiao jijinhui, digital version, 1998), 13.
28. See Erik Zürcher, *The Buddhist Conquest of China: The Spread and Adaptation of Buddhism in Early Medieval China* (1959; repr., Leiden: Brill, 2007); Kenneth Ch'en, *Buddhism in China: A Historical Survey* (Princeton, NJ: Princeton University Press, 1964); Standaert, "Christianity in Late Ming and Early Qing China," 81–116; John Kieschnick, *The Impact of Buddhism on Chinese Material Culture* (Princeton, NJ: Princeton University Press, 2003); Pierce Salguero, *A Global History of Buddhism and Medicine* (New York: Columbia University Press, 2022).
29. The government of the People's Republic of China (PRC) identified its people as having a total of fifty-six ethnicities in an ethnic classification project in the 1950s, of which Han was the majority. In English, "Chinese" can translate both "inhabitants of China" (*Zhongguoren* 中國人) and "ethnically Han Chinese" (*Hanren* 漢人). I use "Han Tibetan Buddhist" to refer to those who were ethnically Han and religiously Tibetan Buddhists. I use "Chinese Buddhist" to refer to adherents who practiced the Buddhist tradition that was transmitted in China since the first century CE—which can also be rendered as "Northern Buddhism" (Beichuan fojiao 北傳佛教), or "Han Buddhism" (Hanchuan fojiao 漢傳佛教). In some cases, I also use "Chinese Buddhists" to refer to "Buddhists in China," or the large Chinese Buddhist communities that consisted of various sects and lineages, including the Han Tibetan Buddhists.
30. Ganzi is culturally part of Kham, Eastern Tibet. It was under the administration of Xikang 西康 Province during the Republican era, and now is an autonomous prefecture in Sichuan.

INTRODUCTION

31. In Nenghai's later years, he named his lineage the Great Prajñāpāramitā Sect (Daborezong 大般若宗). He saw Prajñāpāramitā as the most fundamental teaching in his philosophical framework. See Nenghai, *Xianzheng zhuangyan lun qingliang ji* 現證莊嚴論清涼記 (Lectures delivered on Mount Wutai on the *Ornament of Realization*) (Shanghai: Shanghai foxue shuju, 1994), 8.
32. Data collected in 2016.
33. For example, during the Sino-Japanese War, Nenghai was invited to conduct rituals with other renowned Chinese monks to "protect the nation and pacify calamity." See "Bingzi xizai fahui tekan" 丙子息災法會特刊 (Special issue on the Assembly of Pacifying Calamity in 1936), *Foxue banyuekan* 佛學半月刊 (Buddhist study semimonthly) 127 (May 1936): 1–7; *MFQ* 52: 243–249.
34. John Powers, *Introduction to Tibetan Buddhism* (Ithaca, NY: Snow Lion Publications, 2007), 249–252.
35. "Tantric" can be used to define the pantheon, scriptures, architecture, institutions, ideology, rituals, material culture, and so on. See Charles Orzech, Richard Payne, and Henrik H. Sørensen, "Introduction: Esoteric Buddhism and the Tantras in East Asia: Some Methodological Considerations," in *Esoteric Buddhism and the Tantras in East Asia*, ed. Charles Orzech, Henrik Sørensen, and Richard K. Payne (Leiden and Boston: Brill, 2011), 13. For a summary of the scholastic debate on the terminology of Esoteric and Tantric Buddhism, see Henrik H. Sørensen, "On Esoteric Buddhism in China: A Working Definition," in *Esoteric Buddhism and the Tantras in East Asia*, 156–175.
36. About the Chinese Buddhists' interaction with the Japanese Buddhists, see Welch, *The Buddhist Revival in China*, 160–174.
37. Chen and Deng attribute the shift of interest to the growth of nationalism against the Japanese imperialist threat, as well as to Chinese Buddhists' suspicion of Zhenyan esoteric teachings; see Chen Bing and Deng Zimei, *Ershi shiji Zhongguo fojiao*, 348–355. The introduction of esoteric teachings stimulated discussion among Chinese Buddhist intellectuals. Mei further examined Chinese Buddhists' conflicts with the esoteric masters; see Mei Jingxuan, "Minguo zaoqi xianmi fojiao chongtu de tantao" 民國早期顯密佛教衝突的探討 (Conflicts between esoteric and exoteric Buddhism in the early Republican period), *Chung-Hwa Buddhist Studies* 3 (March 1999): 251–270.
38. For studies on Tantrism, see: Ronald Davidson, *Indian Esoteric Buddhism: A Social History of the Tantric Movement* (New York: Columbia University Press, 2002); Geoffrey Samuel, *The Origins of Yoga and Tantra: Indic Religions to the Thirteenth Century* (Cambridge: Cambridge University Press, 2008); Hugh Urban, *Tantra: Sex, Secrecy, Politics, and Power in the Study of Religion* (Berkeley: University of California Press, 2003). For the history of Tibetan Buddhism, see Ronald Davidson, *Tibetan Renaissance: Tantric Buddhism in the Rebirth of Tibetan Culture* (New York: Columbia University Press, 2005); Matthew Kapstein, *The Tibetan Assimilation of Buddhism: Conversion, Contestation, and Memory* (New York: Oxford University Press, 2000); David Snellgrove, *Indo-Tibetan Buddhism: Indian Buddhists and their Tibetan Successors* (Boston: Shambhala, 1987).

39. According to Welch, most Chinese monks were skeptical of Tantric techniques and doubted whether it was an impure form with a mixture of Brahmanism and magic. See Welch, *The Buddhist Revival in China*, 177.
40. See Yinshun, *Yi fofa yanjiu fofa* 以佛法研究佛法 (Study Buddhism through Buddhism) (Taipei: Zhengwen chubanshe, 2000), 151–152.
41. See Robert Campany, "Religious Repertoires and Contestation: A Case Study Based on Buddhist Miracle Tales," 104–105. Campany's study of the social memory of ascetics shows that narratives help us to understand the environment in which they were created and circulated, and the individuals and groups who contributed to the process. See Robert Campany, *Making Transcendents: Ascetics and Social Memory in Early Medieval China* (Honolulu: University of Hawai'i Press, 2009), 21–22.
42. According to Gray Tuttle, "Lamaism" (*lama jiao* 喇嘛教) was the most common term to refer to the Tibetan beliefs and practices into the 1930s. See Gray Tuttle, *Tibetan Buddhists in the Making of Modern China* (New York: Columbia University Press, 2005), 4.
43. For example, Taixu was not a Tantric practitioner, but he envisioned the revival of esoteric Buddhism as part of making an inclusive amalgam of Buddhism that embraced all components of Buddhism, both esoteric and exoteric. Taixu was enthusiastic in advancing cross-tradition communications. He opened a school for Tibetan learning in Beijing in 1924 and the Sino-Tibetan Buddhist Institute (Hanzang jiaoliyuan 漢藏教理院) in Chongqing in 1931 to train students and prepare them for going to Tibet for further study. See Welch, *The Buddhist Revival in China*, 197–199; Tuttle, *Tibetan Buddhists in the Making of Modern China*, 72–73.
44. See Welch, *The Buddhist Revival in China*, 199.
45. See Chen and Deng, *Ershi shiji Zhongguo fojiao*, 347–381; Mei Jingxuan, "Minguo yilai de hanzang fojiao guanxi," 251–288; Huang Ying-chieh 黃英傑, *Minguo mizong nianjian* 民國密宗年鑑 (Chronicle history of Tantrism during the Republican era) (Taipei: Quanfo wenhua chubanshe, 1992); Françoise Wang-Toutain, "Quand les maîtres chinois s'éveillent au bouddhisme tibétain," *Bulletin de l'École française d'Extrême-Orient* 87 (January 2000): 707–727; Ester Bianchi, "The Tantric Rebirth Movement in Modern China: Esoteric Buddhism Re-vivified by the Japanese and Tibetan Traditions," *Acta Orientalia Academiae Scientiarum Hungaricae* 57, no. 1 (April 2004): 31–54.
46. Tuttle, *Tibetan Buddhists in the Making of Modern China*, 18–19. For the religion and politics of modern Tibet, see Tom Grunfeld, *The Making of Modern Tibet* (Armonk, NY: M.E. Sharpe, 1996); Melvyn Goldstein, *A History of Modern Tibet, 1913–1951: The Demise of the Lamaist State* (Berkeley: University of California Press, 1989), and *A History of Modern Tibet, 1951–1955: The Calm before the Storm* (Berkeley: University of California Press, 2007); Alex McKay, ed., *The Modern Period: 1895–1959, the Encounter with Modernity* (New York: RoutlegeCurzon, 2003); Tsering Shakya, *The Dragon in the Land of Snows: A History of Modern Tibet since 1947* (New York: Columbia University Press, 2000); Elliot Sperling, *The Tibet-China Conflict: History and Polemics* (Washington, DC: East-West Center, 2004); Wang Lixiong and Tsering Shakya, *The Struggle for Tibet* (New York: Verso Books, 2009).

INTRODUCTION

47. Martino Dibeltulo, "The Revival of Tantrism: Tibetan Buddhism and Modern China," PhD dissertation, University of Michigan, 2015.
48. See Chen Bing and Deng Zimei, *Ershi shiji Zhongguo fojiao*, 347–381; Mei Jingxuan, "Minguo yilai de hanzang fojiao guanxi," 251–288.
49. Chen and Deng estimated that, of approximately 2,600 types of Tibetan tantras, only one-tenth (200 to 300), had been translated into Chinese. See Chen Bing and Deng Zimei, *Ershi shiji de zhongguo fojiao*, 373.
50. Many late Qing Buddhist leaders criticized Buddhist monks' excessive involvement in death rituals, for such participation not only distracted them from more serious religious practices but also created a superstitious, irrational image of Buddhism. Taixu promoted an ideal of Humane Buddhism, claiming to shift the focus from death to the living. See Yinshun, *Taixu dashi nianpu* 太虛大師年譜 (Chronological biography of Master Taixu) (1950; repr., Taipei: Zhengwen chubanshe, 2000), 246–247.
51. For example, Nenghai and Fazun translated the *Ornament of Realization* (Xianzheng zhuangyan lun 現證莊嚴論; Skt., Abhisamayālankāra; Wylie: *mngon rtogs rgyan*), a treatise on the Perfection of Wisdom literature. It constitutes one of the five principal works in the curriculum of Gelug seminaries. See discussion in chapter 6.
52. See discussion in chapter 1. The two canonical traditions varied in their selection of scriptures, translation style, and size. According to a comparative study by Kanben, the Chinese Buddhist canonical tradition conserved more texts of early Indian Buddhism, or texts that assorted to the Small Vehicle, and the Tibetan Buddhist canonical tradition conserved more texts of the Great Vehicle and the Vajra Vehicle. Kanben also discussed the different Chinese and Tibetan Buddhist canons developed throughout history. See Kanben 侃本, *Hanzang fojing fanyi bijiao yanjiu* 漢藏佛經翻譯比較研究 (A comparative study of the translation of Chinese and Tibetan Buddhist scriptures) (Beijing: Zhongguo zangxue chubanshe, 2008), 91–106.
53. See Kanben, *Hanzang fojing fanyi bijiao yanjiu*, 107–115.
54. For the intellectual history of modern Chinese Buddhism, see Chan Sin-Wai, *Buddhism in Late Ch'ing Political Thought* (Hong Kong: Chinese University Press, 1985); Erik Hammerstrom, *The Science of Chinese Buddhism: Early Twentieth-Century Engagements* (New York: Columbia University Press, 2015); Jiang Canteng 江燦騰, *Zhongguo jindai fojiao sixiang yanjiu* 中國近世佛教思想研究 (Research on modern Chinese Buddhist thought) (Taipei: Daoxiang chubanshe, 1989); Ma Tianxiang 麻天祥, *Wanqing foxue yu jindai shehui sichao* 晚清佛學與近代社會思潮 (Buddhist thought in late Qing and ideologies in modern society) (Taipei: Wenjin chubanshe, 1992).
55. The *Ngagrim Chenmo* (The great treatise on the Tantric stages; Wylie: *Sngags rim chen mo*; Ch. *Mizong daocidi guanglun* 密宗道次第廣論), composed by Tsongkhapa about esoteric practices, was also translated by Fazun and modified by Yinshun in 1939. See Tsongkhapa, *Mizong daocidi guanglun*, trans. Fazun (Shanghai: Shanghai foxue shuju, 1998). However, *Lamrim Chenmo*, in particular its exoteric parts, received far more attention by the Chinese Buddhist scholars. See discussion in chapter 5.

56. See discussion in chapter 6.
57. Nenghai created a five-hall training system in Jinci Monastery. See Ren Jie 任傑, "Nenghai shangshi dechen qinwen lu" 能海上師德塵親聞錄 (Reminiscence of Guru Nenghai), in *Nenghai shangshi yonghuai lu* 能海上師永懷錄 (Permanent memory of Master Nengha), ed. Shanghai jingang daochang yijing zu (Shanghai: Shanghai foxue shuju, 1997), 58–69.
58. Regarding the different sets of monastic codes, see Akira Hirakawa 平川彰, *Ritsuzō no kenkyū* 律蔵の研究 (A study of the Vinaya collection) (Tōkyo: Sankibō busshorin, 1960); Yifa, *The Origins of Buddhist Monastic Codes in China: An Annotated Translation and Study of the Chanyuan qinggui* (Honolulu: University of Hawai'i Press, 2002).
59. For a collection of memoirs written by Nenghai's disciples, see Shanghai jingang daochang yijing zu, ed., *Nenghai shangshi yonghuai lu* (Shanghai: Shanghai foxue shuju, 1997). For another biography written by Nenghai's disciples, see Dingzhi 定智, *Nenghai shangshi zhuan* 能海上師傳 (Biography of Master Nenghai) (Shanghai: Shanghai foxue shuju, 2007). For a chronicle of Nenghai's activities, see Shen Quji 沈去疾, *Nenghai shangshi nianpu* 能海上師年譜 (Chronological biography of Nenghai) (Hong Kong: Tianma tushu, 2004). For an album of Nenghai and his lineage, see Chen Shidong 陳士東, *Nenghai shangshi xingji lu* 能海上師行跡錄 (Memory of Master Nenghai) (Hongkong: Tianma tushu, 2004).
60. For collections of newspapers and journals in the Republican period, see *MFQ*; *MFQB*; and Yu Ruihua 于瑞華 ed., *Minguo mizong qikan wenxian jicheng* 民國密宗期刊文獻集成 (Collection of Republican-era Tantric periodical literature), 42 volumes (Beijing: Dongfang chubanshe, 2008).
61. See Heinz Bechert, *Buddhismus, Staat und Gesellschaft in den Ländern des Theravāda-Buddhismus: Birma, Kambodscha, Laos, Thailand* (Frankfurt: Metzner, 1966), 7.
62. See David McMahan, *The Making of Buddhist Modernism* (New York: Oxford University Press, 2008), 7.
63. See, for example, Gombrich and Obeyesekere, *Buddhism Transformed*, 13–14.
64. See Charles Taylor, *Sources of the Self: The Making of the Modern Identity* (Cambridge, MA: Harvard University Press, 1989), 215.
65. See McMahan, *The Making of Buddhist Modernism*, 4.
66. See McMahan, *The Making of Buddhist Modernism*, 63–67.
67. See Rebecca Nedostup, *Superstitious Regimes: Religion and the Politics of Chinese Modernity* (Cambridge, MA: Harvard University Asia Center, 2009), 15.
68. "Beiping shilun jingang fahui ji" 北平時輪金剛法會紀 (Report of the Kālacakra Vajra Dharma-Assembly at Beiping), *Haichao yin* 海潮音 (*Voice of the Sea Tide, HCY*) 13, no. 12 (December 1932): 169–171; *MFQ* 182: 467–469.
69. With some exceptions, those who had the time and money to travel to Tibet were monks. Most enthusiasts studied with the lamas visiting from Mongol and Tibet, or the returning Han lamas. See "Banchan Dashi lilin neidi hou gong jian jiuci miaode shilun jingang fahui" 班禪大師蒞內地後共建九次妙德時輪金剛法會 (Panchen Lama conducted Kālacakra Vajra Dharma-Assembly for nine times after reaching China proper), *Xichui Xuanhuashi gongshu yuekan* 西陲宣化使公署

月刊 (Monthly of the Office of the Propagation Envoy to the Western Borderland) 1, nos. 7-8 (October 1936): 190; *MFQB* 82: 200.
70. See McMahan, *The Making of Buddhist Modernism*, 42-44, 185-188. Robert Sharf, "Experience," in *Critical Terms for Religious Studies*, ed. Mark C. Taylor (Chicago: University of Chicago Press, 1998), 94-116.
71. See McMahan, *The Making of Buddhist Modernism*, 50-59.
72. See Erik Braun, *The Birth of Insight: Meditation, Modern Buddhism, and the Burmese Monk Ledi Sayadaw* (Chicago: University of Chicago Press, 2013). 123-124, 127, and 193.
73. See McMahan, *The Making of Buddhist Modernism*, 14.
74. This supports McMahan's argument that the non-Western societies have entailed creative adaptations to some aspects of modernity, while selectively resisting others. See McMahan, *The Making of Buddhist Modernism*, 14.
75. Taixu, "Zhengli sengqie zhidu lun," 13.

1. Chinese Buddhism in Transition

1. The ceremony was widely reported in journals and newspapers, such as "Ji shilun jingang fahui" 紀時輪金剛法會 (Report on the Kālacakra Vajra Dharma-Assembly), *Foxue Banyuekan* 42 (November 1932): 239; *MFQ* 47: 473-474.
2. The guests included Wu Peifu 吳佩孚, Zhang Xueliang 張學良, Duan Qirui 段祺瑞, Sun Chuangfang 孫傳芳, and Xiong Xiling 熊希齡. Wu Peifu (1874-1939) and Sun Chuanfang (1885-1935) were major warlords of the Zhili Army. Zhang Xueliang (1901-2001) led the army of Manchuria but withdrew to Beijing after the Mukden Incident in 1931. Duan Qirui (1865-1936) was the provisional chief executive of the Republic of China from 1924 to 1926. Xiong Xiling (1870-1937) was the republic's premier from 1913 to 1914. See "Beiping shilun jingang fahui ji" 北平時輪金剛法會紀 (Report of the Kālacakra Vajra Dharma-Assembly at Beiping). *Haichao yin* 海潮音 (*Voice of the Sea Tide*, HCY) 13, no. 12 (December 1932): 169-171; *MFQ* 182: 467-469.
3. The Panchen Lama conducted the Kālacakra ceremony nine times between 1927 and 1936, including five ceremonies in Inner Mongolia and two in the Amdo regions. The number of people in the audiences at these places ranged from 37,000 (in Inner Mongolia, 1932) to 175,000 (in Inner Mongolia, 1927). The Beijing ceremony was ranked the second largest in terms of attendees, drawing one hundred thousand. See "Banchan Dashi lilin neidi hou gong jian jiuci miaode shilun jingang fahui," 班禪大師蒞內地後共建九次妙德時輪金剛法會 (Panchen Lama conducted Kālacakra Vajra Dharma-Assembly for nine times after reaching China proper). *Xichui Xuanhuashi gongshu yuekan* 西陲宣化使公署月刊 (Monthly of the Office of the Propagation Envoy to the Western Borderland) 1, nos. 7-8 (October 1936): 190.
4. Changxing was then the president of the Bailin Buddhist College (Bailin jiaoliyuan 柏林教理院) in Beijing. See Changxing 常惺, "Shilun fahui quan faqi wen"

1. CHINESE BUDDHISM IN TRANSITION

時輪法會勸發起文 (Vow to initiate the Kālacakra [Vajra] Dharma-Ceremony), HCY 12, no. 12 (December 1931): 88–93; MFQ 179: 480–485.
5. Duo Linque 多燐却, "Shishi xinbao lun shilun jingang fahui" 時事新報論時輪金剛法會 (Comments on Shishi xinbao about the Kālacakra Vajra Dharma Assembly), HCY 15, no. 4 (December 1934): 1–4; MFQ 186: 451–454.
6. "Shilun jingang fahui" 時輪金剛法會 (Kālacakra Vajra Dharma-Assembly), Shishi xinbao 時事新報 (China Times), March 20, 1934.
7. See Vincent Goossaert and David Palmer, *The Religious Questions in Modern China* (Chicago: University of Chicago Press, 2011), 43–90.
8. Yoshiko Ashiwa and David Wank, eds., *Making Religion, Making the State: The Politics of Religion in Modern China* (Stanford, CA: Stanford University Press, 2009), 3–10.
9. Some of the local associations began in the nineteenth century, but the Chinese Buddhist Federation was the first nation-wide organization. The federation was established in 1912 but did not gain government approval until the Beijing government approved its "Founding Regulation" (zhangcheng 章程) in February 1914. See Chen Bing and Deng Zimei, *Ershi shiji Zhongguo fojiao* (Chinese Buddhism in twentieth-century China) (Beijing: Minzu chubanshe, 2000), 37.
10. Regarding the Nationalist strategy about Tibet and the early interactions, see Gray Tuttle, *Tibetan Buddhists in the Making of Modern China* (New York: Columbia University Press, 2005), 43–56, 68–79.
11. The monk Jingan 敬安, the first president of the Chinese Buddhist Federation, passed away when he was petitioning in Beijing in 1912. See "Zhonghua fojiao zonghui tuiju Zhangjia huofo jiaru benhui wei huizhang" 中華佛教總會推舉章嘉活佛加入本會為會長 (The Zhonghua Buddhist Federation elected Changkya Khutukhtu as the president of the federation), *Fojiao yuebao* 佛教月報 (Buddhist monthly) 4 (October 1913): 5–8; MFQ 6: 263–266.
12. Sun Yat-sen was the first provisional president of the Republic of China after its founding in 1912. See "Zhonghua fojiao zonghui tuiju Zhangjia huofo jiaru benhui wei huizhang," 5–8; MFQ 6: 263–266.
13. See "Shang da zongtong cheng" 上大總統呈 (Petition to the president), *Fojiao yuebao*, no. 4 (October 1913): 1–2; MFQ 6: 259–260.
14. See Holmes Welch, *Buddhist Revival in China* (Cambridge, MA: Harvard University Press, 1968), 1; Chen Bing and Deng Zimei, *Ershi shiji Zhongguo fojiao*, 79–82.
15. See Welch, *Buddhist Revival in China*, 1–11. In the mid-nineteenth century, the Taiping Rebellion swept across central eastern China, destroying much of the religious establishments, including many Buddhist and Daoist temples and their texts.
16. Taixu was a student at Yang Wenhui's school at Nanjing. See Welch, *Buddhist Revival in China*, 9–11, 15. For Taixu's life and reform, see Don Alvin Pittman, *Toward a Modern Chinese Buddhism: Taixu's Reforms* (Honolulu: University of Hawai'i Press, 2001), 2. See also Justin Ritzinger, *Anarchy in the Pure Land: Reinventing the Cult of Maitreya in Modern Chinese Buddhism* (New York: Oxford University Press, 2017).
17. Erik Schicketanz has shown that the sect-centered view of Chinese Buddhist history was developed by Japanese scholars in the late nineteenth and early

1. CHINESE BUDDHISM IN TRANSITION

twentieth centuries. Yang Wenhui, Taixu, and other Chinese Buddhist reformers adopted this perspective to frame their discourses of Buddhist decline and revival. Since the disappearance of most of the thirteen (or eight or ten) sectarian schools were interpreted as a decline of Chinese Buddhism, the revival entailed restoration of the sects. See Erik Schicketanz, *Daraku to fukkō no kindai Chugoku bukkyō: Nihon bukkyō to no kaiko to sono rekishizō no kōchiku* (Between decline and revival: Historical discourse and modern Chinese Buddhism's encounter with Japan) (Kyoto: Hōzōkan, 2016); Erik Schicketanz, "Narratives of Buddhist Decline and the Concept of the Sect (*zong*) in Modern Chinese Buddhist Thought," *Studies in Chinese Religions* 3, no. 3 (2017), 281–300.

18. Taixu, "Zhengli sengqie zhidu lun" (The reorganization of the sangha system), in vol. 9, *Taixu dashi quanshu* (Collected works of Venerable Master Taixu) (1915; repr., Taipei: Miaoyun ji wenjiao jijinhui, digital version, 1998), 15.
19. For the history of three masters, see Geoffrey Goble, *Chinese Esoteric Buddhism: Amoghavajra, the Ruling Elite, and the Emergence of a Tradition* (New York: Columbia University Press, 2019), 15–58.
20. The status of the Zhenyan school stood as a full-fledged, self-conscious sectarian institution is subject to dispute. For Sørensen, esoteric Buddhism stood as a distinct sectarian denomination in the Zhenyan phase during the mid to late Tang, and later remained part of Mahāyāna Buddhism but with distinctive form and emphasis on practice. See Henrik Sørensen, "On Esoteric Buddhism in China: A Working Definition," in *Esoteric Buddhism and the Tantras in East Asia*, ed. Charles Orzech, Henrik H. Sørensen, and Richard K. Payne (Leiden: Brill, 2011), 157–158, 175. But recent studies have challenged the concept of "esoteric Buddhism" as an institutionalized school distinct from Mahāyāna Buddhism throughout history. Some scholars argue that later sectarian circumstances in Japan and Tibet led to an imposition of sectarian templates on eighth- and ninth-century China. See Robert Sharf, *Coming to Terms with Chinese Buddhism: A Reading of the Treasure Store Treatise* (Honolulu: University of Hawai'i Press, 2002), 263–278.
21. Taixu, *Zhengli sengqie zhidu lun*, 15.
22. Taixu attributed the banning of esoteric Buddhism in the Hongwu period (1368–1398) of the early Ming dynasty to some Tibetan monks' discrepant moral practices during the preceding Mongol Yuan dynasty (1271–1368). Compared to the Sakya school transmitted by Phagpa in the Yuan dynasty, Taixu's evaluation of the Gelug school was more positive, saying that if not for Tsongkhapa's reform in monastic disciplines, Tibetan Buddhism would have had declined. See Taixu, "Zhongguo xianshi mizong fuxing zhi qushi" 中國現時密宗復興之趨勢 (The contemporary current of esoteric revival in China), *HCY* 6, no. 8 (October 1925): 12–17; *MFQ* 163: 18–23.
23. Originated in Indian Mahāyāna Buddhism, esoteric Buddhist practices were gradually formulated into systemized ritualistic programs from the sixth century onward. Systemized esoteric Buddhism developed with concepts of lineage and a variety of liturgy to ensure the transmission of these secret teachings. Esoteric rituals of various forms and stages were transmitted to China via

Central Asia in the sixth and seventh centuries, and to Japan in the eighth century. With the absorption of rituals from traditional Indian and various tribal groups, the ritual practices and doctrines were fully integrated in India in the seventh century, and esoteric Buddhism reached its peak with a more systematized formulation of tantras in the eighth century. Due to religious persecution in the late Tang, much of the tantras developed in the later phases of Indian Buddhism did not transmit to China but were conserved in Tibet. See Sørensen, "On Esoteric Buddhism in China: A Working Definition," 157–175.

24. See Roy Rappaport, *Ritual and Religion in the Making of Humanity* (Cambridge: Cambridge University Press, 1999), 58, 275, 285.
25. Ronald Davidson, "Abhiṣeka," in *Esoteric Buddhism and the Tantras in East Asia*, 71–75.
26. Taixu, "Zhengli sengqie zhidu lun," 13. Bernard Faure showed that in Chan Buddhism, discourse of genealogy is central to a lineage's claim of orthodoxy. Chan Buddhism's patriarchal tradition came into formulation around the seventh to eighth centuries, with a surge of genealogy literature such as chronicles and transmission records to delineate unbroken lines from the Indian master Bodhidharma to more recent patriarchs. See Bernard Faure, *The Will to Orthodoxy: A Critical Genealogy of Northern Chan Buddhism* (Stanford, CA: Stanford University Press, 1997), 1–2.
27. See Taixu, "Zhengli sengqie zhidu lun," 13. Luo Tongbing analyzed Taixu's thoughts on esoteric Buddhism, suggesting that Taixu's changing attitude resulted from his personal, religious, institutional, and political interests. See Luo Tongbing, "The Reformist Monk Taixu and the Controversy about Exoteric and Esoteric Buddhism in Republican China," in *Images of Tibet in the 19th and 20th Centuries*, ed. Monica Esposito (Paris: École française d'Extrême-Orient, 2008), 471. As I show in chapter 3, Taixu's changing attitude was also relevant to the degree of knowledge about Japanese and Tibetan esoteric Buddhism. After Dayong reported the observed divergences of Japanese Buddhism in practice, Taixu changed his stand.
28. See Taixu, "Zhengli sengqie zhidu lun," 13.
29. See Chen Bing and Deng Zimei, *Ershi shiji Zhongguo fojiao*, 353.
30. Gonda Raifu was then an influential priest scholar. He served as the chief priest of the Buzan sect of Shingon in 1901, and he held the office of the president of Taisho University from 1928 to 1930. See Gonda Raifu, *Mikkyō kōyō* (Tōkyō: Heigo shuppansha, 1916).
31. Gonda Raifu, *Mizong gangyao* 密宗綱要 (The essentials of esoteric Buddhism), trans. Wang Hong Yuan (1919; repr., Taipei: Tianhua chuban she, 1999). For a study on Wang, see Erik Schicketanz, "Wang Hongyuan and the Import of Japanese Esoteric Buddhism to China During the Republican Period," in *Buddhism Across Asia: Networks of Material, Intellectual and Cultural Exchange* 1, ed. Tansen Sen (Singapore: Institute of Southeast Asian Studies, 2014), 403–427.
32. See Taixu, *Taixu zizhuan* 太虛自傳 (Autobiography of Taixu), vol. 31 of *Taixu dashi quanshu* 太虛大師全書 (Complete works of Taixu) (Beijing: Zongjiao wenhua chubanshe, 2004), 228.

1. CHINESE BUDDHISM IN TRANSITION

33. The *Voice of the Sea Tide* was founded by Taixu in January 1920. Wang published Gonda's "Mantuluo tongjie 曼荼羅通解 (Comprehensive introduction to maṇḍala)" in the journal in 1920.
34. The two forms of practice constituted the core praxis in Shingon Buddhism. The practices of the Womb Realm originated from *Dapiluzhena chengfo shenbian jiachi jing* 大毘盧遮那成佛神變加持經, also known as *Dari jing* 大日经 (Mahāvairocana Sūtra), trans. Śubhakarasiṃha 善無畏 and Yixing, *T* 848. The practices of the Diamond Realm were based on the *Jingangding yiqie rulai zhenshi she dasheng xianzheng dajiaowang jing* 金剛頂一切如來真實攝大乘現證大教王經 (Vajraśekhara Sūtra, also known as *Jingang ding jing* 金剛頂經), trans. Amoghavajra 不空. *T* 865.
35. Wang's status as a lay *ācārya* elicited criticism from conservative monks, as I discuss in chapter 3.
36. Gui Bohua 桂伯華 (1861–1915) was the first layman known to travel abroad to study Shingon in 1910, but he passed away in Japan in 1915. Dayong consulted Wang about learning Japanese and traveling to study at Mount Kōya. Wang replied to Dayong's questions in detail. See Wang Hongyuan, "Fu Shi Dayong shu" 復釋大勇書 (Reply to Venerable Dayong), *Foxin congkan* 佛心叢刊 (Collection of Buddha heart) 1 (January 1922): 1–2; *MFQ* 8: 359–360.
37. "Mijiao zhongxin zhi ji" 密教中興之機 (Chance for the restoration of Esotericism), *HCY* 5, no. 1 (January 1924): 3–4; *MFQ* 158: 166–167. The eighteen-method initiation ritual is a fundamental Shingon offerings ritual. Though the ritual follows common Indic liturgical patterns, the provenance of this ritual remains unclear. Shingon exegetes attributed the root manuals to Kūkai's Chinese teacher Huiguo, but some ritual manuals were possibly composed in Japan after Kūkai's death. On the history, text, and steps of the eighteen-methods ritual, see Robert Sharf, "Thinking Through Shingon Ritual," *Journal of International Association of Buddhist Studies* 26, no.1 (2003): 62–69.
38. See Taixu, "Zhongguo xianshi mizong fuxing zhi qushi," 12–17.
39. Taixu proposed that the number of esoteric temples be limited to "at most, one temple in a parish," to avoid rampant transmission. Taixu, "Zhongguo xianshi mizong fuxing zhi qushi," 12–17.
40. Taixu, "Zhongguo xianshi mizong fuxing zhi qushi," 12–17.
41. Taixu, "Zhongguo xianshi mizong fuxing zhi qushi," 12–17.
42. See Paul Williams and Anthony Tribe, *Buddhist Thought: A Complete Introduction to the Indian Tradition* (New York: Routledge, 2000), 194.
43. According to Paul Williams and Anthony Tribe, over 1,500 Sanskrit texts survived. See Williams and Tribe, *Buddhist Thought*, 195.
44. See Williams and Tribe, *Buddhist Thought*, 195.
45. See Kanben, *Hanzang fojing fanyi bijiao yanjiu*, 106–115.
46. See Williams and Tribe, *Buddhist Thought*, 204.
47. See Williams and Tribe, *Buddhist Thought*, 212.
48. See Williams and Tribe, *Buddhist Thought*, 212–217.
49. See Fandeng 梵燈, "Song zangwen xueyuan quanti liuxue Xizang xu" 送藏文學院全體留學西藏序 (Seeing off the group from Tibetan College to study in Tibet),

1. CHINESE BUDDHISM IN TRANSITION

Shijie fojiao jushilin linkan 世界佛教居士林林刊, *SFJL* 14 (October 1926): 5–6; *MFQB* 9: 319–320.

50. See Huizhong 會中, "Song tongyuan Dagang Wuyi fashi deng ru Beijing fojiao zangwen xueyuan" 送同院大剛晤一法師等入北京佛教藏文學院 (Seeing classmates Dagang and Wuyi to Tibetan College in Beijing), *HCY* 6, no. 2 (March 1925): 9–10; *MFQ* 161: 345–346.
51. Lama Bai Puren was a Mongolian monk who grew up in Rehe Province. For a biography of Lama Bai Puren, see Jinghuan 景桓, "Bai Puren dashi shi lue" 白普仁大師事略 (About Master Bai Puren), *Dayun* 大雲 (Great Cloud) 67 (May 1926): 37–44; *MFQ* 11: 39–46.
52. See Taixu, "Puti dao cidi luelun xu" 菩提道次第略論序 (Preface to the brief treatise of the stages of the path), in *Taixu dashi quanshu*, vol. 19, 780–781.
53. Dayong, "Dayong sheli fu Xianyin fashi han" 大勇闍梨覆顯蔭法師函 (Ācārya Dayong's reply to Master Xianyin), *SFJL* 7 (August 1924): 2; *MFQB* 8: 304.
54. Dayong and Lama Bai had a retreat at the Shanyuan Temple (Shanyuanan 善緣庵), where they practiced fire offering together. This experience exposed Dayong to Tibetan esoteric Buddhism. See Fazun, "Zhuzhe ru zang de jingguo" 著者入藏的經過 (The writer's experience in entering Tibet), in *Fazun fashi foxue lunwenji* 法尊法師佛學論文集 (Collected works of Buddhist studies of Fazun), ed. Lü Tiegang 呂鉄鋼 and Hu Heping 胡和平 (Beijing: Zhongguo fojiao wenhua yanjiusuo, 1990), 358–371.
55. "Beijing zangwen xueyuan jiang zhaokao" 北京藏文學院將招考 (Entrance examination of Beijing Tibetan College), *Foyin* 佛音 (*Voice of Buddhism*) 1, nos. 8–9 (November 1924): 4; *MFQ* 145: 374.
56. "Beijing zangwen xueyuan zhi faqi" 北京藏文學院之發起 (The founding of Beijing Tibetan College), *SFJL* 7 (October 1924): 2–3; *MFQB* 8: 294–295.
57. The teacher Chong Zhenru 充珍儒 was also known as Chong Baolin 充寶琳. He grew up in Kangding County. After Dayong traveled to Kangding, Mr. Chong returned to Kangding. See Huang Ying-Chieh, *Minguo mizong nianjian* 民國密宗年鑑 (Chronicle history of Tantrism during the Republican era) (Taipei: Quanfo wenhua chubanshe, 1992), 45.
58. Dayong planned for the language training from September 1924 to May 1928. See "Beijing zangwen xueyuan zhi faqi," 2–3.
59. See "Beijing zangwen xueyuan zhi faqi," 2–3.
60. Dingzhi, *Nenghai shangshi zhuan* 能海上師傳 (Biography of Master Nenghai) (1984; repr., Shanghai: Shanghai foxue shuju, 2007), 5.
61. See Wang Yuji, "Wang Yuji jushi huanying Banchan han" 王與楫居士歡迎班禪函 (Layman Wang Yuji's welcome letter to the Panchen Lama), *SFJL* 8 (February 1925): 1; *MFQB* 8: 471. About some Chinese scholars' learning of Tibetan Yogācāra thought, see Yao Zhihua, "Tibetan Learning in the Contemporary Chinese Yogācāra School," in *Buddhism Between Tibet and China*, ed. Matthew Kapstein (Boston: Wisdom, 2009), 281–294.
62. See Yanding 嚴定, "Fojiao zangwen xueyuan liuzang xuefa tuan dizi zhi Duo zunzhe han" 佛教藏文學院留藏學法團弟子致多尊者函 (Letters from the group of disciples entering Tibet and the Buddhist Tibetan College to Venerable Duo),

1. CHINESE BUDDHISM IN TRANSITION

Xinan heping fahui tekan 西南和平法會特刊 (Special issue on the Peace Dharma Assembly in the outhwest) (December 1931): 23–24; *MFQB* 42: 443–444.
63. Melvyn Goldstein attributed the Panchen Lama's flee to his futile effort to maintain the independence of his estate in economic and military reforms initiated by the elites in Lhasa. For politics in modern Tibet, see Melvyn Goldstein, *A History of Modern Tibet, 1913-1951: The Demise of the Lamaist State* (Berkeley: University of California Press, 1989), 110–112, 260–230.
64. Khenpo is a degree for higher Buddhist studies in Tibetan Buddhism.
65. "Zangwen xueyuan huanying Banchan daibiao" 藏文學院歡迎班禪代表 (Tibetan college welcomed the Panchen Lama's representative), *SFJL* 8 (February 1925): 1–3; *MFQB* 8: 471–473.
66. See "Fojiao zangwen xueyuan quanti jinjian Banchan ji" 佛教藏文學院全體覲見班禪記 (Record on all people of Tibetan College's meeting with the Panchen Lama), *HCY* 15, no. 4 (April 1925): 12–14; *MFQ* 161: 448–450.
67. According to Fazun, Taixu worried that the Nationalist army would launch an expedition to the north in the spring of 1925, so he ordered Dayong to set off. See Fazun, "Lue shu Taixu dashi zhi beiyuan ji weiye" 略述太虛大師之悲願及偉業 (A brief account of the compassionate wishes and the great endeavor of Master Taixu), in *Fazun fashi foxue lunwen ji*, 349–350.
68. Fandeng, "Song zangwen xueyuan quanti liuxue Xizang xu," 5–6.
69. Huizhong, "Song tongyuan Dagang Wuyi fashi deng ru Beijing fojiao zangwen xueyuan," 9–10.
70. See Dayong, "Fojiao zangwen xueyuan Dayong fashi zi Xikang zhi Sichuan foxuehui tongren han" 佛教藏文學院大勇法師自西康致四川佛學會同仁函 (Letter from Venerable Dayong of Tibetan College in Western Kham to colleagues in Sichuan Buddhist Society), *SFJL* 14 (October 1926): 1–2; *MFQB* 9: 299–300.
71. See "Fojiao zangwen xueyuan zai Kang gaizu ji di Zang fenzhu xiuxue zhi guiyue" 佛教藏文學院在康改組及抵藏分住修學之規約 (Regulation on the reorganization of Tibetan College in Kham and the separate residence and study in Tibet), *Sichuan fojiao xunkan* 四川佛教旬刊 (Ten-day Journal of Sichuan Buddhism) 51 (October 1926): 3; *MFQ* 128: 258.
72. In the 1920s and 1930s, the Lhasa government adopted a policy of isolation and tightened border control. Regarding the interaction between Lhasa and the Nationalist government, see Melvyn Goldstein, *A History of Modern Tibet, 1913-1951*, 65–88. For Lhasa's border policy, see Alex McKay, *Tibet and the British Raj: the Frontier Cadre, 1904-1947* (Richmond, Surrey: Curzon, 1997), 1–8. On the border conflicts, see Hsiao-ting Lin, *Tibet and Nationalist China's Frontier: Intrigues and Ethnopolitics, 1928-49* (Vancouver: UBC Press, 2006), 51–85.
73. See Dagang, "Fojiao zangwen xueyuan Shi Dagang zhi Daofu xian zhishi Ouyang Fushan shu" 佛教藏文學院釋大剛致道孚縣知事歐陽苿杉書 (Letter from Dagang of Tibetan College to the magistrate Ouyang Fushan of the Daofu County), *Fohua xunkan* 佛化旬刊 (Ten-day journal of Buddhism) 91 (November 1927): 8; *MFQ* 17: 364.
74. See "Fojiao zangwen xueyuan zai Kang gaizu ji di Zang fenzhu xiuxue zhi guiyue," 3.

1. CHINESE BUDDHISM IN TRANSITION

75. The Dalai Lama's letter was attached in a letter from Dayong. See Dayong, "Fojiao zangwen xueyuan yuanzhang Shi Dayong you Ganzi zhi Beijing Hu Zihu Yang Mingchen liang xiansheng shu" 佛教藏文學院院長釋大勇由甘孜致北京胡子笏楊明塵兩先生書 (A letter from the principal Shi Dayong of Tibetan College from Ganzi to Mr. Hu Zihu and Mr. Yang Mingchen in Beijing), *Fohua xunkan* 102 (February 1928): 8; *MFQ* 17: 450.
76. See Dayong, "Fojiao zangwen xueyuan yuanzhang Shi Dayong you Ganzi zhi Beijing Hu Zihu Yang Mingchen liang xiansheng shu xu qian" 佛教藏文學院院長釋大勇由甘孜致北京胡子笏楊明塵兩先生書（續前）(A letter from the principal Shi Dayong of Tibetan College from Ganzi to Mr. Hu Zihu and Mr. Yang Mingchen in Beijing [part 2]), *Fohua xunkan* 101 (February 1928): 8; *MFQ* 17: 442.
77. Kangding is located in the present-day Ganzi prefecture. Ganzi was culturally part of Kham in Eastern Tibet. Some sources say that Lama Jampa was ethnically Han Chinese. His temple continued to house Han monks. In the 1930s, Kangding had seven public Tibetan temples, including two large Gelug temples, two small Nyingma temples, and three Kagyu temples. In 1935, about forty Tibetan lamas and twenty Han Buddhists resided in the temple. About the religious circumstances in Kangding in the 1930s, see Yanglei 羊磊, "Kangding chengqu ba lamasi diaocha" 康定城區八喇嘛寺調查 (A survey of the eight lamaseries in town of Kangding), *Chuanbian jikan* 川邊季刊 (Sichuan border quarterly) 1, no 2 (June 1935): 207.
78. For the number of monks and temples in Kham, see a 1935 survey conducted by the Xikang government, "Xikang simiao diaocha" 西康寺廟調查 (A survey of the temples in Western Kham), *Chuanbian jikan* 1, no 4 (December 1935): 286–287. See also another survey on the monastics in sixteen counties in the Kham region, "Xikang lama diaocha" 西康喇嘛調查 (A survey of the lamas in Western Kham), *Chuanbian jikan* 2, no. 2 (June 1936): 201. It showed that approximately 34,700 lamas living in 293 temples.
79. Dayong, "Fojiao zangwen xueyuan," 8.
80. See Wuyi 晤一, "Wuyi shi shang Taixu fashi" 晤一師上太虛法師 (A letter from Venerable Wuyi to Master Taixu), *HCY* 7, no. 6 (July 1926): 8–9; *MFQ* 165: 364–365.
81. See Wuyi, "Wuyi shi shang Taixu fashi," 7.
82. The ordained received various levels of disciplinary codes, from the novice precepts to the full precepts for the ordained monks, the precepts of bodhisattva, and the esoteric precepts. See Wuyi, "Wuyi shi shang Taixu fashi," 7.
83. Known as Jampel Rolpai Lodro ('Jam dpal rol pa'i blo gros), Amdo Geshe was a guest monk at Drakkar Monastery in 1928 and he was met by Fazun.
84. The other three monks were Langchan 朗禪, Changguang 常光, and Huishen 慧深. Fazun, "Zhuzhe ru zang de jingguo," 358–371.
85. See Dingzhi, *Nenghai shangshi zhuan*, 7.
86. See Dingzhi, *Nenghai shangshi zhuan*, 7.
87. Fazun, "Zhuzhe ru zang de jingguo," 358–371.
88. According to the monk Chaoyi, who arrived in Lhasa in 1928, at least eight monks were studying in Lhasa in 1931. They were Chaoyi, Fazun, Tianran 天然, Nenghai, Yongguang, Yongleng 永楞, Yongyan 永严, and Langchan. See Chaoyi,

"Putuo si Chaoyi shang Taixu dashi shu" 普陀寺超一上太虛大師書 (Letter to Master Taixu from Monk Chaoyi of Putuo Temple), *HCY* 13, no. 1 (January 1932): 115–117; *MFQ* 180: 125–127.

89. See "Dayong fashi yuanji" 大勇法師圓寂 (The passing away of Venerable Dayong), *Xiandai sengqie* 現代僧伽 (Modern sangha), nos. 43–44 (June 1930): 79; *MFQB* 39: 271.

2. The Lamas and the Rituals

1. See "Ning yuan ge jie huanying Bai Lama" 寧垣各界歡迎白喇嘛 (All social circles at Ningbo City welcomed Lama Bai), *Shenbao* 申報, April 3, 1926.
2. The practice of Golden Light (Jinguangmingfa 金光明法) does not originate from the highest tantra, nor is it based on a belief in major deities of the Gelug tradition. This chapter does not intend to argue for its status in Tibetan esoteric Buddhism, but rather focus on its representation in a particular Chinese circumstance.
3. See "Sun Chuanfang deng zancheng jinguangming hui" 孫傳芳等贊成金光明會 (Sun Chuanfang and others embraced the Golden Light Ceremony), *Shenbao*, January 10, 1926.
4. See "Bai Lama li xiang qingxing" 白喇嘛蒞湘情形 (The situation of Lama Bai's visit to Hunan), *Shenbao*, February 2, 1926.
5. See "Xiang yihui tiyi quzhu Bai Lama" 湘議會提議驅逐白喇嘛 (The Hunan Council proposed to expel Lama Bai), *Shenbao*, February 3, 1926.
6. See "Xiang yihui tiyi quzhu Bai Lama."
7. The famine struck Yueyang, Linxiang, and Xiangyin. In Yueyang County, over five hundred people suffered from starvation. See Hunansheng difang zhi bianzuan weiyuan hui 湖南省地方誌編纂委員會, *Hunan tongjian* 湖南通鑒 (Chronicle of Hunan) (Hunan: Hunan renmin chuban she, 2008), 998.
8. See "Bai Lama li xiang qingxing."
9. See "Bai Lama li xiang qingxing."
10. See "Xiang yihui tiyi quzhu Bai Lama."
11. See "Bai Lama li xiang qingxing."
12. As much as I hoped to find information about women's voices and the responses of illiterate persons to the rituals, the current records mainly reflect male and educated individuals' voices. The available materials simply do not cover the demographic range. Even though the female and less educated may have constituted a large body of the attendants, they did not leave documents. But the tropes generated here still inform us of the tensions in the rise of esoteric rituals.
13. See Robert Sharf, "On Esoteric Buddhism in China," appendix, in *Coming to Terms with Chinese Buddhism: A Reading of the Treasure Store Treatise* (Honolulu: University of Hawai'i Press, 2002), 263–278.
14. Ronald Davidson explains the rise of esoteric Buddhism as a Buddhist response to social changes in early medieval India (500–1200 CE). Abhiṣeka is an important

2. THE LAMAS AND THE RITUALS

esoteric ritual that enables access to esoteric practice. Davidson argues that the formality of this ritual mimicked the process of coronation, with politicized metaphors in its ritual language, actions, and symbols. See Ronald Davidson, "Abhiṣeka," in *Indian Esoteric Buddhism*, 113–115. See also Charles Orzech and Henrik Sørensen, "Mudrā, Mantra, and Maṇḍala," in *Esoteric Buddhism and the Tantras in East Asia* (Leiden: Brill, 2011), 76.

15. Catherine Bell, *Ritual Theory, Ritual Practice* (1992; repr., New York: Oxford University Press, 2009), 81, 100.
16. For a study of the ninth Panchen Lama, see Fabienne Jagou, *Le 9e Panchen Lama (1883-1937): Enjeu Des Relations Sino-Tibétaines* (Paris: École française d'Extrême-Orient, 2004).
17. The meeting was intended to foster an agreement among various military cliques, political organizations, and public bodies on how to deal with the aftermath of the Beijing coup. The meeting lasted from February 1 to April 21, 1925.
18. The slogan "five races under one union" emphasized harmony among the five major ethnic groups in China including the Han, the Manchus, the Mongols, the Hui, and the Tibetans. See "Banchan zhi xiao mi zhan huo tan" 班禪之消弭戰禍談 (The Panchen Lama's talk on dispersing the calamity of war), *HCY* 6, no. 4 (April 1925): 13–14; *MFQ* 162: 47–48.
19. See "Banchan jin jian Duan zhizheng" 班禪覲見段執政 (The Panchen Lama met with Chief Executive Duan), *HCY* 6, no. 3 (April 1925): 21–22; *MFQ* 161: 457–458. See also, "Banchan chu jing fu Hang" 班禪出京赴杭 (The Panchen Lama left Beijing toward Hangzhou), *HCY* 6, no. 4 (April 1925): 20–21; *MFQ* 162: 54–55.
20. As depicted in chapter 1, the Panchen Lama encouraged Dayong and his students to pursue the study of Tibetan Buddhism.
21. Xiong Xiling served as premier of the Republic of China from July 1913 to February 1914.
22. See "Banchan zhu zhong guowen zhi zhenxiang" 班禪注重國文之真象 (The truth about Panchen Lama's emphasis on the national script), *HCY* 6, no. 4 (April 1925): 14–15; *MFQ* 162: 48–49.
23. See "Banchan zhu zhong guowen zhi zhenxiang," 14–15.
24. See "Banchan chu jing fu Hang," 20–21.
25. See "Banchan chu jing fu Hang," 20–21. Regarding the Panchen Lama's activities, see also, Tuttle, *Tibetan Buddhists in the Making of Modern China* (New York: Columbia University Press, 2005), 88–93.
26. Gilbert Reid, also known as Li Jiabai 李佳白, founded the International Institute of China to promote cultural and religious understanding between the Westerners and the Chinese.
27. See "Ge jiao daibiao can ye Banchan" 各教代表參謁班禪 (Different religious representatives paid a visit to Banchan), *HCY* 6, no. 4 (April 1925): 17–18; *MFQ* 162: 51–52.
28. See "Shangxian tang huanying Banchan zhi qingxing" 尚賢堂歡迎班禪之情形 (The situation of the International Institute of China's reception of Banchan), *HCY* 6, no. 4 (April 1925): 15–17; *MFQ* 162: 49–51.
29. See "Banchan dian fu Sun Chuanfang" 班禪電覆孫傳芳 (Banchan's telegram reply to Sun Chuanfang), *HCY* 6, no. 4 (April 1925): 14; *MFQ* 162: 48.

2. THE LAMAS AND THE RITUALS

30. See "Banchan chu jing fu Hang," 20–21.
31. See "Banchan zhuanche guo Ji" 班禪專車過濟 (The Panchen Lama's special train passed through Jinan), *HCY* 6, no. 4 (April 1925): 21–22; *MFQ* 162: 55–56.
32. See "Ning guan shen yingsong Banchan ji" 寧官紳迎送班禪記 (The record of Ningbo's officers and gentlemen's welcoming and seeing off Panchen), *HCY* 6, no. 5 (May 1925): 14–15; *MFQ* 162: 178–179.
33. See "Banchan fu Putuo zhi shengkuang" 班禪赴普陀之盛況 (The grand reception of Panchen at Putuo), *HCY* 6, no. 5 (May 1925): 13; *MFQ* 162: 177.
34. Yinguang, "Putuo shan Pujisi Banchan she qian seng zhai shang tang fayu" 普陀山普濟寺班禪設千僧齋上堂法語 (The Dharma talk at the banquet for a thousand monks offered by Panchen at the Puji Temple at Putuo Mountain), *SFJL* 10 (August 1925): 1; *MFQ* 14: 501.
35. The reception was led by Wang Yiting 王一亭, an influential lay Buddhist leader in Shanghai. The attendees were representatives from the general Chamber of Commerce, Shanghai Commercial Association, World Lay Buddhist Society, Zhonghua Buddhist Association, and Chinese Social Welfare Organization (Jishenghui 濟生會), the Charity Assembly of Associated Righteousness (Lianyi shanhui 聯義善會), Buddhist Relief Association (Fojiao weichihui 佛教維持會), and monks from the Putuo Island. See "Shanghai guanshang huanying Banchan zhi yanhui" 上海官商歡迎班禪之宴會 (Shanghai officers and merchants' welcome party for Panchen), *HCY* 6, no. 5 (May 1925): 10–12; *MFQB* 2: 433–436.
36. See "Banchan di Hu xu zhi" 班禪抵滬續誌 (The second record of Panchen's visit to Shanghai), *HCY* 6, no. 5 (May 1925): 27–30; *MFQ* 162: 61–64.
37. For discussion of the Zen rhetoric of immediacy, see Robert Sharf, "Buddhist Modernism and the Rhetoric of Meditative Experience," *Numen* 42, no.3 (1995): 228–283.
38. Sharf has shown that doctrine was always secondary to ritual procedures in the monastic curriculum, posing a challenge for the Japanese Buddhist reformers. Robert Sharf, "Thinking through Shingon Ritual," *Journal of International Association of Buddhist Studies* 26, no. 1 (2003): 55–56.
39. Regarding Taixu's critique, see Taixu, "Rensheng fojiao kaiti" 人生佛教開題 (The opening to humanistic Buddhism), *HCY* 26, no. 1 (January 1945): 36–37; *MFQ* 202: 36–37.
40. David L. McMahan, *The Making of Buddhist Modernism* (New York: Oxford University Press, 2008), 17–20.
41. *Shi ji jing* 世記經 (Accounts of the world), translated by Buddhayaśas 佛陀耶舍 and Zhu Fonian 竺佛念 between 399 and 416, *T* no. 1, 1: 144–145.
42. Kang Jiyao 康寄遙, "Qidao xizai, lun qidao" 祈禱息災: 論祈禱 (Pray for pacifying disaster, about praying), *Dayun* 99 (July 1930): 7–10; *MFQB* 21: 305–308.
43. See "Bai fashi hongfa ji" 白法師弘法記 (A record of Master Bai's dissemination of Dharma), in Jinguangming fahui editorial committee ed., *Tianjin jinguangming fahui tekan* 天津金光明法會特刊 (Special issue on the Tianjin Golden Light Ceremony, *TJJGM*) (Tianjin: Tianjin yinshua gongsi, 1928): 1–4; *MFQB* 15: 263–264.
44. See "Bai fashi hongfa ji," *TJJGM*, 1–4.
45. "Bai fashi hongfa ji," *TJJGM*, 2.

2. THE LAMAS AND THE RITUALS

46. See Jinghuan, "Bai Puren dashi shi lue," *Dayun* 67 (May 1926): 37–44; *MFQ* 11: 39–46.
47. See Tao Tao 陶陶, "Lama Bai yu Li Chun zhi tanhua" 白喇嘛與李純之談話 (Lama Bai's dialogue with Li Chun), *Dayun* 69 (July 1926): 70–73; *MFQB* 17: 490–494.
48. For an introduction to the content, see Donald Lopez, *Buddhist Scriptures* (London: Penguin Books, 2004), chap. 5, 37–45. See also *Jinguangming jing*, T no. 245.
49. The Han disciples received initiations from him at the Golden Light ceremonies. The ritual included receiving initiation, making offerings, learning to make hand signs (such as hand signs of offering while making a mental image of vast offering), and learning dozens of mantras (such as the mantra of Amitābha Buddha and the six-syllable mantra). Lama Bai did not mention the origin of the Golden Light ritual that he performed. He may have received it from a revelation at Mount Wutai. He also integrated some basic practices into this procedure. For the details of the procedure, see "Bai Lama xiufa zhong zhi canguanji" 白喇嘛修法中之參觀記 (A record of visiting Lama Bai in performing Dharma), in *TJJGM*: 6–7; *MFQB* 15: 268–269.
50. He was practicing Yaochadajiangfa 藥叉大將法 (the practice of the yaksha generals). See "Bai fashi hongfa ji," 3.
51. See "Bai fashi hongfa ji," 1–4.
52. See "Banchan fo Yingtai chuanfa ji" 班禪佛瀛台傳法記 (A record of Panchen's transmission of Dharma at Yingtai), *Xindeng* 心燈 (The lamp for heart) 19 (November 1926): 99–101; *MFQB* 16: 99–101.
53. The Shanghai ceremony was patronized by the Shanghai Lay Buddhist Society, and the Hangzhou ceremony was held at the Inviting Sages Temple (Zhaoxiansi 招賢寺) for three days. See "Jinguangming hui zhi faqi" 金光明會之發起 (The initiation of the Golden Light Ceremony), *Shenbao*, July 20, 1925.
54. "Nanjing jiang kai jinguangming hui" 南京將開金光明會 (Nanjing will organize Golden Light Ceremony), *Shishi xinbao*, December 28, 1925.
55. See "Wu sheng jinguangming hui choubei jinxing xun" 五省金光明會籌備進行訊 (News on the five provinces' organization of the Golden Light Ceremony), *HCY* 7, no. 2 (April 1926): 7–10; *MFQ* 164: 384–385.
56. See Qiu Liao 秋蓼, "Bai Lama fu Hang zhi zhenwen" 白喇嘛赴杭之珍聞 (Special news on Lama Bai's trip to Hangzhou), *Dayun* 70 (August 1926): 57–58; *MFQ* 137: 479–480.
57. See "Sun Chuanfang tongling jintu sanri" 孫傳芳通令禁屠三日 (Sun Chuanfang ordered closing butchery for three days), *Shenbao*, April 2, 1926; see also "Ning yuan ge jie huanying Bai Lama," *Shenbao*, April 3, 1926.
58. See "Nanjing jiang kai jinguangming hui."
59. See "Nanjing kuaixin" 南京快信 (News from Nanjing), *Shenbao*, April 17, 1926.
60. See "Nanjing kuaixin."
61. See Huiguan 慧觀, "Jiaxing choubei huanying Bai Lama suowen" 嘉興籌備歡迎白喇嘛瑣聞 (Bits of news on the preparation of the reception of Lama Bai at Jiaxing), *Dayun* 69 (July 1926): 54–55.
62. See "Jiaxing 嘉興," *Shenbao*, June 22, 1926.

2. THE LAMAS AND THE RITUALS

63. See Huiguan, "Bai Lama lai He zhi xingxing sese" 白喇嘛來禾之形形色色 (Miscellaneous records of Lama Bai's visit to Jiaxing), *Shenbao*, June 28, 1926.
64. See Huiguan, "Jiaxing choubei huanying Bai Lama suowen," 54–55.
65. See Renhong 仁宏, "Pi Hunan sheng yiyuan Ye Dequan qing qu zhu Bai Lama wen" 闢湖南省議員葉德權請驅逐白喇嘛文 (A rejection to the proposal of Hunan councilor Ye Dequan's proposal to evict Lama Bai), *HCY* 7, no. 4 (May 1926): 16–17; *MFQ* 165: 126–127.
66. Norlha, a high lama of Nyingma school, sought protection from the Nanjing government in 1923 or 1924. See Manhua 曼華, "Xizai fahui kai tan" 息災法會開壇 (The opening of the platform for the Calamity-Pacifying Ceremony), *Shishi xinbao*, May 17, 1933. See also "Nuona huofo zuo di jing" 諾那活佛昨抵京 (Norlha Tulku arrived at the capital yesterday), *Shishi xinbao*, June 13, 1934.
67. See "Nuona zai Yue juxing guanding hui" 諾那在粵行灌頂會 (Norlha organized initiation ceremony at Guangdong), *Shishi xinbao*, May 17, 1934.
68. See Wang Hongchi 王宏持, "Wen xinan heping fahui jiang chu tekan jingshen faxi" 聞西南和平法會將出特刊敬申法喜 (Congratulations to the publication of the Special issue of the Southwest Peace Ceremony), *Xinan heping fahui tekan*, 1–6; *MFQB* 42: 245–250. Details about the ceremony, see Tuttle, *Tibetan Buddhists in the Making of Modern China*, 114–118.
69. "Jinsheng tuoluoni xizai daochang lai jian" 金勝陀羅尼息災道場來件 (Report from Jinsheng Dhāraṇī Calamity-Pacifying Place of Rituals), Special issue, *Chenzhong* 晨鐘 (Morning bell) 3 (May 1928): 1–3; *MFQB* 32: 489–491.
70. The *Humane Kings Sutra* was a third- or fourth-century CE composition exhorting court elites to support Buddhism. See *Renwang huguo bore boluomi jing* 仁王護國般若波羅密經 (Prajñāpāramitā Sutra of Humane Kings and Protection of Nation), T no. 245. Its translation was attributed to Kumārajīva (first version) and Amoghavajra (second version). Orzech regarded this scripture as an apocryphon that combines Buddhist concepts with the traditional Confucian ideal of kingship. See Charles Orzech, "Puns on the Humane King: Analogy and Application in an East Asian Apocryphon," *Journal of the American Oriental Society* 109, no. 1 (1989): 17–24.
71. Weiyin 畏因, "Qidao xizai, shuo qidao" 祈禱息災，說祈禱 (Pray for pacifying disaster, about praying), *Dayun* 99 (July 1930): 3–5; *MFQB* 21: 301–305.
72. Dai Jitao, "Zhi Henan Li zhuxi dian" 致河南李主席電 (Telegram to Henan's Chairman Li), in vol. 3 of *Dai Jitao xiansheng wencun* 戴季陶先生文存 (Extant Writings of Dai Jitao), ed. Chen Tianxi (Taipei: Zhongguo guomindang zhongyang weiyuanhui, 1959), 1293. Letter dated March 4, 1942. For details about Dai's involvement, see also Tuttle, *Tibetan Buddhists in the Making of Modern China*, 72, 84, 136–144, 161–170.
73. The full title is "Huguo Xuanhua Guanghui Dashi" 護國宣化廣慧大師 (Nation-Protector, Propagation Envoy, Great Master of Vast Wisdom Master).
74. See "Jiang weiyuan zhang chuxi zhixun" 蔣委員長出席致訓 (Chairman Chiang attended and gave instruction), *Shishi xinbao*, June 26, 1935.

2. THE LAMAS AND THE RITUALS

75. The commission opened an office for Norlha at Nanjing after his arrival. See "Xikang Nuona Hutuketu" 西康諾那呼圖克圖 (Norlha Qutughtu of Western Kham), *Shishi xinbao*, February 12, 1930.
76. Duara claimed that by the time of the New Life Movement in the mid-1930s, the anti-superstition campaign produced an "elite tradition" that elevated Confucianism and organized religions over a realm of popular religion and superstition. See Prasenjit Duara, *Rescuing History from the Nation*, 110. See also Rebecca Nedostup, *Superstitious Regimes: Religion and the Politics of Chinese Modernity* (Cambridge, MA: Harvard University Asia Center, 2009), 4.
77. "Shenci cunfei biaozhun" 神祠存廢標準 (Standards for preserving and abandoning gods and shrines), in *Zhonghua minguo fagui huibian* 中華民國法規彙編 (Collection of regulations of the Republic of China) (Shanghai: Zhonghua shuju, 1934), 807.
78. The edict aimed to destroy cults that worshipped meaningless deities and natural deities, and cults that collected money in the name of religion. See "Shenci cunfei biaozhun," 807.
79. Liaokong 了空, "Hubei sheng fojiao hui changwei Xiaolan deng cheng" 湖北省佛教會常委曉嵐等呈 (Hubei Provincial Buddhist Association's petition), *Zhongguo fojiaohui yuekan* 中國佛教會月刊 (Chinese Buddhist Association monthly), nos. 5–6 (December 1929): 107.
80. Dongchu, *Zhongguo fojiao jindai shi*, 142.
81. For campaigns at the local level, see Duara, *Rescuing History from the Nation*, 107; and "Anhui zhengshou jingchan mixin juan renwei yiduan huozhong" 安徽收經懺迷信捐認為異端惑眾 (Anhui levied tax on funeral rites and superstition for the confusion caused to the public by the heterodoxy), *Xiandai sengqie* 2, nos. 43–44 (June 1930): 81–82; *MFQB* 39: 273–274.
82. On November 12, 1928, local elites in Zhejiang founded an anti-superstition society to purge what they identified as superstition, even though these practices were widely practiced in both popular and licensed institutional religious activities. See Dongchu, *Zhongguo fojiao jindai shi* 中國佛教近代史 (The modern history of Chinese Buddhism) (1974. repr., Taipei: Zhonghua fojiao wenhua guan, 1987), 142.
83. See Taixu, "Neizheng bu jin po zhuzhong zongjiao" 內政部今頗注重宗教 (The Ministry of Interior recently attended to religion), *HCY* 14, no. 11 (November 1933): 1–2; *MFQ* 185: 289–290.
84. See Kang Jiyao, "Pochu mixin" 破除迷信 (Discard superstition), *Fohua suikan* 佛化隨刊 (Jottings of Buddhism), nos. 10–11 (December 1928): 2–8; *MFQB* 22: 318–324.
85. See Shi Jiezong 釋玠宗, "Foxue shi zhengxin juefei mixin" 佛學是正信絕非迷信 (Buddhist teachings are righteous belief, not superstition), *Taiwan fojiao xinbao* 臺灣佛教新報 (Newspaper of Taiwan Buddhism) 1, no. 6 (December 1925): 2–3; *MFQB* 4: 445–446.
86. See Huang Jianliu 黃健六, "Na xueli lai yanjiu mixin juan" 拿學理來研究迷信捐 (Use doctrines to study superstition tax), *SFJL* 26 (August 1930): 7–17; *MFQB* 11: 41–51.

87. See "Shuo jingchan bingfei mixin" 說經懺並非迷信 (Scripture chanting and penitential offering are not superstition), *Fohua xunkan* 3, no. 91 (November 1927): 1–2; *MFQ* 17: 357–358.
88. See Holmes Welch, *Buddhist Revival in China* (Cambridge, MA: Harvard University Press, 1968), 143–145. Welch claimed that this proposal was raised by a Tibetan representative of Panchen Lama. About Panchen Lama's interaction with Dai Jitao and Taixu, see Dongchu, *Zhongguo fojiao jindai shi*, 377–386.
89. See Tuttle, *Tibetan Buddhists in the Making of Modern China*, 156–158.
90. Dai Jitao, "Renwang huguo fahui fayuan wen" 仁王護國法會發願文 (Vows for the Humane Kings Country-Protection Dharma-Assembly), in *Dai Jitao xiansheng wencun*, vol. 3, ed. Chen Tianxi (Taipei: Zhongguo guomindang zhongyang weiyuanhui, 1959), 1176–1177, dated November 16, 1931.
91. See "Jingang huguo xizai fahui yuanqi" 金剛護國息災法會緣起 (Origin of the Vajra Country-Protection Dharma Assembly), *Zhengxin* 正信 (True belief) 1, no. 2 (April 1932): 6; *MFQB* 43: 22.
92. See "Banchan Dashi lilin neidi hou gongjian jiuci miaode shilun jingang fahui," 190. For details about the Panchen Lama's ceremonies, see Gray Tuttle, "Tibet as the Source of Messianic Teachings to Save Republican China," in *The Images of Tibet in the 19th and 20th Centuries*, ed. Monica Esposito (Paris: École française d'Extrême-Orient, 2008), 329–356.
93. Lu Xun 魯迅, "Zhenjia Tangji hede" 真假堂吉訶德 (True and fake Don Quixote), in *Nanqiang beidiao ji* 南腔北調集 (Southern tone and northern accent) (Shanghai: Tongwen shuju, 1934), 116–118.
94. Hu Shuibo 胡水波, "Shilun jingang fahui xunli" 時輪金剛法會巡禮 (Visit the Kālacakra Vajra Dharma-Assembly), *Xinsheng zhoukan* 新生週刊 (Journal of new life) 1, no. 40 (April 1934): 269–271.
95. See Yikong 一孔, "Guoji xuanchuan" 國際宣傳 (International propaganda), *Shishi xinbao*, May 11, 1933.
96. See Liu Fuqing 劉複頃, "Amituofo Dai Chuanxian" 阿彌陀佛戴傳賢 (Amitābha Dai Chuanxian), *Shishi xinbao*, May 16, 1934.
97. See Manhua, "Dagui" 打鬼 (Beating the ghosts), *Shishi xinbao*, September 2, 1936.
98. Zhang Yingchao 張英超, "Shilun jingang fahui guanguang yinxiang" 時輪金剛法會觀光印象 (Impression of Kālacakra Vajra Dharma-Assembly), *Shidai Manhua* 時代漫畫 (Caricature of time) 5 (May 1934).
99. In addition to holding ceremonies, Chinese Buddhist monks were involved in anti-Japanese military skirmishes and wars in various forms. They organized philanthropic events, provided medical services to Chinese armies, and some monks even participated in skirmishes. See Xueyu, *Buddhism, War, and Nationalism: Chinese Monks in the Struggle against Japanese Aggressions, 1931-1945* (New York: Routledge, 2005), 105–150.
100. Duo Linque, "*Shishi xinbao* lun shilun jingang fahui" 時事新報論時輪金剛法會 (Comments on *Shishi xinbao* about the Kālacakra Vajra Dharma-Assembly), *HCY* 15, no. 4 (December 1934): 1–4; *MFQ* 186: 451–454.
101. For example, Miaoguang criticized Lama Bai for eating meat and drinking alcohol, thus breaking basic Buddhist precepts and lacking compassion. See

Miaoguang 妙光, "Duiyu Bai Puren Lama zhi gongdao ping" 對於白普仁喇嘛之公道評 (Fair criticism of Lama Bai Puren), *HCY* 7, no. 4 (May 1926): 10–11; *MFQ* 165: 120–121.
102. Taixu pointed out that the Huayan Sūtra was believed to be obtained from the Dragon King's court, and the Lotus Sutra from Treasure Tower. Taixu, "Douzheng jiangu zhong lue lun Shilun Jingang Fahui" 鬥諍堅固中略論時輪金剛法會 (Comments on the Kālacakra Vajra Dharma-Assembly in contentious dissensions), *HCY* 15, no. 5 (May 1934): 1–2; *MFQ* 187: 9–10. See *Miaofa lianhua jing* 妙法蓮華經 (Skt. Saddharmapuṇḍarīka Sūtra; The Lotus Sutra), trans. Kumārajīva, *T* no. 262; *Huayan jing* 華嚴經 (Skt. The Avataṃsaka Sūtra; Flower Ornament Sutra), trans., Sikṣānanda, *T* no. 278.
103. See Changxing, "Shilun fahui quan faqi wen," 時輪法會勸發起文 (Vow to initiate the Kālacakra [Vajra] Dharma-Ceremony), *HCY* 12, no. 12 (December 1931): 88–93; *MFQ* 179: 480–485.

3. Esoteric Buddhism for Laypeople

1. The survey provided information about the names, routine activities, and locations of the organizations. About two hundred organizations developed in the Yangtze River region: fifty in Zhejiang, twenty-three in Anhui, nine in Jiangxi, eleven in Hubei, eleven in Hunan, and twenty-seven in Sichuan. About thirty-nine organizations were in the Yellow River region: twenty-five in Hebei, four in Shandong, four in Henan, five in Shanxi and Shaanxi. Fifteen organizations were located in northeast China: six in Liaoning, seven in Jilin, and two in Heilongjiang. See "Fojiao jiguang diaocha lu" 佛教機關調查錄 (Survey of Buddhist Organizations), *SFJL* 20 (August 1928): 16–21; *MFQB* 10: 96–101; "Fojiao jiguang diaocha lu," *SFJL* 21, (November 1928): 11–14; *MFQB* 10: 211–214; "Fojiao jiguan diaocha lu," *SFJL* 23 (1929): 14–19; *MFQB* 10: 322–327.
2. "Beijing shi guanli Yiheyuan shiwu suo guanyu Ding Shuqiu gouzhi dimu de cheng ji Beijing Wanshou shan Yuchun yuan jushilin zuzhi dagang" 北京市管理頤和園事務所關於丁淑秋購置地畝的呈及北京萬壽山毓春園居士林組織大綱" (The administrative office of the Summer Palace in Beijing, about Ding Shuqiu's request to purchase land and the organization principles of the Lay Society in the Garden of Nurturing Spring on Mount of Longevity), April 1928, J021-001-00012, Beijing Municipal Archives. Hereafter referenced as "Yuchun yuan jushilin zuzhi dagang."
3. "Yuchun yuan jushilin zuzhi dagang."
4. "Yuchun yuan jushilin zuzhi dagang." The society owned a woodland of twenty-four *mu* 畝 at the Western Hill of Beijing and also owned fifteen offices, which they rented to provided additional income.
5. Ding Wenjun 丁文雋, "Beiping xiaoxi" 北平消息 (News about Beijing), *SFJL* 30 (September 1931): 10; *MFQB* 11: 322.

3. ESOTERIC BUDDHISM FOR LAYPEOPLE

6. The hereditary temples were usually small in size and could not provide sufficient education to the resident members. See Ding Wenjun, "Hu Zihu jushi zhuan" 胡子笏居士傳 (Biography of layman Hu Zihu), *Jue youqing* 覺有情 (Awaken the sentient beings), nos. 107–108 (February 1944): 13–14; *MFQB* 62: 173–174.
7. "Beijing zangwen xueyuan zhi faqi," 北京藏文學院之發起 (The founding of Beijing Tibetan College), *SFJL* 7 (August 1924): 2–3; *MFQB* 8: 294–295.
8. In a letter dated March 22, 1926, Dayong wrote to Hu about the budget of the journey. Dayong, "Dayong fashi zi Xikang zhi Beijing liuzang xuefa houyuan hui ganshi Hu Zihu jushi han" 大勇法師自西康致北京留藏學法後援會幹事胡子笏居士函 (Letter from Master Dayong in Xikang to Hu Zihu, the manager of Beijing supporters' Association for the Study at Tibet), *SFJL* 14 (October 1926): 2–3; *MFQB* 9: 300–301. See also, Dayong, "Dayong fashi zhi Hu Zihu Yang Mingchen liang xiansheng shu" 大勇法師致胡子笏楊明塵兩先生書 (Letter from Master Dayong to Hu Zhihu and Yang Mingchen), *SFJL* no. 23 (1929): 3–6; *MFQB* 10: 273–276.
9. The society changed its name to "Beiping Lay Buddhist Society" (Beiping Jushilin 北平居士林) in 1946 and "Beijing Lay Buddhist Society" (Beijing Jushilin 北京居士林) in 1949. See Zhou Shujia 周叔迦, "Shenqing shu 申請書" (Application), 196-002-00290, July 1951, Beijing Municipal Archives.
10. Beijing Jushilin Committee, ed., *Beijing fojiao jushilin lishi yu yange* 北京佛教居士林歷史與沿革 (History and development of Beijing Lay Buddhist Society) (Beijing: Beijing fojiao jushilin, 2010), 3–4. For the organization's principles, see "Huabei jushilin guanyu chengbao gaixuan zhiyuan qingxing jushilin zhangcheng de chengwen ji shehuiju de pishi" 華北居士林關於呈報改選職員情形居士林章程的呈文及社會局的批示 (The Huabei Lay Buddhist Society's report about reelection of officers, organization principles, and reply from the bureau of the society), July 1938, J002-003-00828, Beijing Municipal Archives.
11. Beijing Jushilin Committee, ed., *Beijing fojiao jushilin lishi yu yange*, 14.
12. Regarding Taixu's leaving Wuchang and coming to Beijing to build the World Buddhist Institute, see Yuanguang 圓光, "Bailin foxue yanjiushe gaizu shijie foxueyuan jiaoliyuan de jingguo" 柏林佛學研究社改組世界佛學苑教理院的經過 (The procedure of transforming the Buddhist Research Society of Cypress Forest to World Buddhist Institute), *Fojiao pinglun* 佛教評論 (Buddhist Review) 1, no. 1 (January 1931), 69–72; *MFQ* 46: 189–192.
13. Beijing jushilin committee, ed., *Beijing fojiao jushilin lishi yu yange*, 1.
14. See Nenghai, *Putitang risong* (Beijing: Beiping huabei jushilin, 1934); Nenghai, *Guiyi faxin sheyao song* (Beijing: Beiping huabei jushilin, 1934).
15. See Nenghai "Putidao cidi ke song jiangji" 菩提道次第科頌講記 (Lecture notes on the Compendium of Lamrim), in *Sanxue jianglu*, 1–164.
16. See "Huabei jushilin qingde Zongkaba dashi zhenxiang" 華北居士林請得宗喀巴大師真像 (Huabei Lay Buddhist Society obtained a painting of the true image of Master Tsongkhapa), *Foxue banyuekan* 121 (February 1936), 20; *MFQ* 52: 110.
17. See "Huabei jushilin qingde Zongkaba dashi zhenxiang," 20.
18. Hu's grandson became a novice monk in Nenghai's lineage at the age of nine. Information collected in an interview with Hu's grandson and granddaughter

3. ESOTERIC BUDDHISM FOR LAYPEOPLE

in September 2013. About Hu's life, see also "Hu Zihu shiji" 胡子笏示寂 (Obituary of Hu Zihu), *Jue youqing*, nos. 105–106 (January 1944): 16; *MFQB* 62: 160.
19. Chen Bing and Deng Zimei, *Ershi shiji zhongguo fojiao* (Chinese Buddhism in twentieth-century China) (Beijing: Minzu chubanshe, 2000), 353.
20. "Shantou mijiao chongxinghui jinxun" 汕頭密教重興會近訊 (Recent news about the Shantou Society of Restoring Chinese Esoteric Buddhism), *Foxue banyuekan* 88 (October 1934): 10; *MFQ* 50: 72.
21. "Benhui zhangchen" 本會章程 (Principles of our society), *Shideng foxue yuekan* 1 (July 1934): 51; *MFQB* 48: 239.
22. Wang Hongyuan, "Fakan ci" 發刊詞 (Foreword), *Shideng foxue yuekan* 1 (July 1934): 1–2; *MFQB* 48: 189–190.
23. Zhou Zhicheng 周志誠, "Mijiao jushilin yuanqi bing jianyue" 密教居士林緣起並簡約 (The origin of the Esoteric Lay Buddhist Society and regulation), *Fojiao zazhi* 佛教雜誌 (Buddhist Magazine) no. 24 (December 1935): 45–52; *MFQ* 64: 541–548.
24. "Xianggang Li Yizhen jushi rumi yinyuan ji Zhenyanzong jushilin zhi laili" 香港黎乙真居士入密因緣及真言宗居士林之來歷 (Layman Li Yizhen's entry into Esoteric Buddhism and the founding of Zhenyan Lay Buddhist Society), *Siming xian fojiao hui huikan* 思明縣佛教會會刊 (Journal of the Buddhist Association in Siming County) 2 (1932): 83–84; *MFQB* 42: 89–90.
25. Lama Bai remained active in Beijing and Tianjin until his passing away in Beijing on August 7, 1929. See "Bai Lama yuanji" 白喇嘛圓寂 (Bai Lama Passed Away), *Shenbao*, August 9, 1929.
26. Deng Jiquan 鄧繼佺, "Tianjin jinguangming fahui tebie bian yan" 天津金光明法會特別弁言 (Preface to the Special Issue on the Tianjin Golden Light Dharma Ceremony), *Tianjin jinguangming fahui tekan* 天津金光明法會特刊 (*Special Issue on the Tianjin Golden Light Dharma Ceremony*; *TJJGM*) (Tianjin: Tianjin yinshua gongsi, 1928), 1–3; *MFQB* 15: 85–87.
27. See "Chongxiu Yonghegong yuanqi" 重修雍和宮緣起 (Origin of rebuilding Yonghe Temple), *TJJGM*, 1–2; *MFQB* 15: 295–296.
28. See "Chongxiu Yonghegong dianyu gongcheng jihua shu" 重修雍和宮殿宇工程計畫書 (Project proposal to rebuild the halls in Yonghe Temple), *TJJGM*, 4–9; *MFQB* 15: 298–303.
29. When Yuan Shikai passed away in 1916, Li, who at the time was vice president, took over the presidency. Li had served two times as president (1916 to 1917, and 1922 to 1923). Xu Shichang was the president from 1918 to 1922. Xu's brother Xu Shiguang 徐世光 led the organizing committee, which had over twenty patrons. Former president Li passed away in June 1928, but the Golden Light Ceremony was dedicated to him, as the event was organized in his mansion. Li's wife Wu Jingjun 吳敬君 and his eldest son Li Shaoji 黎紹基 were the principal patrons of the ceremony. See Deng Jiquan, "Tianjin jinguangming fahui tebie bian yan," 1–3.
30. The *Special Issue* has 249 pages. The title of the *Special Issue* was written by Liang Qichao 梁啟超 and Zhang Binglin 章炳麟, two influential literati in the late Qing and early Republican period.
31. Deng Jiquan, "Tianjin jinguangming fahui tebie bian yan," 1–3.

3. ESOTERIC BUDDHISM FOR LAYPEOPLE

32. Deng Jiquan, "Tianjin jinguangming fahui tebie bian yan," 1–3.
33. Deng Jiquan, "Tianjin jinguangming fahui tebie bian yan," 1–3.
34. Deng Jiquan, "Tianjin jinguangming fahui tebie bian yan," 1–3.
35. The Longevity Buddha, also known as Amitābha Buddha or Amitāyus Buddha, was one of the most worshipped Buddhas in the Chinese Buddhist world.
36. Deng Jiquan, "Tianjin jinguangming fahui tebie bian yan," 1–3.
37. For details, see "Wuliang shou fo chengjiu fa," 4–9.
38. The translators, Chen Lansheng 陳瀾生 and Li Ciwu 李次武 explained that the Chinese transliteration could not fully capture the pronunciation of the Tibetan sound, so the Romanization would better help readers. See "Bai fashi guanding chuanfa lu," 7–27.
39. See "Gong tan foxiang biao fa zhi yiyi" 壇供佛像表法之意義 (The meanings of the Dharma expressed in the Buddha statues on the altar), *TJJGM*, 4–5; *MFQB* 15: 192–193.
40. The *Special Issue* was priced at 1 yuan.
41. For example, on October 13th, Lama Bai taught the following practices: three-syllable visualization, the four refuges, the vow of bodhicitta, the four infinite minds, the mantra of the Infinite life Buddha, the heart mantra of Amitābha Buddha, the six-syllable mantra, the Great White Parasol mantra, the Yellow Tara mantra, the one hundred-syllable mantra, the dedication, the auspicious mantra, and the mantra of getting rebirth. See "Bai fashi guanding chuanfa lu" 白法師灌頂傳法錄 (The record of Master Bai's initiation and transmission of Dharma), *TJJGM*, 7–27; *MFQB* 15: 127–142.
42. For details, see "Wuliang shou fo chengjiu fa" 無量壽佛成就法 (The accomplishing Dharma of the Infinite Life Buddha), *TJJGM*, 4–9; *MFQB* 15: 121–125.
43. See He Jianming 何建明, "Luelun Qingmo minchu de zhongguo fojiao nüzhong" 略論清末民初的中國佛教女眾 (A brief study of Buddhist women in the Late Qing and early Republican period), *Foxue yanjiu* 佛學研究 (Buddhist Studies) 6 (1997): 203–209.
44. As I show in chapter 6, Longlian 隆蓮 (1909–2006) was a head disciple in Nenghai's lineage. Ester Bianchi's study on Longlian has greatly expanded our knowledge about the nuns who were practicing esoteric Buddhism. See Ester Bianchi, "Subtle Erudition and Compassionate Devotion: Longlian, 'The Most Outstanding Bhikṣuṇī' in Modern China," in *Making Saints in Modern China*, ed. David Ownby, Vincent Goosaert, Ji Zhe (New York: Oxford University Press, 2017), 272–311.
45. See Deng Jiazhou 鄧家宙, *Xianggang fojiaoshi* 香港佛教史 (History of Buddhism in Hong Kong) (Hongkong: zhonghua shuju, 2015), 66–68; Wang Gengwu 王賡武, *Xianggang shi xinbian* 香港史新編 (A new history of Hong Kong) (Hongkong: Joint Publishing, 2016), 919–920.
46. Li rented a house in 1925 and raised funds to purchase a permanent site for the society in 1928. See "Xianggang Li Yizhen jushi rumi yinyuan ji Zhenyanzong jushilin zhi laili," 84.
47. "Xianggang Li Yizhen jushi rumi yinyuan ji Zhenyanzong jushilin zhi laili," 83–84.

3. ESOTERIC BUDDHISM FOR LAYPEOPLE

48. Chen Lidian 陳歷典, "Gengwu Chaozhou kaitan guanding ji" 庚午潮州開壇灌頂記 (The consecration in Chaozhou in 1930), in *Mijiao jiangxi lu*, vol. 5, ed. Yu Ruihua (Beijing: Huaxia chubanshe, 2009), 265-266.
49. Wang Huilan, "Renshen benhui diliu ci guanding ji," 壬申本會第六次灌頂記 (The sixth consecration of our society in 1932), in *Mijiao jiangxi lu*, vol. 5, 275-278.
50. Wang Huilan, "Renshen benhui diliu ci guanding ji," 275-278.
51. Wang Hongyuan, "Wang da a she li kaishi" 王大阿闍黎開示 (Sermon by great Ācārya Wang), in *Mijiao jiangxi lu*, vol. 5, 293-296. After Wang conferred consecration on monastic followers, Yao openly criticized Wang. See Yao Taofu 姚陶馥, "Hufa tongyan" 護法痛言 (Criticism in defense of Dharma), *HCY* 14, no. 7 (July 1933): 45-49; *MFQ* 184: 311-315.
52. Wang Fuhui 王福慧, "Benhui diwuci guanding ji" 本會第五次灌頂記 (The fifth consecration of our society), in *Mijiao jiangxi lu*, vol. 5, 267-270.
53. The custom of breaking the toes of young girls and then tightly binding the toes under the soles their feet was considered a rite of passage to prepare for womanhood as well as a way to limit a woman's mobility and power; it existed in China for nearly a millennia. Anti-footbinding campaigns were conducted in the early twentieth century, and the practice was officially banned in 1912.
54. Wang Fuhui, "Benhui diwuci guanding ji," 267-270.
55. Wang Hongyuan had two sons and three daughters. For more about Wang's family, see Du Tengying 杜騰英, "Ji Wang Hongyuan jushi zhi jiating" 記王弘願居士之家庭 (Layman Wang Hongyuan's family), *Shideng foxue yuekan* 3 (September 1934), 12-13; *MFQB* 48: 386-387.
56. Wang Huilan and Wang Hongyuan's niece, who was then ten years old, gave the talk openly on the street on April 16. For the talk, see Wang Huilan and Wang Ruo'e 王若娥, "Wang Huilan, Wang Ruo'e er tongnü jingtu wenda" 王慧蘭王若娥二童女淨土問答 (Dialogues between two girls, Wang Huilan and Wang Ruo'e, about Pure Land), *HCY* 2, no.6 (May 1921): 10-12; *MFQ* 151: 128-130.
57. See Wang Huilan, Wang Ruo'e, and Xing Huizhao 邢慧昭, "Wang Huilan, Wang Ruo'e, Xing Huizhao san tongnü he shuo sida jiekong" 王慧蘭王若娥邢慧昭三童女合說四大皆空 (Wang Huilan, Wang Ruo'e, and Xing Huizhao, three girls' talk on the emptiness of the Four Great Elements), *HCY* 2, no. (August 1921): 6-8; *MFQ* 151: 454-456.
58. See Wang Huilan, "Dajixiang tiannü baoxiang" 大吉祥天女寶相 (Sacred image of Mahālakṣmī), *Jue youqing* 11, no. 12 (December 1950), front cover; *MFQB* 63: 303. Also, see Wang Huilan, "Fomu Dakongquemingwang xiang," 佛母大孔雀明王像 (Image of Mahāmayūrī), *Jue youqing* 11, no. 11 (November 1950), front cover; *MFQB* 63: 279.
59. Kōken Itō 伊藤弘憲 and Akiyama Hidenori 秋山秀典, *Shingon shū shōshi* 真言宗小史 (Brief history of Shingon Buddhism) (Tokyo: Shinkō sha, 1926). Wang Huilan translated the booklet at her father's request. See Wang Huilan, "Yiteng Hongxian Qiushan Xiudian zhu Wang Huilan yi Zhenyanzong xiaoshi" 伊藤弘憲秋山秀典著王慧蘭譯《真言宗小史》 (Brief history of Shingon Buddhism, composed by Kōken Itō and Akiyama Hidenori, translated by Wang Huilan), *Shideng foxue yuekan* 2 (August 1936): 71; *MFQB* 48: 357.

3. ESOTERIC BUDDHISM FOR LAYPEOPLE

60. For sermons given by Shen Shuwen, see Long Zhaoyu 龍昭宇, ed., *Zixing guangming: jingang shangshi Gongga Laoren kaishilu* 自性光明: 金剛上師貢噶老人開示錄 (The self-nature bright light: Record of Vajra Master Elder Gongga's teaching) (Taipei: Zhengfayan chubanshe, 1993).
61. For a biography of Shen Shuwen, see Tong Lizhou 童麗舟, *Baiyun jian de chuanqi: jingang shangshi Gongga Laoren xueshan xiuxing ji* 白雲間的傳奇: 金剛上師貢噶老人雪山修行記 (A legend amongst the clouds: Record of the cultivation of Vajra Master Gongga in the snowy mountains) (Taipei: Zhengfayan chubanshe, 1961).
62. After getting engaged in 1919, she renounced her marriage in 1920. She then spent her time in building schools and religious cultivation. For a detailed study of Gongga Laoren's life, see Fabienne Jagou, *Gongga Laoren (1903-1997): Her Role in the Spread of Tibetan Buddhism in Taiwan* (Leiden: Brill, 2021), especially 10-35.
63. For a timeline of Gongga Laoren's life, see Jagou, *Gongga Laoren (1903-1997)*, 143-146.
64. Gongga Laoren took nun's vow with the 16th Karmapa in New York in 1980. For a discussion of her legitimacy, see Jagou, *Gongga Laoren (1903-1997)*, 64-69.
65. See Xue Rongxiang 薛榮祥, "Zangchuan fojiao daochang zai Taiwan de fazhan gaikuang" 藏傳佛教道場在台灣的發展概況 (Basic situation of the development of Tibetan Buddhist sites in Taiwan), *Taiwan wenxian* 臺灣文獻 (Taiwan historica) 56, no. 2 (2005): 129-152, especially 147-149.
66. For a study of Shen's transmissions in Taiwan, see Jagou, *Gongga Laoren (1903-1997)*, 41-69.
67. See Huang Ying-chieh, "Taiwan zangchuan fojiao yinjing hui xiankuang fenxi" 台灣藏傳佛教印經會現況分析 (An analysis of the publication societies of Tibetan Buddhism in Taiwan), *Fojiao tushuguan guankan* 佛教圖書館館刊 (Journal of Buddhist libraries) 50 (December 1998): 6-14.
68. For an in-depth study of Shen Shuwen and her lineage, see Jagou, *Gongga Laoren (1903-1997)*. See also Stephania Travagnin, "Elder Gongga (1903-1997) Between China, Tibet and Taiwan: Assessing Life, Mission and Mummification of a Buddhist Woman," *Journal of the Irish Society for the Academic Study of Religions* 3, no. 1 (June 2016): 250-272.
69. For an interview of Fang Yu about her life and career, see Liu Zuwu 劉祖武 and Qian Boli 錢波麗, "Beican shijie de yizhe" 《悲慘世界》的譯者 (Translators of *Les Misérables*), *Wenhui bao* 文匯報, July 10, 2001.
70. Li Dan studied literature and music in France in the 1920s. Fang and Li translated the first two volumes of *Les Misérables* in 1929 and completed the other volumes in the 1980s. See Victor Hugo, *Beican shijie* 悲慘世界, trans. Li Dan and Fang Yu (Beijing: Renmin chubanshe, 1984). For details about her translation, see Liu Zuwu and Qian Boli, "*Beican shijie* de yizhe," 1.
71. According to one source, Fang became sick after giving birth in 1934, was healed after receiving treatment from a monk, and went on to cultivate faith in Buddhism.
72. Gangkar Rinpoche visited Kunming in 1940 and 1948. See "Gongga Shangshi di Kunming jiangjing xinzhong zhongduo" 貢噶上師抵昆明講經信眾眾多 (Guru

Gangkar arrived in Kunming and his lecture attracted a mass), *Jueyouqing* 9 (September 1948): 25; *MFQB* 90: 25.
73. See Wang Jiaqi, "Kunming Lianhua jingshe jianzao jinianbei" 昆明蓮華精舍建造紀念碑 (Monument in honor of the building of the Lotus Vihāra in Kunming), *Jueyouqing* 11 (November 1950): 10; *MFQB* 63: 288.
74. See Kunming shi fojiao xiehui 昆明市佛教協會, ed., *Kunming fojiao shi* 昆明佛教史 (History of Buddhism in Kunming) (Kunming: Yunnan minzhu chuban she, 2001), 124–125.
75. For the lay translators and their works in early-twentieth-century China (1931–1951), see Gray Tuttle, "Translating Buddhism from Tibetan to Chinese in Early-Twentieth-Century China (1931–1951)," in *Buddhism Between Tibet and China*, ed. Matthew Kapstein (Boston: Wisdom Publication, 2009), 241–280.
76. See Dorje Jueba and Zhang Xinruo, *Misheng fahai* (1930; repr., Taipei: Xinwenfeng chuban she, 1987). As Tuttle has pointed out, the actual editor was Zhang Xinruo 張心若, a lay disciple of Dorje Jueba. See Gray Tuttle, "Translating Buddhism from Tibetan to Chinese in Early-Twentieth-Century China (1931–1951)," 241–280. A variety of manuals published from the 1930s to 1950s were also compiled into five volumes of *Zangmi xiufa midian*. See Lü Tiegang 呂鐵鋼 and Zhou Shaoliang 周紹良, eds., *Zangmi xiufa midian* (The secret scriptures of Tibetan Esoteric Dharma practices), 5 vols. (Beijing: Huaxia chubanshe, 1996).
77. For the Western representation of Tibet in the early twentieth century, see Harry Oldmeadow, *Journeys East: 20th Century Western Encounters with Eastern Religious Traditions* (Bloomington, IN: World Wisdom, 2004), 125–154.
78. See Donald Lopez, *The Tibetan Book of the Dead: A Biography* (Princeton, NJ: Princeton University Press, 2011), 1–12.
79. For the intermediate states and the ritual programs described in the text, see Bryan Cuevas, *The Hidden History of* The Tibetan Book of the Dead (New York: Oxford University Press, 2003), 39–68.
80. See Walter Evans-Wentz, *The Tibetan Book of the Dead* (Oxford: Oxford University Press, 1927). Evans-Wentz's interpretation of the Tibetan texts was controversial. For a critique of Evans-Wentz's translation, see Donald Lopez, chap. 2, in *Prisoners of Shangri-La: Tibetan Buddhism and the West* (Chicago: University of Chicago Press, 1999).
81. William McGuire, "Jung, Evans-Wentz and Various other Gurus," *Journal of Analytical Psychology* 48, no. 4 (September 2003): 433–445.
82. Zhao Hongzhu 趙洪鑄 and Dai Chuanxian 戴傳賢, "Zhongyou wenjiao dedu mifa erze" 中有聞教得度密法序二則 (Two essays on the secret teaching of liberation through hearing during the intermediate state), *Jue youqing*, nos. 199–200 (December 1947): 13; *MFQ* 89: 305.
83. Walter Evans-Wentz, *Zhongyin jiudu mifa*, trans. Zhang Miaoding (Shashi: Wenda kanyinshe, 1936; repr., Taipei: Leming fayuan, 1992), originally published as *The Tibetan Book of the Dead* (Oxford: Oxford University Press, 1927).
84. Zhang Miaoding, "Zhongyin jiudu mifa shangjuan chongyi chugao zixu" 中陰救度密法上卷重譯初稿自序 (Author's preface to the retranslation of the first volume of the secret teaching of bardo liberation), *Foxue banyuekan* 133 (August 1936):

3. ESOTERIC BUDDHISM FOR LAYPEOPLE

16–17; *MFQ* 52: 474–475. Zhang argued that the Chinese canonical works such as *Yuqie shidi lun* 瑜伽師地論 (Discourse on the stages of concentration practice, Yogacārabhūmi-śāstra) did not provide detailed teachings on death.
85. Zhang Miaoding, "Zhongyin jiudu mifa shangjuan chongyi chugao zixu," 16–17.
86. Zhang Miaoding, "Zhongyin jiudu mifa shangjuan chongyi chugao zixu," 16–17.
87. Zhang Miaoding, "Zhongyin jiudu mifa shangjuan chongyi chugao zixu," 16–17.
88. For Chinese Buddhists' reception of *lamrim* teaching, see the discussion in chapter 5.
89. Zhang Miaoding, "Zhongyin jiudu mifa shangjuan chongyi chugao zixu," 16–17.
90. Evans-Wentz, *Zhongyou wenjiao dedu mifa.*
91. Zhao Hongzhu and Dai Chuanxian, "Zhongyou wenjiao dedu mifa erze," 13.
92. Based on Kazi Dawa-Samdup's rendering, Evans-Wentz edited and wrote annotations for the seven Tibetan texts on yogic practice. The book was published as *Tibetan Yoga and Secret Doctrines*, which was also known as *Seven Books of Wisdom of the Great Path*. See Walter Evans-Wentz, *Tibetan Yoga and Secret Doctrines* (London: Oxford University Press, 1935). For the influence of theosophy, see Donald Lopez, "Foreword," *Tibetan Yoga and Secret Doctrines: Seven Books of Wisdom of the Great Path, According to the Late Lama Kazi Dawa-Samdup's English Rendering* (New York: Oxford University Press, 2000).
93. Walter Evans-Wentz, "Xizang fabao guanzhu" 西藏法寶貫珠 (String of jewels in Tibetan Buddhist Teachings), trans. Zhao Hongzhu *HCY* 28, no. 3 (March 1947): 21–23; *MFQ* 203: 317–319.
94. Dai was the minister of the Examination Ministry from 1928 to 1947 and in charge of civil servants' selection for the Republican government (see chapter 2). Dai openly patronized many Tibetan and Mongolian Buddhist leaders, including the ninth Panchen Lama. For Dai's patronizing of Buddhism, see Xueyu, *Buddhism, War, and Nationalism*, 114; Gregory Scott, "The Buddhist Nationalism of Dai Jitao," *The Journal of Chinese Religions* 39 (June 2011): 55–81; Tuttle, *Tibetan Buddhists in the Making of Modern China*, 156–178.
95. Zhao Hongzhu and Dai Chuanxian, "Zhongyou wenjiao dedu mifa erze," 13.
96. Li noticed that Evans-Wentz's annotations did not always align with the conventional Buddhist stands, yet Li explained them as exegesis. See Li Jinxi 黎錦熙, "Zhongyou wenjiao dedu mifa xu" 中有聞教得度密法序 (Preface to the liberation through hearing during the intermediate state), *Wenjiao congkan* 文教叢刊 (Collection of culture and education) 1, nos. 3–4 (December 1945): 116–117; *MFQ* 99: 342–343.
97. Li Jinxi, "Zhongyou wenjiao dedu mifa xu," 116–117.
98. See Padmasambhava, *Zhongyou jiaoshou tingwen jietuo mifa* 中有教授聽聞解脫密法 (The secret teaching of liberation through hearing during the intermediate state), trans. Sun Jingfeng (Shanghai: Shanghai foxue shuju, 1960).
99. See Li Jinxi, "Zhongyou wenjiao dedu mifa xu," 116–117.
100. Sun titled it *Fanzanghan zonghe dacidian* 梵藏漢綜合大辭典 (A synthesized dictionary of Sanskrit, Tibetan, and Chinese). See Sun Jingfeng, "Yu Zhu Tongsheng jushi shu" 與朱同生居士書 (Letter to layman Zhu Tongsheng), *Jue youqing* 12, no.1 (January 1951): 16–17; *MFQB* 63: 342–343.

101. See Sun Jingfeng, "Zhi Zhang Miaoding jushi shu" 致張妙定居士書 (Letter to layman Zhang Miaoding), *Foxue banyuekan*156 (August 1937): 14; *MFQ* 54: 244.
102. Affiliated with Henan Provincial Buddhist Association (Henan Fojiaohui 河南佛教會), the Kaifeng Buddhist Seminary was opened in 1931. See "Kaifeng foxueyuan xingjiang chengli" 開封佛學院行將成立 (The founding of the Kaifeng Seminary), *Xiandai sengqie* 現代僧伽 (Modern sangha) 4, no. 2 (June 1931): 185; *MFQ* 67: 101.
103. Sun Jingfeng, "Yu Zhu Tongsheng jushi shu," 16–17.
104. Following the convention of esoteric Buddhism, Sun controlled the circulation of high tantra manuals that he translated. He requested that readers receive consecration before reading these manuals. For the qualified practitioners who had received consecration, he would print a certain number of copies to help their practice. See Sun Jingfeng, "Fu Qian Xianyi jushi han," 覆錢顯毅居士函 (Letter to layman Qian Xianyi), *Foxue banyuekan* 198 (February 1940): 10–11; *MFQ* 55: 210–211.
105. Sun Jingfeng, "Zhi Zhang Miaoding jushi shu," 14.
106. Padmasambhava, *Zhongyou jiaoshou tingwen jietuo mifa*.
107. Sun tried to raise funds to publish a collection of tantric manuals. He listed twenty-five manuals that he had prepared for public circulation. See Sun Jingfeng, "Muyin xinyi Xizang wen jingji qi" 募印新譯西藏文經籍啟 (Raising funds to publish the newly translated Tibetan scriptures), *Foxue banyuekan* 208 (July 1940): 9–11; *MFQ* 55: 333–335.

4. Debates on Esoteric Buddhism

1. This proposal was integrated into his plan of building Kaiyuan Temple to revive esoteric Buddhism. See Taixu, "Zhengli sengqie zhidu lun," (The reorganization of the sangha system), vol. 9 in *Taixu dashi quanshu* (Collected works of Venerable Master Taixu), 1915 (repr., Taipei: Miaoyun ji wenjiao jijinhui, Digital version, 1998), 180–181.
2. The monks regularly reported their experience in Chinese Buddhist journals and translated texts to inform the readers about Japanese Buddhist teachings and practices. See, for example, Xianyin, "Shi ba dao jiaxing zuofa miji" 十八道加行作法秘記 (Procedures of the eighteen-paths preliminary rituals), *SFJL* 5 (1924 April): 1–13; *MFQB* 7: 301–313.
3. Dayong first traveled to Japan in 1921. He came back to China to raise funds and went to Japan again to resume study in the winter of 1922. He returned to Shanghai in October 1923. Dayong and Chisong learned esoteric rituals related to the Womb Realm and the Diamond Realm at the Temple of Heavenly Merit (Tentokuin 天德院), and also learned Sanskrit at Kōyasan University under the guidance of Kaneyama Bokushō. Xianyin visited Mount Kōya in 1923. About Chisong, see Yu Lingbo 于淩波, "Chisong," in *Minguo gaoseng zhuan chubian* 民國高僧傳初編 (Prominent monks of the Republican period) (Taipei: Zhi shu fang chubanshe, 2005), 393–400.

4. DEBATES ON ESOTERIC BUDDHISM

4. See Mei Jingxuan, "Minguo yilai de hanzang fojiao guanxi" (Relationship between Chinese and Tibetan Buddhism in the Republican period, 1912–1949), *Chung-Hwa Buddhist Studies* 2 (March 1998): 251–288; Mei Jingxuan, "Minguo zaoqi xianmi fojiao chongtu de tantao" (Conflicts between esoteric and exoteric Buddhism in the early Republican period), *Chung-Hwa Buddhist Studies* 3 (March 1999): 251–270.
5. According to Luo, Taixu's attitude changed from introducing non-Chinese traditions to defend the Chinese temples against expropriation, harmonizing the different traditions, seeing the different disciplinary conducts and sectarian arrogance in Japanese and Tibetan Buddhist traditions as a threat to the reform, and rejecting esoteric practices as irrelevant for modern Buddhism. See Luo Tongbing, "The Reformist Monk Taixu and the Controversy about Exoteric and Esoteric Buddhism in Republican China," in *Images of Tibet in the 19th and 20th Centuries*, ed. Monica Esposito (Paris: École française d'Extrême-Orient, 2008), 433–471. Huang Ying-chieh's study on the Wuchang Buddhist Seminary shows that the monastic and lay disciples' fascination with esoteric Buddhism increased frictions among the clergy in competition for patronage and administrative power at the institute. See Huang Ying-chieh, "Taixu dashi de xianmi jiaoliu chutan, yi Riben mizong wei li" 太虛大師的顯密交流初探, 以日本密宗為例 (Master Taixu's communication of exoteric and esoteric Buddhism: The case of Japanese esoteric school), *Hsuan Chuang Journal of Buddhism* 14 (September 2010): 135–164.
6. Kenneth Ch'en and Peter Gregory acknowledged Huiguan 慧觀 (365–436) as one of the earliest to propose a doctrinal classification system. Huiguan learned with the famous translator Kumārajīva (334–413). In light of a series of debates with Daosheng 道生 (355–434) about the nature of enlightenment and Buddha's convenient teachings, Huiguan proposed that the Buddhist teachings should be divided into "sudden teachings" and "gradual teachings." Huiguan went further to categorize the gradual teachings in terms of five periods. Huiguan identified the Avataṃsaka Sūtra, the scripture preached by Śākyamuni Buddha right after he realized enlightenment, as the "sudden teachings," and all other scriptures as "gradual teachings." Huiguan's classifications affected the Tiantai patriarch Zhiyi 智顗 (538–597) and the early Huayan patriarch Zhiyan 智儼 (602–668). See Peter Gregory, ed., *Sudden and Gradual: Approaches to Enlightenment in Chinese Thought* (Honolulu: University of Hawai'i Press, 1987), 3. See also Kenneth Ch'en, *Buddhism in China: A Historical Survey*, 180–183.
7. For the history of Chinese Buddhist doctrinal classification, see Peter Gregory, *Tsung-Mi and the Sinification of Buddhism* (Princeton, NJ: Princeton University Press, 1964), 93–114.
8. The five bibliographical categories of Huayan doctrinal classification are: Hīnayāna (or the Smaller Vehicle, *xiaoshengjiao* 小乘教); beginning Mahāyāna (*dasheng shijiao* 大乘始教); final Mahāyāna (*dasheng zhongjiao* 大乘終教); sudden (*dunjiao* 頓教), and perfect (*yuanjiao* 圓教). The Tiantai philosophy is based on the teaching of the Lotus Sutra (Miaofa lianhua jing 妙法蓮華經). See *Tiantai Si Jiao Yi* 天臺四教儀 (Outline of the Tiantai Fourfold Teachings), T no. 1931, ed.

4. DEBATES ON ESOTERIC BUDDHISM

Diguan 諦觀 (ca. 970). In the Tiantai classification, "secret teaching" (*mimijiao* 秘密教) is listed under one of the four methods (*sihuayi* 四化儀) rather than a separate teaching. See Li Silong 李四龍, "Lue lun Zhiyi de mijiao si xiang" 略論 智顗的"秘教"思想 (Introduction to Zhiyi's thought about secret teaching), *Zhongguo zhexue shi* 中國哲學史 (History of Chinese philosophy) 2 (2009): 25–31.

9. Kūkai studied with the esoteric masters in the capital of the Tang dynasty and returned to Japan in 806.
10. When transmitting Buddhism from China to Japan, Kūkai attempted to establish esotericism as a legitimate category and to characterize it as a new form of Buddhism. Ryûichi Abé found that Kūkai shunned using *shū* (sect) to posit Shingon as a school but framed the esoteric as a *yāna* (vehicle) or *piṭaka* (collection). See Ryûichi Abé, *The Weaving of Mantra: Kūkai and the Construction of Esoteric Buddhist Discourse* (New York: Columbia University Press, 1999), 202–204.
11. Abé has shown that Kūkai's works were a response to the six officially recognized schools (Risshū, Kusha, Jōjitsu, Hossō, Sanron, Kegon) in Nara and the Tendai school. See Abé, *The Weaving of Mantra*, 202.
12. The conceptualization of Buddha evolved from a human teacher in early Buddhism to a more sophisticated notion of the embodiment of the ultimate ontological reality in Mahāyāna Buddhism. The *trikāya* theory was developed to address the various dimensions of Buddhahood: *dharmakāya* refers to *tathatā*, the fundamental nature of all transcendental and mundane existences; *nirmāṇakāya* denotes attributes and events in connection with the historical Śākyamuni Buddha; *sambhogakāya* connotes more transcendental merit and achievement of the Buddha. See Guangxing, *The Concept of the Buddha: Its Evolution from Early Buddhism to the Trikāya Theory* (London: RoutledgeCurzon, 2005), 1–52.
13. *Benkenmitsu nikyōron* 弁顯密二教論 (Distinguishing the Two Teachings of the Exoteric and Esoteric, hereafter *Distinguishing*), Kūkai 空海, T no. 2427, 77: 374. For an English translation of the text, see Kūkai, *On the Differences between the Exoteric and Esoteric Teachings*, trans. Rolf Giebel and Dale Todaro (Moraga, CA: Bukkyō Dendō Kyōkai, 2004).
14. *Distinguishing*, T no. 2427, 77: 375.
15. Ōchō Enichi assumed that doctrinal classification was unique to Chinese Buddhism. Peter Gregory also identified doctrinal classification as a definitive feature of Chinese Buddhist scholasticism. See Ōchō Enichi, "The Beginnings of Tenet Classification in China," *The Eastern Buddhist* 14, no. 2 (1981): 71–94. Peter Gregory, *Tsung-Mi and the Sinification of Buddhism* (Princeton, NJ: Princeton University Press, 1991), 93.
16. *Himitsu mandara jūjū shinron* (The ten abiding stages of mind according to the secret mandalas), Kūkai, T no. 2425.
17. The Mahāvairocana Sūtra elaborates on the ten stages of the mind to depict the consciousness of various sentient beings. See *Dapiluzhena jing yan mi chao* 大毗 盧遮那經演密鈔 (Exegesis on the Mahāvairocana Sūtra), Jueyuan 覺苑 (ca. 1077), T no. 848. Kūkai took the ten-stages terminology to classify the teachings of various philosophical schools. Kasulis's study shows that Kūkai ranked the

traditions according to how deeply their followers conceptually recognize and experientially fathom the existence of reality. For Kūkai, the Tendai and Kegon schools provide insights about transcendental reality but lack esoteric practices that enable the practitioners truly to experience such microcosmic existence. See Thomas Kasulis, "Truth Words: The Basis of Kūkai's Theory of Interpretation," in *Buddhist Hermeneutics*, ed. Donald Lopez (Honolulu: University of Hawai'i Press, 1988), 257–272.

18. Dayong learned the Lotus Sutra with Taixu at Mount Wutai in 1921; Chisong was educated at Huayan College (Huayan Daxue 華嚴大學) from 1913 to 1916 under the renowned master Yuexia 月霞 (1858–1917). Xianyin studied Tiantai philosophy with Dixian 諦閒 (1858–1932) at the Guanzong Society (Guanzong Xueshe 觀宗學社) from 1918 to 1920.

19. Inclusiveness, a doctrine that stresses the mutual interpenetration of all phenomena, is one of the most influential doctrines in Chinese Buddhism. This doctrine draws on the Indian scripture the Avataṃsaka Sūtra and is developed by philosophers of the Chinese Huayan school. After Dushun 杜順 (557–640), the first patriarch of the Chinese Huayan school, theorized the inclusiveness principle in an essay on the Dharma realm, generations of Huayan philosophers appropriated it to argue for a totalistic view of reality. This view emphasizes the interpenetrating and reciprocal aspects of existence. From this perspective, no single event can be adequately understood without an understanding of the totality of its connections to all other events. For Dushun's view of totality, see Garma C. C. Chang, *The Buddhist Teaching of Totality: The Philosophy of Hwa Yen Buddhism* (University Park: The Pennsylvania State University Press, 1971), 121–135. For the influence of Huayan thought on East Asian Buddhist practice, see Robert Gimello, ed., *Avatamsaka Buddhism in East Asia* (Wiesbaden: Harrassowitz Verlag, 2012).

20. The Tiantai and Huayan traditions regard the Lotus Sutra and the Avataṃsaka Sūtra respectively as superior teachings that reveal most of the ultimate truth. Yet both scriptures are labeled as the eighth and ninth of the ten stages in Kūkai's classification and as inferior to the Shingon teachings.

21. Dayong regularly communicated with his teacher Taixu, reporting his progress and providing information on the major lineages and temples in Japan. Taixu published the letters in Buddhist periodicals in 1922 and 1923. See Dayong, "Liuxue Riben mizong zhi baogao" 留學日本密宗之報告 (Reports about Studying Esoteric Buddhism in Japan), HCY 3, no. 9 (November 1922): 2; MFQ 154: 314.

22. See Dayong, "Liuxue Riben Zhenyan zong zhi tongxin" 留學日本真言宗之通信 (Reports about Study in Japanese Shingon School), HCY 4, no. 8 (September 1924): 1–2; MFQ 157: 61–62. Letter to Taixu dated June 20, 1924.

23. See Dayong, "Liuxue Riben Zhenyan zong zhi tongxin," 1–2. Dayong used the integration of *shi* (or *shixiang* 事相) and *li* 理 (principle) to argue that principles are manifested in all phenomena, including in rituals. In Tiantai and Huayan philosophies, *shi* and *li* refer to appearances and reality. Before the advent of Buddhism, Chinese thinkers had already used the terms widely in Chinese metaphysics. Buddhist writers used *shi* and *li* to denote manifest events and the

4. DEBATES ON ESOTERIC BUDDHISM

more general principles behind these discrete phenomena. For the development of the terms, see Brook Ziporyn, *Beyond Oneness and Difference: Li and Coherence in Chinese Buddhist Thought and its Antecedents* (Albany: State University of New York Press, 2013), 185–261.

24. Dayong, "Liuxue Riben Zhenyan zong zhi tongxin," 1–2. On Dayong's reading, Yixing only mentioned that esotericism transcends teachings of "the three vehicles" of śrāvaka, pratyekabuddha, and bodhisattva. *Dapiluzhena chengfo jingshu* 大毘盧遮那成佛經疏 (Commentary on the Mahāvairocana-abhisaṃbodhi tantra), T no. 1796.
25. Dayong, "Da Taixu fashi shu er" 答太虛法師書二 (Second Letter in Reply to Master Taixu), HCY 4, no. 9 (September 1924): 1–4. Letter dated July 10, 1924. Dayong referred to the works of Vasubandu, Fazang, and Yixing to argue that the fruits of Buddha's enlightenment are ineffable. *Shidi jing lun* 十地經論 (Treatise of the Daśabhūmika Sūtra, T no. 1522) is attributed to Vasubandu (fourth century), one of the most important theorists in Indian Buddhism. The treatise was translated into Chinese by Bodhiruci in the sixth century. *Huayan wujiao zhang* 華嚴五教章 (The essay on the five teachings of Huayan; T no. 1866, 45) was written by Fazang 法藏 in the seventh century, who was later regarded as the third patriarch of the Huayan school.
26. Also, quoting Gonda Raifu's *The Essentials of Esoteric Buddhism*, Dayong pointed out that Gonda Raifu also found Kūkai's reading of the Mahāvairocana Sūtra different from the stands of Śubhakarasiṃha and Yixing. Dayong, "Da Taixu fashi shu er," 4.
27. Dayong, "Da Taixu fashi shu er," 4.
28. Dayong, "Da Taixu fashi shu er," 4.
29. See Taixu, "Zhengli sengqie zhidu lun," 180–181.
30. Taixu, "Zhongguo xianshi mizong fuxing zhi qushi," 12–17.
31. Buddhist scriptures use different categories to measure spiritual progress and accomplished states. Some stipulate that three incalculable eons (*san da a seng qi jie* 三大阿僧祇劫) are needed for the cultivation. For example, *Pusa yingluo benye jing* 菩薩瓔珞本業經 (Sūtra of the primary activities that serve as necklaces of the bodhisattvas) (T no. 1485) identifies fifty-two stages in the path of cultivation. Zhiyi, the sixth-century Tiantai patriarch, adopted the terminology of the fifty-two stages to explain the procedure. In Zhiyi's classification, the practitioners are worldlings (*fan* 凡) in the first ten stages of faith (*shixinwei* 十信位). The eleventh stage is a significant turning point when practitioners change into worthies (*xian* 賢) and give rise to a thought of enlightenment after having eliminated the conceptual illusions of the three realms of existence (*duan sanjie jianhuo jin* 斷三界見惑盡). From the eleventh stage to the fiftieth stage of the ten-ground bodhisattvas, practitioners nurture the six perfections for three great eons. In the last two stages of saints (*sheng* 聖), the adepts practice for hundreds of eons to cultivate the great marks of Buddhahood (*xianghao* 相好). "Three great *kalpas* (eons)" are a general index but the actual time taken to reach ultimate liberation depends on practitioners' capacity and diligence. See *Tiantai si jiao yi* 天臺四教儀 (Outline of the Tiantai Fourfold Teachings), T no. 1931.

4. DEBATES ON ESOTERIC BUDDHISM

32. *Sokushin jōbutsu gi* 即身成佛義 (Treatise on becoming Buddha in this very body), Kūkai, T no. 2428.
33. Wang proclaimed the doctrinal superiority of esotericism. He argued that although exoteric teachings claim that all sentient beings have Buddha nature, only esoteric Buddhism elaborates about achieving Buddhahood in this lifetime. Wang Hongyuan, "Guangzhou fojiao jiexing jingshe kaimu tekan xu" 廣州佛教解行精舍開幕特刊序 (Preface to the special issue about the opening of Vihāra of Understanding and Practice in Guangzhou), *Mijiao jiangxi lu* 6, no. 7 (July 1932): 149–170.
34. Taixu, "Lun jishen chengfo" 論即身成佛 (About realizing Buddhahood in this very body), *HCY* 6, no. 8 (October 1925): 17–23; *MFQ* 163: 23–29.
35. Understanding these notions as alternative designations to describe different stages of cultivation, Taixu analyzed them by using the terminology of the Tiantai school, particularly the "six identities" (*liu ji* 六即) or the six ways to become Buddha. The Tiantai master Zhiyi coined the "six identities" to denote six stages of bodhisattva cultivation in the Tiantai category of perfect teachings (*yuanjiao liu ji* 圓教六即). The six are (1) "principle identity" (*li ji* 理即), understanding that all sentient beings are of Buddha nature; (2) "nominal identity" (*mingzi ji* 名字即), learning teachings through the nominations; (3) "meditation identity" (*guanxing ji* 觀行即), perceiving through meditation; (4) "semblance identity" (*xiangsi ji* 相似即), purifying six faculties and seeing Buddhahood; (5) "identity of discrimination of truth" (*fenzheng ji* 分證即), perceiving reality and getting rid of illusions gradually; (6) "identity of perfection" (*jiujing ji* 究竟即). About the six identities, see *Mohe zhiguan* 摩訶止觀 (The great calming and contemplation), Zhiyi, T no. 1911, 46: 128.
36. The notion of "becoming a Buddha at once" comes from a public case (*gong'an* 公案) in the Chan tradition, which tells that a butcher reached enlightenment as soon as he put down his knife. See *Wudeng huiyuan* 五燈會元 (The compendium of five lamps), ed. Puji 普濟 in 1252, X no. 1565, 80: 411. Nominal designation (*jiaming yanxiang* 假名言相, Skt. *prajñapti*) is an important Mahāyāna notion, see *Dasheng qixin lun* 大乘起信論 (Treatise of the awakening of Mahāyāna faith), ed. Zhendi, T no. 1666, 32: 577. Phenomenal things are without inherent nature, but nominal labels are attached to them for the sake of communication and teaching. Taixu explained the rhetorical devices by referring to the nominal identity. That is, practitioners increasingly understand the Buddha nature of all beings through learning and reading.
37. Taixu, "Lun jishen chengfo," 17–23.
38. Six fundamental elements that constitute all things are earth, water, fire, air, space, and consciousness.
39. Taixu, "Lun jishen chengfo," 17–23.
40. Taixu refers to the third stage of "meditation identity" (*guanxing ji*) that denotes the bodhisattvas' practicing of meditation to experience true reality. Taixu emphasized that meditation methods of other Buddhist schools also offer effective ways to perceive the ultimate truth. See Taixu, "Lun jishen chengfo," 17–23.

4. DEBATES ON ESOTERIC BUDDHISM

41. Regarding the legend of Kūkai's manifestation as a Buddha, Taixu argued that appearance does not affirm Kūkai's attainment of Buddhahood, since demons and gods of miraculous powers are also capable of rendering such "supernormal manifestations (*shenbian* 神變)." See Taixu, "Lun jishen chengfo," 17–23. In Tiantai meditation theory, an adept can manifest supernormally after having purified the six faculties. The Lotus Sutra also states that reading, chanting, preaching, and writing the sūtra result in the merit of six pure faculties, *T* no. 262, 9:51. Tiantai writers assigned purification of the six pure faculties to the resemblance identity (the fourth stage of the six identities), or the ten stages of faith (*shi xin wei*) of the fifty-two stages. See Diguan, *Tiantai sijiao yi*, *T* no. 1931, 46:779.
42. Taixu led thirty representatives to attend the Buddhist Conference of East Asia (Dongya fojiao dahui 東亞佛教大會) in Tokyo in November of 1925. They also visited Kōyasan University. For the trip to Japan, see Taixu, *Taixu zizhuan* (Autobiography of Taixu), vol. 31 of *Taixu dashi quanshu* 太虛大師全書 (Complete works of Taixu) (Beijing: Zongjiao wenhua chubanshe, 2004), 254–255, 269–271.
43. Kaneyama acknowledged that except for a few fundamental mantras, most of the esoteric texts expound on ritualistic practices rather than doctrines. Yet he argued that esoteric Buddhism focused not only on ritualistic practice but also on doctrinal learning. Kaneyama Bokushō, "Hongfa Dashi zhi fojiao guan" 弘法大師之佛教觀 (Master Kūkai's view on esoteric Buddhism)," trans. Tang Qingliang, in *Haichao yin wenku* 海潮音文庫 (Collection of *Voice of the Sea Tide*), vol. 2, ed. Taixu, Fan Gunong 范古農, and Ciren Shi Zhuren 慈忍室主人. Tapei: xinwenfeng chubanshe, 1985, 54.
44. Kaneyama Bokushō, "Hongfa Dashi zhi fojiao guan," 54.
45. Taixu, "Gaoyeshan daxue yanjiangci" 高野山大學講演辭 (Presentation at Kōyasan University), *HCY* 6, no. 12 (February 1926): 19–20; *MFQ* 164: 53–54.
46. Mei and Luo have discussed Taixu's changing attitude toward esoteric Buddhism. See Mei Jingxuan, "Minguo zaoqi xianmi fojiao chongtu de tantao," 251–270; Luo Tongbing, "The Reformist Monk Taixu and the Controversy about Exoteric and Esoteric Buddhism in Republican China," 433–471.
47. Buddhist monasteries function as educational and liturgical centers. On monastic and lay Buddhists' routine activities in the Republican period, see Holmes Welch, *The Practice of Chinese Buddhism* (Cambridge, MA: Harvard University Press, 1967), 357–366. Sets of precepts instruct the laity to respect and patronize the clergy, through which they can cultivate merit. See *Youposai jie jing* 優婆塞戒經 (Skt., Upāsaka-śīla-sūtra, *The Sūtra of Upāsaka Precepts*), *T* no. 1488, trans. Dharmakṣema (385–433). In this text, Buddha explains precepts and bodhisattva vows for laypersons.
48. In the late nineteenth and early twentieth century, lay Buddhists played an increasingly important role in reprinting scriptures, initiating organizations, and establishing educational institutions. Buddhist intellectuals such as Yang Wenhui advanced reprinting the Buddhist canon and initiating Buddhist education. Regarding lay Buddhism in the late Qing, see Dongchu, *Zhongguo fojiao jindai shi* (The Modern History of Chinese Buddhism) (1974; repr., Taipei:

4. DEBATES ON ESOTERIC BUDDHISM

Zhonghua fojiao wenhua guan, 1987), 39–46. Taixu proposed that the clergy should take initiatives in restoring esoteric Buddhism in China. See Taixu, "Zhongguo xianshi mizong fuxing zhi qushi," 12–17. Holmes Welch argued that with the participation of the laity in Buddhist activities, the distinction between clergy and laity became weakened in the Republican period. See Holmes Welch, *The Buddhist Revival in China* (Cambridge, MA: Harvard University Press, 1968), 82–86.

49. In esoteric Buddhism, both monastic and lay adherents have to go through the same consecration ritual to be admitted to various levels of practice. Underlying the ritual is a transmission narrative, according to which esoteric teachings were bestowed by a cosmic Buddha and should be passed down in an unbroken lineage. Spiritual masters who have been authorized to perform the ritual are therefore essential to the proper transmission.

50. Wang Hongyuan, "Jinggao hainei foxue jia" 敬告海內佛學家 (Announcement to Buddhists throughout the Country), *HCY* 4, no. 11 (November 1923): 8–9; *MFQ* 157: 443–444.

51. There are consecrations of varying functions. In esoteric Buddhism, four consecrations are designed for (1) consecration of eliminating obstacles (*chunan* 除難); (2) consecration of achievement (*chengjiu* 成就) which helps adepts to gain blessings; (3) consecration of improving conditions (*zengyi jishen* 增益己身); (4) consecration of attaining the state of *ācārya*. For details see *Rui xi ye jing* 甤呬耶經, trans. Amoghavajra (705–774), *T* no. 897, 18: 772.

52. Taixu also doubted Gonda Raifu's legitimacy as *ācārya* because of his lapse in ethical observance. Taixu, "Zhi Wang Hongyuan jushi shu" 致王弘願居士書 (Letter to Wang Hongyuan), *HCY* 5, no. 2 (February 1924): 1; *MFQ* 158: 339.

53. Xianyin was then studying at Mount Kōya and Manshu Jiedi was at Tamon-in. Xianyin speculated that Gonda agreed to consecrate Wang only because he expected Wang to enter the monastic order. Xianyin exhorted Wang to join the clergy as soon as possible to avoid criticism. See Xianyin, "Xianyin fashi zhi Wang Hongyuan jushi han" 顯蔭法師致王弘願居士函 (Letter from Master Xianyin to Wang Hongyuan), *SFJL* 8 (July 1924): 7–8; *MFQB* 8: 133–134.

54. Like Xianyin, Manshu Jiedi attributed the public censure of Zhenyan esotericism to Wang's improper reception. Manshu Jiedi claimed that if Wang chose to become a fully ordained monk, the public outcry would soon quiet down. See Manshu Jiedi, "Yu Wang Hongyuan lun mijiao shu" 與王弘願論密教書 (Discussion with Wang Hongyuan about Esotericism), *HCY* 14, no. 2 (February 1933): 79–84; *MFQ* 183: 209–214.

55. *Liangbu dafa xiangcheng shizi fufa ji* 兩部大法相承師資付法記 (Record of the Transmission of the Two Great Tantras), Haiyun, *T* no. 2081. Wang wrongly interpreted the iconographic representation of the cosmic Mahāvairocana Buddha, arguing that the depiction of Mahāvairocana Buddha as a layman suggests a justification of the lay *ācārya*. See Wang Hongyuan, "Zaifu Xianyin a she li shu" 再復顯蔭阿闍梨書 (A response to Ācārya Xianyin), *SFJL* 7 (August 1924): 9; *MFQB* 8: 311.

56. Dongchu, *Zhongguo fojiao jindai shi*, 428.

4. DEBATES ON ESOTERIC BUDDHISM

57. Dayong discussed it with layman Liu Xianxiu. Liu Xianxiu 劉顯休, "Liu Xianxiu jushi laihan" 劉顯休居士來函 (Letter from Liu Xianxiu), *HCY* 6, no. 1 (March 1925): 4–5; *MFQ* 161: 228–229.
58. Manshu Jiedi argued that ancient laity might receive the consecration of Dharma-transmission to assist in the consecration ceremony when there was a shortage of monastic assistants. The lay adepts were not supposed to confer consecration to others. See Manshu Jiedi, "Yu Wang Hongyuan lun mijiao shu," 79–84.
59. See Liu Xianxiu, "Liu Xianxiu jushi laihan," 4–5. Manshu Jiedi doubted Wang's capacity and kept exhorting Wang to join the clergy. See Manshu Jiedi, "Yu Wang Hongyuan lun mijiao shu," 79–84.
60. See Chen Lidian 陳歷典, "Yuanwu jushi Wang Hongyuan xiansheng zhi lishi" 圓五居士王弘願先生之歷史 (Biography of layman Wang Hongyuan), in *Mijiao jiangxi lu* 密教講習錄 (Records of sermons on esotericism), ed. Yu Ruihua 于瑞華 (Beijing: Huaxia chubanshe, 2009), vol. 5, 52–54.
61. For example, in April 1932, a nun, forty-one laymen, and thirty-two laywomen came to receive consecration from Wang. Among them, sixty received the consecration of the Womb Realm and fourteen received the consecration of the Diamond Realm. Wang's daughter recorded the details about the ceremony. See Wang Huilan, "Renshen benhui diliu ci guanding ji" (The sixth consecration of our society in 1932), in *Mijiao jiangxi lu* (Records of sermons about esotericism), vol. 5, 275.
62. *HCY* published a special issue regarding critiques of esotericism, see "Mizong wenti zhuanhao" 密宗問題專號 (Special issue about esotericism), *HCY* 14, no. 7 (July 1933). See also Chenyin 塵隱, "Du da Haichaoyin mizong wenti zhuanhao fasheng zhi ganxiang" 讀答海潮音密宗問題專號發生之感想 (My thought on reply to the special issue about esotericism), *HCY* 15, no. 6 (June 1934); *MFQ* 187: 201–210. "Wang Shiyu zhengchao zhong de xianhua" 王師愈靜潮中的閒話 (A talk about the dissensions regarding Wang Hongyuan), *HCY* 15, no. 3 (March 1934): 34–42; *MFQ* 186: 345–352.
63. See Feng Zhongxi 馮重熙, "Renshen Guangzhou kaitan ji" 王申廣州開壇記 (Record of the opening of the altar in Guangzhou in 1932), in *Mijiao jiangxi lu* (Records of sermons about esotericism), vol. 5, 278–297.
64. Chen Lidian, "Yuanwu jushi Wang Hongyuan xiansheng zhi lishi," 52–54.
65. *Huayan shu xu* 華嚴疏序 (The Preface to Commentary on the *Avataṃsaka Sūtra*), Chengguan (ca. 737–838), *X* no. 227.
66. Wang viewed esotericism as superior to the prevalent Chinese Buddhist philosophies for providing a more profound and complete perspective on ultimate truth. Wang claimed that, according to the doctrinal classification of the Huayan school, the state of Buddha as described in the lower teachings only equals the state of bodhisattva in the greater teachings, and only Huayan teachings provide the most complete vision of Buddhahood. Wang argued that the Buddhahood described in Huayan literature is lower than the state of the highest achievements through esoteric practices. See Wang Hongyuan, "*Huayan shu xu* kou yi ji" 華嚴疏序口義記 (Exposition on *The Preface to Commentary on the*

4. DEBATES ON ESOTERIC BUDDHISM

Avataṃsaka Sūtra), in *Mijiao jiangxi lu* (Records of sermons about esotericism), vol. 1, 279.
67. Chisong visited Japan to attend the East Asian Buddhist Assembly in the fall of 1925, after which he stayed at Mount Kōya and studied with Gonda Raifu. In 1926, he visited Mount Hiei to study Tendai esotericism.
68. Chisong wrote the article after returning from his first study trip to Mount Kōya in 1923. In the article, Chisong challenged Kūkai's doctrinal classification on ten different points. An editor copied the article and published it in *HCY* in 1928. Chisong, "Xian mi jiao heng" 賢密教衡 (The evaluation of the Huayan and esoteric teachings), *HCY* 9, no. 4 (May 1928): 1–11; *MFQ* 170: 127–137.
69. *Dapiluzhena chengfo jing shu* 大毘盧遮那成佛經疏 (Commentary on the Mahāvairocana Sūtra), Yixing, *T* no. 1796.
70. Fazang, *Huayan wujiao zhang*, *T* no. 1866, 45. Fazang posited that there is no differentiation of the teachings for the three vehicles, but there is only one vehicle to teach all beings by numerous skillful means toward Buddhahood.
71. Chisong, "Xian mi jiao heng," 130.
72. Chisong, "Xian mi jiao heng," 130. Ocean and tides are a common simile used to refer to the principle and phenomena in Huayan philosophy, see *Huayan jing shu*, *T* no. 1735, 35: 503.
73. Adopting Chengguan's doctrinal classification, an eleventh-century Chinese scholar Jueyuan 覺苑 developed the point. But Chisong disagreed with Jueyuan about the differentiation of esoteric Buddhism and exoteric Buddhism. See, *Dapiluzhena jing yan mi chao*, *X* no. 439, 23.
74. Chisong, "Xian mi jiao heng," 130.
75. Annen 安然 (841–915), a famous Japanese Tendai philosopher, classified the Lotus Sutra as "secret of the principle" (*rihimitsu* 理祕密) and the esoteric teachings as "secret of both principle and phenomena" (*jirikumitsu* 事理俱密). Chisong disagreed with Annen and claimed that the Avataṃsaka Sūtra goes beyond the bifurcation of esoteric Buddhism and exoteric Buddhism.
76. Chisong, "Xian mi jiao heng," *HCY* 9, no. 6 (July 1928): 31–42; *MFQ* 170: 389–400.
77. Cheng Zhai'an 程宅安, *Mizong yaoyi* 密宗要義 (Essentials of esotericism) (1929; repr., Chengdu: Bashu shushe, 2011).
78. Wang was referring to Jueyuan's exposition. Jueyuan claimed that even if the adepts are chanting spells and visualizing the deities, the three mysteries are incomplete if the adepts are not making the proper hand gestures. See *Dapiluzhena jing yan bian mi chao*, *X* no. 439, 23: 626.
79. Wang Hongyuan, "Fu Li Lianshe lao jushi shu" 復李蓮舌老居士書 (Letter to layman Li Lianshe), in *Mijiao jiangxi lu* (Records of sermons about esotericism), vol. 5, 149. Letter dated October 5, 1930.
80. Wang Hongyuan, "Heng xian mi jiao heng" 衡賢密教衡 (Evaluation of the evaluation of Huayan and esoteric teachings), *Mijiao jiangxi lu* 19 (1929): 227–268. Wang also sent this article to Gonda and received Gonda's approval of his interpretation. Gonda Raifu, "Fu Wang Hongyuan jushi han" 復王弘願居士函 (Reply to Wang Hongyuan), in *Mijiao jiangxi lu* (Records of sermons about esotericism), vol. 5, 86. Letter dated the fourth day of October, in the third year of Showa (1928).

4. DEBATES ON ESOTERIC BUDDHISM

81. Wang Hongyuan, "Heng xian mi jiao heng," 227–268.
82. Chisong, "Xianmi jiao heng shi huo" 賢密教衡釋惑 (Clarifications on the Evaluation of Huayan and Esoteric Teachings), *HCY* 10, no. 3 (April 1929): 1–7; *MFQ* 172: 349–354.
83. Fazun, "Fazun fashi zixu" 法尊法師自敘 (Autobiography of Fazun), in *Fazun fashi foxue lunwen ji*, ed. Lü Tiegang 呂鐵鋼 and Hu Heping 胡和平 (Beijing: Zhongguo fojiao wenhua yanjiusuo, 1990), 372–376.
84. The monk Chaoyi estimated a budget of four hundred *yuan* a year to cover the expenditure of four monks. When they ran out of money, Chaoyi left Lhasa in 1931 and took the sea route from Calcutta to Singapore and Hong Kong, hoping to raise funds for them to resume their studies. But at Taixu's invitation, Chaoyi went to teach at the Sino-Tibetan Institute at Chongqing and never returned to Lhasa. See Chaoyi, "Putuo si Chaoyi shang Taixu dashi shu" (Letter to Master Taixu from Monk Chaoyi of Putuo Temple), *HCY* 13, no. 1 (January 1932): 115–117; *MFQ* 180: 125–127.
85. For details about Fazun's life at Lhasa, see Fazun, "Zhuzhe ru Zang de jingguo" 著者入藏的經過 (The writer's experience in entering Tibet), in *Fazun fashi foxue lunwen ji*, 365. See also Brenton Sullivan, "Blood and Teardrops: The Life and Travels of Venerable Fazun (1901–1980)," in *Buddhists: Understanding Buddhism Through the Lives of Practitioners*, ed. Todd Lewis (Malden, MA: Wiley-Blackwell, 2014), 296–304.
86. Langchan fell ill and on several occasions received medical treatment from the Dalai Lama's doctors. Unfortunately, Langchan passed away in a temple outside Lhasa before the doctors' arrival. See Fazun, "Zhuzhe ru Zang de jingguo," 366.
87. In the letter, Chaoyi provided the curriculum of the three major seminaries in Lhasa. See Chaoyi, "Putuo si Chaoyi shang Taixu dashi shu," 115–117.
88. See Chen Xueqin 陳學勤, "Chaoyi shangshi sishi nian ji lue" 超一上師四十年紀略 (Forty years of Guru Chaoyi), *Fohaideng* 佛海燈 (Light over the Buddhist ocean) 2, no. 9–10 (August 1937): 4–8; *MFQ* 79: 406–410.
89. Even though Fazun yearned for more years of training in Lhasa, he didn't get to return to Lhasa. After 1950, Fazun moved to Beijing. He served as a vice president of the Chinese Buddhist Seminary, which was founded in Beijing in 1956. Fazun, "Fazun fashi zixu," 376.
90. Huiding wrote a series of essays on *Foxue banyuekan* from January to July 1935. See Huiding, "Zang mi da wen" 藏密答問 (Answers to questions about Tibetan esotericism), *Foxue banyuekan* 94 (January 1935): 5–8; *MFQ* 50: 249–252.
91. See Huiding, "Zang mi da wen," 5–8.
92. See Fazun, "Ping Zang mi da wen" 評藏密答問 (Comments on answers to questions about Tibetan esotericism), *HCY* 16, no. 6 (June 1935): 20–25; *MFQ* 190: 440–445.
93. See Huiding, "Zang mi da wen," *Foxue banyuekan* 95 (January 1935): 6–8; *MFQ* 50: 278–280. See also Huiding, "Zang mi da wen," *Foxue banyuekan* 106 (July 1935): 14–15; *MFQ* 51: 148.

4. DEBATES ON ESOTERIC BUDDHISM

94. See Yuanfang, "Ping Zang mi da wen zhi yi duan" 評藏密答問之一段 (Comments on a paragraph of answers to questions about Tibetan esotericism), *Foxue banyuekan* 108 (August 1935): 27–28; MFQ 51: 227–229.
95. Among the different types of consecrations, the wisdom empowerments in the Mahāyoga and Yoginī tantras involved sexual elements, making them controversial in India. See Paul Williams and Anthony Tribe, *Buddhist Thought* (London: Routledge, 2013), 176–178.
96. See Huiding, "Zang mi da wen," 6–8.
97. See Fazun, "Ping Zang mi da wen."
98. The first successive line of reincarnation was traditionally recognized as the reincarnation of Karmapa, the head of the Karma Kagyu lineage in the thirteenth century. Cabezón showed that the practice might have begun in the late eleventh and early twelfth centuries. See José Cabezón, "On Tulku Lineages," *Revue d'Etudes Tibétaines* 38 (2017), 1–28, especially 1–2. Gamble analyzed the autobiographies of Rangjung Dorje (1284–1339) to examine the invention of the institution of reincarnation. See Ruth Gamble, *Reincarnation in Tibetan Buddhism* (New York: Oxford University Press, 2018), 77–98.
99. The disciples also made offerings to the Tibetan lamas in memory of Dayong. The boy unfortunately passed away in Lhasa in 1945. See Hengyan 恆演, "Dayong a she li bing zhuanshi hu du tu hezhuan" 大勇阿闍黎並轉世呼都圖合傳 (Joint biographies of Ācārya Dayong and his reincarnation), *HCY* 27, no. 9 (September 1946): 28–29; MFQ 203: 68–69.
100. Huiyuan was remembered as the first patriarch of the Chinese Pure Land school. Regarding the evolution of Huiyuan's story, see Charles Jones, *Chinese Pure Land Buddhism: Understanding a Tradition of Practice* (Honolulu: University of Hawai'i Press, 2019), 148–168.
101. See Huiding, "Zang mi da wen," *Foxue banyuekan*, 5–8.
102. Rongkong wrote on Pure Land Buddhism in relation to esoteric Buddhism. See Rongkong, "Jing mi huo wen" 淨密或問 (Questions about Pure Land Buddhism and esoteric Buddhism), *Foxue banyuekan* 92 (December 1934): 3–6; MFQ 50: 191–194. Rongkong also criticized Fazun's positions, claiming that for the adepts, rebirth was hazardous for their spiritual development since they may not maintain the intellect of their past lives. An adept could choose to first be reborn in the Land of Bliss and then be subsequently reborn in this world. See Rongkong, "Yue Bi Xiao Shi Zhu ping Zang mi da wen" 閱避囂室主評藏密答問 (Reading Fazun's comments on answers to the questions about Tibetan esotericism), *Foxue banyuekan* 109 (August 1935): 11–14; MFQ 51: 243–246.
103. See Taixu, "Yue Zang mi huo wen" 閱藏密或問 (Reading the questions about Tibetan esotericism), *HCY* 16, no. 3 (March 1935): 20–21; MFQ 190: 26–27.
104. See Fazun, "Ping Zang mi da wen," *HCY*, 20–25.
105. The ancient patriarchs ardently promoted the chanting of Amitābha Buddha's name as an easy way that was accessible to all believers. Regarding the notions of self-power and other power, see Charles Jones, *Chinese Pure Land Buddhism*, 61–84.
106. Tanya Zivkovic's study explores the Tibetans' faith in the presence of the lamas through continuous rebirths in worldly existence. The doctrinal foundation of

the reincarnated lamas is based on the Buddha's hagiographies that depict his past lives, the three bodies of the Buddha, and the gradual journey of bodhisattva cultivation. The theory of the Buddha's three bodies is important, for it suggests that enlightened beings could manifest themselves in different forms. See Tanya Zivkovic, *Death and Reincarnation in Tibetan Buddhism: In-Between Bodies* (London: Routledge, 2013), 1–14.

107. Cabezón showed that there existed many accounts of Tibetans identified as Tibetan saints, Indian masters, or enlightened beings. See Cabezón, "On Tulku Lineages," 2.

108. The editors of the *Foxue banyuekan* printed two thousand copies of the booklet. See "Zang mi da wen lei bian" 藏密答問類編 (References to the answers to questions about Tibetan esotericism), *Foxue banyuekan* 155 (July 1937): 11; *MFQ* 54: 209.

5. The Path to Enlightenment

1. Some materials from this chapter have been presented at the 2016 international conference on Sino-Tibetan Buddhism at Renmin University and the Princeton Forum on Modern Chinese Buddhism in 2016.
2. See Chen Bing and Deng Zimei, *Ershi shiji de zhongguo fojiao* (Chinese Buddhism in Twentieth-Century China) (Beijing: Minzu chubanshe, 2000), 373.
3. The truth of the path (Skt. *mārga-satya*) is the fourth of the four noble truths preached by the Buddha in the first discourse after he attained liberation. The Buddha preached the eightfold paths, or eight correct practices that can bring about the result of liberation. Different traditions developed a variety of theories to show the path to liberation. Mahāyāna Buddhism upholds the bodhisattva ideal and elaborates on the bodhisattva path. Mahāyāna literature often describes the path in terms of six *pāramitā*, or six perfections of generosity, morality, patience, diligence, contemplation, and wisdom. For the development of the path doctrine, see Carl Olson, *The Different Paths of Buddhism: A Narrative Historical Introduction* (New Brunswick, NJ: Rutgers University Press, 2005).
4. Nāgārjuna (around the second and third centuries) and Asaṅga (fourth century) were esteemed thinkers for the philosophical development of Mahāyāna Buddhism. Atiśa brought the *lamrim* teaching to Tibet, based on which his disciples founded the Kadampa tradition. Atiśa's teaching became the source of inspiration for the *lamrim* doctrinal tradition in Tibet. For an English version, see Atiśa, *Atisha's Lamp for the Path to Enlightenment*, trans. Sonam Rinchen and Ruth Sonam (Ithaca, NY: Snow Lion, 1997).
5. For an English version, see Tsongkhapa, *The Great Treatise on the Stages of the Path to Enlightenment*, trans. *Lamrim* Translation Committee (Ithaca, NY: Snow Lion, 2000).
6. Dayong preached the *Brief Treatise* to his cohort in 1927. The translation was recorded by layman Hu Zhizhan 胡智湛. See Fazun, "Puti dao cidi guanglun de zaozuo fanyi neirong he tijie" 菩提道次第廣論的造作、翻譯、內容和題解 (The

Composition, Translation, Content, and Title of *Lamrim Chenmo*), in *Fazun fashi foxue lunwen ji* (Beijing: Zhongguo fojiao wenhua yanjiu suo, 1990), 260. For a collection of Fazun's translated works, see Fazun, *Fazun fashi yiwenji* 法尊法師譯文集 (Collected translated works of Fazun), ed. Lü Tiegang, Hu Heping, and Wu Limin 吳立民 (Hongkong: Zhongguo fojiao wenhua chuban youxian gongsi, 2000).

7. Fazun learned *Lamrim Chenmo* in 1932 and *Ngagrim Chenmo* in 1933. See Fazun, "Zhuzhe ru Zang de jingguo" (The writer's experience in entering Tibet), in *Fazun fashi foxue lunwenji* (Collected works of Buddhist studies of Fazun), ed. Lü Tiegang and Hu Heping (Beijing: Zhongguo fojiao wenhua yanjiusuo, 1990), 364–365.

8. For the institute, see *Hanzang jiaoliyuan li'an wenjian huibian* 漢藏教理院立案文件彙編 (Collected material of the Sino-Tibetan Buddhist Institute) (Chongqing: Hanzang jiaoli yuan, 1936); *Shijie foxueyuan hanzang jiaoliyuan tekan* 世界佛學苑漢藏教理院特刊 (Special issue on the Sino-Tibetan Buddhist Institute) (Chongqing: Hanzang jiaoli yuan, 1944). For the school's faculty, staff, curriculum, and publication, see Gray Tuttle, *Tibetan Buddhists in the Making of Modern China* (New York: Columbia University Press, 2005), 194–204.

9. Taixu wrote a preface for the Chinese translation. See Tsongkhapa, *Putidao cidi guanglun*, trans. Fazun (Chongqing: Hanzang jiaoliyuan, 1935). For Fazun and his career at Sino-Tibetan Buddhist Institute, see Brenton Sullivan, "Venerable Fazun at the Sino-Tibetan Buddhist Studies Institute (1932–1950) and Tibetan Gelug Buddhism in China," *The Indian International Journal of Buddhist Studies* 9 (2008): 199–241.

10. For Dayong's translation of the *Lamrim mdor bsdus*, see Hengyan, "Dayong a she li bing zhuanshi hudutu hezhuan," *HCY* 27, no. 9 (September 1946): 28; *MFQ* 203: 68–69. See Tsongkhapa, *Mizong daocidi lun*, trans. Fazun (Shanghai: Shanghai foxue shuju, 1998).

11. Fazun visited the lay supporters in Beijing and Tianjin to raise funds to publish *Lamrim Chenmo*. According to Fazun, the Sino-Tibetan College produced an oil-printed version before 1935. See Fazun, "Puti dao cidi guanglun de zaozuo fanyi neirong he tijie," 260.

12. Fazun, "Puti dao cidi guanglun de zaozuo fanyi neirong he tijie," 259.

13. The Panchen Lama planned to promote education to the Chinese Buddhists in Tibetan Buddhist doctrines (see chapter 1). But at least in the early 1920s, few extant documents show that the Chinese monks were receiving training about Tibetan commentaries from the Tibetan lamas.

14. Fazun mentioned that he came to faith in Tibetan Buddhism mainly for its philosophical sophistication, rather than for its tantras. Fazun, "Zhuzhe ru Zang de jingguo," 363.

15. Fazun, "Zhuzhe ru Zang de jingguo," 363.

16. Fazun, "Puti dao cidi guanglun de zaozuo fanyi neirong he tijie," 259.

17. Fazun, "Puti dao cidi guanglun de zaozuo fanyi neirong he tijie," 265.

18. Fazun, "Cong Xizang fojiao xuepai xingshuai de yanbian shuodao Zhongguo fojiao de jianli" 從西藏佛教學派興衰的演變說到中國佛教的建立 (From the

5. THE PATH TO ENLIGHTENMENT

changing history of Tibetan scholasticism to the establishment of Chinese Buddhism), in *Fazun fashi foxue lunwen ji*, 27.
19. Fazun, "Cong Xizang fojiao xuepai xingshuai de yanbian shuodao Zhongguo fojiao de jianli," 27.
20. Fazun, "Cong Xizang fojiao xuepai xingshuai de yanbian shuodao Zhongguo fojiao de jianli," 27.
21. Fazun, "Puti dao cidi guanglun de zaozuo fanyi neirong he tijie," 265.
22. Fazun, "Zongkaba dashi de puti dao cidi lun" 宗喀巴大師的《菩提道次第論》 (Master Tsongkhapa's *Lamrim Chenmo*), in *Fazun fashi foxue lunwen ji*, 269.
23. Taixu criticized the different schools for their neglect of doctrinal learning. For example, Taixu criticized the Chan practitioners for stubbornly adhering to some Chan canonical texts and ignoring all other teachings, the Tiantai and Huayan schools for promoting a particular scripture over other scriptures, and the Japanese Tendai and Pureland schools for chanting only a scripture title or a Buddha's name. Taixu, "Xuwen" 序文 (Preface), in *Puti dao cidi guanglun* (1935; repr., Putian, Fujian: Putian guanghua si, 1992), 1–2. He also rejected the Zhenyan practitioners' promotion of the superiority of esoteric teachings. For more on this, see the discussion in chapter 2.
24. Taixu, "Xuewen," 1–2.
25. Taixu, "Xuwen," 1–2.
26. See Chaoyi, "Puti dao cidi lun ji lue song" 菩提道次第論極略頌 (The succinct verses from *Lamrim Chenmo*), *HCY* 14, no. 2 (February 1933): 35–36; *MFQ* 183: 165–166. See Chaoyi, "Puti dao cidi lun she song ke pan" 菩提道次第論攝頌科判 (An outline of the verses of *Lamrim Chenmo*), *HCY* 14, no. 2 (February 1933): 169–170; *MFQ* 183: 169–170.
27. For example, Fazun visited Chongqing Foxueshe to talk about *lamrim* for a month, and then he was invited to speak at Chengdu Foxueshe. Chaoyi was invited to Xian and Qinghai to speak on *lamrim*. See "Gedi fashi jiangjing yishu" 各地法師講經一束 (Information about masters' lectures in different places), *HCY* 18, no. 6 (June 1937): 97; *MFQ* 197: 105–107.
28. The three persons are defined according to their levels of motivations or capacities. The teaching of the path to enlightenment is divided into five categories: (1) preliminary instructions to the stages of the three persons; (2) practice of the person of inferior capacity; (3) practice of the person of medium capacity; (4) practice of high capacity; (5) practice of the esoteric vehicle. See Nenghai, "Puti dao cidi ke song jiangji," 11.
29. Nenghai claimed that *lamrim* encompasses all the thirty-seven practices that the Buddha taught in his early days. See Nenghai, "Puti dao cidi ke song jiangji," 1.
30. "Nenghai fashi Beiping jiang puti dao" 能海法師北平講菩提道 (Venerable Nenghai lectured on *Lamrim* in Beijing), *HCY* 17, no. 1 (January 1936): 104; *MFQ* 192: 364.
31. Zhang Mengliang 張夢良, "Nenghai fashi jin zaijing jiang putidao cidi qinei bing guanding chuanfa" 能海法師近在京講菩提道次第期內併灌頂傳法 (Venerable

Nenghai gave lectures on *Lamrim* and offered initiations in Nanjing), *Zhengxin* 8, nos. 1-2 (April 1936): 14; *MFQB* 44: 208.
32. Ren Jie, "Nenghai shangshi zhushu mulu ji daodu" 能海上師著述目錄及導讀 (A catalog of works of Master Nenghai with introduction). Unpublished manuscript. Dated: summer 2009.
33. Nenghai collated verses from *Lamrim Chenmo* in *Puti dao cidi xinlun* 菩提道次第心論 (Essence of *Lamrim*) to assist the disciples' recitation. See Nenghai, *Puti dao cidi xinlun* (Tainan: Heyu chubanshe, 1996). He also translated a manual titled *Puti dao cidi qiandao liu jiaxing fa* 菩提道次第前導六加行法 (The six preparatory practices of *Lamrim*) to guide the disciples' meditative practice. See *Puti dao cidi qiandao liu jiaxing fa*, unpublished manuscript.
34. Nenghai delivered the lectures in 1935 at Huabei Lay Buddhist Society, which were recorded by a lay disciple named Ren Dingxun 任定詢. For a printed edition, see Nenghai, "Puti dao cidi kesong jiangji," in *Sanxue jianglu* 三學講錄 (Lecture notes on the three teachings), ed. Nenghai shangshi quanji bianweihui (Shanghai: Shanghai foxue shuju, 2005), 1–164.
35. Nenghai, "Puti dao cidi kesong jiangji," 25.
36. Nenghai, "Puti dao cidi kesong jiangji," 31.
37. Nenghai, "Puti dao cidi kesong jiangji," 7.
38. Nenghai, "Puti dao cidi kesong jiangji," 31.
39. Nenghai, "Puti dao cidi kesong jiangji," 7.
40. Nenghai, "Puti dao cidi kesong jiangji," 7.
41. Nenghai, *Xianzheng zhuangyan lun qingliang ji*, 118.
42. They adopted the conventional Mahāyāna notion that it takes eons for an ordinary being to reach Buddhahood. See chapter 4.
43. Nenghai, "Puti dao cidi kesong jiangji," 107.
44. Nenghai, "Puti dao cidi kesong jiangji," 107.
45. Nenghai, "Puti dao cidi kesong jiangji," 155.
46. Nenghai, "Puti dao cidi kesong jiangji," 9.
47. Nenghai, "Puti dao cidi kesong jiangji," 11.
48. Nenghai, "Puti dao cidi kesong jiangji ngji," 9.
49. Christian Meyer examined the emergence of the Science of Religion as an academic field in China in the late nineteenth and early twentieth centuries. In the 1920s, new debates emerged calling for the establishment of the discipline of the Science of Religion as an outcome of the intellectual New Culture Movement. See Christian Meyer, "How the 'Science of Religion' (*zongjiaoxue*) as a Discipline Globalized 'Religion' in Late Qing and Republican China, 1890–1949—Global Concepts, Knowledge Transfer, and Local Discourses," in *Globalization and the Making of Religious Modernity in China*, ed. Thomas Jansen, Thoralf Klein, and Christian Meyer (Leiden: Koninklijke Brill, 2014), 305–306, 312–313.
50. Welch, *The Buddhist Revival in China* (Cambridge, MA: Harvard University Press, 1968), 202.
51. Ouyang Jingwu (1871–1943) delivered the speech at the opening ceremony of the Sino Academy of Inner Studies (Zhina neixueyuan 支那內學院) in

Nanjing in 1922. Ouyang promulgated the scholarly study of mind-only thought. In the speech, he enumerated five obstacles in the area of Buddhist Studies: (1) some Chan practitioners neglected doctrinal study; (2) the Buddhist scholarship was too generalized and biased; (3) scholars of the Tiantai and Huayan schools narrowed the scope of research and specialized only in their traditions; (4) scholars often misunderstood philosophical works composed in the Tang dynasty; and (5) scholars did not develop research methods and they stuck to religious stances. See Ouyang Jingwu, "Weishi jueze tan," 唯識抉擇談 (Selected works on the mind-only thought), in *Ouyang Jian xuanji* 歐陽漸選集 (Selected works of Ouyang Jian), vol. 51 of *Xiandai foxue daxi* 現代佛學大系, ed. Lan Jifu 藍吉富 (Taipei: Mile chuban she, 1984), 291–293.

52. Zhang Kecheng was a scholar known for research in mind-only thought. For a biography of Zhang, see Jiang Weiqiao 蔣維喬, "Zhang Kecheng xiansheng zhuan" 張克誠先生傳 (Biography of Zhang Kecheng), *HCY* 3, no. 2 (August 1922): 3–4. For Nenghai's study with Zhang, see Dingzhi, *Nenghai shangshi zhuan* (Biography of Master Nenghai) (1984; repr., Shanghai: Shanghai foxue shuju, 2007), 3; *MFQ* 153: 461–462.
53. After attending the lectures, Nenghai befriended Zhang and continued to study with him, see Dingzhi, *Nenghai shangshi zhuan*, 3.
54. Nenghai gave the lectures at Jinci Monastery in 1942 and the notes were taken down by Longlian. Nenghai did not specify the scholars he was criticizing. See Nenghai, "Dingdao ziliang song jianglu" 定道資糧頌講錄 (Notes on the preparation for the path of concentration), in *Sanxue jianglu*, 170.
55. Nenghai, "Shelifu apitanlun chanding pin xueji jianglu," 338–339.
56. Nenghai, "Shelifu apitanlun chanding pin xueji jianglu," 338.
57. The triadic model of hearing, thinking, and meditating originated in Indian Buddhist scholarship. In particular, Vasubandhu and the Sautrāntika tradition greatly influenced the Gelug discussion about the wisdom arising from the three types of practice. See Leah Zahler, *Study and Practice of Meditation: Tibetan Interpretations of the Concentrations and Formless Absorptions* (Ithaca, NY: Snow Lion, 2009), 12–16. Anne Klein also showed that in Gelug scholarship on the Sautrāntika philosophy, the scholars emphasized the significance of inferential cognition in revealing the reality of phenomena. They generally agreed that understanding derived from conceptual thought increases the understanding derived from direct perception. See Anne Klein, *Knowledge and Liberation: Tibetan Buddhist Epistemology in Support of Transformative Religious Experience* (Ithaca, NY: Snow Lion, 1986), 32.
58. While all types of Buddhist meditation aim to reach enlightenment, the different traditions express the immediate goals in quite a variety of ways. For example, early Indian Buddhists focused on realizing the emptiness of all conditioned phenomena and attaining liberation from suffering, but the Chinese Chan meditators emphasized sudden and intuitive enlightenment. For the varied expressions of the meditative goals, see Edward Conze, *Buddhist Meditation*, 2nd ed. (New York: Routledge Publication, 2008), 12–13.

5. THE PATH TO ENLIGHTENMENT

59. Yoshihide Yoshizu points out that the term *guan* 觀 has a variety of meanings in Chinese Buddhist literature. In early translations, it denotes insight meditation in contrast to stabilization meditation. In later periods, the Tiantai philosophers used *guan* to indicate meditation in contrast with teaching (*jiao* 教), whereas most other Buddhists used the term to suggest a unity of meditation and wisdom. See Yoshihide Yoshizu, "The Relation between Chinese Buddhist History and Soteriology," trans. and ed. Paul Groner, in *Paths to Liberation: The Mārga and its Transformations in Buddhist Thought*, ed. and trans. Robert Buswell and Robert Gimello (Honolulu: University of Hawai'i Press, 1992), 315–316.
60. Regarding the order of meditative cultivation of calm abiding and insight, according to Leah Zahler, most Gelug texts agree that cultivation of calm abiding precedes that of insight meditation. See Leah Zahler, *Study and Practice of Meditation*, 66–69.
61. See, for example, Anne Klein, *Knowledge and Liberation*, 17. Robert Gimello also showed that mystical experience is shaped by religious and cultural backgrounds. Robert Gimello, "Mysticism and Meditation," in *Mysticism and Philosophical Analysis*, ed. Steven Katz (New York: Oxford University Press, 1978), 176. See also, Robert Gimello, "Mysticism in its Contexts" in *Mysticism and Religious Traditions*, ed. Steven Katz (New York: Oxford University Press, 1983), 61–88.
62. Paul Williams, "A Note on Some Aspects of Mi bskyod rdo rje's critique of dGe lugs pa Madhyamaka," *Journal of Indian Philosophy* 11 (1983): 128.
63. Nenghai used the terms *jueguan* and *xunsi* 尋伺 (Skt. vitarka-vicāra) interchangeably. Nenghai taught meditation methods based on a chapter of Chinese canonical text on meditation. His thoughts on meditation were most systematically shown in his writing about the ninth chapter in the *Shelifu a pi tan lun* 舍利弗阿毗曇論 (Śāriputrābhidharma) (T no. 1548: 620–624). This chapter explains various meditative methods the Buddha taught his disciples. Nenghai's notes were collected and published as "Shelifu apitanlun chanding pin xueji" 舍利弗阿毗曇論禪定品學記 (Lecture Records on the Notes on the Samādhi Chapter in the Śāriputrābhidharma)," in *Jiedinghui jiben sanxue*, ed. Nenghai shangshi quanji bianwei hui (Shanghai: Shanghai foxue chubanshe, 2005): 215–310. He also delivered lectures on the chapter, and the notes were taken down by his nun disciple Longlian. Nenghai, "Shelifu apitanlun chanding pin xueji jianglu" 舍利弗阿毗曇論禪定品學記講錄 (Notes on the Samādhi Chapter in the Śāriputrābhidharma), in *Sanxue jianglu*, 278–354.
64. Regarding the attributes of the four noble truths, see *Jushe lun* 俱舍論 (Abhidharma-kośa), T no. 1558: 119. The treatise enumerates the sixteen attributes of the four truths to be contemplated in meditation. Each truth respectively connotes four attributes. In meditation, these qualities are taken as objects of meditation. Practitioners contemplate them until they receive direct realization. The first noble truth of suffering connotes impermanence, misery, emptiness, and no-self; the second noble truth of origination suggests cause, gathering, continuation, and conditioning; the third truth of the cessation of

5. THE PATH TO ENLIGHTENMENT

suffering suggests annihilation of affliction, calming, subtleness, detachment; the fourth truth of path includes the path to cessation, suitability, activity leading to liberation, and transcendence. For the meditation of sixteen aspects of four truths, see Bhikkhu KL Dhammajoti, *Sarvāstivāda Abhidharma* (Hong Kong: University of Hong Kong Press, 2009), 433–470.

65. Nenghai, "Shelifu apitanlun chanding pin xueji jianglu," 334–335.
66. Nenghai, "Shelifu apitanlun chanding pin xueji jianglu," 338–339.
67. Nenghai, "Shelifu apitanlun chanding pin xueji jianglu," 334.
68. Nenghai, "Qingliangji" 7.
69. Nenghai, "Qingliangji," 7.
70. Among a variety of Prajñāpāramitā Sūtras in the Chinese Buddhist canon, the Mahāprajñāpāramitā Sūtra translated by Xuangzang is the largest, with six-hundred fascicles. See *Da bore boluomiduo jing* 大般若波羅蜜多經 (Skt. Mahāprajñāpāramitā Sūtra), T no. 220, 5: 1b.
71. The *Testament of Ba* is an account of the establishment of Buddhism in Tibet. Its origins and dating remain controversial. It is traditionally attributed to Ba Salnang and possibly formulated in the ninth or tenth century, but some modern scholars claim that it was compiled after the tenth century. See Matthew Kapstein, *The Tibetan Assimilation of Buddhism: Conversion, Contestation, and Memory* (New York: Oxford University Press, 2000), 23–36.
72. Kim Hwa-shang was a Silla monk of the northern Chan school. He was active in Yizhou 益州, where the five Tibetans encountered him. Master Kim was described as a monk skillful in meditation and having some sort of supernatural power. He correctly predicted the forthcoming death of the Tibetan king and the establishment of Buddhism in Tibet. Chan discourses attributed to Kim Hwa-shang were found in Dunhuang Tibetan Chan manuscripts. Master Kim emphasized intuitive realization (*jue* 覺). See Jeffrey Broughton, "Early Ch'an Schools in Tibet," in *Studies in Ch'an and Hua-yen*, ed. Robert Gimello and Peter Gregory (Honolulu: University of Hawai'i Press, 1983), 1–68.
73. For discussion on later Tibetan historians' dismissal of the episode, see Kapstein, *The Tibetan Assimilation of Buddhism*, 72–74.
74. Recent scholarship has posed questions to the narrative recorded in the *Testament of Ba*. Some scholars suspected that a Tibetan Chan lineage may have survived in Dunhuang region to the ninth century. For the Tibetan Chan tradition, see Luis Gomez, "The Direct and Gradual Approaches of Zen Master Mahāyāna: Fragments of the Teachings of Mo-ho-yen," in *Studies in Ch'an and Huayan*, 69–169. See also Kapstein, *The Tibetan Assimilation of Buddhism*, 69–77. For some recently translated Tibetan Chan texts see Sam van Schaik, *Tibetan Zen: Discovering a Lost Tradition* (Boston: Snow Lion, 2015).
75. Recent scholarship found that some elements of Moheyan's lineage survived in eastern Tibet after the contest. For example, some scholars suggested that the Great Perfection (*rdzogs chen*) systems of the Nyingma order, the Mahāmudrā of the Kagyu order, and other systems presumably adsorbed certain elements from Chan teaching. For example, see David Germano, "Architecture and Absence in the Secret Tantric History of rDzogs Chen," *Journal of*

5. THE PATH TO ENLIGHTENMENT

the *International Association of Buddhist Studies* 17, no. 2 (1994): 203–335. Sakya Paṇḍita once criticized the Kagyu Mahāmudrā for absorbing inspiration from Chan, see Roger Jackson, "Sa skya Paṇḍita's Account of the bSam yas Debate: History as Polemic," *Journal of the International Association of Buddhist Studies* 5, no. 1 (1982): 89–99.

76. In the Republican period, most monasteries and monks nominally belonged to the Chan tradition. Holmes Welch, *The Practice of Chinese Buddhism* (Cambridge, MA: Harvard University Press, 1967), 3–4.
77. Nenghai, "Qingliang xuji," 17.
78. This is a well-known *gong'an* in the Chan literature. See *Wudeng huiyuan* 五燈會元, X no. 1565: 411.
79. Nenghai, "Qingliang xuji," 3–4.
80. Nenghai, "Qingliang xuji," 4.
81. Esoteric rituals involve the usage of the three mysteries of body, speech, and mind. Visualization involves the generation of mental images. See Paul Copp, "Visualization and Contemplation," in *Esoteric Buddhism and the Tantras in East Asia*, ed. Charles Orzech, Henrik Sørensen, and Richard Payne (Leiden: Brill, 2011), 141–145.
82. Nenghai translated *Wenshu Daweide jingang benzun xiuxing chengjiu fa* 文殊大威德金剛本尊修行成就法 (The completion of the practice of Mañjuśrī Yamāntaka) on his second trip to Lhasa in 1941. He translated *Daweide cidi song lue yin* 大威德次第頌略引 (A preliminary guide to the verses of the stages of Yamāntaka) in Jixiang Monastery in 1957.
83. Nenghai, "Qingliang ji," 127–129.
84. *Zuo chan sanmei jing* (*T* no. 614) was compiled by Kumārajīva. It collates a variety of meditative techniques, including the remembrance of the Buddha. In this type of meditation, the meditator is instructed to look at an image or statue of Buddha and contemplate the physical signs and merit of the Buddha to develop calmness and insight. See Shengyan 聖嚴, *Chanyao* 禪鑰 (The key to Zen) (Taipei: Fagun wenhua chubanshe, 1996), 40. See also, Liao Yixuan 廖乙璿, "Zuochan sanmei jing chanfa jianjie"《坐禪三昧經》禪法簡介 (A brief introduction to the *Sūtra on the Samādhi of Sitting Meditation*), *Fuyan Buddhist Studies* 10 (2015): 40–77.
85. Nenghai, "Qingliang ji," 110–129.
86. *Zhenzhou Linji Huizhao chanshi yulu* 鎮州臨濟慧照禪師語錄 (Discourses of Chan Master Linji Huizhao from the prefecture of Zhen), *T* no. 1985: 500.
87. Chan master Shengyan explained that, the *gong'an* suggests that meditators should not attach to anything, including the appearances of Buddha. See Shengyan, *Shengyan fashi jiao huatou chan* 聖嚴法師教話頭禪 (Huatou Chan taught by Master Shengyan) (Taipei: Fagu wenhua shiye, 2009), 22.
88. Nenghai, "Qingliang xuji," 21.
89. Nenghai, "Qingliang xuji," 21.
90. Nenghai, "Shelifu apitanlun chanding pin xueji jianglu," 334–335.
91. Nenghai, "Shelifu apitanlun chanding pin xueji jianglu," 334–335.
92. Nenghai, "Shelifu apitanlun chanding pin xueji jianglu," 339–341.

6. Tibetan Buddhism Among Han Chinese

1. Some portions of this chapter were presented at the annual meeting of the American Academy of Religion (AAR) in Atlanta in 2015.
2. Mount Wutai became the sacred site for Chinese Buddhists in the fifth century. From the seventh century onward, pilgrims from India, Kashmir, Tibet, Japan, and Korea also visited this sacred mountain. See Karl Debreczeny, "Wutai Shan: Pilgrimage to Five Peak Mountain," *Journal of the International Association of Tibetan Studies* 6 (2011): 1–133. See also Gray Tuttle, "Tibetan Buddhism at Ri bor-tse Inga/Wutai shan in Modern Times," *Journal of the International Association of Tibetan Studies* 2 (2006), 1–35. For Mongolian pilgrims, see Isabelle Charleux, *Nomads on Pilgrimage: Mongols on Wutaishan (China), 1800-1940* (Leiden: Brill, 2015), 255–276.
3. Holmes Welch, *The Buddhist Revival in China* (Cambridge, MA: Harvard University Press, 1968), 196–200.
4. Nenghai's sister, who was ten years older than him, married into a family that run a soy sauce shop in Mianzhu. Tan Tian interviewed Nenghai's family members in the 2000s and revealed some facets about his secular life. See Tan Tian 譚天, *Nenghai shangshi zhuan* (Biography of Guru Nenghai) (Beijing: Zhongyang wenxian chubanshe, 2008), 40–55.
5. For Nenghai's early life, see Zhang Jiyin 張繼寅, "Nenghai fashi zhuan" 能海法師傳 (Biography of Master Nenghai), in *Nenghai shangshi yonghuai lu*, 88.
6. Various sources provided different information about the time of Nenghai's entering the military school. He entered the Land Force Lower-Ranking Officer Unit in 1905 or 1906, although 1906 seems more plausible since the school recruited the first batch of students that year. Some students transferred to the newly opened Intense Military School in 1908. Nenghai graduated from the Military School in 1909. For the history of the military schools in Sichuan, see Sichuan sheng wenshi yanjiu guan, ed., *Sichuan junfa shiliao* 四川軍閥史料 (Historical materials on Sichuan warlords) (Chengdu: Sichuan renmin chubanshe, 1981), 6–7. See also Zhou Kaiqing 周開慶, *Minguo Sichuan shishi* 民國四川史事 (History of Sichuan during the Republican period) (Taipei: Taiwan shangwu yinshuguan, 1969), 91–92.
7. Robert A. Kapp studied the common features of the first generation of Sichuan warlords who were in power between 1911 and 1927. Most of them were born between 1875 and 1880. Some received military training in Japan, where they may have established contact with the Nationalists. See Robert Kapp, *Szechwan and the Chinese Republic: Provincial Militarism and Central Power, 1911-1938* (New Haven, CT: Yale University Press, 1973), 11–13.
8. See Robert Kapp, *Szechwan and the Chinese Republic*, 11.
9. According to a memoir, many of Nenghai's friends were Nationalists and were persecuted by military supporters of Yuan Shikai. See Zhang Jiyin, "Nenghai fashi zhuan," 91.
10. See Zhang Jiyin, "Nenghai fashi zhuan," 92.

6. TIBETAN BUDDHISM AMONG HAN CHINESE

11. See Likong 力空, "Nenghai fashi zai Wutaishan jiangwan Yulanpeng jing biguan xiufa" 能海法師在五臺山講完盂蘭盆經閉關修法 (Master Nenghai practiced in reclusion after preaching on the Yulanpeng Sūtra at Wutai), *Shanxi fojiao zazhi* 山西佛教雜誌 (Journal of Shanxi Buddhism) 1, no. 9 (September 1934): 67; *MFQ* 140: 235.
12. See Dingzhi, *Nenghai shangshi zhuan* 能海上師傳 (Biography of Master Nenghai) (Shanghai: Shangha foxue shuju, 2007), 2.
13. Dingzhi, *Nenghai shangshi zhuan*, 2.
14. Nenghai's first wife was the seventh daughter of the Zhuang family and his third wife was the eighth daughter. Tan Tian, *Nenghai shangshi zhuan*, 95, 123.
15. The five largest public temples in Chengdu area were Mañjuśrī Monastery, Monastery of Great Compassion (Dacisi 大慈寺), Monastery of Thatched Cottage (Caotangsi 草堂寺), Monastery of Saintly Glory (Yaoguangsi 堯光寺), and Monastery of Luminous Enlightenment (Zhaojuesi 昭覺寺). Before 1949, there were 112 Buddhist temples (including 107 private temples and 5 public temples) and six lay Buddhist societies in Chengdu region. See United Front Work Department of Chengdu, "Guanyu Chengdu shi fojiao qingkuang de ziliao" 關於成都市佛教情況的資料 (Materials about Buddhism in Chengdu), June 11, 1955, Sichuan Provincial Archives, Jianchuan 050-01-038.
16. Other cofounders were Zeng Ziyu 曾子玉, Huang Sufang 黃肅方, and Pi Huaibai 皮懷白. For the founding history of the society, see Chengdu shi difangzhi bianzuan weiyuanhui 成都市地方誌編纂委員會 (Committee of gazetteer compilation in Chengdu), ed., *Chengdu shizhi zongjiao zhi* 成都市志宗教志 (Religious history of Chengdu), vol. 8 of *Chengdu shizhi* 成都市志 (Gazetteer of Chengdu) (Chengdu: Sichuan cishu chubanshe, 1993), 113.
17. Buddhist scholars, including Liu Zhuyuan 劉洙源, Yu Shayuan 余沙園, and Shao Mingshu 邵明叔, often gave lectures in the society. Dingzhi, "Nenghai shangshi zhuan," 4.
18. Lady Zhang was ordained at Mañjuśrī Monastery; her Dharma name was Nengxing 能興. She lived afterward at a private temple in Guanghan 廣漢. Lady Zhuang was ordained by a nun named Longshou 隆壽 at the Hall of Aidao. Nenghai's daughter was later adopted by the Chen family in Chengdu. For Nenghai's family, see Tan Tian, *Nenghai shangshi zhuan*, 32–35, 130–142. See also Dingzhi, *Nenghai shangshi zhuan*, 2.
19. Tan Tian, *Nenghai shangshi zhuan*, 132.
20. Nenghai might have been to the Kham region several times. These trips could have helped him to increase his contact with Tibetans, which facilitated his later trips to study with Tibetan lamas. According to a 1935 article written by Nenghai's former colleague (the magistrate of Jiangjin 江津 County in Sichuan), Nenghai was deployed to the Kham region around 1915. See Huweng 湖翁, "Ting Nenghai fashi jiangyan hou" 聽能海法師講演後 (Reflection on Master Nenghai's lecture), *Chuanbian jikan* 川邊季刊 (Quarterly of Sichuan border) 5, no 1, (April 1926): 18–20.

21. Nenghai, "Dingdao ziliang song jianglu (Notes on the preparation for the path of concentration). In *Sanxue jianglu* (Notes on the three teachings), 170–277, vol. 2 of *Nenghai shangshi quanji* (*NHSS*), 172–173.
22. In 1915, commissioned by the Sichuan warlord Liu Xiang 劉湘 (1890–1938), Nenghai went to Japan on a business tour to "study the politics and industry." See Dingzhi, *Nenghai shangshi zhuan*, 2. See also Likong, "Nenghai fashi zai Wutaishan jiangwan yulanpeng jing biguan xiufa," 67.
23. Nenghai, "Dingdao ziliang song jianglu," 172.
24. For the thriving of religious printing in the early twentieth century, see Gregory Scott, "Navigating the Sea of Scriptures: The Buddhist Studies Collectanea, 1918–1923," in *Religious Publishing and Print Culture in Modern China: 1800–2012*, ed. Philip Clart and Gregory Adam Scott (Boston: De Gruyter, 2015), 91–139.
25. Nenghai, "Dingdao ziliang song jianglu," 172.
26. Huang Chanhua 黃懺華, the elder brother of Huang Shuyin, was a well-known Buddhist scholar who composed *Zhongguo fojiaoshi* 中國佛教史 (The history of Chinese Buddhism) (Shanghai: shangwu yinshuguan, 1947). The Huang brothers both studied with Ouyang Jingwu at Jinling Scriptural Press. Huang Shuyin taught Sanskrit at Peking University before his death in 1925. For an obituary of Huang, see Huang Chanhua, "Huang Shuyin jushi shi lue" 黃樹因居士事略 (About layman Huang Shuyin), *SFJL*, nos. 3–4 (October 1925), 3–4; *MFQB* 7: 205.
27. Alexander von Stael-Holstein (1877–1937) opened courses on Sanskrit at Peking University, which facilitated scholarship in Indian Studies among the modern Chinese Buddhist intellectuals. For a biography of Alexander von Stael-Holstein, see Wang Qiling, *The Academic Knight Between East and West: A Biography of Alexander Staël von Holstein* (Singapore: Cengage Learning Asia, 2014).
28. The four monks were Yongguang, Chuanpin 傳品, Guoyao 果瑤, and Guoyu 果玉. An ordination-ceremony assistant named Hengliang 恒亮 also joined them. Nenghai, "Dingdao ziliang song jianglu," 172.
29. They left for Lhasa in June 1928 and arrived in September. The other three monks were Yongguang, Yonglun, and Yongyan. For the general situation at Sera, Drepung, and Ganden (the three major Gelug monasteries in Lhasa), see Melvyn Goldstein, *A History of Modern Tibet, 1913–1951: The Demise of the Lamaist State* (Berkeley: University of California Press, 1989), 24–34.
30. Dingzhi, *Nenghai shangshi zhuan*, 11–13. As a result of patronage from the Qing imperial court, Yamāntaka (a wrathful form of Mañjuśrī in esoteric Buddhism) has been widely worshipped in the Gelug temples in Beijing, Manchuria, and Mongolia. See Bulcsu Siklós, "The Evolution of the Buddhist Yama," *The Buddhist Forum* 4 (1996): 165–189.
31. Buddhist practice can be divided into three categories of training: morality, concentration, and wisdom. Disciplinary codes for monastic members are listed in vinaya. Vinaya describes rules of proper conduct and deportment, offenses of varying gravity, and penalties ranging from repentance to expulsion from the monastic order. Vinaya also describes the procedures of important ecclesiastical ceremonies, such as conferring precepts and repentance. Various ancient Buddhist schools in India developed their distinctive versions.

6. TIBETAN BUDDHISM AMONG HAN CHINESE

Regarding the different types of Vinaya, see Akira Hirakawa, *Ritsuzō no kenkyū* 律蔵の研究 (A study of the Vinaya collection) (Tokyo: Sankibō Busshorin, 1960).

32. A number of scriptures related to Prajñāpāramitā emerged between the first and tenth century in India. See Edward Conze, "The Development of Prajñāpāramitā Thought," in *Thirty Years of Buddhist Studies: Selected Essays by Edward Conze* (Oxford: Bruno Cassirer Publishers, 1967), 122–124.
33. According to the tradition, Maitreya revealed the *Ornament* to Asaṅga in the fourth century. About the commentary tradition in Indian, see Conze, "The Development of Prajñāpāramitā Thought," 123–147.
34. For the translation, see Maitreya, *Xianguan zhuangyan lun* 現觀莊嚴論 (*Ornament of realization*), trans. Fazun (Chongqing: Hanzang jiaoli yuan, 1937).
35. Nenghai gave sixty-two sermons on the topic in 1958 and 1959. The notes were published as *Xianzheng zhuangyan lun qingliang ji*. For his other works, see Nenghai, *Xianzheng zhuangyan lun sanzhong hekan* (Collation of three texts on the *Ornament of Realization*) (Shanghai: Shanghai foxue shuju, 2001).
36. *Da bore boluomiduo jing* (Mahāprajñāpāramitā Sūtra, Sutra of Great Perfection), trans. Xuanzang, *T* no. 220, 5–7.
37. See Nenghai, "Qingliang ji," 1–3. For details about Nenghai's interpretation of the *Ornament*, see Wei Wu, "Approaching the Perfection of Wisdom: Nenghai's Interpretation of the *Ornament of Realization*," in *Sino-Tibetan Buddhism Across the Ages*, eds. Ester Bianchi and Weirong Shen (Leiden: Brill, 2021), 253–277.
38. The talk was given at the Monastery of the Heavenly Jewel (Tianbaosi) in Zhenjiang Province. See Nenghai, "Puti dao cidi kesong," (Lecture notes on the compendium of *Lamrim*) , 51.
39. Dingzhi, *Nenghai shangshi zhuan*, 7.
40. Nenghai, "Synopsis of *Lamrim Chenmo*," 51.
41. See Nenghai, "Puti dao cidi xinlun," in *Jiaoli chuji* 教理初基 (Basic teachings), vol. 3 of *Nenghai shangshi quanji* 能海上師全集 (Collective work of Nenghai), ed. Nenghai shangshi quanji bianwei hui (Shanghai: Shanghai foxue shuju, 1989–2001), 305–364.
42. Nenghai, "Puti dao cidi xinlun," 304.
43. See Nenghai, "Nenghai fashi zhi Guanyi heshang jian" 能海法師致貫一和尚緘 (Letter from Master Nenghai to Master Guanyi), *Fohua xunkan* 103 (March 1928): 8; *MFQ* 17: 458.
44. See Dingzhi, *Nenghai shangshi zhuan*, 13.
45. "Bingzi xizai fahui yuanqi" 丙子息災法會緣起 (Origin of the calamity-pacifying Dharma Assembly in 1936), *Foxue banyue kan* 126 (May 1936): 243–249; *MFQ* 52: 243–249.
46. The abbot Guanghui 廣慧 invited Nenghai to Guangji Monastery (now known as the Monastery of the Green Mountains, Bishansi 碧山寺). See Chenkong 塵空, "Wutaishan Guangji maopeng zhi guoqu yu xianzai" 五臺山廣濟茅蓬之過去與現在 (The past and present of the Thatched Cottage of Vast Salvation at Mount Wutai), *HCY* 17, no.7 (July 1936): 79–82; *MFQ* 194: 235–238. In terms of operation and property ownership, Chinese Buddhist temples can be classified as public monasteries (also known as "temple of ten directions") and hereditary

temples. Traditionally, because its property was collectively shared by the monastic order, a public temple was open to all monastic members. Its abbot was elected among the resident monks or nuns. In a hereditary temple, its property was owned by the abbot and passed down to his Dharma descendants. About the two types of temples, see Welch, *The Practice of Chinese Buddhism*, 3.

47. Xu Weiru 徐蔚如, "Shanxi Wutaishan beitai ding Guangji maopeng mukuan gouzhi zhaitian qi" 山西五臺山北台頂廣濟茅蓬募款購置齋田啟 (Raise funds to purchase land for the Thatched Cottage of Vast Salvation on the northern peak of Mount Wutai), *Tianjin fojiao jushilin linkan* 天津佛教居士林林刊 (Journal of the Lay Buddhist Society of Tianjin) 4 (July 1927): 71–72; *MFQB* 34: 483–484.
48. About the routine at public temples, see Holmes Welch, *The Practice of Chinese Buddhism*, 47–89.
49. Xu Weiru, "Shanxi Wutaishan beitai ding Guangji maopeng mukuan gouzhi zhaitian qi," 71–72.
50. See Dingzhi, *Nenghai shangshi zhuan*, 14. Hu Zihu was also an important patron of Guangji Monastery. As the president of Huabei Lay Buddhist Society, Hu supported Taixu and Dayong's introduction of Tibetan Buddhism. See chapter 1 and chapter 3.
51. For Nenghai's translation of the tantras, see Ester Bianchi, "Yamāntaka-Vajrabhairava in Modern China: Analysis of 20th Century Translations from Tibetan," in *Buddhist Asia* 2, ed., G. Orofino and S. Vita (Kyoto: Italian School of East Asian Studies, 2010): 99–140.
52. Zhaotong, "Suishi Haigong shangshi huiyilu" 隨侍海公上師回憶錄 (Memoir of serving Guru Nenghai), in *Nenghai shangshi yonghuai lu*, 29–40. Before coming to Mount Wutai in the spring of 1936, Zhaotong studied at the Dharma-Realm Learning Society (Fajie xueshe 法界學社) in Fujian Province. Zhaotong became a senior disciple in the lineage and accompanied Nenghai on his second trip to Tibet in 1940.
53. See Zhongren 中人, *Nenghai shangshi ji qi dizi shengping shiji huiji* 能海上師及其弟子生平事蹟彙集 (Accounts of Guru Nenghai and His Disciples) (Henan Anyang: Dingguosi, 2004), 28.
54. See Zhaotong, "Sui shi Haigong shangshi huiyi lu," 32.
55. See Chenkong, "Wutaishan Guangji maopeng zhi guoqu yu xianzai," 79–82.
56. Some monks who did not want to practice either Chan meditation or visualization were allowed to practice their own way during the retreat. Zhaotong, "Suishi Haigong shangshi huiyilu," 32–33.
57. Zhaotong, "Suishi Haigong shangshi huiyilu," 32–33.
58. Zhaotong, "Suishi Haigong shangshi huiyilu," 32.
59. Zhaotong, "Suishi Haigong shangshi huiyilu," 32–33.
60. The official residence of Jasagh Lama was located on the Summit of Bodhisattva (Pusading 菩薩頂). After his retirement, he resided at the Sudhana Cave. See Ren Jie, "Huiyi Zhasake Lao Lama" 回憶札薩克老喇嘛 (Memory of Zhasake Lama), unpublished manuscript, dated in the summer of 1995.
61. Zhaotong, "Suishi Haigong shangshi huiyilu," 29–40.

6. TIBETAN BUDDHISM AMONG HAN CHINESE

62. As shown by Ester Bianchi's study, the nunnery manifests a synthesis of Chinese and Tibetan Buddhist elements. Nenghai's nun disciples adopted the Chinese Buddhist ceremony calendars and set the same positions in the monastic administration, but they practiced esoteric Buddhism. See Ester Bianchi, *The Iron Statue Monastery: A Buddhist Nunnery of Tibetan Tradition in Contemporary China* (Firenze: Leo S. Olschki, 2001); Bianchi, "Tiexiangsi," in *Innovative Buddhist Women: Swimming Against the Stream*, ed. Karma Lekshe (Tsomo Richmond: Curzon, 2000), 130–141.
63. In the 1930s, the major public temples in Chengdu were all associated with Chan. See United Front Work Department of Chengdu, "Guanyu Chengdu shi fojiao qingkuang de ziliao," Sichuan Provincial Archives, Jianchuan 050-01-038. A local gazetteer listed over 270 Buddhist temples and Daoist temples in Chengdu in 1909. Most of these temples were private temples. See Fu Chongju 傅崇矩, *Chengdu tonglan* 成都通覽 (Overview of Chengdu) (1909; repr., Chengdu: Bashu shushe, 1987), 110–111.
64. Kuanlin 寬霖, "Wenshu yuan gaikuang" 文殊院概況 (Overview of Mañjuśrī Monastery), January 22, 1951, Sichuan Provincial Archives, Jianchuan 050-01-197.
65. Dingzhi, "Nenghai shangshi zhuan," 17.
66. Kuanlin, "Wenshu yuan gaikuang," Sichuan Provincial Archives, Jianchuan 050-01-197.
67. A few resident monks were managing the nearby farmland belonging to Mañjuśrī Monastery. See Kuanlin, "Wenshu yuan gaikuang," Sichuan Provincial Archives, Jianchuan 050-01-197.
68. Guangwen 廣文, "Nenghai fashi de yili" 能海法師的毅力 (Perseverance of Nenghai), *Sichuan fojiao yuekan* 8, no. 3 (March 1938): 2; MFQ 60: 2.
69. Dingzhi, *Nenghai shangshi zhuan*, 17.
70. Nenghai, "Dingdao ziliang song jianglu," 190.
71. Dingzhi, *Nenghai shangshi zhuan*, 17.
72. During wartime, the Hall of the Novice Monks provided shelter for young boys. For example, one of the earliest residents in the novice monk hall was a refugee boy from Shanghai. After his mother died during Japanese bombing, his father took him to escape to Sichuan. His father couldn't support him, however, so he sent him to the temple. See Ren Jie, "Jinci si jiafeng" 近慈寺家風 (The style of Jinci Monastery), unpublished manuscript dated summer 2007.
73. When a novice monk turned twenty, he would receive full ordination at Jinci Monastery. The monks who newly joined Jinci were placed in the Hall of Precept Learning. Nenghai also invited Jasagh Lama from Mount Wutai to Jinci Monastery. The lama lived at the temple and transmitted teachings to the disciples from 1948 to 1951. See Ren Jie 任傑, "Nenghai shangshi dechen qinwen lu," 58–69. See also, Dingzhi, *Nenghai shangshi zhuan*, 37–38.
74. Ren Jie, "Nenghai shangshi dechen qinwen lu," 58–69.
75. Ren Jie, "Nenghai shangshi dechen qinwen lu," 58–69.
76. The temple was also known as Temple of Enlightenment in Clouds (Yunwusi 雲悟寺). In the early 1950s, it accommodated over one hundred resident monks. See Chengdu Department of Religious Affairs, "Chengdu Mianzhu deng di

guanyu fodaojiao simiao daoguan qingkuang diaocha baogao" 成都綿竹等地關於佛道教寺廟道觀情況調查報告 (Survey of the Buddhist and Daoist Temples in Chengdu and Mianzhu), January 19, 1960, Sichuan Provincial Archives, Jianchuan 051-01-314; Xingfa 興法, "Guanyu chengdu jincisi he yunwusi de guanxi jianjie" 關於成都近慈寺和雲悟寺的關係簡介 (An introduction to the relationship between Jinci Monastery and Yunwu Temple), in *Nenghai shangshi yonghuai lu* (Shanghai: Shanghai foxue shuju, 1997), 52–54.

77. Dingzhi, *Nenghai shangshi zhuan*, 52.
78. Ren Jie, "Nenghai shangshi dechen qinwen lu," 60.
79. Chengdu Department of Religious Affairs, "Chengdu Mianzhu dengdi guanyu fodaojiao simiao daoguan qingkuang diaocha baogao," See also Dingzhi, *Nenghai shangshi zhuan*, 20.
80. Renci 仁慈, "Nenghai fashi zai Shu jinkuang" 能海法師在蜀近況 (Recent situation of Master Nenghai in Sichuan), *Jueyouqing*, nos. 167–168 (August 1946): 2; MFQB 63: 2.
81. See Lama Zopa, *The Heart of the Path: Seeing the Guru as Buddha* (Weston, MA: Lama Yeshe Wisdom Archives, 2009), 26.
82. In the devotional practice known as "guru yoga," the practitioner visualizes the guru as the embodiment of the Buddha. The disciple's unfailing faith helps to cement the karmic relationship with the guru, which helps to increase her chance of meeting with the guru in future lives. See Lama Zopa, *The Heart of the Path*, 176. The centrality of the guru also has to do with the oral and textual transmission of esoteric practices. Composed in "twilight language," many tantric texts require instruction from skillful teachers to decode them. See, for example, Judith Simmer-Brown, *Dakini's Warm Breath: The Feminine Principle in Tibetan Buddhism* (Boston: Shambhala, 2001), xvi.
83. Dingzhi, *Nenghai shangshi zhuan*, 80. Also see Ren Jie, "Jinci si jiafeng."
84. Nenghai's claim of dual sectarian identities, simultaneously affirming the Gelug and Chan transmission, is important for the lineage's expansion and acceptance in the larger Chinese Buddhist community. See Wei Wu, "Making a Tibetan Sect in Twentieth-Century China," *Studies in Chinese Religions* no. 3 (Nov. 2017): 242–257.
85. Zhaotong, an attendant of Nenghai on his second trip to Lhasa, provided many details about Nenghai's activities. See Zhaotong, "Suishi Haigong shangshi huiyilu," 29–40.
86. Dingzhi, *Nenghai shangshi zhuan*, 27.
87. Nenghai was said to receive over four-hundred types of esoteric practices. Dingzhi, *Nenghai shangshi zhuan*, 26–32.
88. See Zhaotong, "Suishi Haigong shangshi huiyilu," 29–40.
89. See Ren Jie, "Jinci si jiafeng."
90. See Ren Jie, "Jinci si jiafeng."
91. His sermons and writings on Vinaya were also based on the Four-Part Vinaya, but he often cited the Gelug works to illuminate the points. See Nenghai, "Qingliang xuji," in *Xianzheng zhuangyan lun qingliang ji* (The notes collected on Mount Wutai on the *Ornament of Realization*) (Shanghai: Shanghai foxue shuju, 1994),

322. About the practice of vinaya by Nenghai's tradition, see Ester Bianchi, "Yi jie wei shi 以戒為師: Theory and Practice of Monastic Discipline in Modern and Contemporary Chinese Buddhism," *Studies in Chinese Religions* 3, no. 2 (2017), 111–141.

92. See Mingxin 明心, "Nenghai fashi zai Beiping shuofa" 能海法師在北平說法 (Master Nenghai is Preaching in Beijing), *Foxue banyue kan* (November 1935): 21; *MFQ* 51: 439.

93. "Shanxi sheng fojiaohui jiang lü fahui dunqing Nenghai fashi jiang sifen lü" 山西省佛教會講律法會敦請能海法師講四分律 (Shanxi Provincial Buddhist Association invited Master Nenghai to preach the Four-Part Vinaya at the Vinaya-Preaching Assembly), *Fojiao zazhi* 佛教雜誌 (Journal of Buddhism) 20 (August 1935): 74–75; *MFQ* 137: 242–243.

94. Daowu was the abbot of Mañjuśrī Monastery; Kuanlin later also became the abbot of Mañjuśrī Monastery. For Changyuan and his promotion of monastic education in Sichuan Buddhism, see Stefania Travagnin, "Monk Changyuan 昌圓 (1879–1945), Nuns in Chengdu, and Revaluation of Local Heritage: Voicing Local (In)Visible Narratives of Modern Sichuan Buddhism," *Journal of Chinese Religions* 49, no. 2 (November 2021): 191–239.

95. See "Fojiao shiren hui zhi Changyuan fashi" 佛教時人彙誌：昌圓法師 (Accounts of contemporary Buddhists, Master Changyuan), *Zhengxin* 10, no. 3 (August 1937): 3; *MFQB* 44: 325.

96. The precept-giving ceremony is one of the most important ecclesiastical rites in Chinese Buddhism; receiving full precepts marks a person's being fully ordained.

97. Well-educated in Chinese and Tibetan Buddhist literature, Longlian not only contributed to the compilation of Nenghai's works, but also presided over the Nunnery of the Iron Statue in Chengdu. See Ester Bianchi, "Subtle Erudition and Compassionate Devotion: Longlian, 'The Most Outstanding Bhikṣuṇī' in Modern China," in *Making Saints in Modern China*, ed. David Ownby, Vincent Goosaert, Ji Zhe (New York: Oxford University Press, 2017), 272–311. For a biography of Longlian, see Qiu Shanshan 裘山山, *Dangdai diyi biqiuni: Longlian fashi zhuan* 當代第一比丘尼：隆蓮法師傳 (The principal nun in contemporary times: Biography of Master Longlian) (Shanghai: Shanghai cishu, 2007).

98. Nenghai had known them when he was serving in the Sichuan army before joining the order. Liu, Pan, and Deng were military leaders and assumed important political roles in Sichuan. Pan Wenhua acted as the mayor of Chongqing from 1929 to 1935, Liu Wenhui became the president of the Sichuan provincial government in 1936, and Deng Xihou was the president of the Sichuan provincial government in 1946.

99. The Pengzhou Stūpa was originally constructed in the fifth century. When thunder hit the stūpa in 1922, half of it collapsed. The stūpa in Luzhou didn't survive. Besides the two in Deyang and Pengzhou, the other extant stūpa was in the Jewel Light Monastery in Xindu. See Nenghai et al., "Pei xiu Deyang Xiaoganta mujuan xu" 培修德陽孝感塔募捐序 (Announcement about raising funds to repair Deyang's Xiaogan Stūpa), *Sichuan fojiao yuekan* 5, no. 2 (February 1935):

11; *MFQ* 58: 392. See also, Nenghai, "Chong jian gu Yizhou Longxing shelita yuan qi" 重建古益州龍興舍利塔緣起 (Conditions of rebuilding the Rising Dragon Stūpa of the ancient Yi Prefecture), *Jue you qing* 9, no. 6 (June 1948): 2–3; *MFQ* 89: 426–427.
100. See "Nenghai fashi hongfa jin xun" 能海法師宏法近訊 (Recent news about Master Nenghai spreading Dharma), *Foxue banyue kan* 168 (November 1938): 7; *MFQB* 65: 7.
101. Dingzhi, "Nenghai shangshi zhuan," 36.
102. Qingding, "Wushang dabao enshi Nenghai lao fashi dexing ji shi" 無上大寶恩師能海老法師德行紀實 (Memoir of the merits of the Ultimate Great Master Nenghai), in *Nenghai shangshi yonghuai lu*, 3–19.
103. Qingding, "Wushang dabao enshi Nenghai lao fashi dexing ji shi," 12.
104. Qingding, "Wushang dabao enshi Nenghai lao fashi dexing ji shi," 9–11; Dingzhi, "Nenghai shangshi zhuan," 36.
105. Qingding, "Wushang dabao enshi Nenghai lao fashi dexing ji shi," 10–12.
106. Dingzhi, "Nenghai shangshi zhuan," 39.
107. Dingzhi, "Nenghai shangshi zhuan," 47.
108. See Ester Bianchi, "Sino-Tibetan Buddhism, Continuities and Discontinuities: The Case of Nenghai's Legacy in the Contemporary Era," in *Chinese and Tibetan Esoteric Buddhism*, ed. Yael Bentor and Meir Shahar (Leiden: Brill, 2017), 300–318.
109. Regarding the translated works of Liu Mingyuan and Ren Jie, see Zhongren, *Nenghai shangshi ji qi dizi shengping shiji huiji*, 43–55.

Conclusion

1. Ashiwa and Wank have shown that, influenced by the discourse of modernity, the Republican and Communist governments both accepted the five world religions as orthodox religions, and the institutionalization of religion and state-making formation supported each other. See Yoshiko Ashiwa and David L. Wank, eds., *Making Religion, Making the State: The Politics of Religion in Modern China* (Stanford, CA: Stanford University Press, 2009), 8–18. Tuttle has also shown that the Republican and Communist governments both recognized the significance of religion in connecting with the Tibetans. See Tuttle, *Tibetan Buddhists in the Making of Modern China* (New York: Columbia University Press, 2005), 230.
2. For an account of Khenpo Jigme Phuntsok, see David Germano, "Re-membering in the Dismembered Body of Tibet: Contemporary Tibetan Visionary Movements in the People's Republic of China," in *Buddhism in Contemporary Tibet: Religious Revival and Cultural Identity*, ed. Melvyn Goldstein and Matthew Kapstein (Berkeley: University of California Press, 1998), 53–95. According to Smyer Yu, by the summer of 2000 approximately two thousand Han Chinese monastic and lay disciples became long-term residents in Larung Academy. See Dan Smyer Yu, *The Spread of Tibetan Buddhism in China: Charisma, Money, Enlightenment* (London; New York: Routledge, 2012), 2.

CONCLUSION

3. In Matthew Kapstein's description, the phenomenon of "shangrilafication" or idealization of Tibet, in spite of criticism in the West, has just begun in China. See Matthew Kapstein, "A Thorn in the Dragon's Side: Tibetan Buddhist Culture in China," in *Governing China's Multiethnic Frontiers*, ed. Morris Rossabi (Seattle: University of Washington Press, 2004), 230–259, particularly 259. For public images of Tibetan culture and the recent development of Tibetan tourism, see Yu, *The Spread of Tibetan Buddhism in China*, 178. Tibetan religious sites were often used to market tourism for the region; see Ashild Kolas, *Tourism and Tibetan Culture in Transition: A Place Called Shangrila* (New York: Routledge, 2008), 106. See also Charlene Makley, "Minzu, Market, and the Mandala: National Exhibitionism and Tibetan Buddhist Revival in Post-Mao China," in *Faiths on Display: Religion, Tourism, and the Chinese State*, ed. Tim Oakes and Donald S. Sutton (Lanham, MD: Rowman and Littlefield Publishers, 2010), 127–156. For the negative impacts of tourism in Tibet, such as creating a fake culture and the ecological problems caused by railroad construction, see Tsering Woeser and Wang Lixiong, *Voices from Tibet: Selected Essays and Reportage* (Honolulu: University of Hawai'i Press, 2014), 19–32.
4. For a discussion of the media and religion in the Chinese Buddhist community, see Stefania Travagnin, ed., *Religion and Media in China: Insights and Case Studies from the Mainland, Taiwan and Hong Kong* (New York: Routledge, 2016); Raoul Birnbaum, "Buddhist China at the Century's Turn," *The China Quarterly* 174 (June 2003): 428–450, especially 448–449.
5. Khenpo Sodargye (1962–), is an example of a Buddhist teacher who uses new media to create transnational Buddhist communities. See Amy Holmes-Tagchungdarpa, "Beyond Living Buddhas, Snowy Mountains and Mighty Mastiffs: Imagining Tibetan Buddhism in Contemporary China's Mediascape," in *Religion and Media in China*, ed., Stefania Travagnin (New York: Routledge, 2016), 256–274.
6. *Lamrim Chenmo* and its abbreviated version *Lamrim Dordu* have become textbooks in Chongqing Buddhist Seminary, Guangdong Buddhist Seminary for the Nuns, Fujian Buddhist Seminary, Minnan Buddhist Seminary, Jiechuang Buddhist Seminary in Jiangsu, and others.
7. The text recorded Pabongkha Rinpoche's lectures over twenty-four days in 1921. Fazun and other Han monks also studied the *lamrim* teaching with him when visiting Lhasa. For an English translation, see Pabongkha Rinpoche, *Liberation in the Palm of Your Hand: A Concise Discourse on the Path to Enlightenment*, ed. Trijang Rinpoche, trans. Michael Richards (Somerville, MA: Wisdom, 2006). See Pabongkha Rinpoche, *Zhangzhong jietuo*, trans. Jiangbo 江波 (Taipei: Baifaluo chubanshe, 2000).
8. For example, in seminaries that included *Lamrim Chenmo* in the curriculum, the learners often focused their study on the beginning chapters instead of reading through the whole book. Their discussion only covered the common Buddhist teachings (especially the Mahāyāna teachings) and ended at the section about bodhisattva practice, skipping the subsequent parts on the more advanced teachings of meditation and wisdom.

[263]

9. Jiqun 濟群 is one of the most productive Buddhist scholars promulgating *lamrim* literature to Chinese Buddhists. He has been teaching at several large seminaries since 1984 and served as president at the Jiechuang Buddhist Institute (Jiechuang Foxue Yanjiusuo 戒幢佛學研究所) in Jiangsu. For a collection of Jiqun's series lectures on the *lamrim* teaching in 2004, see Jiqun, *Puti dadao* 菩提大道 (The great way to enlightenment), 3 vols., (Suzhou: Jiechuang foxue yanjiu suo, 2010). See also Jiqun, *Fofa xiuxue cidi* 佛法修學次第 (Stages of Buddhist practice) (Suzhou: Jiechuang foxue yanjiusuo, 2007); Jiqun, *Daocidi zhi dao* 道次第之道 (The way of the stages of the path) (Suzhou: Jiechuang foxue yanjiusuo, 2009). For Jiqun's reflection on Chinese Buddhist institution, see Jiqun, *Puti lu manman, hanchuan fojiao de sikao* 菩提路漫漫: 漢傳佛教的思考 (The long journey to enlightenment, a reflection on Chinese Buddhism) (Beijing: Zongjiao wenhua chubanshe, 2006).

Bibliography

Abbreviations

T Chinese Buddhist Electronic Text Association. The Taishō Shinshū Daizōkyō 大正新脩大藏經 [Revised version of the Tripiṭaka of the Taishō period]. http://www.cbeta.org/.
HCY *Haichao yin* 海潮音 [*Voice of the Sea Tide*].
MFQ Huang, Xianian 黃夏年 and Li Yangquan 李陽泉, eds. *Minguo fojiao qikan wenxian jicheng* 民國佛教期刊文獻集成 [Collection of Republican-era Buddhist periodical literature]. 204 volumes. Beijing: Quanguo tushuguan wenxian suowei fuzhi zhongxin, 2006.
MFQB Huang, Xianian, ed. *Minguo fojiao qikan wenxian jicheng bubian* 民國佛教期刊文獻集成補編 [Supplementary collection of Republican-era Buddhist periodical literature]. 83 volumes. Beijing: Zhongguo shudian, 2008.
NHSS *Nenghai shangshi quanji* 能海上師全集 [Collective work of Nenghai].
SFJL *Shijie fojiao jushilin linkan* 世界佛教居士林林刊 [Journal of the World Lay Buddhists' Society].
TJJGM *Tianjin jinguangming fahu tekan* 天津金光明法會特刊 [The Special Issue on the Tianjin Golden Light Dharma Ceremony].
X Chinese Buddhist Electronic Text Association. *Xuzangjing* 續藏經 [Supplemental Tripiṭaka]. http://www.cbeta.org/.

Canonical Works

Benkenmitsu nikyōron 弁顯密二教論 [Distinguishing the two teachings of the exoteric and esoteric]. Kūkai 空海. T no. 2427.

BIBLIOGRAPHY

Da bore boluomiduo jing 大般若波羅蜜多經 [Skt. Mahāprajñāpāramitā Sūtra, Sutra of the Wisdom of Great Perfection]. Translated by Xuanzang. *T* no. 220.

Dapiluzhena chengfo jing shu 大毘盧遮那成佛經疏 [Commentary on the Mahāvairocana Sūtra]. Yixing 一行. *T* no. 1796.

Dapiluzhena chengfo shenbian jiachi jing 大毘盧遮那成佛神變加持經 [Mahāvairocana Sūtra]. Translated by Śubhakarasiṃha 善無畏 and Yixing. *T* no. 848.

Dapiluzhena jing yan mi chao 大毗盧遮那經演密鈔 [Exegesis on the Mahāvairocana Sūtra]. Jueyuan 覺苑. *X* no. 439.

Dasheng qixin lun 大乘起信論 [Treatise of the awakening of Mahāyāna faith]. Translated by Zhendi 眞諦 [Skt. Paramārtha, 499–569]. *T* no. 1666.

Himitsu mandara jūjū shinron 秘密曼荼羅十住心論 [The ten abiding stages of mind according to the secret mandalas]. Kūkai. *T* no. 2425.

Huayan jing 華嚴經 [Skt. Avataṃsaka Sūtra; Flower Ornament Sutra]. Translated by Śikṣānanda 實叉難陀. *T* no. 278.

Huayan jing shu 華嚴經疏 [Commentary on the Avataṃsaka Sūtra]. Chengguan 澄觀. *T* no. 1735.

Huayan shu xu 華嚴疏序 [The preface to commentary on the Avataṃsaka Sūtra]. Chengguan. *X* no. 227.

Huayan wujiao zhang 華嚴五教章 [The essay on the five teachings of Huayan]. Fazang 法藏. *T* no. 1866.

Jingangding yiqie rulai zhenshi she dasheng xianzheng dajiaowang jing 金剛頂一切如來真實攝大乘現證大教王經 [Vajraśekhara Sūtra]. Translated by Amoghavajra 不空. *T* 865.

Jinguangming jing 金光明經 [The Sutra of Golden Light]. *T* no. 245.

Jushe lun 俱舍論 [Abhidharma-kośa]. *T* no. 1558.

Liangbu dafa xiangcheng shizi fufa ji 兩部大法相承師資付法記 [Record of the transmission of the two great tantras]. Haiyun 海雲. *T* no. 2081.

Miaofa lianhua jing 妙法蓮華經 [Saddharmapuṇḍarīka Sūtra; The Lotus Sutra]. Translated by Kumārajīva. *T* no. 262.

Mohe zhiguan 摩訶止觀 [The great calming and contemplation]. Zhiyi 智顗. *T* no. 1911.

Pusa yingluo benye jing 菩薩瓔珞本業經 [Sutra of the primary activities that serve as necklaces of the bodhisattvas]. *T* no. 1485.

Renwang huguo bore boluomi jing 仁王護國般若波羅密經 [Prajñāpāramitā Sūtra of Humane Kings and Protection of Nation]. *T* no. 245.

Rui xi ye jing 蕤呬耶經 [Guhya Sūtra]. Translated by Amoghavajra. *T* no. 897.

Shelifo a pi tan lun 舍利弗阿毗曇論 [Śāriputrābhidharma śāstra]. *T* no. 1548.

Shidi jing lun 十地經論 [Treatise of the Daśabhūmika Sūtra]. *T* no. 1522.

Shi ji jing 世記經 [Accounts of the world]. *T* no. 1.

Sokushin jōbutsugi 即身成佛義 [Treatise on becoming Buddha in this very body]. Kūkai. *T* no. 2428.

Tiantai si jiao yi 天臺四教儀 [Outline of the Tiantai fourfold teachings]. Recorded by Diguan 諦觀. *T* no. 1931.

Wudeng huiyuan 五燈會元 [The compendium of five lamps]. Edited by Puji. *X* no. 1565.

Youposai jie jing 優婆塞戒經 [Upāsaka-śīla Sūtra, The Sutra of Upāsaka precepts]. Translated by Dharmakṣema 曇無讖. *T* no. 1488.

Yuqie shidi lun 瑜伽師地論 [Yogacārabhūmi śāstra; Discourse on the stages of concentration practice]. Translated by Xuanzang. *T* no. 1579.

Zhenzhou Linji Huizhao chanshi yulu 鎮州臨濟慧照禪師語錄 [Discourses of Chan Master Linji Huizhao from the prefecture of Zhen]. *T* no. 1985.

Zuo chan sanmei jing 坐禪三昧經 [The Sutra on Samādhi of Sitting Meditation]. *T* no. 614.

Other Primary Works

"Anhui zhengshou jingchan mixin juan renwei yiduan huozhong" 安徽徵收經懺迷信捐認為異端惑眾 [Anhui levied tax on funeral rites and superstition for the confusion caused to the public by the heterodoxy]. *Xiandai sengqie* 2, nos. 43–44 (June 1930): 81–82; *MFQB* 39: 273–274.

Atiśa. *Atisha's Lamp for the Path to Enlightenment*. Translated by Sonam Rinchen and Ruth Sonam. Ithaca, NY: Snow Lion, 1997.

"Bai fashi guanding chuanfa lu" 白法師灌頂傳法錄 [The record of Master Bai's initiation and transmission of Dharma]. In *Tianjin jinguangming fahui tekan* 天津金光明法會特刊 [Special issue on the Tianjin Golden Light Ceremony, *TJJGM*]. Edited by Jinguangming fahui editorial committee, 7–27. Tianjin: Tianjin yinshua gongsi, 1928; *MFQB* 15: 127–142.

"Bai fashi hongfa ji" 白法師弘法記 [A Record of Master Bai's Dissemination of Dharma]. In *TJJGM*, 1–4; *MFQB* 15: 263–264.

"Bai Lama li xiang qingxing" 白喇嘛蒞湘情形 [The situation of Lama Bai's visit to Hunan]. *Shenbao* 申報, February 2, 1926.

"Bai Lama xiufa zhong zhi canguanji" 白喇嘛修法中之參觀記 [A record of visiting Lama Bai in performing Dharma], in *TJJGM*, 6–7; *MFQB* 15: 268–269.

"Bai Lama yuanji" 白喇嘛圓寂 [Bai Lama passed away], *Shenbao*, August 9, 1929.

"Banchan chu jing fu Hang" 班禪出京赴杭 [The Panchen Lama left Beijing toward Hangzhou]. *Haichao yin* 海潮音 (*Voice of the Sea Tide*, *HCY*) 6, no. 4 (April 1925): 20–21; *MFQ* 162: 54–55.

"Banchan Dashi lilin neidi hou gong jian jiuci miaode shilun jingang fahui" 班禪大師蒞內地後共建九次妙德時輪金剛法會 [Panchen Lama conducted Kālacakra Vajra Dharma-Assembly for nine times after reaching China proper]. *Xichui Xuanhuashi gongshu yuekan* 西陲宣化使公署月刊 [Monthly of the Office of the Propagation Envoy to the Western Borderland] 1, nos. 7–8 (October 1936): 190; *MFQB* 82: 200.

"Banchan di Hu xu zhi" 班禪抵滬續誌 [The second record of Panchen's visit to Shanghai]. *HCY* 6, no. 5 (May 1925): 27–30; *MFQ* 162: 61–64.

"Banchan dian fu Sun Chuanfang" 班禪電覆孫傳芳 [Banchan's telegram reply to Sun Chuanfang]. *HCY* 6, no. 4 (April 1925): 14; *MFQ* 162: 48.

"Banchan fo Yingtai chuanfa ji" 班禪佛瀛台傳法記 [A record of Panchen's transmission of Dharma at Yingtai]. *Xindeng* 心燈 [The lamp for heart], no. 19 (November 1926): 99–101; *MFQB* 16: 99–101.

"Banchan fu Putuo zhi shengkuang" 班禪赴普陀之盛況 [The grand reception of Panchen at Putuo]. *HCY* 6, no. 5 (May 1925): 13; *MFQ* 162: 177.

"Banchan jin jian Duan zhizheng" 班禪覲見段執政 [The Panchen Lama met with Chief Executive Duan], *HCY* 6, no. 3 (April 1925): 21–22; *MFQ*161: 457–458.

"Banchan zhi xiao mi zhan huo tan" 班禪之消弭戰禍談 [The Panchen Lama's talk on dispersing the calamity of war]. *HCY* 6, no. 4 (April 1925): 13–14; *MFQ* 162: 47–48.

"Banchan zhu zhong guowen zhi zhenxiang" 班禪注重國文之真象 [The truth about Panchen Lama's emphasis on the national script]. *HCY* 6, no. 4 (April 1925): 14–15; *MFQ* 162: 48–49.

"Banchan zhuanche guo Ji" 班禪專車過濟 [The Panchen Lama's special train passed through Jinan]. *HCY* 6, no. 4 (April 1925): 21–22; *MFQ* 162: 55–56.

"Beijing shi guanli Yiheyuan shiwu suo guanyu Ding Shuqiu gouzhi dimu de cheng ji Beijing Wanshou shan Yuchun yuan jushi lin zuzhi dagang" 北京市管理頤和園事務所關於丁淑秋購置地畝的呈及北京萬壽山毓春園居士林組織大綱 [The administrative office of Summer Palace in Beijing, about Ding Shuqiu's request to purchase land and the organization principles of the Lay Society in the Garden of Nurturing Spring on Mount of Longevity], April 1928, J021-001-00012, Beijing Municipal Archives.

"Beijing zangwen xueyuan jiang zhaokao" 北京藏文學院將招考 [Entrance examination of Beijing Tibetan College]. *Foyin* 佛音 (Voice of Buddhism) 1, nos. 8–9 (November 1924): 4; *MFQ* 145: 374.

"Beijing zangwen xueyuan zhi faqi" 北京藏文學院之發起 [The founding of Beijing Tibetan College]. *SFJL*, no. 7 (October 1924): 2–3; *MFQB* 8: 294–295.

"Beiping shilun jingang fahui ji" 北平時輪金剛法會紀 [Report of the Kālacakra Vajra Dharma-Assembly at Beiping]. *HCY* 13, no. 12 (December 1932): 169–171; *MFQ* 182: 467–469.

"Benhui zhangchen" 本會章程 [Principles of our society]. *Shideng foxue yuekan*, no. 1 (July 1934): 51; *MFQB* 48: 239.

"Bingzi xizai fahui tekan" 丙子息災法會特刊 [Special issue on the Assembly of Pacifying Calamity in 1936]. *Foxue banyuekan*, no.127 (May 1936): 1–7; *MFQ* 52: 243–249.

"Bingzi xizai fahui yuanqi" 丙子息災法會緣起 [Origin of the Calamity-Pacifying Dharma Assembly in 1936]. *Foxue banyue kan* 佛學半月刊 [Buddhist study semimonthly], no. 126 (May 1936): 243–249; *MFQ* 52: 243–249.

Changxing 常惺. "Shilun fahui quan faqi wen" 時輪法會勸發起文 [Vow to initiate the Kālacakra Dharma Ceremony]. *HCY* 12, no. 12 (December 1931): 88–93; *MFQ* 179: 480–485.

Chaoyi 超一. "Puti dao cidi lun ji lue song" 菩提道次第論極略頌 [The succinct verses from *Lamrim Chenmo*]. *HCY* 14, no. 2 (February 1933): 35–36; *MFQ* 183: 165–166.

———. "Puti dao cidi lun she song ke pan" 菩提道次第論攝頌科判 [An outline of the verses of *Lamrim Chenmo*]. *HCY* 14, no. 2 (February 1933): 169–170; *MFQ* 183: 169–170.

———. "Putuo si Chaoyi shang Taixu dashi shu" 普陀寺超一上太虛大師書 [Letter to Master Taixu from Monk Chaoyi of Putuo Temple]. *HCY* 13, no. 1 (January 1932): 115–117; *MFQ* 180: 125–127.

Chen Lidian 陳歷典. "Gengwu Chaozhou kaitan guanding ji" 庚午潮州開壇灌頂記 [The consecration in Chaozhou in 1930]. In *Mijiao jiangxi lu* 密教講習錄 [Records of sermons about esotericism]. Vol. 5, 265–266. Edited by Yu Ruihua. Beijing: Huaxia chubanshe, 2009.

———. "Yuanwu jushi Wang Hongyuan xiansheng zhi lishi" 圓五居士王弘願先生之歷史 [Biography of layman Wang Hongyuan]. In *Mijiao jiangxi lu* [Records of sermons about esotericism]. Vol. 5, 52–54.

Chen Xueqin 陳學勤. "Chaoyi shangshi sishi nian ji lue" 超一上師四十年紀略 [Forty years of Guru Chaoyi]. *Fohaideng* 佛海燈 [Light over the Buddhist ocean] 2, no. 9–10 (August 1937): 4–8; *MFQ* 79: 406–410.

Cheng Zhai'an 程宅安. *Mizong yaoyi* 密宗要義 [Essentials of esotericism]. 1929. Reprint. Chengdu: Bashu shushe, 2011.

Chengdu Department of Religious Affairs. "Chengdu Mianzhu dengdi guanyu fodaojiao simiao daoguan qingkuang diaocha baogao" 成都綿竹等地關於佛道教寺廟道觀情況調查報告 [Survey of the Buddhist and Daoist temples in Chengdu and Mianzhu], January 19, 1960, Sichuan Provincial Archives, Jianchuan 051-01-314.

Chenkong 塵空. "Wutaishan Guangji maopeng zhi guoqu yu xianzai" 五臺山廣濟茅蓬之過去與現在 [The past and present of the Thatched Cottage of Vast Salvation at Mount Wutai]. *HCY* 17, no.7 (July 1936): 79–82; *MFQ* 194: 235–238.

Chenyin 塵隱. "Du da Haichaoyin mizong wenti zhuanhao fasheng zhi ganxiang" 讀答海潮音密宗問題專號發生之感想 [My thought on reply to the special issue about esotericism]. *HCY* 15, no. 6 (June 1934); *MFQ* 187: 201–210.

"Chongxiu Yonghegong dianyu gongcheng jihua shu" 重修雍和宮殿宇工程計畫書 [Project proposal to rebuild the halls in Yonghe Temple]. In *TJJGM*, 4–9; *MFQB* 15: 298–303.

"Chongxiu Yonghegong yuanqi" 重修雍和宮緣起 [Origin of rebuilding Yonghe Temple]. In *TJJGM*, 1–2; *MFQB* 15: 295–296.

Chisong 持松. "Xian mi jiao heng" 賢密教衡 [Evaluation of the Huayan and esoteric teachings]. *HCY* 9, no. 4 (May 1928): 1–11; *MFQ* 170: 127–137.

———. "Xianmi jiao heng" 賢密教衡 [Evaluation of the Huayan and esoteric teachings]. *HCY* 9, no. 6 (July 1928): 31–42; *MFQ* 170: 389–400.

———. "Xianmi jiao heng shi huo" 賢密教衡釋惑 [Clarifications on the evaluation of Huayan and esoteric teachings]. *HCY* 10, no. 3 (April 1929): 1–7; *MFQ* 172: 349–354.

Dagang 大剛. "Fojiao zangwen xueyuan Shi Dagang zhi Daofu xian zhishi Ouyang Fushan shu" 佛教藏文學院釋大剛致道孚縣知事歐陽莆杉書 [Letter from Dagang of Tibetan College to the magistrate Ouyang Fushan of the Daofu County]. *Fohua xunkan* 佛化旬刊 [Ten-day Journal of Buddhism], no. 91 (November 1927): 8; *MFQ* 17: 364.

Dai Jitao 戴季陶. "Renwang huguo fahui fayuan wen" 仁王護國法會發願文 [Vows for the Humane Kings Country-Protection Dharma-Assembly]. In *Dai Jitao xiansheng wencun* 戴季陶先生文存 [Extant writings of Dai Jitao]. Vol. 3. Edited by Chen Tianxi, 1176–1177. Taipei: Zhongguo guomingdang zhongyang weiyuanhui, 1959.

———. "Zhi Henan Li zhuxi dian" 致河南李主席電 [Telegram to Henan's Chairman Li]. In *Dai Jitao xiansheng wencun*. Vol. 3, 1293.

"Dayong fashi yuanji" 大勇法師圓寂 [The passing away of Venerable Dayong]. *Xiandai sengqie* 現代僧伽 [Modern sangha], nos. 43–44 (June 1930): 79; *MFQB* 39: 271.

Dayong 大勇. "Da Taixu fashi shu er" 答太虛法師書二 [Second letter in reply to Master Taixu]. *HCY* 4, no. 9 (September 1924): 1–4.

———. "Dayong fashi zhi Hu Zihu Yang Mingchen liang xiansheng shu" 大勇法師致胡子笏楊明塵兩先生書 [Letter from Master Dayong to Hu Zhihu and Yang Mingchen]. *SFJL* no. 23 (1929): 3–6; *MFQB* 10: 273–276.

———. "Dayong fashi zi Xikang zhi Beijing liuzang xuefa houyuan hui ganshi Hu Zihu jushi han" 大勇法師自西康致北京留藏學法後援會幹事胡子笏居士函 [Letter from Master Dayong in Xikang to Hu Zihu, the manager of Beijing Supporters' Association for the Study at Tibet]. *SFJL*, no. 14 (October 1926): 2–3; *MFQB* 9: 300–301.

———. "Dayong sheli fu Xianyin fashi han" 大勇闍梨覆顯蔭法師函 [Ācārya Dayong's reply to Master Xianyin]. *SFJL*, no. 7 (August 1924): 2; *MFQB* 8: 304.

———. "Fojiao zangwen xueyuan Dayong fashi zi Xikang zhi Sichuan foxuehui tongren han" 佛教藏文學院大勇法師自西康致四川佛學會同仁函 [Letter from Venerable Dayong of Tibetan College in western Kham to colleagues in Sichuan Buddhist Society]. *SFJL*, no. 14 (October 1926): 1–2; *MFQB* 9: 299–300.

———. "Fojiao zangwen xueyuan yuanzhang Shi Dayong you Ganzi zhi Beijing Hu Zihu Yang Mingchen liang xiansheng shu" 佛教藏文學院院長釋大勇由甘孜致北京胡子笏楊明塵兩先生書 [A letter from the principal Shi Dayong of Tibetan College from Ganzi to Mr. Hu Zihu and Mr. Yang Mingchen in Beijing]. *Fohua xunkan*, no. 102 (February 1928): 8; *MFQ* 17: 450.

———. "Fojiao zangwen xueyuan yuanzhang Shi Dayong you Ganzi zhi Beijing Hu Zihu Yang Mingchen liang xiansheng shu xu qian" 佛教藏文學院院長釋大勇由甘孜致北京胡子笏楊明塵兩先生書（續前）[A letter from the principal Shi Dayong of Tibetan College from Ganzi to Mr. Hu Zihu and Mr. Yang Mingchen in Beijing (part 2)]. *Fohua xunkan*, no. 101 (February 1928): 8; *MFQ* 17: 442.

———. "Liuxue Riben mizong zhi baogao" 留學日本密宗之報告 [Reports about studying esoteric Buddhism in Japan]. *HCY* 3, no. 9 (November 1922): 2; *MFQ* 154: 314.

———. "Liuxue Riben Zhenyan zong zhi tongxin" 留學日本真言宗之通信 [Reports about study in Japanese Shingon school]. *HCY* 4, no. 8 (September 1924): 1–2; *MFQ* 157: 61–62.

Deng Jiquan 鄧繼佺. "Tianjin jinguangming fahui tebie bian yan" 天津金光明法會特別弁言 [Preface to the special issue on the Tianjin Golden Light Dharma Ceremony]. In *TJJGM*, 1–3; *MFQB* 15: 85–87.

Ding Wenjun 丁文雋. "Beiping xiaoxi" 北平消息 [News about Beijing]. *SFJL*, no. 30 (September 1931): 10; *MFQB* 11: 322.

———. "Hu Zihu jushi zhuan" 胡子笏居士傳 [Biography of Layman Hu Zihu]. *Jue youqing* 覺有情 [Awaken the sentient beings], nos. 107–108 (February 1944): 13–14; *MFQB* 62: 173–174.

Du Tengying 杜騰英. "Ji Wang Hongyuan jushi zhi jiating" 記王弘願居士之家庭 [Layman Wang Hongyuan's family]. *Shideng foxue yuekan*, no. 3 (September 1934), 12–13; *MFQB* 48: 386–387.

Duo Linque 多僯卻. "*Shishi xinbao* lun shilun jingang fahui" 時事新報論時輪金剛法會 [Comments on *Shishi xinbao* about the Kālacakra Vajra Dharma-Assembly]. *HCY* 15, no. 4 (December 1934): 1–4; *MFQ* 186: 451–454.

Duojie Jueba 多傑覺拔 and Zhang Xinruo 張心若. *Misheng fahai* 密乘法海 [The Dharma ocean of the esoteric vehicle]. 1930. Reprint. Taipei: Xinwenfeng chuban gongsi, 1987.

Esler, Joshua. *Tibetan Buddhism among Han Chinese: Mediation and Superscription of the Tibetan Tradition in Contemporary Chinese Society.* Lanham, MD: Lexington Press, 2020.

Evans-Wentz, Walter. *The Tibetan Book of the Dead.* Oxford: Oxford University Press, 1927.

———. *Tibetan Yoga and Secret Doctrines.* London: Oxford University Press, 1935.

———. "Xizang fabao guanzhu" 西藏法寶貫珠 [String of jewels in Tibetan Buddhist teachings]. Translated by Zhao Hongzhu 趙洪鑄. *HCY* 28, no.3 (March 1947): 21–23; *MFQ* 203: 317–319.

———. *Zhongyin jiudu mifa* 中陰救度密法 [Secret teaching of bardo liberation]. Translated by Zhang Miaoding 張妙定. Shashi, Hubei: wenda kanyinshe, 1936. Reprint, *Zhongyin jiudu mifa.* Taipei: Leming fayuan, 1992. Originally published as *The Tibetan Book of the Dead.* Oxford: Oxford University Press, 1927.

———. *Zhongyou wenjiao dedu mifa* 中有聞教得度密法 [Secret teaching of liberation through hearing during the intermediate state]. Translated by Zhao Hongzhu. 1945. Reprint. Taipei: Xinwenfeng chubanshe, 1980. Originally published as *The Tibetan Book of the Dead.* Oxford: Oxford University Press, 1927.

Fandeng 梵燈. "Song zangwen xueyuan quanti liuxue Xizang xu" 送藏文學院全體留學西藏序 [Seeing off the group from Tibetan College to study in Tibet]. *SFJL*, no. 14 (October 1926): 5–6; *MFQB* 9: 319–320.

Fazun. "Cong Xizang fojiao xuepai xingshuai de yanbian shuodao Zhongguo fojiao de jianli" 從西藏佛教學派興衰的演變說到中國佛教的建立 [From the changing history of Tibetan scholasticism to the establishment of Chinese Buddhism]. In *Fazun fashi foxue lunwen ji* [Collected works of Buddhist studies of Fazun]. Edited by Lü Tiegang 呂鉄鋼 and Hu Heping 胡和平. Beijing: Zhongguo fojiao wenhua yanjiusuo, 1990. 18–30.

———. *Fazun fashi foxue lunwenji* 法尊法師佛學論文集 [Collected works of Buddhist studies of Fazun]. Edited by Lü Tiegang and Hu Heping. Beijing: Zhongguo fojiao wenhua yanjiusuo, 1990.

———. *Fazun fashi yiwenji* 法尊法師譯文集 [Collected translated works of Fazun]. Edited by Lü Tiegang, Hu Heping, and Wu Limin 吳立民. Hongkong: Zhongguo fojiao wenhua chuban youxian gongsi, 2000.

———. "Fazun fashi zixu" 法尊法師自敘 [Autobiography of Fazun]. In Fazun, *Fazun fashi foxue lunwen ji*, 372–376.

———. "Lue shu Taixu dashi zhi beiyuan ji weiye" 略述太虛大師之悲願及偉業 [A brief account of the compassionate wishes and the great endeavor of Master Taixu]. In Fazun, *Fazun fashi foxue lunwen ji*, 249–357.

———. "Ping Zang mi da wen" 評藏密答問 [Comments on answers to questions about Tibetan esotericism]. *HCY* 16, no. 6 (June 1935): 20–25; *MFQ* 190: 440–445.

———. "Puti dao cidi guanglun de zaozuo fanyi neirong he tijie" 菩提道次第廣論的造作、翻譯、內容和題解 [The composition, translation, content, and title of *Lamrim Chenmo*]. In Fazun, *Fazun fashi foxue lunwen ji*, 259–265.

———. "Zhuzhe ru Zang de jingguo" 著者入藏的經過 [The writer's experience in entering Tibet]. In Fazun, *Fazun fashi foxue lunwenji*, 358–371.

———. "Zongkaba dashi de puti dao cidi lun" 宗喀巴大師的《菩提道次第論》[Master Tsongkhapa's *Lamrim Chenmo*]. In Fazun, *Fazun fashi foxue lunwen ji*, 266–280.

Feng Zhongxi 馮重熙. "Renshen Guangzhou kaitan ji" 壬申廣州開壇記 [Record of the opening of the altar in Guangzhou in 1932]. In *Mijiao jiangxi lu* [Records of sermons about esotericism]. Edited by Yu Ruihua. Vol. 5, 278–297. Beijing: Huaxia chubanshe, 2009.

"Fojiao jiguang diaocha lu" 佛教機關調查錄 [Survey of Buddhist organizations]. *SFJL*, no. 20 (August 1928): 16–21; *MFQB* 10: 96–101.

———. *SFJL*, no. 21, (November 1928): 11–14; *MFQB* 10: 211–214.

———. *SFJL*, no. 23 (1929): 14–19; *MFQB* 10: 322–327.

"Fojiao shiren hui zhi Changyuan fashi" 佛教時人彙誌：昌圓法師 [Accounts of contemporary Buddhists, Master Changyuan]. *Zhengxin* 10, no. 3 (August 1937): 3; *MFQB* 44: 325.

"Fojiao zangwen xueyuan quanti jinjian Banchan ji" 佛教藏文學院全體覲見班禪記 [Record on all people of Tibetan College's meeting with the Panchen Lama]. *HCY* 15, no. 4 (April 1925): 12–14; *MFQ* 161: 448–450.

"Fojiao zangwen xueyuan zai Kang gaizu ji di Zang fenzhu xiuxue zhi guiyue" 佛教藏文學院在康改組及抵藏分住修學之規約 [Regulation on the reorganization of Tibetan College in Kham and the separate residence and study in Tibet]. *Sichuan fojiao xunkan* 四川佛教旬刊 [Ten-day journal of Sichuan Buddhism], no. 51 (October 1926): 3; *MFQ* 128: 258.

"Gedi fashi jiangjing yishu" 各地法師講經一束 [Information about masters' lectures in different places]. *HCY* 18, no. 6 (June 1937): 97; *MFQ* 197: 105–107.

"Ge jiao daibiao can ye Banchan" 各教代表參謁班禪 [Different religious representatives paid a visit to Banchan]. *HCY* 6, no. 4 (April 1925): 17–18; *MFQ* 162: 51–52.

Gonda Raifu. "Fu Wang Hongyuan jushi han" 復王弘願居士函 [Reply to Wang Hongyuan]. In *Mijiao jiangxi lu* [Records of sermons about esotericism], vol. 5, 86.

———. *Mizong gangyao* 密宗綱要 [The essentials of esoteric Buddhism]. Translated by Wang Hongyuan. 1919. Reprint. Taipei: Tianhua chuban she, 1999.

"Gong tan foxiang biao fa zhi yiyi" 壇供佛像表法之意義 [The meanings of the Dharma expressed in the Buddha statues on the altar]. In *TJJGM*, 4–5; *MFQB* 15: 192–193.

"Gongga Shangshi di Kunming jiangjing xinzhong zhongduo" 貢噶上師抵昆明講經信眾眾多 [Guru Gangkar arrived in Kunming and his lecture attracted a mass]. *Jueyouqing*, no. 9 (September 1948): 25; *MFQB* 90: 25.

Guangwen 廣文. "Nenghai fashi de yili" 能海法師的毅力 [Perseverance of Nenghai]. *Sichuan fojiao yuekan* 8, no.3 (March 1938): 2; *MFQ* 60: 2.

Hanzang jiaoliyuan li'an wenjian huibian 漢藏教理院立案文件彙編 [Collected material of the Sino-Tibetan Buddhist Institute]. Chongqing: Hanzang jiaoli yuan, 1936.

Hengyan 恆演. "Dayong a she li bing zhuanshi hu du tu hezhuan" 大勇阿闍黎並轉世呼都圖合傳 [Joint biographies of Ācārya Dayong and his reincarnation]. *HCY* 27, no. 9 (September 1946): 28–29; *MFQ* 203: 68–69.

Hu Shuibo 胡水波. "Shilun jingang fahui xunli" 時輪金剛法會巡禮 [Visit the Kālacakra Vajra Dharma-Assembly]. *Xinsheng zhoukan* 新生週刊 [Journal of new life] 1, no. 40 (April 1934): 269–271.

"Hu Zihu shiji" 胡子笏示寂 [Obituary of Hu Zihu]. *Jue youqing*, nos. 105–106 (January 1944): 16; *MFQB* 62: 160.

"Huabei jushilin guanyu chengbao gaixuan zhiyuan qingxing jushilin zhangcheng de chengwen ji shehuiju de pishi" 華北居士林關於呈報改選職員情形居士林章程的

BIBLIOGRAPHY

呈文及社會局的批示 [The Huabei Lay Buddhist Society's report about reelection of officers, organization principles, and reply from the bureau of the society], July 1938, J002-003-00828, Beijing Municipal Archives.

"Huabei jushilin qingde Zongkaba dashi zhenxiang" 華北居士林請得宗喀巴大師真像 [Huabei Lay Buddhist Society obtained a painting of the true image of Master Tsongkhapa]. *Foxue banyuekan*, no. 121 (February 1936), 20; MFQ 52: 110.

Huang Jianliu 黃健六. "Na xueli lai yanjiu mixin juan" 拿學理來研究迷信捐 [Use doctrines to study superstition tax]. *SFJL* 26 (August 1930): 7–17; MFQB 11: 41–51.

Huiding 慧定. "Zang mi da wen" 藏密答問 [Answers to questions about Tibetan esotericism]. *Foxue banyuekan*, no. 94 (January 1935): 5–8; MFQ 50: 249–252.

———. "Zang mi da wen." *Foxue banyuekan*, no. 95 (January 1935): 6–8; MFQ 50: 278–280.

———. "Zang mi da wen." *Foxue banyuekan*, no. 106 (July 1935): 14–15; MFQ 51: 148.

Huiguan 慧觀. "Bai Lama lai He zhi xingxing sese" 白喇嘛來禾之形形色色 [Miscellaneous records of Lama Bai's visit to Jiaxing]. *Shenbao*, June 28, 1926.

———. "Jiaxing choubei huanying Bai Lama suowen" 嘉興籌備歡迎白喇嘛瑣聞 [Bits of news on the preparation of the reception of Lama Bai at Jiaxing]. *Dayun*, no. 69 (July 1926): 54–55.

Huizhong 會中. "Song tongyuan Dagang Wuyi fashi deng ru Beijing fojiao zangwen xueyuan" 送同院大剛晤一法師等入北京佛教藏文學院 [Seeing classmates Dagang and Wuyi to Tibetan College in Beijing]. *HCY* 6, no. 2 (March 1925): 9–10; MFQ 161: 345–346.

Huweng 湖翁. "Ting Nenghai fashi jiangyan hou" 聽能海法師講演後 [Reflection on Master Nenghai's lecture]. *Chuanbian jikan* 川邊季刊 [Sichuan border quarterly] 5, no 1, (April 1926): 18–20.

"Ji shilun jingang fahui" 紀時輪金剛法會 [Report on the Kālacakra Vajra Dharma-Assembly]. *Foxue Banyuekan* 42 (November 1932): 239; MFQ 47: 473–474.

"Jiang weiyuan zhang chuxi zhixun" 蔣委員長出席致訓 [Chairman Chiang attended and gave instruction]. *Shishi xinbao*, June 26, 1935.

Jiang Weiqiao 蔣維喬. "Zhang Kecheng xiansheng zhuan" 張克誠先生傳 [Biography of Zhang Kecheng]. *HCY* 3, no. 2 (August 1922): 3–4.

"Jiaxing 嘉興." *Shenbao*, June 22, 1926.

"Jingang huguo xizai fahui yuanqi" 金剛護國息災法會緣起 [Origin of the Vajra Country-Protection Dharma Assembly]. *Zhengxin* 正信 [True belief] 1, no. 2 (April 1932): 6; MFQB 43: 22.

Jinghuan 景桓. "Bai Puren dashi shi lue" 白普仁大師事略 [About Master Bai Puren]. *Dayun* 大雲 [Great cloud], no. 67 (May 1926): 37–44; MFQ 11: 39–46.

"Jinguangming hui zhi faqi" 金光明會之發起 [The Initiation of the Golden Light Ceremony]. *Shenbao*, July 20, 1925.

"Jinsheng tuoluoni xizai daochang lai jian" 金勝陀羅尼息災道場來件 [Report from Jinsheng Dhāraṇī Calamity-Pacifying place of rituals]. Special Issue, *Chenzhong* 晨鐘 [Morning bell], no. 3 (May 1928): 1–3; MFQB 32: 489–491.

Kaneyama Bokushō. "Hongfa Dashi zhi fojiao guan" 弘法大師之佛教觀 [Master Kūkai's View on Buddhism]. Translated by Tang Qingliang. In *Haichao yin wenku* 海潮音文庫 [Collection of *Voice of the Sea Tide*]. Vol. 2, 54. Edited by Taixu, Fan Gunong 范古農, and Ciren Shi Zhuren 慈忍室主人. Tapei: xinwenfeng chubanshe, 1985.

Kang Jiyao 康寄遙. "Pochu mixin" 破除迷信 [Discard Superstition]. *Fohua suikan* 佛化隨刊 [Jottings of Buddhism], nos. 10–11 (December 1928): 2–8; *MFQB* 22: 318–324.

———. "Qidao xizai, lun qidao" 祈禱息災: 論祈禱 [Pray for pacifying disaster, about praying]. *Dayun*, no. 99 (July 1930): 7–10; *MFQB* 21: 305–308.

"Kaifeng foxueyuan xingjiang chengli" 開封佛學院行將成立 [The founding of the Kaifeng Seminary]. *Xiandai sengqie* 現代僧伽 [Modern sangha] 4, no. 2 (June 1931): 185; *MFQ* 67: 101.

Kuanlin 寬霖. "Wenshu yuan gaikuang" 文殊院概況 [Overview of Mañjuśrī Monastery], January 22, 1951, Sichuan Provincial Archives, Jianchuan 050-01-197.

Kūkai 空海. *On the Differences Between the Exoteric and Esoteric Teachings*. Translated by Rolf Giebel and Dale Todaro. Moraga, CA: Bukkyō Dendō Kyōkai, 2004.

Li Jinxi 黎錦熙. "Zhongyou wenjiao dedu mifa xu" 中有聞教得度密法序 [Preface to the Liberation through hearing during the intermediate state]. *Wenjiao congkan* 文教叢刊 [Collection of culture and education] 1, nos. 3–4 (December 1945): 116–117; *MFQ* 99: 342–343.

Liaokong 了空. "Hubei sheng fojiao hui changwei Xiaolan deng cheng" 湖北省佛教會常委曉嵐等呈 [Hubei Provincial Buddhist Association's petition]. *Zhongguo fojiaohui yuekan* 中國佛教會月刊 [Chinese Buddhist Association monthly], nos. 5–6 (December 1929): 107.

Liu Fuqing 劉複頃. "Amituofo Dai Chuanxian" 阿彌陀佛戴傳賢 [Amitābha Dai Chuanxian]. *Shishi xinbao*, May 16, 1934.

Liu Xianxiu 劉顯休. "Liu Xianxiu jushi laihan" 劉顯休居士來函 [Letter from Liu Xianxiu]. *HCY* 6, no. 1 (March 1925): 4–5; *MFQ* 161: 228–229.

Liu Zuwu 劉祖武 and Qian Boli 錢波麗. "Beican shijie de yizhe" 《悲慘世界》的譯者 [Translators of *Les Misérables*], *Wenhui bao* 文匯報, July 10, 2001.

Maitreya. *Xianguan zhuangyan lun* 現觀莊嚴論 [Ornament of realization]. Translated by Fazun. Chongqing: Hanzang jiaoli yuan, 1937.

Manhua 曼華. "Dagui" 打鬼 [Beating the ghosts]. *Shishi xinbao*, September 2, 1936.

———. "Xizai fahui kai tan" 息災法會開壇 [The opening of the platform for the Calamity-Pacifying Ceremony]. *Shishi xinbao*, May 17, 1933.

Manshu Jiedi 曼殊揭諦. "Yu Wang Hongyuan lun mijiao shu" 與王弘願論密教書 [Discussion with Wang Hongyuan about esotericism]. *HCY* 14, no. 2 (February 1933): 79–84; *MFQ* 183: 209–214.

Miaoguang 妙光. "Duiyu Bai Puren Lama zhi gongdao ping" 對於白普仁喇嘛之公道評 [Fair criticism of Lama Bai Puren]. *HCY* 7, no. 4 (May 1926): 10–11; *MFQ* 165: 120–121.

"Mijiao zhongxin zhi ji" 密教中興之機 [Chance for the restoration of esotericism]. *HCY* 5, no. 1 (January 1924): 3–4; *MFQ* 158: 166–167.

Mingxin 明心. "Nenghai fashi zai Beiping shuofa" 能海法師在北平說法 [Master Nenghai is preaching in Beijing]. *Foxue banyue kan* (November 1935): 21; *MFQ* 51: 439.

"Mizong wenti zhuanhao" 密宗問題專號 [Special issue about esotericism], *HCY* 14, no. 7 (July 1933).

"Nanjing jiang kai jinguangming hui" 南京將開金光明會 [Nanjing will organize Golden Light Ceremony]. *Shishi xinbao*, December 28, 1925.

"Nanjing kuaixin" 南京快信 [News from Nanjing]. *Shenbao*, April 17, 1926.

BIBLIOGRAPHY

"Nenghai fashi Beiping jiang puti dao" 能海法師北平講菩提道 [Venerable Nenghai lectured on *Lamrim* in Beijing]. *HCY* 17, no. 1 (January 1936): 104; *MFQ* 192: 364.

"Nenghai fashi hongfa jin xun" 能海法師宏法近訊 [Recent news about Master Nenghai spreading Dharma]. *Foxue banyue kan*, no. 168 (November 1938): 7; *MFQB* 65: 7.

Nenghai. "Chong jian gu Yizhou Longxing shelita yuan qi" 重建古益州龍興舍利塔緣起 [Conditions of rebuilding the Rising Dragon Stūpa of the ancient Yi prefecture]. *Jue you qing* 9, no. 6 (June 1948): 2–3; *MFQ* 89: 426–427.

———. *Dingdao ziliang song jianglu* 定道資糧頌講錄 [Notes on the preparation for the path of concentration]. In *Sanxue jianglu* 三學講錄 [Notes on the three teachings], 170–277. Vol. 2 of Nenghai shangshi quanji [*NHSS*].

———. *Guiyi faxin sheyao song* 皈依發心攝要誦 [Compendium of verses for taking refuge and making vows]. Beijing: Beiping huabei jushilin, 1934.

———. *Jiaoli chuji* 教理初基 [Basic teachings]. Vol. 3 of *NHSS*. Shanghai: shanghai foxue chubanshe, 1998.

———. *Jiedinghui jiben sanxue* 戒定慧基本三學 [The basic three teachings of precept, concentration, and wisdom]. Vol. 1 of *NHSS*. Shanghai: shanghai foxue chubanshe, 2005.

———. "Nenghai fashi zhi Guanyi heshang jian" 能海法師致貫一和尚緘 [Letter from Master Nenghai to Master Guanyi]. *Fohua xunkan*, no. 103 (March 1928): 8; *MFQ* 17: 458.

———. *Nenghai shangshi quanji* 能海上師全集 [Collective work of Nenghai, *NHSS*]. 5 vols. Edited by Nenghai shangshi quanji bianwei hui. Shanghai: Shanghai foxue shuju, 1989–2001.

———. "Puti dao cidi kesong" 菩提道次第科頌 [Lecture notes on the compendium of *Lamrim*]. Unpublished manuscript.

———. "Puti dao cidi kesong jiangji" 菩提道次第科頌講記 [Lecture notes on the compendium of *Lamrim*]. In Nenghai, *Sanxue jianglu* [Lecture notes on the three teachings]. Edited by Nenghai shangshi quanji bianweihui. Shanghai: Shanghai foxue shuju, 2005, 1–164.

———. "Puti dao cidi qiandao liu jiaxing fa" 菩提道次第前導六加行法 [The six preparatory practices of *Lamrim*]. Unpublished manuscript.

———. "Puti dao cidi xinlun" 菩提道次第心論 [Core of Lamrim Chenmo]. In *Jiaoli chuji* [Basic teachings], 305–364. Edited by Nenghai shangshi quanji bianweihui. Shanghai: Shanghai foxue shuju, 1998.

———. *Putitang risong* 菩提堂日誦 [Daily chanting at the Hall of Bodhi]. Beijing: Beiping huabei jushilin, 1934.

———. "Qingliang ji" 清涼記 [Lecture notes on Mount Wutai]. In *Xianzheng zhuangyan lun qingliang ji* [The notes collected on Mount Wutai on the *Ornament of Realization*], 1–235. Edited by Nenghai shangshi quanji bianweihui. Shanghai: shanghai foxue shuju, 1994.

———. "Qingliang xuji" 清涼續記 [Added lecture notes on Mount Wutai]. In Nenghai, *Xianzheng zhuangyan lun qingliang ji*, 236–376.

———. *Sanxue jianglu* 三學講錄 [Lectures on the three teachings]. Vol. 2 of NHSS. Shanghai: Shanghai foxue shuju, 1997.

———. "Shelifu apitanlun chanding pin xueji" 舍利弗阿毗曇論禪定品學記 [Notes on the Samādhi chapter in the *Śāriputrābhidharma*]. In *Jiedinghui jiben sanxue*, 215–310.

———. "Shelifu apitanlun chanding pin xueji jianglu" 舍利弗阿毗曇論禪定品學記講錄 [Lecture records on the notes on the Samādhi chapter in the Śāriputrābhidharma]. In Nenghai, *Sanxue jianglu*, 278–354.

———. *Xianzheng zhuangyan lun qingliang ji* 現證莊嚴論清涼記 [The notes collected on Mount Wutai on the *Ornament of Realization*]. Shanghai: Shanghai foxue shuju, 1994.

———. *Xianzheng zhuangyan lun sanzhong hekan* 現證莊嚴論三種合刊 [Collation of three texts on the *Ornament of Realization*]. Shanghai: Shanghai foxue shuju, 2001.

———, trans. *Daweide cidi song lue yin* 大威德次第頌略引 [A preliminary guide to the verses of the stages of Yamāntaka]. Chengdu: Jincisi, 1957.

———, trans. *Wenshu Daweide jingang benzun xiuxing chengjiu fa* 文殊大威德金剛本尊修行成就法 [The Completion of the Practice of Mañjuśrī Yamāntaka]. Chengdu: Jincisi, 1941.

Nenghai et al. "Pei xiu Deyang Xiaoganta mujuan xu" 培修德陽孝感塔募捐序 [Announcement about Raising Funds to Repair the Xiaogan Stūpa in Deyang]. *Sichuan fojiao yuekan* 5, no. 2 (February 1935): 11; *MFQ* 58: 392.

"Ning guan shen yingsong Banchan ji" 寧官紳迎送班禪記 [The record of Ningbo's officers and gentlemen's welcoming and seeing off Panchen]. *HCY* 6, no. 5 (May 1925): 14–15; *MFQ* 162: 178–179.

"Ning yuan ge jie huanying Bai Lama" 寧垣各界歡迎白喇嘛 [All social circles at Ningbo City welcomed Lama Bai]. *Shenbao*, April 3, 1926.

"Nuona huofo zuo di jing" 諾那活佛昨抵京 [Norlha Tulku arrived at the capital yesterday]. *Shishi xinbao*, June 13, 1934.

"Nuona zai Yue juxing guanding hui" 諾那在粵行灌頂會 [Norlha organized initiation ceremony at Guangdong]. *Shishi xinbao*, May 17, 1934.

Padmasambhava. *Zhongyou jiaoshou tingwen jietuo mifa* 中有教授聽聞解脫密法 [The secret teaching of liberation through hearing during the intermediate state]. Translated by Sun Jingfeng. Shanghai: Shanghai foxue shuju, 1960.

Qingding 清定. "Wushang dabao enshi Nenghai lao fashi dexing ji shi" 無上大寶恩師能海老法師德行紀實 [Memoir of the merits of the Ultimate Great Master Nenghai]. In *Nenghai shangshi yonghuai lu*, 3–19. Shanghai: Shanghai foxue shuju, 1997.

Qiu Liao 秋蓼. "Bai Lama fu Hang zhi zhenwen" 白喇嘛赴杭之珍聞 [Special news on Lama Bai's trip to Hangzhou]. *Dayun*, no. 70 (August 1926): 57–58; *MFQ* 137: 479–480.

Renci 仁慈. "Nenghai fashi zai Shu jinkuang" 能海法師在蜀近況 [Recent Situation of Master Nenghai in Sichuan]. *Jueyouqing*, nos. 167–168 (August 1946): 2; *MFQB* 63: 2.

Renhong 仁宏. "Pi Hunan sheng yiyuan Ye Dequan qing qu zhu Bai Lama wen" 闢湖南省議員葉德權請驅逐白喇嘛文 [A rejection to the proposal of Hunan Councilor Ye Dequan's Proposal to Evict Lama Bai]. *HCY* 7, no. 4 (May 1926): 16–17; *MFQ* 165: 126–127.

Rongkong 融空. "Jing mi huo wen" 淨密或問 [Questions on Pure Land Buddhism and esoteric Buddhism]. *Foxue banyuekan*, no. 92 (December 1934): 3–6; *MFQ* 50: 191–194.

———. "Yue Bi Xiao Shi Zhu ping Zang mi da wen" 閱避囂室主評藏密答問 [Reading Fazun's Comments on Answers to the Questions about Tibetan esotericism]. *Foxue banyuekan*, no. 109 (August 1935): 11–14; *MFQ* 51: 243–246.

"Shang da zongtong cheng" 上大總統呈 [Petition to the president]. *Fojiao Yuebao*, no. 4 (October 1913): 1–2; *MFQ* 6: 259–260.

"Shanghai guanshang huanying Banchan zhi yanhui" 上海官商歡迎班禪之宴會 [Shanghai officers and merchants' welcome party for Panchen]. *HCY* 6, no. 5 (May 1925): 10–12; *MFQB* 2: 433–436.

"Shanxi sheng fojiaohui jiang lü fahui dunqing Nenghai fashi jiang sifen lü" 山西省佛教會講律法會敦請能海法師講四分律 [Shanxi Provincial Buddhist Association invited Master Nenghai to preach the Four-Part Vinaya at the Vinaya-Preaching Assembly]. *Fojiao zazhi* 佛教雜誌 [Journal of Buddhism], no. 20 (August 1935): 74–75; *MFQ* 137: 242–243.

"Shangxian tang huanying Banchan zhi qingxing" 尚賢堂歡迎班禪之情形 [The situation of the International Institute of China's reception of Banchan]. *HCY* 6, no. 4 (April 1925): 15–17; *MFQ* 162: 49–51.

Shi Jiezong 釋玠宗. "Foxue shi zhengxin juefei mixin" 佛學是正信絕非迷信 [Buddhist teachings are righteous belief, not superstition]. *Taiwan fojiao xinbao* 臺灣佛教新報 [Newspaper of Taiwan Buddhism] 1, no. 6 (December 1925): 2–3; *MFQB* 4: 445–446.

"Shuo jingchan bingfei mixin" 說經懺並非迷信 [Scripture chanting and penitential offering are not superstition]. *Fohua xunkan* 3, no. 91 (November 1927): 1–2; *MFQ* 17: 357–358.

"Sun Chuanfang deng zancheng jinguangming hui" 孫傳芳等贊成金光明會 [Sun Chuanfang and others embraced the Golden Light Ceremony]. *Shenbao*, January 10, 1926.

"Sun Chuanfang tongling jintu sanri" 孫傳芳通令禁屠三日 [Sun Chuanfang ordered closing butchery for three days]. *Shenbao*, April 2, 1926.

Sun Jingfeng 孫景風. "Fu Qian Xianyi jushi han," 覆錢顯毅居士函 [Letter to layman Qian Xianyi]. *Foxue banyuekan*, no.198 (February 1940): 10–11; *MFQ* 55: 210–211.

———. "Muyin xinyi Xizang wen jingji qi" 募印新譯西藏文經籍啟 [Raising funds to publish the newly translated Tibetan scriptures]. *Foxue banyuekan*, no. 208 (July 1940): 9–11; *MFQ* 55: 333–335.

———. "Yu Zhu Tongsheng jushi shu" 與朱同生居士書 [Letter to layman Zhu Tongsheng]. *Jue youqing* 12, no.1 (January 1951): 16–17; *MFQB* 63: 342–343.

———. "Zhi Zhang Miaoding jushi shu" 致張妙定居士書 [Letter to layman Zhang Miaoding]. *Foxue banyuekan*, no.156 (August 1937): 14; *MFQ* 54: 244.

"Shantou mijiao chongxinghui jinxun" 汕頭密教重興會近訊 [Recent news about the Shantou Society restoring Chinese esoteric Buddhism]. *Foxue banyuekan*, no. 88 (October 1934): 10; *MFQ* 50: 72.

Taixu 太虛. "Douzheng jiangu zhong lue lun Shilun Jingang Fahui" 鬥諍堅固中略論時輪金剛法會 [Comments on the Kālacakra Vajra Dharma-Assembly in contentious dissensions]. *HCY* 15, no. 5 (May 1934): 1–2; *MFQ* 187: 9–10.

———. "Gaoyeshan daxue yanjiangci" 高野山大學講演辭 [Presentation at Kōyasan University]. *HCY* 6, no. 12 (February 1926): 19–20; *MFQ* 164: 53–54.

———. "Lun jishen chengfo" 論即身成佛 [About realizing Buddhahood in this very body]. *HCY* 6, no. 8 (October 1925): 17–23; *MFQ* 163: 23–29.

———. "Neizheng bu jin po zhuzhong zongjiao" 內政部今頗注重宗教 [The Ministry of Interior recently attended to religion]. *HCY* 14, no. 11 (November 1933): 1–2; *MFQ* 185: 289–290.

———. "Rensheng fojiao kaiti" 人生佛教開題 [The opening to humanistic Buddhism]. *HCY* 26, no. 1 (January 1945): 36–37; *MFQ* 202: 36–37.

———. "Xuwen" 序文 [Preface]. In *Puti dao cidi guanglun* 菩提道次第廣論 [The great treatise on the stages of the path to enlightenment], 1–2. 1935. Reprint. Putian, Fujian: Putian guanghua si, 1992.

———. "Puti dao cidi lue lun shi" 菩提道次第略論序 [Preface to the brief treatise of the stages of the path]. In *Taixu dashi quanshu* 太虛大師全書 [Complete works of Taixu]. Vol. 19, 780–781. Beijing: Zongjiao wenhua chubanshe, 2004.

———. *Taixu zizhuan* 太虛自傳 [Autobiography of Taixu]. Vol. 31 of *Taixu dashi quanshu* [Complete works of Taixu].

———. "Yue Zang mi huo wen" 閱藏密或問 [Reading the questions about Tibetan esotericism]. *HCY* 16, no. 3 (March 1935): 20–21; *MFQ* 190: 26–27.

———. "Zhengli sengqie zhidu lun" 整理僧伽制度論 [The reorganization of the sangha system]. Vol. 9 of *Taixu dashi quanshu* 太虛大師全集 [Collected works of Venerable Master Taixu]. 1915. Reprint. Taipei: Miaoyun ji wenjiao jijinhui, Digital version, 1998.

———. "Zhi Wang Hongyuan jushi shu" 致王弘願居士書 [Letter to Wang Hongyuan]. *HCY* 5, no. 2 (February 1924): 1; *MFQ* 158: 339.

———. "Zhongguo xianshi mizong fuxing zhi qushi" 中國現時密宗復興之趨勢 [The contemporary current of esoteric revival in China], *HCY* 6, no. 8 (October 1925): 12–17; *MFQ* 163: 18–23.

Tao Tao 陶陶. "Lama Bai yu Li Chun zhi tanhua" 白喇嘛與李純之談話 [Lama Bai's dialogue with Li Chun]. *Dayun*, no. 69 (July 1926): 70–73; *MFQB* 17: 490–494.

Tsongkhapa. *Mizong daocidi guanglun* 密宗道次第廣論 [The great treatise on the Tantric stages]. Translated by Fazun. Shanghai: shanghai foxue shuju, 1998.

———. *Puti dao cidi guanglun* 菩提道次第廣論 [The great treatise on the stages of the path to enlightenment]. Translated by Fazun. 1935. Reprint. Putian, Fujian: Putian Guanghuasi, 1992.

———. *The Great Treatise on the Stages of Path to Enlightenment*. Translated by the *Lamrim* Translation Committee. Ithaca, NY: Snow Lion, 2000.

United Front Work Department of Chengdu. "Guanyu Chengdu shi fojiao qingkuang de ziliao" 關於成都市佛教情況的資料 [Materials about Buddhism in Chengdu], June 11, 1955. Sichuan Provincial Archives, Jianchuan 050-01-038.

Wang Hongchi 王宏持. "Wen xinan heping fahui jiang chu tekan jingshen faxi" 聞西南和平法會將出特刊敬申法喜 [Congratulations to the publication of the special issue of the Southwest Peace Ceremony]. *Xinan heping fahui tekan*, 1–6; *MFQB* 42: 245–250.

Wang Fuhui 王福慧. "Benhui diwuci guanding ji" 本會第五次灌頂記 [The fifth consecration of our society]. In *Mijiao jiangxi lu* [Records of sermons about esotericism]. Edited by Yu Ruihua. Vol. 5, 267–270. Beijing: Huaxia chubanshe, 2009.

Wang Hongyuan 王弘願. "Fakan ci" 發刊詞 [Foreword]. *Shideng foxue yuekan*, no. 1 (July 1934): 1–2; *MFQB* 48: 189–190.

———. "Fu Li Lianshe lao jushi shu" 復李蓮舌老居士書 [Letter to layman Li Lianshe]. In *Mijiao jiangxi lu* [Records of sermons about esotericism]. Edited by Yu Ruihua. Vol. 5, 149.

———. "Fu Shi Dayong shu" 復釋大勇書 [Reply to Venerable Dayong]. *Foxin congkan* 佛心叢刊 [Collection of Buddha heart], no. 1 (January 1922): 1–2; *MFQ* 8: 359–360.

———. "Guangzhou fojiao jiexing jingshe kaimu tekan xu" 廣州佛教解行精舍開幕特刊序 [Preface to the special issue about the opening of Vihāra of Understanding and Practice in Guangzhou]. *Mijiao jiangxi lu* 6, no. 7 (July 1932): 149–170.

———. "Heng xian mi jiao heng" 衡賢密教衡 [Evaluation of the evaluation of Huayan and esoteric teachings]. *Mijiao jiangxi lu* 19 (1929): 227–268.

———. "Huayan shu xu kou yi ji" 華嚴疏序口義記 [Exposition on The Preface to Commentary on the Avataṃsaka Sūtra]. In *Mijiao jiangxi lu* [Records of sermons about esotericism]. Edited by Yu Ruihua. Vol. 1, 279.

———. "Jinggao hainei foxue jia" 敬告海內佛學家 [Announcement to Buddhists throughout the country]. *HCY* 4, no. 11 (November 1923): 8–9; *MFQ* 157: 443–444.

———. "Wang da a she li kaishi" 王大阿闍黎開示 [Sermon by Great Ācārya Wang]. In *Mijiao jiangxi lu* [Records of sermons about esotericism]. Edited by Yu Ruihua. Vol. 5, 293–296.

———. "Zaifu Xianyin a she li shu" 再復顯蔭阿闍梨書 [A response to Ācārya Xianyin]. *SFJL*, no. 7 (August 1924): 9; *MFQB* 8: 311.

Wang Huilan 王慧蘭. "Dajixiang tiannü baoxiang" 大吉祥天女寶相 [Sacred image of Mahālakṣmī]. *Jue youqing* 11, no. 12 (December 1950), front cover; *MFQB* 63: 303.

———. "Fomu Dakongquemingwang xiang," 佛母大孔雀明王像 [Image of Mahāmayūrī]. *Jue youqing* 11, no. 11 (November 1950), front cover; *MFQB* 63: 279.

———. "Renshen benhui diliu ci guanding ji," 壬申本會第六次灌頂記 [The sixth consecration of our society in 1932]. In *Mijiao jiangxi lu* [Records of sermons about esotericism]. Edited by Yu Ruihua. Vol. 5, 275–278.

———. "Yiteng Hongxian Qiushan Xiudian zhu Wang Huilan yi Zhenyanzong xiaoshi" 伊藤弘憲秋山秀典著王慧蘭譯《真言宗小史》[Brief history of Shingon Buddhism, composed by Kōken Itō and Akiyama Hidenori, translated by Wang Huilan]. *Shideng foxue yuekan*, no. 2 (August 1936): 71; *MFQB* 48: 357.

Wang Huilan and Wang Ruo'e 王若娥. "Wang Huilan, Wang Ruo'e er tongnü jingtu wenda" 王慧蘭王若娥二童女淨土問答 [Dialogues between two girls, Wang Huilan and Wang Ruo'e, about Pure Land]. *HCY* 2, no. 6 (May 1921): 10–12; *MFQ* 151: 128–130.

Wang Huilan, Wang Ruo'e, and Xing Huizhao 邢慧昭. "Wang Huilan, Wang Ruo'e, Xing Huizhao san tongnü he shuo sida jiekong" 王慧蘭王若娥邢慧昭三童女合說四大皆空 [Wang Huilan, Wang Ruo'e, and Xing Huizhao, three girls' talk on the emptiness of the four great elements]. *HCY* 2, no. (August 1921): 6–8; *MFQ* 151: 454–456.

Wang Jiaqi 王家齊. "Kunming Lianhua jingshe jianzao jinianbei" 昆明蓮華精舍建造紀念碑 [Monument in honor of the building of the Lotus Vihāra in Kunming], *Jueyouqing*, no. 11 (November 1950): 10; *MFQB* 63: 288.

Wang Yuji 王與楫. "Wang Yuji jushi huanying Banchan han" 王與楫居士歡迎班禪函 [Layman Wang Yuji's welcome letter to the Panchen Lama]. *SFJL*, no. 8 (February 1925): 1; *MFQB* 8: 471.

Weiyin 畏因. "Qidao xizai, shuo qidao" 祈禱息災，說祈禱 [Pray for pacifying disaster, about praying]. *Dayun*, no. 99 (July 1930): 3–5; *MFQB* 21: 301–305.

"Wu sheng jinguangming hui choubei jinxing xun" 五省金光明會籌備進行訊 [News on the five provinces' organization of the Golden Light Ceremony]. *HCY* 7, no. 2 (April 1926): 7–10; *MFQ* 164: 384–385.

"Wuliang shou fo chengjiu fa" 無量壽佛成就法 [The accomplishing Dharma of the Infinite Life Buddha]. In *TJJGM*, 4–9; *MFQB* 15: 121–125.

Wuyi 晤一. "Wuyi shi shang Taixu fashi" 晤一師上太虛法師 [A letter from Venerable Wuyi to Master Taixu]. *HCY* 7, no. 6 (July 1926): 8–9; *MFQ* 165: 364–365.

Xianyin 顯蔭. "Shi ba dao jiaxing zuofa miji" 十八道加行作法秘記 [Procedures of the eighteen paths preliminary rituals]. *SFJL*, no. 5 (1924 April): 1–13; *MFQB* 7: 301–313.

———. "Xianyin fashi zhi Wang Hongyuan jushi han" 顯蔭法師致王弘願居士函 [Letter from Master Xianyin to Wang Hongyuan]. *SFJL* 8 (July 1924): 7–8; *MFQB* 8: 133–134.

"Xiang yihui tiyi quzhu Bai Lama" 湘議會提議驅逐白喇嘛 [The Hunan Council proposed to expel Lama Bai]. *Shenbao*, February 3, 1926.

"Xianggang Li Yizhen jushi rumi yinyuan ji Zhenyanzong jushilin zhi laili" 香港黎乙真居士入密因緣及真言宗居士林之來歷 [Layman Li Yizhen's entry into esoteric Buddhism and the founding of Zhenyan Lay Buddhist Society]. *Siming xian fojiao hui huikan* 思明縣佛教會會刊 [Journal of the Buddhist Association in Siming County], no. 2, (1932): 83–84; *MFQB* 42: 89–90.

Xingfa 興法. "Guanyu chengdu jincisi he yunwusi de guanxi jianjie" 關於成都近慈寺和雲悟寺的關係簡介 [An introduction to the relationship between Jinci Monastery and Yunwu Temple]. In *Nenghai shangshi yonghuai lu*, 52–54. Shanghai: Shanghai foxue shuju, 1997.

"Xikang Nuona Hutuketu" 西康諾那呼圖克圖 [Norlha Qutughtu of Western Kham]. *Shishi xinbao*, February 12, 1930.

"Xikang lama diaocha" 西康喇嘛調查 [A survey of the lamas in western Kham]. *Chuanbian jikan* 2, no. 2 (June 1936): 201.

"Xikang simiao diaocha" 西康寺廟調查 [A survey of the temples in western Kham]. *Chuanbian jikan* 1, no 4 (December 1935): 286–287.

Xu Weiru 徐蔚如. "Shanxi Wutaishan beitai ding Guangji maopeng mukuan gouzhi zhaitian qi" 山西五臺山北台頂廣濟茅蓬募款購置齋田啟 [Raise funds to purchase land for the Thatched Cottage of Vast Salvation on the northern peak of Mount Wutai]. *Tianjin fojiao jushilin linkan* 天津佛教居士林林刊 [Journal of the Lay Buddhist Society of Tianjin], no. 4 (July 1927): 71–72; *MFQB* 34: 483–484.

Yanding 嚴定. "Fojiao zangwen xueyuan liuzang xuefa tuan dizi zhi Duo zunzhe han" 佛教藏文學院留藏學法團弟子致多尊者函 [Letters from the group of disciples entering Tibet and the Buddhist Tibetan College to Venerable Duo]. *Xinan heping fahui tekan* 西南和平法會特刊 [Special issue on the Peace Dharma Assembly in the southwest] (December 1931): 23–24; *MFQB* 42: 443–444.

Yanglei 羊磊. "Kangding chengqu ba lamasi diaocha" 康定城區八喇嘛寺調查 [A survey of the eight lamaseries in town of Kangding]. *Chuanbian jikan* 1, no 2 (June 1935): 207.

Yao Taofu 姚陶馥. "Hufa tongyan" 護法痛言 [Criticism in defense of Dharma]. *HCY* 14, no. 7 (July 1933): 45–49; *MFQ* 184: 311–315.

BIBLIOGRAPHY

Yikong 一孔. "Guoji xuanchuan" 國際宣傳 [International propaganda]. *Shishi xinbao*, May 11, 1933.

Yinguang 印光. "Putuo shan Pujisi Banchan she qian seng zhai shang tang fayu" 普陀山普濟寺班禪設千僧齋上堂法語 [The Dharma talk at the banquet for a thousand monks offered by Panchen at the Puji Temple at Putuo Mountain]. *SFJL* 10 (August 1925): 1; *MFQ* 14: 501.

Yu Ruihua 于瑞華, ed. *Minguo mizong qikan wenxian jicheng* 民國密宗期刊文獻集成 [Collection of Republican-era Tantric periodical literature]. 42 volumes. Beijing: Dongfang chubanshe, 2008.

——, ed. *Mijiao jiangxi lu* 密教講習錄 [Records of sermons about esotericism]. 5 volumes. Beijing: Huaxia chubanshe, 2009.

Yuanfang 圓方. "Ping Zang mi da wen zhi yi duan" 評藏密答問之一段 [Comments on a paragraph of answers to questions about Tibetan esotericism]. *Foxue banyuekan*, no. 108 (August 1935): 27–28; *MFQ* 51: 227–229.

Yuanguang 圓光. "Bailin foxue yanjiushe gaizu shijie foxueyuan jiaoliyuan de jingguo" 柏林佛學研究社改組世界佛學苑教理院的經過 [The procedure of transforming the Buddhist Research Society of Cypress Forest to World Buddhist Institute]. *Fojiao pinglun* 佛教評論 [Buddhist review] 1, no. 1 (January 1931), 69–72; *MFQ* 46: 189–192.

"Zang mi da wen lei bian" 藏密答問類編 [References to the answers to questions about Tibetan esotericism]. *Foxue banyuekan*, no. 155 (July 1937): 11; *MFQ* 54: 209.

"Zangwen xueyuan huanying Banchan daibiao" 藏文學院歡迎班禪代表 [Tibetan College welcomed the Panchen Lama's representative]. *SFJL*, no. 8 (February 1925): 1–3; *MFQB* 8: 471–473.

Zhang Mengliang 張夢良. "Nenghai fashi jin zaijing jiang putidao cidi qinei bing guanding chuanfa" 能海法師近在京講菩提道次第期內併灌頂傳法 [Venerable Nenghai gave lectures on *Lamrim* and offered initiations in Nanjing]. *Zhengxin* 8, nos. 1–2 (April 1936): 14; *MFQB* 44: 208.

Zhang Miaoding 張妙定. "Zhongyin jiudu mifa shangjuan chongyi chugao zixu" 中陰救度密法上卷重譯初稿自序 [Author's preface to the retranslation of the first volume of the secret teaching of bardo liberation]. *Foxue banyuekan*, no.133 (August 1936): 16–17; *MFQ* 52: 474–475.

Zhang Yingchao 張英超. "Shilun jingang fahui guanguang yinxiang" 時輪金剛法會觀光印象 [Impression of Kālacakra Vajra Dharma-Assembly]. *Shidai manhua* 時代漫畫 [Caricature of time], no. 5 (May 1934).

Zhao Hongzhu 趙洪鑄 and Dai Chuanxian 戴傳賢. "Zhongyou wenjiao dedu mifa erze" 中有聞教得度密法序二則 [Two essays on the secret teaching of liberation through hearing during the intermediate state]. *Jue youqing*, nos. 199–200 (December 1947): 13; *MFQ* 89: 305.

Zhaotong 昭通. "Suishi Haigong shangshi huiyilu" 隨侍海公上師回憶錄 [Memoir of serving Guru Nenghai]. In *Nenghai shangshi yonghuai lu*, 29–40. Shanghai: Shanghai foxue shuju, 1997.

"Zhonghua Fojiao zonghui tuiju Zhangjia huofo jiaru benhui wei huizhang" 中華佛教總會推舉章嘉活佛加入本會為會長 [The Zhonghua Buddhist Federation elected Changkya Khutukhtu as the president of the federation]. *Fojiao yuebao* 佛教月報 [Buddhist monthly], no. 4 (October 1913): 5–8; *MFQ* 6: 263–266.

Zhou Shujia 周叔迦. "Shenqing shu 申請書" [Application], 196-002-00290, July 1951, Beijing Municipal Archives.

Zhou Zhicheng 周志誠. "Mijiao jushilin yuanqi bing jianyue" 密教居士林緣起並簡約 [The Origin of the Esoteric Lay Buddhist Society and regulation]. *Fojiao zazhi* no. 24 (December 1935): 45–52; *MFQ* 64: 541–548.

Secondary Works

Ashiwa, Yoshiko, and David L. Wank, eds. *Making Religion, Making the State: The Politics of Religion in Modern China*. Stanford, CA: Stanford University Press, 2009.

Bediako, Kwame. "A Variety of African Responses (2): John Mbiti, or Christ as the Redeemer of the African heritage." In *Theology and Identity: The Impact of Culture upon Christian Thought in the Secondary Century and in Modern Africa*. Carlisle, CA: Regnum Books, 1992.

———. *Christianity in Africa: The Renewal of a Non-Western Religion*. Edinburgh, UK: Edinburgh University Press, 1995.

Beijing Jushilin Committee, ed. *Beijing fojiao jushilin lishi yu yange* 北京佛教居士林歷史與沿革 [History and development of Beijing Lay Buddhist Society]. Beijing: Beijing fojiao jushilin, 2010.

Bevans, Stephen B. *Models of Contextual Theology*. Maryknoll, NY: Orbis, 1996.

Bechert, Heinz. *Buddhismus, Staat und Gesellschaft in den Ländern des Theravāda-Buddhismus: Birma, Kambodscha, Laos, Thailand*. Frankfurt: Metzner, 1966.

Bell, Catherine. *Ritual Theory, Ritual Practice*. 1992. Reprint. New York: Oxford University Press, 2009.

Bhikkhu KL Dhammajoti. *Sarvāstivāda Abhidharma*. Hong Kong: University of Hong Kong Press, 2009.

Bianchi, Ester. "Sino-Tibetan Buddhism: Continuities and Discontinuities: The Case of Nenghai's Legacy in the Contemporary Era." In *Chinese and Tibetan Esoteric Buddhism*. Edited by Meir Shahar and Yael Bentor, 200–319. Leiden: Brill, 2017.

———. "Subtle Erudition and Compassionate Devotion: Longlian, 'The Most Outstanding Bhikṣuṇī' in Modern China." In *Making Saints in Modern China*. Edited by David Ownby, Vincent Goosaert, Ji Zhe, 272–311. New York: Oxford University Press, 2017.

———. "The 'Chinese Lama' Nenghai." In *Buddhism Between Tibet and China*. Edited by Matthew Kapstein, 295–348. Boston: Wisdom Publication, 2009.

———. *The Iron Statue Monastery: A Buddhist Nunnery of Tibetan Tradition in Contemporary China*. Firenze: Olschki, 2001.

———. "Tiexiangsi." In *Innovative Buddhist Women: Swimming Against the Stream*. Edited by Karma Lekshe Tsomo, 130–141. Richmond: Curzon, 2000.

———. "The Tantric Rebirth Movement in Modern China: Esoteric Buddhism Revivified by the Japanese and Tibetan Traditions." *Acta Orientalia Academiae Scientiarum Hung* 57, no. 1 (April 2004): 31–54.

———. "Yamāntaka-Vajrabhairava in Modern China. Analysis of 20th Century Translations from Tibetan." In *Buddhist Asia 2*. Edited by G. Orofino and S. Vita, 99–140. Kyoto: Italian School of East Asian Studies, 2010.

———. "Yi jie wei shi 以戒為師: Theory and Practice of Monastic Discipline in Modern and Contemporary Chinese Buddhism." *Studies in Chinese Religions* 3, no. 2 (2017), 111–141.

Bianchi, Ester, and Weirong Shen, eds. *Sino-Tibetan Buddhism Across the Ages*. Leiden: Brill, 2021.

Birnbaum, Raoul. "Buddhist China at the Century's Turn." *The China Quarterly*, no. 174 (June 2003): 428–450.

Braun, Erik. *The Birth of Insight: Meditation, Modern Buddhism, and the Burmese Monk Ledi Sayadaw*. Chicago: University of Chicago Press, 2013.

Broughton, Jeffrey. "Early Ch'an Schools in Tibet." In *Studies in Ch'an and Hua-yen*. Edited by Robert Gimello and Peter Gregory, 1–68. Honolulu: University of Hawai'i Press, 1983.

Cabezón, José. "On Tulku Lineages." *Revue d'Etudes Tibétaines*, no. 38 (2017), 1–28.

Cadonna, Alfredo, and Ester Bianchi, eds. *Facets of Tibetan Religious Tradition and Contacts with Neighbouring Cultural Areas*. Firenze: Oslchki, 2002.

Campany, Robert. *Making Transcendents: Ascetics and Social Memory in Early Medieval China*. Honolulu: University of Hawai'i Press, 2009.

———. "Religious Repertoires and Contestation: A Case Study Based on Buddhist Miracle Tales," *History of Religions* 52, no. 2 (November 2012): 99–141.

Chan Sin-Wai. *Buddhism in Late Ch'ing Political Thought*. Hong Kong: Chinese University Press, 1985.

Chang, Garma C. C. *The Buddhist Teaching of Totality: The Philosophy of Hwa Yen Buddhism*. University Park: The Pennsylvania State University Press, 1971.

Chandler, Stuart. *Establishing a Pure Land on Earth: The Foguang Buddhist Perspective on Modernization and Globalization*. Honolulu: University of Hawai'i Press, 2004.

Charleux, Isabelle. *Nomads on Pilgrimage: Mongols on Wutaishan (China), 1800-1940*. Leiden: Brill, 2015.

Chen Bing 陳兵 and Deng Zimei 鄧子美. *Ershi shiji Zhongguo fojiao* 二十世紀中國佛教 [Chinese Buddhism in Twentieth-Century China]. Beijing: Minzu chubanshe, 2000.

Chen, Shidong 陳士東. *Nenghai shangshi xingji lu* 能海上師行跡錄 [Memory of Master Nenghai]. Hongkong: Tianma tushu, 2004.

Ch'en, Kenneth. *Buddhism in China: A Historical Survey*. Princeton, NJ: Princeton University Press, 1964.

Chengdu shi difangzhi bianzuan weiyuanhui 成都市地方誌編纂委員會 [Committee of Gazetteer Compilation in Chengdu] ed., *Chengdu shizhi zongjiao zhi* 成都市志宗教志 [Religious history of Chengdu], vol. 8 of *Chengdu shizhi* 成都市志 [Gazetteer of Chengdu]. Chengdu: Sichuan cishu chubanshe, 1993.

Chou, Wen-Shing Lucia. *Mount Wutai: Visions of a Sacred Buddhist Mountain*. Princeton, NJ: Princeton University Press, 2018.

Coe, Choki. "Contextualizing Theology." In *Mission Trends No. 3: Third World Theologies*. Edited by Gerald H. Anderson and Thomas F. Stransky, 19–24. New York: Paulist Press, 1976.

Conze, Edward. *Buddhist Meditation*. 2nd ed. New York: Routledge Publication, 2008.

———. "The Development of Prajñāpāramitā Thought." In *Thirty Years of Buddhist Studies: Selected Essays by Edward Conze*. Oxford: Bruno Cassirer Publishers, 1967.

Copp, Paul. "Visualization and Contemplation." In *Esoteric Buddhism and the Tantras in East Asia*. Edited by Charles Orzech, Henrik Sørensen, and Richard Payne, 141–145. Leiden: Brill, 2011.

Covell, Stephen. *Japanese Temple Buddhism: Worldliness in a Religion of Renunciation*. Honolulu: University of Hawai'i Press, 2005.

Cuevas, Bryan. *The Hidden History of* The Tibetan Book of the Dead. New York: Oxford University Press, 2003.

Davidson, Ronald M. "Abhiṣeka." In *Esoteric Buddhism and the Tantras in East Asia*. Edited by Charles Orzech, Henrik Sørensen, and Richard Payne, 71–75. Leiden: Brill, 2011.

———. *Indian Esoteric Buddhism: A Social History of the Tantric Movement*. New York: Columbia University Press, 2002.

———. *Tibetan Renaissance: Tantric Buddhism in the Rebirth of Tibetan Culture*. New York: Columbia University Press, 2005.

Debreczeny, Karl. "Wutai Shan: Pilgrimage to Five Peak Mountain." *Journal of the International Association of Tibetan Studies* 6 (2011): 1–133.

Deng Jiazhou 鄧家宙. *Xianggang fojiaoshi* 香港佛教史 [History of Buddhism in Hong Kong]. Hongkong: zhonghua shuju, 2015.

Dibeltulo, Martino. "The Revival of Tantrism: Tibetan Buddhism and Modern China." PhD dissertation. The University of Michigan, 2015.

Dingzhi 定智. *Nenghai shangshi zhuan* 能海上師傳 [Biography of Master Nenghai]. 1984. Reprint. Shanghai: Shanghai foxue shuju, 2007.

Gomez, Luis. "The Direct and Gradual Approaches of Zen Master Mahāyāna: Fragments of the Teachings of Mo-ho-yen." in *Studies in Ch'an and Huayan*. Edited by Robert Gimello and Peter Gregory, 69–169. Honolulu: University of Hawai'i Press, 1984.

Dongchu 東初. *Zhongguo fojiao jindai shi* 中國佛教近代史 [The modern history of Chinese Buddhism]. 1974. Reprint, Taipei: Zhonghua fojiao wenhua guan, 1987.

Duara, Prasenjit. *Rescuing History from the Nation: Questioning Narratives of Modern China*. Chicago: University of Chicago Press, 1995.

Faure, Bernard. *The Will to Orthodoxy: A Critical Genealogy of Northern Chan Buddhism*. Stanford: Stanford University Press, 1997.

Fu Chongju 傅崇矩. *Chengdu tonglan* 成都通覽 [Overview of Chengdu]. 1909; reprint. Chengdu: Bashu shushe, 1987.

Gamble, Ruth. *Reincarnation in Tibetan Buddhism*. New York: Oxford University Press, 2018.

Germano, David. "Architecture and Absence in the Secret Tantric History of rDzogs Chen." *Journal of the International Association of Buddhist Studies* 17, no. 2 (1994): 203–335.

———. "Re-membering in the Dismembered Body of Tibet: Contemporary Tibetan Visionary Movements in the People's Republic of China." In *Buddhism in Contemporary Tibet: Religious Revival and Cultural Identity*. Edited by Melvyn Goldstein and Matthew Kapstein, 53–95. Berkeley: University of California Press, 1998.

Gimello, Robert. "Mysticism and Meditation." In *Mysticism and Philosophical Analysis*. Edited by Steven Katz, 170–199. New York: Oxford University Press, 1978.

———. "Mysticism in its Contexts." In *Mysticism and Religious Traditions*. Edited by Steven Katz, 61–88. New York: Oxford University Press, 1983.

Gimello, Robert, ed. *Avatamsaka Buddhism in East Asia*. Wiesbaden: Harrassowitz Verlag, 2012.

Gimello, Robert, and Peter Gregory, eds. *Studies in Ch'an and Hua-yen*. Honolulu: University of Hawai'i Press, 1983.

Goble, Geoffrey. *Chinese Esoteric Buddhism: Amoghavajra, the Ruling Elite, and the Emergence of a Tradition*. New York: Columbia University Press, 2019.

Goldstein, Melvyn. *A History of Modern Tibet, 1913-1951: The Demise of the Lamaist State*. Berkeley: University of California Press, 1989.

———. *A History of Modern Tibet, 1951-1955: The Calm before the Storm*. Berkeley: University of California Press, 2007.

Gombrich, Richard. *Theravada Buddhism: A Social History from Ancient Benares to Modern Colombo*. London: Routledge, 1988.

Gombrich, Richard, and Gananath Obeyesekere. *Buddhism Transformed: Religious Changes in Sri Lanka*. Princeton, NJ: Princeton University Press, 1988.

Goossaert, Vincent, and David Palmer. *The Religious Question in Modern China*. Chicago: University of Chicago Press, 2011.

Gregory, Peter. *Tsung-Mi and the Sinification of Buddhism*. Princeton, NJ: Princeton University Press, 1991.

———, ed. *Sudden and Gradual: Approaches to Enlightenment in Chinese Thought*. Honolulu: University of Hawai'i Press, 1987.

Grunfeld, Tom. *The Making of Modern Tibet*. Armonk, New York: M. E. Sharpe, 1996.

Guangxing. *The Concept of the Buddha: Its Evolution from Early Buddhism to the Trikāya Theory*. London: RoutledgeCurzon, 2005.

Hammerstrom, Erik. *The Science of Chinese Buddhism: Early Twentieth-Century Engagements*. New York: Columbia University Press, 2015.

He Jianming 何建明. "Luelun Qingmo minchu de zhongguo fojiao nüzhong" 略論清末民初的中國佛教女眾 [A brief study of Buddhist women in the late Qing and early Republican period]. *Foxue yanjiu* 佛學研究 [Buddhist studies], no. 6 (1997): 203–209.

Heine, Steven, and Charles S. Prebish, eds. *Buddhism in the Modern World: Adaptations of an Ancient Tradition*. New York: Oxford University Press, 2003.

Hirakawa, Akira 平川彰. *Ritsuzō no kenkyū* 律蔵の研究 [A study of the Vinaya collection]. Tokyo: Sankibō Busshorin, 1960.

Holmes-Tagchungdarpa, Amy. "Beyond Living Buddhas, Snowy Mountains and Mighty Mastiffs: Imagining Tibetan Buddhism in Contemporary China's Mediascape." In *Religion and Media in China*. Edited by Stefania Travagnin, 256–274. New York: Routledge, 2016.

Huang Chanhua 黃懺華. "Huang Shuyin jushi shi lue" 黃樹因居士事略 [About layman Huang Shuyin]. *SFJL*, nos. 3–4 (October 1925), 3–4; *MFQB* 7: 205.

———. *Zhongguo fojiaoshi* 中國佛教史 [The history of Chinese Buddhism]. Shanghai: shangwu yinshuguan, 1947.

Huang Ying-chieh 黃英傑. *Minguo mizong nianjian* 民國密宗年鑑 [Chronicle history of Tantrism during the Republican era]. Taipei: Quanfo wenhua chubanshe, 1992.

———. "Taiwan zangchuan fojiao yinjing hui xiankuang fenxi" 台灣藏傳佛教印經會現況分析 [An Analysis of the Publication Societies of Tibetan Buddhism in Taiwan]. *Fojiao tushuguan guankan* 佛教圖書館館刊 [Journal of Buddhist libraries], no. 50 (December 1998): 6–14.

———. "Taixu dashi de xianmi jiaoliu chutan, yi Riben mizong wei li" 太虛大師的顯密交流初探, 以日本密宗為例 [Master Taixu's communication of exoteric and esoteric Buddhism: The case of Japanese esoteric school]. *Hsuan Chuang Journal of Buddhism* 14 (September 2010): 135–164.

Hugo, Victor. *Beican shijie* 悲慘世界. Translated by Li Dan and Fang Yu. Beijing: Renmin chubanshe, 1984.

Hunansheng difang zhi bianzuan weiyuan hui 湖南省地方誌編纂委員會. *Hunan tongjian* 湖南通鑒 [Chronicle of Hunan]. Hunan: Hunan renmin chuban she, 2008.

Jackson, Roger. "Sa skya Paṇḍita's Account of the bSam yas Debate: History as Polemic." *Journal of the International Association of Buddhist Studies* 5, no. 1 (1982): 89–99.

Jagou, Fabienne. *Gongga Laoren (1903–1997): Her Role in the Spread of Tibetan Buddhism in Taiwan*. Leiden: Brill, 2021.

———. *Le 9e Panchen Lama (1883–1937): Enjeu Des Relations Sino-Tibétaines*. Paris: École française d'Extrême-Orient, 2004.

Jagou, Fabienne, ed. *The Hybridity of Buddhism: Contemporary Encounters Between Tibetan and Chinese Traditions in Taiwan and the Mainland*. Études thématiques 29. Paris: École française d'Extrême-Orient, 2018.

Jiang Canteng 江燦騰. *Zhongguo jindai fojiao sixiang yanjiu* 中國近世佛教思想研究 [Research on modern Chinese Buddhist thought]. Taipei: Daoxiang chubanshe, 1989.

Jiqun 濟群. *Daocidi zhi dao* 道次第之道 [The way of the stages of the path]. Suzhou: Jiechuang foxue yanjiusuo, 2009.

———. *Fofa xiuxue cidi* 佛法修學次第 [Stages of Buddhist practice]. Suzhou: Jiechuang foxue yanjiusuo, 2007.

———. *Puti dadao* 菩提大道 [The great way to enlightenment], 3 volumes. Suzhou: Jiechuang foxue yanjiu suo, 2010.

———. *Puti lu manman, hanchuan fojiao de sikao* 菩提路漫漫: 漢傳佛教的思考 [The long journey to enlightenment, a reflection on Chinese Buddhism]. Beijing: Zongjiao wenhua chubanshe, 2006.

Jones, Charles. *Chinese Pure Land Buddhism: Understanding a Tradition of Practice*. Honolulu: University of Hawai'i Press, 2019.

Kanben 侃本. *Hanzang fojing fanyi bijiao yanjiu* 漢藏佛經翻譯比較研究 [A comparative study of the translation of Chinese and Tibetan Buddhist scriptures]. Beijing: Zhongguo zangxue chubanshe, 2008.

Kane, Ross. *The Syncretism of Tradition: Reappraising Cultural Mixture in Christianity*. New York: Oxford University Press, 2020.

Kapp, Robert. *Szechwan and the Chinese Republic: Provincial Militarism and Central Power, 1911–1938*. New Haven, CT: Yale University Press, 1973.

Kapstein, Matthew, "A Thorn in the Dragon's Side: Tibetan Buddhist Culture in China." In *Governing China's Multiethnic Frontiers*. Edited by Morris Rossabi, 230–259. Seattle: University of Washington Press, 2004.

———. *The Tibetan Assimilation of Buddhism: Conversion, Contestation, and Memory*. New York: Oxford University Press, 2000.
Kapstein, Matthew, ed. *Buddhism Between Tibet and China*. Boston: Wisdom Publication, 2009.
Kasulis, Thomas. "Truth Words: The Basis of Kūkai's Theory of Interpretation." In *Buddhist Hermeneutics*. Edited by Donald Lopez, 252–272. Honolulu, HI: University of Hawai'i Press, 1988.
Kieschnick, John. *The Impact of Buddhism on Chinese Material Culture*. Princeton, NJ: Princeton University Press, 2003.
King, Sallie. *Socially Engaged Buddhism*. Honolulu: University of Hawai'i Press, 2009.
Klein, Anne. *Knowledge and Liberation: Tibetan Buddhist Epistemology in Support of Transformative Religious Experience*. Ithaca, NY: Snow Lion, 1986.
Kolas, Ashild. *Tourism and Tibetan Culture in Transition: A Place Called Shangrila*. New York: Routledge, 2008.
Lama Zopa. *The Heart of the Path: Seeing the Guru as Buddha*. Weston, MA: Lama Yeshe Wisdom Archives, 2009.
Lawrence, Bruce. *Defenders of God: The Fundamentalist Revolt against the Modern Age*. San Francisco: Harper and Row, 1989.
Laliberté, André. *Politics of Buddhist Organizations in Taiwan*. New York: RoutledgeCurzon, 2004.
Lin, Hsiao-ting, *Tibet and Nationalist China's Frontier: Intrigues and Ethnopolitics, 1928-49*. Vancouver: UBC Press, 2006.
Li Silong 李四龍. "Lue lun Zhiyi de mijiao si xiang" 略論智顗的"秘教"思想 [Introduction to Zhiyi's thought about secret teaching]. *Zhongguo zhexue shi* 中國哲學史 [History of Chinese philosophy], no. 2 (2009): 25–31.
Liao Yixuan 廖乙璿. "Zuochan sanmei jing chanfa jianjie" 《坐禪三昧經》禪法簡介 [A brief introduction to the Sutra on the Samādhi of Sitting Meditation]. *Fuyan Buddhist Studies*, no. 10 (2015): 40–77.
Likong 力空. "Nenghai fashi zai Wutaishan jiangwan yulanpeng jing biguan xiufa" 能海法師在五臺山講完盂蘭盆經閉關修法 [Master Nenghai practiced in reclusion after preaching on the Yulanpeng Sūtra at Wutai]. *Shanxi fojiao zazhi* 山西佛教雜誌 [Journal of Shanxi Buddhism] 1, no. 9 (September 1934): 67; *MFQ* 140: 235.
Long Zhaoyu 龍昭宇, ed. *Zixing guangming: jingang shangshi Gongga Laoren kaishilu* 自性光明: 金剛上師貢噶老人開示錄 [The self-nature bright light: Record of Vajra Master Elder Gongga's teaching]. Taipei: Zhengfayan chubanshe, 1993.
Lopez, Donald. *Buddhist Scriptures*. London: Penguin Books, 2004.
———. "Foreword," *Tibetan Yoga and Secret Doctrines: Seven Books of Wisdom of the Great Path, according to the Late Lama Kazi Dawa-Samdup's English Rendering*. New York: Oxford University Press, 2000.
———. *Prisoners of Shangri-La: Tibetan Buddhism and the West*. Chicago: University of Chicago Press, 1999.
———. *The Tibetan Book of the Dead: A Biography*. Princeton, NJ: Princeton University Press, 2011.
Kōken Itō 伊藤弘憲 and Akiyama Hidenori 秋山秀典. *Shingon shū shōshi* 真言宗小史 [Brief history of Shingon Buddhism]. Tokyo: Shinkō sha, 1926.

Kunming shi fojiao xiehui 昆明市佛教協會, ed. *Kunming fojiao shi* 昆明佛教史 [History of Buddhism in Kunming]. Kunming: Yunnan minzhu chuban she, 2001.

Lu Xun 魯迅. "Zhenjia Tangji hede" 真假堂吉訶德 [True and fake Don Quixote]. In *Nanqiang beidiao ji* 南腔北調集 [Southern tone and northern accent], 116–118. Shanghai: Tongwen shuju, 1934.

Luo Tongbing. "The Reformist Monk Taixu and the Controversy about Exoteric and Esoteric Buddhism in Republican China." In *Images of Tibet in the 19th and 20th Centuries*. Edited by Monica Esposito, 433–472. Paris: École française d'Extrême-Orient, 2008.

Lü Tiegang 呂鐵鋼 and Zhou Shaoliang 周紹良, eds. *Zangmi xiufa midian* 藏密修法秘典 [The secret scriptures of Tibetan esoteric Dharma practices]. 5 volumes. Beijing: Huaxia chubanshe, 1996.

McKay, Alex. *Tibet and the British Raj: the Frontier Cadre, 1904–1947*. Richmond, Surrey: Curzon, 1997.

McKay, Alex, ed. *The Modern Period: 1895–1959, the Encounter with Modernity*. Vol. 3 of *The History of Tibet*. New York: RoutlegeCurzon, 2003.

Ma Tianxiang 麻天祥. *Wanqing foxue yu jindai shehui sichao* 晚清佛學與近代社會思潮 [Buddhist thought in Late Qing and ideologies in modern society]. Taipei: Wen jin chubanshe, 1992.

Madsen, Richard. *Democracy's Dharma: Religious Renaissance and Political Development in Taiwan*. Berkeley: University of California Press, 2007.

Makita Tairyō 牧田諦亮. *Chūgoku kinsei Bukkyō shi no kenkyū* 中國近世佛教史の研究 [Studies in the modern history of Chinese Buddhism]. Kyoto: Heirakuji Shoten, 1957.

Makley, Charlene. "Minzu, Market, and the Mandala: National Exhibitionism and Tibetan Buddhist Revival in Post-Mao China." In *Faiths on Display: Religion, Tourism, and the Chinese State*. Edited by Tim Oakes and Donald S. Sutton, 127–156. Lanham, MD: Rowman and Littlefield, 2010.

McKim, Donald K. *The Westminster Dictionary Theological Terms*. Louisville, KY: Westminster John Knox Press, 2014.

McMahan, David. *The Making of Buddhist Modernism*. New York: Oxford University Press, 2008.

McGuire, William. "Jung, Evans-Wentz and Various other Gurus." *Journal of Analytical Psychology* 48, no. 4 (September 2003): 433–445.

Mei Jingxuan 梅靜軒. "Minguo yilai de hanzang fojiao guanxi" 民國以來的漢藏佛教關係1912–1949 [Relationship between Chinese and Tibetan Buddhism in the Republican period, 1912–1949]. *Chung-Hwa Buddhist Studies* 2 (March 1998): 251–288.

———. "Minguo zaoqi xianmi fojiao chongtu de tantao" 民國早期顯密佛教衝突的探討 [Conflicts between esoteric and exoteric Buddhism in the early Republican period]. *Chung-Hwa Buddhist Studies* 3 (March 1999): 251–270.

Meyer, Christian. "How the 'Science of Religion' (zongjiaoxue) as a Discipline Globalized 'Religion' in Late Qing and Republican China, 1890–1949—Global Concepts, Knowledge Transfer, and Local Discourses." In *Globalization and the Making of Religious Modernity in China*. Edited by Thomas Jansen, Thoralf Klein, and Christian Meyer, 297–341. Leiden: Koninklijke Brill, 2014.

Nedostup, Rebecca. *Superstitious Regimes: Religion and the Politics of Chinese Modernity*. Cambridge, MA: Harvard University Asia Center, 2009.

Ōchō Enichi. "The Beginnings of Tenet Classification in China." *The Eastern Buddhist* 14, no. 2 (1981): 71-94.

Oldmeadow, Harry. *Journeys East: 20th Century Western Encounters with Eastern Religious Traditions*. Bloomington, IN: World Wisdom, 2004.

Olson, Carl. *The Different Paths of Buddhism: a Narrative Historical Introduction*. New Brunswick, NJ: Rutgers University Press, 2005.

Orzech, Charles. "Fang Yankou and Pudu: Translation, Metaphor, and Religious Identity." In *Daoist Identity: History, Lineage, and Ritual*. Edited by Livia Kohn and Harold David Roth, 213-234. Honolulu: University of Hawai'i Press, 2002.

———. "Puns on the Humane King: Analogy and Application in an East Asian Apocryphon." *Journal of the American Oriental Society* 109, no. 1 (1989): 17-24.

Orzech, Charles, and Henrik Sørensen, "Mudrā, Mantra, and Maṇḍala." In *Esoteric Buddhism and the Tantras in East Asia*. Ed. Charles Orzech Henrik H. Sørensen, and Richard K. Payne, 76-89. Leiden: Brill, 2011.

Orzech, Charles, Henrik H. Sørensen, and Richard K. Payne, eds. *Esoteric Buddhism and the Tantras in East Asia*. Leiden: Brill, 2011.

Ouyang Jingwu 歐陽竟無. "Weishi jueze tan," 唯識抉擇談 [Selected works on the mind-only thought]. In *Ouyang Jian xuanji* 歐陽漸選集 [Selected Works of Ouyang Jian], vol. 51 of *Xiandai foxue daxi* 現代佛學大系. Edited by Lan Jifu 藍吉富, 291-293. Taipei: Mile chuban she, 1984.

Pabongkha Rinpoche. *Liberation in the Palm of Your Hand: A Concise Discourse on the Path to Enlightenment*. Edited by Trijang Rinpoche, translated by Michael Richards. Somerville, MA: Wisdom, 2006.

———. *Zhangzhong jietuo* 掌中解脫 [Liberation in the palm of your hand]. Translated by Jiangbo 江波. Taipei: Baifaluo chubanshe, 2000.

Pittman, Don Alvin. *Toward a Modern Chinese Buddhism: Taixu's Reforms*. Honolulu: University of Hawai'i Press, 2001.

Powers, John. *Introduction to Tibetan Buddhism*. Ithaca, New York: Snow Lion, 2007.

Qiu Shanshan 裘山山. *Dangdai diyi biqiuni: Longlian fashi zhuan* 當代第一比丘尼: 隆蓮法師傳 [The principal nun in contemporary times: Biography of Master Longlian]. Shanghai: Shanghai cishu, 2007.

Queen, Christopher, Damien Keown, Charles S. Prebish, eds. *Action Dharma: New Studies in Engaged Buddhism*. New York: RoutledgeCurzon. 2003.

Queen, Christopher, and Sallie King. *Engaged Buddhism: Buddhist Liberation Movements in Asia*. Albany: State University of New York Press, 1996.

Rappaport, Roy. *Ritual and Religion in the Making of Humanity*. Cambridge: Cambridge University Press, 1999.

Ren Jie 任傑. "Huiyi Zhasake Lao Lama" 回憶札薩克老喇嘛 [Memory of Zhasake Lama]. Unpublished manuscript. Dated: summer 1995.

———. "Jinci si jiafeng" 近慈寺家風 [The style of Jinci Monastery]. Unpublished manuscript. Dated: summer 2007.

———. "Nenghai shangshi dechen qinwen lu 能海上師德塵親聞錄 [Reminiscence of Guru Nenghai]." In *Nenghai shangshi yonghuai lu*, 58-69. Shanghai: Shanghai foxue shuju, 1997.

———. "Nenghai shangshi zhushu mulu ji daodu" 能海上師著述目錄及導讀 [A catalog of works of Master Nenghai with introduction]. Unpublished manuscript. Dated: summer 2009.

Ritzinger, Justin. *Anarchy in the Pure Land: Reinventing the Cult of Maitreya in Modern Chinese Buddhism*. New York: Oxford University Press, 2017.

Ryûichi Abé. *The Weaving of Mantra: Kūkai and the Construction of Esoteric Buddhist Discourse*. New York: Columbia University Press, 1999.

Salguero, Pierce. *A Global History of Buddhism and Medicine*. New York: Columbia University Press, 2022.

Samuel, Geoffrey. *The Origins of Yoga and Tantra: Indic Religions to the Thirteenth Century*. Cambridge: Cambridge University Press, 2008.

Schicketanz, Erik. *Daraku to fukkō no kindai Chugoku bukkyō: Nihon bukkyō to no kaiko to sono rekishizō no kōchiku* [Between decline and revival: Historical discourse and modern Chinese Buddhism's encounter with Japan]. Kyoto: Hōzōkan, 2016.

———. "Narratives of Buddhist Decline and the Concept of the Sect (*zong*) in Modern Chinese Buddhist Thought." *Studies in Chinese Religions* 3, no. 3 (2017): 281–300.

———. "Wang Hongyuan and the Import of Japanese Esoteric Buddhism to China During the Republican Period." In *Buddhism Across Asia: Networks of Material, Intellectual and Cultural Exchange*. Edited by Tansen Sen, 403–427. Singapore: Institute of Southeast Asian Studies, 2014.

Scott, Gregory. "Navigating the Sea of Scriptures: The Buddhist Studies Collectanea, 1918–1923." In *Religious Publishing and Print Culture in Modern China: 1800–2012*. Edited by Philip Clart and Gregory Adam Scott, 91–139. Boston: De Gruyter, 2015.

———. "The Buddhist Nationalism of Dai Jitao." *The Journal of Chinese Religions* no. 39 (June 2011): 55–81.

Shahar, Meir and Yael Bentor, eds. *Chinese and Tibetan Esoteric Buddhism*. Leiden: Brill, 2017.

Shakya, Tsering. *The Dragon in the Land of Snows: A History of Modern Tibet Since 1947*. New York: Columbia University Press, 2000.

Shanghai jingang daochang yijing zu, ed. *Nenghai shangshi yonghuai lu* 能海上師永懷錄 [Permanent memory of Master Nenghai]. Shanghai: Shanghai foxue shuju, 1997.

Sharf, Robert. "Buddhist Modernism and the Rhetoric of Meditative Experience." *Numen* 42, no. 3 (1995): 228–83.

———. *Coming to Terms with Chinese Buddhism: A Reading of the Treasure Store Treatise*. Honolulu: University of Hawai'i Press, 2002.

———. "Experience." In *Critical Terms for Religious Studies*. Edited by Mark C. Taylor, 94–116. Chicago: University of Chicago Press, 1998.

———. "On Esoteric Buddhism in China." Appendix in *Coming to Terms with Chinese Buddhism: A Reading of the Treasure Store Treatise*, 263–278. Honolulu: University of Hawai'i Press, 2002.

———. "Thinking Through Shingon Ritual." *Journal of International Association of Buddhist Studies* 26, no. 1 (2003): 62–69.

Shen Quji 沈去疾. *Nenghai shangshi nianpu* 能海上師年譜 [Chronological biography of Nenghai]. Hong Kong: Tianma tushu, 2004.

"Shenci cunfei biaozhun" 神祠存廢標準 [Standards for preserving and abandoning gods and shrines]. In *Zhonghua minguo fagui huibian* 中華民國法規彙編 [Collection of regulations of the Republic of China], 807. Shanghai: Zhonghua shuju, 1934.

Shengyan 聖嚴. *Chanyao* 禪鑰 [The key to Zen]. Taipei: Fagun wenhua chubanshe, 1996.

———. *Shengyan fashi jiao huatou chan* 聖嚴法師教話頭禪 [Huatou Chan taught by Master Shengyan]. Taipei: Fagu wenhua shiye, 2009.

Shorter, Aylward. *Toward a Theology of Inculturation*. Eugene, OR: Wipf and Stock, 1999.

Sichuan sheng wenshi yanjiu guan, ed. *Sichuan junfa shiliao* 四川軍閥史料 [Historical materials on Sichuan warlords]. Chengdu: Sichuan renmin chubanshe, 1981.

Siklós, Bulcsu. "The Evolution of the Buddhist Yama." *The Buddhist Forum* 4 (1996): 165–189.

Simmer-Brown, Judith. *Dakini's Warm Breath: The Feminine Principle in Tibetan Buddhism*. Boston: Shambhala, 2001.

Snellgrove, David L. *Indo-Tibetan Buddhism: Indian Buddhists and Their Tibetan Successors*. Boston: Shambhala, 1987.

Sørensen, Henrik. "On Esoteric Buddhism in China: A Working Definition." In *Esoteric Buddhism and the Tantras in East Asia*. Edited by Charles Orzech, Henrik H. Sørensen, and Richard K. Payne, 155–175. Leiden Boston: Brill, 2011.

Sperling, Elliot. *The Tibet-China Conflict: History and Polemics*. Policy Studies 7. Washington, DC: East-West Center, 2004.

Standaert, Nicolas. "Christianity in Late Ming and Early Qing China as a Case of Cultural Transmission." In *China and Christianity*. Edited by Stephen Uhalley and Xiaomin Wu, 81–116. Armonk, New York: M. E. Sharpe, 2000.

Sullivan, Brenton. "Blood and Teardrops: The Life and Travels of Venerable Fazun (1901–1980)." In *Buddhists: Understanding Buddhism Through the Lives of Practitioners*. Edited by Todd Lewis, 296–304. Malden, MA: Wiley-Blackwell, 2014.

———. "Venerable Fazun at the Sino-Tibetan Buddhist Studies Institute (1932–1950) and Tibetan Gelug Buddhism in China." *The Indian International Journal of Buddhist Studies*, no. 9 (2008): 199–241.

Swidler, Ann. "Culture in Action: Symbols and Strategies," *American Sociological Review* 51, no. 2 (April 1986): 273–286.

———. *Talk of Love: How Cultures Matters*. Chicago: University of Chicago Press, 2013.

Tan Tian 譚天. *Nenghai shangshi zhuan* 能海上師傳 [Biography of Guru Nenghai]. Beijing: Zhongyang wenxian chubanshe, 2008.

Tanner, Kathryn. *Theories of Culture: A New Agenda for Theology*. Minneapolis, MN: Fortress Press, 1997.

Taylor, Charles. *Sources of the Self: The Making of the Modern Identity*. Cambridge, MA: Harvard University Press, 1989.

Tong Lizhou 童麗舟. *Baiyun jian de chuanqi: jingang shangshi Gongga Laoren xueshan xiuxing ji* 白雲間的傳奇: 金剛上師貢噶老人雪山修行記 [A legend amongst the clouds: Record of the cultivation of Vajra Master Gongga in the snowy mountains]. Taipei: Zhengfayan chubanshe, 1961.

BIBLIOGRAPHY

Travagnin, Stephania. "Elder Gongga (1903–1997) Between China, Tibet and Taiwan: Assessing Life, Mission and Mummification of a Buddhist Woman." *Journal of the Irish Society for the Academic Study of Religions* 3, no. 1 (June 2016): 250–272.

———. "Monk Changyuan 昌圓 (1879–1945), Nuns in Chengdu, and Revaluation of Local Heritage: Voicing Local (In)Visible Narratives of Modern Sichuan Buddhism." *Journal of Chinese Religions* 49, no. 2 (November 2021): 191–239.

Travagnin, Stephania, ed. *Religion and Media in China: Insights and Case Studies from the Mainland, Taiwan and Hong Kong.* New York: Routledge, 2016.

Tsering Woeser and Wang Lixiong. *Voices from Tibet: Selected Essays and Reportage.* Honolulu: University of Hawai'i Press, 2014.

Tuttle, Gray. "Tibet as the Source of Messianic Teachings to Save Republican China." In *The Images of Tibet in the 19th and 20th Centuries*. Edited by Monica Esposito, 329–356. Paris: École française d'Extrême-Orient, 2008.

———. "Tibetan Buddhism at Ri bortse Inga/Wutai shan in Modern Times." *Journal of the International Association of Tibetan Studies* 2 (2006), 1–35.

———. *Tibetan Buddhists in the Making of Modern China.* New York: Columbia University Press, 2005.

———. "Translating Buddhism from Tibetan to China in Early Twentieth Century China (1931–1951)." In *Buddhism Between Tibet and China*. Edited by Matthew Kapstein, 241–280. Boston: Wisdom Publication, 2009.

Tuttle, Gray and Johan Elverskog, eds. "Wutai Shan and Qing Culture." Special Issue. *Journal of the International Association of Tibetan Studies* (December 2011).

Urban, Hugh. *Tantra: Sex, Secrecy, Politics, and Power in the Study of Religion.* Berkeley: University of California Press, 2003.

Van Schaik, Sam. *Tibetan Zen: Discovering a Lost Tradition.* Boston: Snow Lion Publication, 2015.

Walls, Andrew. *The Missionary Movement in Christian History: Studies in the Transmission of Faith.* Maryknoll, NY: Orbis, 1996.

Wang Gengwu 王賡武. *Xianggang shi xinbian* 香港史新編 [A new history of Hong Kong]. Hongkong: Joint Publishing, 2016.

Wang Lixiong and Tsering Shakya. *The Struggle for Tibet.* New York: Verso Books, 2009.

Wang Qiling. *The Academic Knight between East and West: A Biography of Alexander Staël von Holstein.* Singapore: Cengage Learning Asia, 2014.

Wang-Toutain, Françoise. "Quand les maîtres chinois s'éveillent au bouddhisme tibétain." *Bulletin de l'École française d'Extrême-Orient* 87 (January 2000): 707–727.

Weidner, Marsha, ed. *Cultural Intersections in Later Chinese Buddhism.* Honolulu: University of Hawai'i Press, 2001.

Wu, Wei. "Approaching the Perfection of Wisdom: Nenghai's Interpretation of the *Ornament of Realization*." In *Sino-Tibetan Buddhism Across the Ages*. Edited by Ester Bianchi and Weirong Shen, 253–277. Leiden: Brill, 2021.

———. "Making a Tibetan Sect in Twentieth-Century China." *Studies in Chinese Religions* no. 3 (Nov. 2017): 242–257.

Welch, Holmes. *The Buddhist Revival in China.* Cambridge, MA: Harvard University Press, 1968.

———. *The Practice of Chinese Buddhism.* Cambridge, MA: Harvard University Press, 1967.

Williams, Paul. "A Note on Some Aspects of Mi bskyod rdo rje's critique of dGe lugs pa Madhyamaka." *Journal of Indian Philosophy* 11 (1983): 128.
Williams, Paul, and Anthony Tribe. *Buddhist Thought: A Complete Introduction to the Indian Tradition*. London: Routledge, 2000.
Xue Rongxiang 薛榮祥. "Zangchuan fojiao daochang zai Taiwan de fazhan gaikuang" 藏傳佛教道場在台灣的發展概況 [Basic situation of the development of Tibetan Buddhist sites in Taiwan]. *Taiwan wenxian* 臺灣文獻 [Taiwan historica] 56, no. 2 (2005): 129–152.
Xueyu. *Buddhism, War, and Nationalism: Chinese Monks in the Struggle Against Japanese Aggressions, 1931-1945*. New York: Routledge, 2005.
Yao Zhihua. "Tibetan Learning in the Contemporary Chinese Yogācāra School." In *Buddhism Between Tibet and China*. Edited by Matthew Kapstein. Boston: Wisdom, 2009.
Yifa. *Origins of Buddhist Monastic Codes in China*. Honolulu: University of Hawai'i Press, 2002.
Yinshun 印順. *Taixu dashi nianpu* 太虛大師年譜 [Chronological biography of Master Taixu]. 1950. Reprint. Taipei: Zhengwen chubanshe, 2000.
———. *Yi fofa yanjiu fofa* 以佛法研究佛法 [Study Buddhism through Buddhism]. Taipei: Zhengwen chubanshe, 2000.
Yoshihide Yoshizu. "The Relation between Chinese Buddhist History and Soteriology." Translated and edited by Paul Groner. In *Paths to Liberation: the Mārga and its Transformations in Buddhist Thought*. Edited by Robert Buswell and Robert Gimello, 309–338. Honolulu: University of Hawai'i Press, 1992.
Yu Lingbo 于淩波. *Minguo gaoseng zhuan chubian* 民國高僧傳初編 [Prominent monks of the Republican period]. Taipei: zhi shu fang chubanshe, 2005.
Yu, Dan Smyer. *The Spread of Tibetan Buddhism in China: Charisma, Money, and Enlightenment*. New York: Routledge, 2012.
Zahler, Leah. *Study and Practice of Meditation: Tibetan Interpretations of the Concentrations and Formless Absorptions*. Ithaca, NY: Snow Lion, 2009.
Zhang Jiyin 張繼寅. "Nenghai fashi zhuan" 能海法師傳 [Biography of Master Nenghai]. In *Nenghai shangshi yonghuai lu*. Edited by Dingzhi, 88–100. Shanghai: Shanghai foxue shuju, 2007.
Zhongren 中人. *Nenghai shangshi ji qi dizi shengping shiji huiji* 能海上師及其弟子生平事蹟彙集 [Accounts of Guru Nenghai and his disciples]. Henan Anyang: Dingguosi, 2004.
Zhou Kaiqing 周開慶. *Minguo Sichuan shishi* 民國四川史事 [History of Sichuan during the Republican period]. Taipei: Taiwan shangwu yinshuguan, 1969.
Ziporyn, Brook. *Beyond Oneness and Difference: Li and Coherence in Chinese Buddhist Thought and its Antecedents*. Albany: State University of New York Press, 2013.
Zivkovic, Tanya. *Death and Reincarnation in Tibetan Buddhism: In-Between Bodies*. London: Routledge, 2013.
Zürcher, Erik. *The Buddhist Conquest of China: the Spread and Adaptation of Buddhism in Early Medieval China*. 1959. Reprint. Leiden: Brill, 2007.

Index

Abé, Ryûichi, 236n10–11
Abhidharmakośa (*Jushe lun*), 154
abhiṣeka rituals, 33, 219–20n14
advertisements, 17, 61
Āgama (*A han jing*), 124, 130, 132
agency, human, 4, 21
Aidao Nunnery (Chengdu), 173–74
Amdo Geshe, 45, 113, 114
Amitābha Buddha, 10, 78, 119, 222n49; chanting of name of, 245n105; heart mantra of, 229n41; reincarnation and, 117. *See also* Longevity Buddha (Changshoufo)
Amoghavajra (Bukong), 31, 215n34, 223n70
Annen, 108, 243n75
Annuttarayoga ("highest yoga"), 38
anti-superstition movements, 6, 47, 62–66, 224n76
apprehension and analysis (*jueguan*), 138, 251n63
Asaṅga, 122, 246n4, 257n33
Ashiwa, Yoshiko, 29
Aśoka, 174
Atiśa, 122, 125, 246n4
auspicious mantra, 229n41

Avalokiteśvara, Bodhisattva, 53
Avataṃsaka Sūtra, 99, 100, 107, 235n6, 237n19–20; Chisong's exegetical program and, 108, 109; commentaries on, 108; Nenghai's interpretation of *lamrim* and, 130; in "separate teaching of the perfect teaching" (*bieyuan*) category, 110

Bai Puren, Lama, 39, 56–57, 61, 62, 123, 216n51; criticized for breaking basic Buddhist precepts, 225n101; esoteric practices taught by, 82, 229n41; Golden Light ceremonies and, 48–50, 57–60, 79–83, 222n49; Golden Light Sutra and, 81; Han lay disciples of, 79–80; as ritual specialist, 56
Baohua, Mount (Baohuashan), 67
Bao Khenpo (Bao Kanbu), 93
bardo (intermediate states), 89
Bardo Liberation, 88–89, 92, 93
Ba Salnang, 252n71
"Beating the Ghosts" (article), 68–69
Bechert, Heinz, 18
Bediako, Kwame, 3

[295]

INDEX

Beijing, city of, 24, 48, 53, 173; Chinese Buddhist Seminary, 244n89; Panchen Lama in, 51, 55; spread of Zhenyan school in, 97; Tibetan college in, 23, 37. *See also* Kālacakra Vajra Dharma-Ceremony; Tibetan College in Bejing

Beijing Lay Buddhist Society (Jushilin), 39, 42–43, 44, 74, 126, 157–58; diversification of events, 75–76; name changes, 76, 227n9; spread of esoteric Buddhism in China and, 77

Beijing Supporters' Association for the Pursuit of Dharma in Tibet (Beijing liuzangxuefa houyuanhui), 75

Beiping Lay Buddhist Society of North China (Beiping huabei jushilin), 76

Beiyang army and government, 29, 51, 52

Bell, Catherine, 51

Bevans, Stephen, 5, 204n9, 205n22–23

Bianchi, Ester, 2, 14, 163, 229n44

bodhicitta (*putixin*), 129, 229n41

Bodhidharma, 145, 214n26

Bodhipathapradīpa [Lamp for the path to enlightenment; Ch. *Puti dao deng lun*] (Atiśa), 122

Bodhiruci, 238n25

bodhisattvas, 98, 100, 104, 238n31, 242n66; Avataṃsaka Sūtra and, 110; bodhisattva ideal, 21; chanting names of, 61, 69; six stages of bodhisattva cultivation, 239n35

body mystery (*shenmi*), 110

Boxer Uprising (1899–1901), 57–58

Braun, Erik, 21

Brief treatise of the stages of the path (Wylie: *Lamrim mdor bsdus*; Ch. *Puti dao cidi luelun*). See *Lamrim Dordu*

Buddha, the, 10, 47, 98; chanting of the Buddha's name, 74; evolution of the conceptualization of, 236n12; four noble truths preached by, 246n3; fruits of Buddha's enlightenment, 101, 238n25; guru as embodiment of, 260n82; meditation and, 253n84; middle way doctrine and, 139

Buddhahood, attained in this very body, 102–4, 239n36

Buddha statues, 82

Buddhism: academic study of, 153; de-ritualization trend in, 55; four noble truths, 139, 251–52n64; global Buddhism, 183; as officially recognized religion, 29; pan-Asian religious identity and, 14; responses to Western modernity, 18; as "world religion," 13–14, 23. *See also* Chinese Buddhism; esoteric Buddhism; Japanese Buddhism; Tibetan Buddhism

Buddhist Association of True Beliefs in Hankou (Hankou fojiao zhengxinhui), 77

Buddhist Conference of East Asia [Dongya fojiao dahui] (Tokyo, 1925), 240n42

Buddhist Monthly of the Light of the World (*Shideng foxue yuekan*), 78

Buddhist studies, assemblies for (*foxuehui*), 74

Cai, Lady, 85

Cai E, uprising led by, 150

calamities, pacification of, 56, 61, 67, 157

calm abiding (*śamatha*), 138, 251n60

Campany, Robert, 4, 13, 208n41

Cao Kun, 52

Carya tantra, 38

Catalog of Imported Items, The (Kūkai), 99

Catholicism, 29, 53

Changdu (Wylie: Chab mdo), 45

Changkya Khutukhtu, 30, 63

Changsha, city of, 48, 49

Changxing, 27, 70, 76, 211n4

Changyuan, 164, 173, 174

Chan school, 9, 24, 33, 248n23, 250n58; Buddhahood in this very body, 103; cognitive reason seen as distraction, 146; death/rebirth process and, 90;

INDEX

discourse of genealogy in, 214n26; doctrinal study deemphasized by, 137, 250n51; *gong'an* (paradoxical phrases as teaching tools), 130, 141, 144, 145, 253n87; meditation and, 78, 140, 144, 146, 157, 160, 258n56; middle way doctrine, 139; monastic Buddhism dominated by, 151; Nenghai's engagement with Chan meditation, 140–41, 144–47; primacy of intuitive experience emphasized by, 134, 138; sudden enlightenment, 10, 183, 239n36, 250n58. *See also* Zen Buddhism

chanting, 61, 64

Chaoyi, 114, 121, 218n88, 244n87; initiations received by, 113–14; *lamrim* literature and, 122, 147

Ch'en, Kenneth, 8, 235n6

Chen Bing, 1, 14, 207n37, 209n49

Chengcan, 157

Chengdu, city of, xi, 7; military schools in, 150; Monastery of Approaching Compassion, 11; Nenghai's lineage founded in, 25, 127; public temples of, 151, 255n15, 259n63

Chengdu Society of Buddhist Studies (Chengdu foxueshe), 77

Chengguan, 108, 243n73

Chengshi school, 124

Cheng Zhai'an, 110

Chen Lansheng, 229n38

Chen Taoyi, 59, 60

Chiang Kai-shek, 66

Chicago Parliament of World Religions (1893), 13

Children's Saving-Nation Association (Tongzi jiuguohui), 85

China, People's Republic of (PRC), 11, 177, 206n29

China proper: Buddhism as link with Tibet, 2; defined, 203n1; entry of esoteric Buddhism into, 1, 8; map, xi; Panchen Lama's exile to, 23

China, Republican (Nationalist), 183, 206n26, 253n76; establishment of (1912), 6; failure to keep Qing territories, 29; iconoclastic campaigns (1920s), 19; Japanese invasion of (1931), 67; Nationalist army, 56, 62, 217n67; Northern Expedition, 62, 150; Revolution of 1911 and, 150; Tibetan Buddhism as state-approved religion, 67; tightened control over religions, 63

Chinese Buddhism, 1, 5, 182; anti-superstition campaign and, 62–66; balance of study and practice, 134, 137; canon of, 81; changes of modernity and, 205n25; comparison of canonical traditions with Tibetan Buddhism, 15, 209n52; debated role in Chinese society, 51; decline of scholasticism, 126, 134; defined, 206n29; doctrinal inclusiveness, 183; esoteric meditation and, 21; extensive borrowing from Tibetan and Japanese traditions, 9; reception and reformulation of esoteric Buddhism, 16; revival/restoration of, 14, 22, 54, 119; spiritual solutions from non-Chinese traditions, 28; training in Tibetan seminaries and, 15. *See also* Chan school; Huayan school; Tiantai school

Chinese Buddhist Federation (Zhonghua fojiao zonghui), 29, 212n9, 212n11

Chinese language, 41, 53

Chinese United League (Tongmenhui), 150

Chisong, 10, 96, 183, 237n18; *ācārya* title received by, 36; "Evaluation of the Huayan and Esoteric Teachings" [Xian mi jiao heng], 108, 243n68; in Japan, 35, 97, 99, 234n3, 243n67; Kūkai criticized by, 99–100, 108, 109; open but critical attitude toward esotericism, 119

Chongqing, city of, xi, 7, 114, 130, 176, 180

Chongqing Society of Buddhist Studies (Chongqing Foxueshe), 77

INDEX

Chong Zhenru (Chong Baolin), 216n57
Christianity, 2, 53, 204n13
Ciqin, 164
Cizhou, 76
Clear Meaning Commentary [*Xianguan zhuangyan lun xianmingyishu*, Wylie: 'grel pa don gsal] (Harbhadra), 154
Coe, Choki, 3
commentaries, 1, 5, 17, 40, 153; by ancient Indian philosophers, 44; in Pali, 21; translations of, 23
Commentary on the Mahāvairocana Sūtra (Yixing), 100
Communism, 183
Compassionate Cause Temple (Ciyinsi), in Beijing, 39
connection-establishing consecration (*jieyuan guanding*), rite of, 81
consecration, mantra of, 83
consecration rites, 84, 97; Dharma-transmitting, 97, 105, 106; transmission narrative and, 240n49
contextualization, 3
Creation Era Temple (Kaiyuansi), 35
cross-cultural transmission, 4
Cui Yunzhai, 74
Cultural Revolution, 11, 87, 177, 183, 207n33
cyan temples (*qingmiao*), 148

Dai Jitao, 28, 63, 67
Dalai Lama, 26, 41, 43, 116
Daoism, 13, 29, 53, 64
Daojie, 30
Daosheng, 235n6
Daowu, 173, 261n94
Daoxing, 30
Dapiluzena chengfo shenbian jiachi jing (*Dari jing*, Mahāvairocana Sūtra), 215n34
Davidson, Ronald, 219–20n14
Dayong, 6–10, 14, 37, 75, 152, 183, 184, 227n8; *ācārya* title received by, 35–36; death of, 46, 123; as disciple of Taixu, 35, 95, 237n21; in Japan, 22, 35, 95, 97, 99, 234n3; Kūkai criticized by, 99–100, 101; *lamrim* literature and, 122, 123, 127, 147, 183, 246n6; long delayed travel to Tibet, 43–44, 123; meditation and, 21; open but critical attitude toward esotericism, 119; purported reincarnation of, 116; return from Japan (1923), 113; study with Bai Puren, 39, 216n54; Tibetan college in Beijing built by, 23, 42; Tibetan commentarial tradition and, 15; Tibetan-language training for monks and, 40, 216n58; Tibetan scholasticism and, 182; unfinished translation of *Brief Treatise*, 123
death process, 89, 90
Deng Xihou, 174, 261n98
Deng Zimei, 1, 14, 207n37, 209n49
Dharmagupta Vinaya (Sifenlü, Four-Part Vinaya), 16, 260n91
dharmakāya ("truth body"), 99, 236n12
Dharma lectures, 75, 76
Dharma Ocean of the Esoteric Vehicle, The (*Misheng fahai*), 88
Dharma-Realm Learning Society (Fajie xueshe), 258n52
Dharma-transmitting consecration (*chuanfa guanding*), 97, 105, 106, 242n58
Diamond Realm consecration rite, 84
Dibeltulo, Martino, 14
Ding Xuqiu, 74
Dixian, 237n18
doctrinal classification (*panjiao*), 10, 97–102, 108, 121, 132, 235n8
Dongchu, 1
Dorje Chopa (Duojie Jueba), 40–41, 61, 91
Dorje Jueba, 232n76
Drakkar Temple (Zhajiasi), 43, 45, 46
Drepung Monastery (Lhasa), 11, 45, 113, 116, 153
Duan Qirui, 52, 58, 211n2
Duara, Prasenjit, 63, 224n76
Dunhuang region, 252n72, 252n74

[298]

INDEX

Eastern Esoteric Buddhism (Rimi or Dongmi), 36
Efficacious Valley Temple (Linggusi), 60
elements, six fundamental, 103, 239n38
E'mei, Mount (E'meishan), 174, 176
emptiness of four great elements, doctrine of, 85
Engaged Buddhism, 18
enlightenment, 21, 23, 91; gradual versus faster paths to, 102, 132–33, 141, 144, 146, 183; *lamrim* ("stages of the path") doctrine and, 25, 122–27; realized through spells and rituals, 24; sudden or rapid, 10, 104, 107, 140–41, 239n36, 250n58
Enlightenment, European/Western, 18
epidemics, 49, 50, 56, 71
Esler, Joshua, 2
esoteric Buddhism (*mijiao*), 12, 28, 34–37, 62; adapted to Chinese cultural milieu, 6; "authenticity" of, 5, 47; centrality of guru in transmission narrative of, 170; Chinese translation and interpretation of, 2; comparison and representation of, 22–25; critics of, 24, 119; dialectical process of transmission, 96; doctrinal controversy about (1920s), 24; family conversions to, 84; female adepts and, 83–88; growing interest in, 33–34; Han Buddhists' suspicion of, 127; introduction to China proper, 46; lay Buddhist societies and, 93–94; popularity of, 71; relation to Mahāyāna Buddhism, 213n20; "restoration" of Chinese version, 10; rise of, 1–2, 14, 23; role of lay Buddhist societies in promoting, 78; transmission of, 8, 18, 25, 119, 213–14n23. *See also* exoteric (*xianjiao*)-esoteric (*mijiao*) bifurcation; Tantric Buddhism
esoteric Buddhism, debates on, 9, 19, 95–97, 119–20; attainment of Buddhahood, 102–5; comparison of doctrines, 107–12; disputes over ceremonies, 55–62; doctrinal classification controversy (1920s), 97–102; issues discussed among Han Buddhists, 112–19; patterns of modernity selectively appropriated, 21–22; role of lay teachers, 105–7
Esoteric school (Mizong), 31
Essentials of Esoteric Buddhism [*Mikkyō kōyō*] (Gonda Raifu), 35, 238n26
"Evaluation of the Huayan and Esoteric Teachings" [Xian mi jiao heng] (Chisong), 108, 243n68
Evans-Wentz, Walter, 89, 91, 232n80, 233n92
exoteric (*xianjiao*)–esoteric (*mijiao*) bifurcation, 12, 24, 35, 44, 77, 96; attainment of Buddhahood, 104; Avataṃsaka Sūtra and, 243n75; Huayan school and, 109, 112; Nenghai's interpretation of *lamrim* and, 132, 133; Shingon doctrinal classification system and, 98; Wang Hongyuan on superiority of esotericism, 10, 77, 102–3, 132, 182, 239n33, 242n66
Eyes of the True Dharma (Zhengfayan), 86

Faguang, 164, 173
famines, 49, 50, 56, 71, 219n7
Fandeng, 39
Fang Yu, 86–87, 231n71
Faure, Bernard, 214n26
Fazang, 109, 238n25, 243n70
Fazun, 7, 9, 112–13, 114, 121, 217n67, 218n88; in Beijing, 244n89; at Drepung Monastery, 45, 113; *Lamrim Chenmo* taught by, 127, 183; *lamrim* literature and, 122–25, 147, 183, 247n7, 263n7; meditation and, 21; on reincarnation, 117–18; Rongkong's criticism of, 245n102; Tibetan commentarial tradition and, 15; Tibetan scholasticism and, 182; translations by, 15, 23, 209n51
Feng clique (Fengxi), 48, 53
Feng Yuxiang, 52

[299]

INDEX

"five races under one union" slogan, 52, 54, 220n18
four infinite minds, 83, 229n41
Foyuan, 151, 152
Fozu tongji [Comprehensive Record of Buddhas and Patriarchs] (Zhipan), 32

Gangkar Rinpoche (Gongga Hutuketu), 86, 87, 231n72
Ganzi region, 11, 43, 46, 206n30
Garden of Enlightenment [Jueyuan] (Shanghai), 177
Garden of Nurturing Spring (Yuchunyuan), 74
Gelug (Wylie: Dge lugs) tradition, 7, 11, 16, 25, 121; deities of, 219n2; ethics education in, 45; *lamrim* ("stages of the path") doctrine and, 126; monastic training and, 167; Mongolian and Tibetan monks of, 39; Panchen Lama and, 26, 211n3; rejection of sudden enlightenment, 141; "Yellow-Hat Lineage," 148. *See also* Nenghai, Gelug lineage founded by
getting rebirth, mantra of, 229n41
Gimello, Robert, 251n61
Golden Light ceremonies (Jinguangming fahui), 48–49, 57–60, 67, 219n2; Han disciples' initiation at, 222n49; Lama Bai's bond with laity and, 83; Lu Xun's wartime criticism of, 68; Republican leaders and, 80, 228n29
Golden Light Sutra, 58, 61, 80, 81
Goldstein, Melvyn, 217n63
Gonda Raifu, 77, 84, 214n30, 215n33; consecration conferred on Wang Hongyuan, 97, 105, 106, 241n53; *The Essentials of Esoteric Buddhism*, 35, 238n26; "Mantuluo tongjie," 215n33; Taixu's criticism of, 36
Gongga, Elder (Gongga Laoren), 86
Gongga, Mount, 86
Gongga Vihāra (Gongga Jingshe), 86
Goossaert, Vincent, 29

graduated teachings of the three persons (*sanshi dao*), 130, 133, 248n28
Great Buddha Temple [Dafosi] (Guangzhou), 61
Great Prajñāpāramitā Sect (Daborezong), 207n31
Great Seal (*dashouyin*), 86
Great treatise on the stages of the esoteric path (Wylie: Sngags rim chen mo; Ch. Mizong daocidi guanglun). *See* Ngagrim Chenmo
Great treatise on the stages of the path to enlightenment, The (*Puti dao cidi guanglun*). *See* Lamrim Chenmo
Great White Parasol mantra, 229n41
Gregory, Peter, 235n6, 236n15
Guangdong Province, 77, 84, 97
Guanghui, 257n46
Guangji Monastery (Beijing), 129
Guangji Monastery [Guangjimaopeng] (Mt. Wutai), 157, 158, 160–61, 164, 177, 257n46
Guangzhou, 24, 84
Guanyi, Master, 152
Guanzong Society (Guanzong xueshe), 237n18
Gui Bohua, 215n36
Guide to Visualize the Three Refuges, The, 143
Guiyi faxin sheyao song [Compendium of verses for taking refuge and making vows] (Nenghai), 76
guru yoga, 144–45, 167–69, 172, 260n82

Hall of Aidao [Aidaotang] (Chengdu), 152
Hall of Vairocana (Piludian), 174, 176
halls for chanting of Buddha's name (*nianfo tang*), 74
Han Buddhists, 1, 15, 39, 96, 181, 220n18; diverse teachings learned by, 111; Gelug training program and, 146; Han Tibetan Buddhists defined, 206n29; *lamrim* doctrine and, 147; Tibetan texts selectively translated by, 8
Haribhadra, 154
heart mantra, 83, 229n41

INDEX

Heian period (Japan), 99
Hengxiu, 157
Hermitage of Compassionate Saint [Cisheng'an] (Mt. E'mei), 176
Himitsu mandara jūjū shinron (Ten abiding stages of mind according to the secret mandalas), 99
Hīnayāna (Smaller Vehicle, *xiaoshengjiao*), 130, 131, 133, 235n8
holding ceremonies, 225n99
Hong Kong, *xi*, 24, 78, 83
Huang Chanhua, 256n26
Huang Shuyin, 153, 256n26
Huang Sufang, 255n16
Huang Ying-chieh, 14, 235n5
Huayan school, 9, 24, 96, 99–100, 183, 242n66, 250n51; Avataṃsaka Sūtra and, 237n19; Buddhahood attainment and, 110; doctrinal inclusiveness principle, 10; "five bibliographical categories" of, 98, 235n8; one-vehicle doctrine (*yishengjiao*), 108, 109, 110, 111, 112, 119–20; on *shi* (appearance) and *li* (reality), 237n23; Taixu's criticism of, 248n23
Huayan Sutra, 226n102
Hubei Province, 48, 64, 75, 163; map, *xi*; spread of Zhenyan school in, 97
Huiding, 114–15, 119
Huiguan, 235n6
Huiguo, Master, 31, 215n37
Huiyuan, 117, 245n100
Humane Kings Sutra, 61, 67, 223n70
Humanistic Buddhism, 18
Hunan Province, *xi*, 49, 59, 60
hungry ghosts, 65
Hu Zhizhan, 246n6
Hu Zihu, 44, 75–76, 227n8; family of, 77, 227n18; renovation of Yonghe Temple and, 80; Sino-Tibetan College established by, 77

inclusiveness doctrine, 237n19
inculturation, 3
India, 35, 69, 118, 156, 219n14, 254n2; decline and disappearance of Buddhism from, 38, 115; esoteric Buddhism transmitted to China, 31, 33–34, 213–14n23; Kālacakra scriptures and, 69–70; Prajñāpāramitā literature in ancient India, 154, 257n32; sacred legacy inherited from, 12; sexual tantra in, 245n95; Tibet's geographical proximity to, 39; Vinaya in, 256n31; Xuanzang's journey to, 42
Indian Buddhism, 13, 209n52, 238n25; liberation from suffering as focus, 250n58; Tibetan Buddhism as authentic legacy of, 67; Tibetan practices inherited from, 38; triad of hearing, thinking, and meditation, 250n57; vegetarianism and, 115
indigenization, 3
Infinite life Buddha, mantra of, 229n41
initiation rites, 26–27, 40, 45, 46; eighteen-method (Jūhachidō), 36; Medicine Buddha, 49
insight (*vipaśyanā*), 138, 251n60
International Institute of China (Shangxiantang), 53, 220n26
Inviting Sages Temple (Zhaoxiansi), 222n53
Iron Statue Nunnery [Tiexiangsi] (Chengdu), *162*, 163, 259n62; Longlian as leader of, 176, 261n97; Tsongkhapa Hall, *163*
Islam, 29, 53

Jagou, Fabienne, 2, 86
Jampa, Lama, 44, 116, 153
Jamyang Chopel, 153
Jamyang Chopel Rinpoche, 45
Japan, 1, 18, 254n2; Chinese monks in, 35, 215n36; Heian period, 99
Japanese Buddhism, 2, 5, 12, 70; Chinese Buddhists' engagement with, 22; controversial teachings in Chinese readings, 102; Nichiren, 18; position of ritual and doctrine in, 55, 221n38; as pure successor of Tang esoteric Buddhism, 36; shift in interest to

[301]

INDEX

Japanese Buddhism (*continued*)
  Tibetan Buddhism, 37–38, 39, 42; six officially recognized schools, 236n11; Taixu's criticism of, 126, 248n23; transformations of, 9, 23. *See also* Shingon Buddhism; Tendai school
Japanese language, 7
Jasagh Lama (Zhasake Lama), 161, 258n60, 259n73
Jewel Light Monastery [Baoguangsi] (Xindu), 152, 163, 173, 261n99
Jiangsu Province, 48, 54, 126; Golden Light ceremonies in, 59; map, *xi*
Jiangxi Province, *xi*, 24, 48, 78; Golden Light ceremonies in, 59; spread of Zhenyan school in, 97
Jiechuang Buddhist Institute [Jiechuang Foxue Yanjiusuo] (Jiangsu), 264n9
Jiezong, 65
Jinci Monastery (Chengdu), 25, *136*, 155, 162, 250n54; confluence of Chinese and Tibetan Buddhism at, 167–74, 176–79; five-hall system, 164–67; founded by Nenghai (1938), 149, 156, 170; founding history of, 161, 163, 180; Hall of Learning Skills (Xueshitang), 164; Hall of Novice Monks (Shamitang), 164, 259n72; Hall of Precept Learning (Xuejietang), 164–65, 259n73; Hall of Preparatory Practice (Jiaxingtang), 165; Old Jinci Monastery, *156*; rites and festivals at, 172; six sub-branches of, 176; Tsongkhapa Hall, *168*, *169*; Vajra Hall (Jingangtang), 165–66; Yamāntaka Hall, 169
Jingan, 212n11
Jingangding yiqie rulai zhenshi dashen xianzheng dajiaowang jing (Vajraśekhara Sūtra), 215n34
Jinling Buddhist Scriptural Press (Jinling kejingchu), 153, 256n26
Jinsheng dhāraṇī (*Jinsheng tuoluoni*), 61
Jiqun, 264n9

Jixiang Vinaya Monastery (Mt. Wutai), 158
Jokhang Monastery (Dazhaosi), 171
journalism, Buddhist, 181, 182
Jueyuan, 243n78

Kadampa tradition, 246n4
Kagyu order, 86, 116, 218n77, 245n98; Mahāmudrā, 252–53n75
Kaifeng Buddhist Seminary (Kaifeng foxueyuan), 92, 234n102
Kaiyuan school (Kaiyuanzong), 22, 31, 32. *See also* Zhenyan school (Zhenyangzong)
Kaiyuan Temple, 234n1
Kālacakra ceremonies/scriptures, 67, 68, 69–70
"Kālacakra Ceremony in Contentious Debate" (Taixu), 69
Kālacakra tantra, 38, 70
Kālacakra Vajra Dharma-Ceremony, 20, 26, 27, 67–68, 211nn1–3
Kamalaśila, 140
Kanben, 209n52
Kaneyama Bokushō, 35, 103–4, 240n43
Kangding (Wylie: Dar rtse mdo; Dartsedo), town of, 43, 44, 45, 114, 117; Dayong's team in, 153; temples and sects in, 218n77
Kapp, Robert A., 254n7
Kapstein, Matthew, 263n3
karma, doctrine of, 56, 59, 74, 80, 115, 131
karma, mantra of purifying, 83
karma, societies of pure (*jingye she*), 74
Karma Kagyu lineage, 86, 245n98
Karma Lingpa, 89
Karmapa, 245n98
Kashmir, 254n2
Kasulis, Thomas, 236n17
Kazi Dawa-Samdup, Lama, 89, 91, 233n92
Kegon school, 237n17
Kham region (Tibet), 40, 43, 61, 112, 113, 123, 206n30; Larung Gar Academy, 184; map, *xi*; Nenghai in, 152, 154,

[302]

INDEX

155, 255n20; temples in, 7; Tibetan masters of, 45. *See also* Kangding
Khangsar Rinpoche, 45, 113, 114, 153; death of (1941), 172; as Nenghai's guru, 11, 170–72; stūpa at Mount Wutai for, *160*
Khenpo Jigme Phuntsok, 184
Khenpo Sodargye, 263n5
Khenpo Wangdu (Dbang 'dus), 41, 53
Kieschnick, John, 8
Kim Hwa-shang (Ch. Jin Heshang), 140, 252n72
Klein, Anne, 250n57
KMT (Kuomintang), 11
Korea, 254n2
Kōya, Mount, 35, 84, 103, 215n36, 234n3; as base Shingon monastery, 31; Han monks trained at, 97
Kriya tantra, 38
Kuanlin, 173, 261n94
Kūkai, 31, 35, 98–99, 215n37, 236n9; *The Catalog of Imported Items*, 99; doctrinal classification and, 102, 108; esotericism characterized as new Buddhist vehicle, 99, 236n10; manifestation as Mahāvairocana (attainment of Buddhahood), 102, 103, 104, 240n41; ten-stages terminology of, 99, 100, 236–37n17; on "three bodies of Buddha (*trikāya*)," 99
Kumārajīva, 223n70, 235n6, 253n84
Kunming, city of, *xi*, 87

Lama Chöpa [Wylie: Bla ma mchod pa; Ch. *Shangshi gongyangfa*] (fourth Panchen Lama), 168, 169
lamas, Tibetan and Mongolian, 47, 55, 73, 96, 112; ceremonies performed in Chinese cities, 50, 51, 61; integrated into Chinese state system, 63, 70; laypeople's interactions with, 79; local Buddhists' support for, 62; in Nanjing, 90; reciprocal exchange with disciples, 71–72; reincarnate, 116; as ritual specialists, 56, 61;

vegetarianism not followed by, 36, 69; as "yellow-robe monks," 148
lamrim ("stages of the path") doctrine, 76, 90, 179; commentary tradition and, 182; doctrinal learning integrated with meditative praxis, 134, 137–40; Nenghai's interpretation of, 127, 129–34, 140, 146–47; as path to enlightenment, 25, 122–27; three principal stages, 129, 248n28
Lamrim Chenmo [*Great Treatise*] (Tsongkhapa), 15, 43, 121, 122, 123, 247n7; Chaoyi's translation of, 126; commentaries on, 184; Fazun's translation of, 125; Nenghai's lecture notes on, *142*; Nenghai's translation of, 155; study-practice relationship and, 137–38; taught in seminaries, 263n6, 263n8
Lamrim Dordu [*Brief Treatise*] (Tsongkhapa), 122, 123, 246n6, 263n6
Langchan, 218n88, 244n86
Lankāvatāra Sūtra (*Leng qie jing*), 115
Larung Gar Academy, 184
Lawrence, Bruce, 205n24
lay Buddhist societies, 43, 54, 73–79, 226n1. *See also* Beijing Lay Buddhist Society; Shanghai Lay Buddhist Society
lay practitioners, 79–83, 93–94; debates on role of lay teachers, 7, 105–7, 121; translations of *Tibetan Book of the Dead* by, 88–93; women, 83–88
lecture notes (*biji, ji, jiangji*), 17, 127, 129, 130, *142*
Lessing, Ferdinand, 153
Lhasa, *xi*, 7, 113, 116, 154, 244n89
li (principle, reality), 237n23
Liang Qichao, 228n30
Liberation in the Palm of Your Hand [Ch. *Zhangzhong jietuo*] (Pabongkha Rinpoche), 184
Liberation Through Hearing During the Internediate State (Bardo Thodol; Wylie: *Bar do thos grol*). *See Bardo Liberation*

[303]

INDEX

Li Ciwu, 229n38
Li Dan, 87, 231n70
Li Dingkui, 59
light, mantra of (*guangming zhenyan*), 84
Li Jinxi, 91, 233n96
Li Shaoji, 228n29
literacy and illiteracy, 219n12
Liu Cunhou, 150
Liu Mingyuan, 179
Liu Wenhui, 174, 261n98
Liu Xiang, 256n22
Liu Zhuyuan, 255n17
Li Yizhen, 83–84, 229n46
Li Yuanhong, 80, 228n29
Longevity Buddha (Changshoufo), 81, 229n35. *See also* Amitābha Buddha
Longlian, 179, 229n44, 251n63; at Aidao Nunnery, 174; Iron Statue Nunnery led by, 176, 261n97
lotus societies (*lianshe*), 74
Lotus Sutra (*Miaofa lianhua jing*), 99, 109–10, 226n102, 235n8, 237n18, 237n20, 240n41; in "common teaching of the perfect teaching" (*tongyuan*) category, 110; Nenghai's interpretation of *lamrim* and, 130; as "secret of the principle" (*rihimitsu*), 243n75
Lotus Vihāra (Lianhua jingshe), 87
Luo Tongbing, 214n27, 235n5
Lu Xun, 68

Madhyamakāvatāra (*Ruzhong lun*), 154
Mahāprajñāpāramitā Sūtra, 139, 154, 252n70
Mahāvairocana, 102
Mahāvairocana Sūtra, 100, 108, 110, 236n17; commentaries on, 108; in "perfect teaching" (*yuanjiao*) category, 109
Mahāyāna [Great Vehicle, *dasheng*] (exoteric Buddhism), 21, 51, 213n20; bodhisattva ideal and, 246n3; enlightenment as gradual process, 102; esoteric practices originating in, 213n23; European knowledge of, 90; exoteric, 61–62; Huayan doctrinal classification and, 235n8; ideal of universal salvation, 9; *lamrim* doctrine and, 130; soteriology of, 71; "three bodies of Buddha (*trikāya*)" theory, 99, 236n12; Yogācāra teaching, 40. *See also* exoteric (*xianjiao*)–esoteric (*mijiao*) bifurcation
Mahāyoga tantra, 245n95
Maitreya, 154, 257n33
Making of Buddhist Modernism, The (McMahan), 18
Manchuria, 63
Manchus, 220n18
maṇḍalas (symbolic diagrams), 26, 51, 93
Mañjuśrī, Bodhisattva, 148, 161, 176, 256n30
Mañjuśrī Monastery [Wenshuyuan] (Chengdu), 173, 255n15, 255n18; abbots of, 163–64, 261n94; six subtemples of, 164
Manshu Jiedi, 105, 106, 241n54, 242n58
mantras (spells), 14, 15, 28, 33, 65, 81, 165; of Amitābha Buddha, 222n49; chanted to protect the country, 66–71; as a hallmark of esoteric practice, 51; Lama Bai Puren and, 82, 229n41; Mañjuśrī mantra, 169
"Mantuluo tongjie" [Comprehensive introduction to maṇḍala] (Gonda Raifu), 215n33
Marco Polo Bridge Incident (1937), 162
Ma Xuchang, 49
Mbiti, John, 3, 204n13
McKim, Donald K., 3
McMahan, David, 18, 19, 55–56; on heterogeneity of responses to modernity, 21, 211n74; on meditation and Buddhist cosmology, 21
Medicine Buddha (Yaoshifo), 49, 58
meditation, 20–21, 56; Chan meditation, 78, 140, 144, 146, 157, 160, 258n56; doctrinal study balanced with, 137, 138; four noble truths and, 139, 251–52n64; gradual versus faster

[304]

INDEX

enlightenment and, 146; intuitive, 145, 146; remembrance of the Buddha, 253n84; visualization and, 144
Mei Jingxuan, 1, 14, 97, 207n37
memoirs, 17, 45, 170
Meyer, Christian, 249n49
Miaoguang, 225n101
Military School of the Land Force (Lujun suchengxuetang), 150
mind-only thought, 137, 250n51–52
Ming dynasty, 8, 26, 32, 213n22
modernism, Buddhist, 7, 18–22
modernity, 4, 16, 71; defined, 205n24; in the West, 18
Moheyan, 140–41, 252n75
Monastery of Approaching Compassion [Jincisi] (Chengdu), 11–12
Monastery of Great Compassion [Dacisi] (Chengdu), 255n15
Monastery of Heavenly Jewel [Tianbaosi] (Chongqing), 151
Monastery of Luminous Enlightenment [Zhaojuesi] (Chengdu), 255n15
Monastery of Saintly Glory [Yaoguangsi] (Chengdu), 255n15
Monastery of Thatched Cottage [Caotangsi] (Chengdu), 255n15
Monastery of Vast Salvation [Guangjisi] (Beijing), 173
monastic economy, 1, 6, 206n26
Mongolia, 53, 63
Mongols, 220n18
monks, 10, 17, 39, 105, 106; "cyan-robe monks," 148; involvement in anti-Japanese resistance, 225n99; Jinci Monastery five-hall system and, 164–67; Kālacakra Vajra Dharma-Ceremony and, 27; loss of imperial patronage, 6; Tibetan and Mongolian, 69; travel to Japan by, 35; travel to Tibet by, 112, 113, 122, 153–54, 210n69, 244n84, 256n29
Mount Kōya monastery, 31, 35, 215n36
mudrās (hand gestures), 26, 51, 65, 81, 82, 222n49
Mukden Incident (1931), 211n2

Nāgārjuna, 70, 100, 122, 246n4
Nanjing, city of, *xi*, 48, 60, 90
Nanjing government, 63, 67, 70
Nanjing Lay Buddhist Society (Nanjing jushilin), 92
Nationalist army, 56, 62, 217n67
nationalist movements, 18
Nationalist Party, 150
National People's Convention [Guomin huiyi] (1931), 67
nation-building, 1, 6, 46, 62, 63, 70, 71
Nedostup, Rebecca, 63
Nenghai (Gong Jixi), 7, 8, 9, 11–12, 114, 121; biography and family of, 149–56, 254n4, 255n14; branches of Tibetan Buddhism developed by, 148–49; Buddhism discovered by, 151; commentaries promoted by, 154; death of, 177; dual sectarian identities of, 260n84; graduated training program for disciples, 15, 210n57; *lamrim* interpreted by, 122, 127, 129–34, 154–56, 183, 248n29; lecture notes on *Lamrin Chenmo, 142*; meditation and, 21, 137–39, 251n63; military career of, 149–50, 254n6; move to Mount Wuhai (1934), 77; photographic portrait of, *128*; practical use of *lamrim* and, 134, 137–40; reflection on Chan meditation, 140–41, 144–47; reform at Mount Wutai, 156–58, 160–62; statues of Nenghai in temples, *135–36*; study of esoteric rituals in Tibet, 45, 76, 218n88; stūpas for, *159, 171*; Tibetan commentarial tradition and, 15; Tibetan scholasticism and, 182; translations by, 15, 23, 154, 155, 158, 164, 169, 172, 174, 177, 209n51, 253n82; Vinaya and, 172–73, 174
Nenghai, Gelug lineage founded by, 11, 25, 127, 207n31; building of, 162–67, *162, 163, 165, 166*; rituals and, 15
New Culture Movement, 249n49
New Life Movement, 224n76
Ngagrim Chenmo (Tsongkhapa), 122, 247n7

[305]

INDEX

Nichiren Buddhism, 18
nirmāṇakāya ("body of manifestation"), 99, 236n12
nonduality, Tibetan Buddhist deities and, 65
Norlha Lama, 17, 61, 63, 87, 223n66, 224n75
Northeastern Charity Alliance (Huabei cishan lianhehui), 61
nuns, 83, 105, 106, 176, 259n62. *See also* Iron Statue Nunnery; Longlian
Nyingma school, 61, 89, 223n66, 252n75

Ōchō Enichi, 236n15
one-hundred-syllable mantra, 229n41
Opening Bliss Temple (Kaifusi), 49
Ornament of Realization (Xianzheng zhuangyab lun; Skt. Abhimsmayālankāra; Wylie: *mngon rtogs rgyan*), 154, 209n51, 257n33
Orthodox Catholicism, 53
Orzech, Charles, 12, 205n19, 223n70
Ouyang Jingwu, 137, 153, 249–50n51, 256n26

Pabongka Rinpoche, 113, 184, 263n7
Padmasambhava (Lianhuasheng Dashi), 87, 89
Pali language, 153
Palmer, David, 29
Panchen Lama, fourth (Lobsang Gyaltsen), 168
Panchen Lama, sixth (Lobsang Palden Yeshe), 52
Panchen Lama, ninth (Thubten Choekyi Nyima), 9, 17, 20, 42, 51–55, 62; exile to China proper, 23, 26; flight to Inner Mongolia (1924), 41, 217n63; honorary titles granted by Nanjing government, 63; Kālacakra Vajra Dharma-Ceremony and, 26, 27, 67; Lama Bai Puren and, 58; at National People's Convention (1931), 66–67; promotion of peace, 53, 54; reincarnation and, 116; visibility of Tibetan Buddhism among Chinese Buddhists and, 46, 123; Yogācāra commentaries and, 40
Pan Wenhua, 174, 261n98
Payne, Richard, 12
Perfect Solemnity Temple (Jingyansi), 60
Phagpa, 32, 213n22
philology, European, 14
Pi Huaibai, 255n16
Prajñāpāramitā, 154, 207n31, 257n32
Preface to Interlinear on the Avataṃsaka Sūtra [*Huayan shu xu*] (Chengguan), 108
Propagation Seminary of Mahāyāna Buddhism (Dasheng fojiao honghuayuan), 75
Protestantism, 29
Protestant Reformation, 18
"Provisional Regulations on Temple Management" (Simiao guanli zanxiu tiaoli), 29
Pure Land school, 9, 10, 24, 54, 245n100; death/rebirth process and, 90; as easy path to salvation, 114; reincarnation and, 116–17, 118
Puti dao cidi kesong [Compendium of *lamrim*] (Nenghai), 129
Puti dao cidi kesong jiangji [Lecture Notes on the *Compendium of Lamrim*] (Nenghai), 130
Puti dao cidi xinlun [Core of *Lamrim Chenmo*] (Nenghai), 155
Putitang risong [Daily chanting at the Hall of Bodhi] (Nenghai), 76
Putuo Island, 54
Putuo Mountain (Putuoshan), 53

Qianlong, Emperor, 52
Qingding, 176–77, 179
Qing dynasty, 8, 26, 148; Boxer Uprising and, 57; civil service examination abolished by, 150; decline of, 6; "Eighteen Provinces," 203n1; esoteric teachings in court of, 32; pursuit of learning from Japan during, 97; royal temples of, 39

INDEX

Qing dynasty, collapse of, 1, 2, 14, 23; repatriation of imperial troops from Tibet, 29; Revolution of 1911 and, 29, 75; Yuan Shikai and, 51–52
Qingfo, 158
Qinghai, city of, 54, 126

rationalism, 21
"Record of Lama Bai's Dissemination of Dharma, A," 56
Records of Sermons About Esotericism (Mijiao jiangxi lu), 77
Red School of Tibet, 32
reform, religious, 1, 6; monastic economy and, 206n26; Nenghai's reform at Mount Wutai, 156–58, 160–62; pan-Asian religious identity and, 14
Reid, Gilbert (Li Jiabai), 53, 220n26
reincarnation, 114, 116–19, 121, 245n98; of Tibetan lamas, 10, 245–46n106
religion (*zongjiao*), 29, 61; Republican state control over, 63–66; role in advancing peace, 53; superstition distinguished from, 47
Ren Dingxun, 76, 249n34
Ren Jie, 179
"Reorganization of the Sangha System, The" [Zhengli sengqie zhidu lun] (Taixu), 22, 31
repertoire theory, 2, 4–11
ritual ceremonies, 16, 20, 28, 253n81; authenticity of, 69; eighteen-method (Jūhachidō), 36, 215n37; esoteric rituals seen as superstition, 66; situational and strategic qualities of, 51. *See also* Golden Light ceremonies
Romanticism, 18, 21
Rongkong, 117, 245n102

Śākyamuni Buddha, 27–28, 115, 235n6
Sakya Paṇḍita, 253n75
Sakya school, 213n22
Salguero, Pierce, 8

sambhogakāya ("reward body"), 99, 236n12
Sanlun school, 124
Sanskrit language, 92, 153, 234n3
Sautrāntika tradition, 250n57
Sayadaw, Ledi, 21
Schicketanz, Erik, 212n17
science, 19
Science of Religion, 249n49
scriptures, 81, 98, 153, 238n31; burned during Cultural Revolution, 177; canonical, 5; chanting of, 61, 64; ideal Buddhist community depicted in, 105; place of scriptural circulation (*fojing liutongchu*), 74; places for reading of (*yuejingchu*), 74
Secret Scriptures of Tibetan Esoteric Dharma Practices (Zangmi xiufa midian), 88
Sequence of Masters and Dharma Transmissions (Shizi xiangcheng chuanfa cidi), 106
sermons, 16; by Foyuan, 151; by Khangsar Rinpoche, 171; by Nenghai, 17, 76, 129, 154, 157, 173, 257n35
sexuality, 38, 65, 97, 119; in consecration rites of high tantra, 115–16, 245n95; critics of esoteric Buddhism and, 19; sex yoga (Shuangshenfa), 97
Shambhala Kingdom, myth of, 27, 69
Shandong Province, xi, 54, 153
Shanghai, 7, 24, 76, 130, 163, 177, 180; Golden Light ceremonies in, 58, 60, 222n53; map, xi; Panchen Lama in, 54, 66, 221n35; spread of Zhenyan school in, 97
Shanghai Lay Buddhist Society (Shanghai fojiao jushilin), 40, 77, 222n53
Shantou Society of the Restoration of Esoteric Buddhism (Shantou mijiao chongxinghui), 78
Shanxi Province, 148
Shanxi Provincial Buddhist Association (Shanxi fojiaohui), 173

[307]

INDEX

Shanyuan Temple (Shanyuanan), 216n54
Shaocheng Buddhist Society (Shaocheng foxueshe), 151–52
Shao Mingshu, 255n17
Sharf, Robert, 50, 221n38
Shelifu a pi tan lun (Śāriputrābhidharma), 251n63
Shenbao (newspaper), 50
Shengyan, 253n87
Shen Shuwen (Gongga Laoren), 86, 230n62, 230n64
shi [*shixiang*] (appearance), 237n23
Shidi jing lun [*Treatise of the Daśabhūmika Sūtra*] (attrib. Vasubandu), 238n25
Shijing Temple (Chengdu), 170
Shingon Buddhism, 2, 77, 95; Buzan sect, 35, 214n30; Diamond Realm, 35, 84, 215n34, 234n3; doctrinal classification system of, 97–98; fruits of Buddha's enlightenment, 101; mythological elements purged from, 55; as successor to Kaiyuan school, 32; transformations in Japan, 34; Womb Realm, 35, 84, 215n34, 234n3. *See also* Japanese Buddhism; Kōya, Mount; Zhenyan school (Zhenyangzong)
Shishi shinbao (newspaper), 50
Shorter, Aylward, 3
Sichuan army, 137
Sichuan Buddhist Association (Sichuan fojiaohui), 164, 173
Sichuan Buddhist Seminary (Sichuan foxueyuan), 173
Sichuan Buddhist Society (Sichuan foxuehui), 43
Sichuan Nun Seminary [Sichuan nizhong foxueyuan] (Chengdu), 179
Sichuan Province, 126, 150, 152; map, *xi*; Nenghai's Gelug lineage in, 7, 11, 17, 163, 176, 180; Nenghai's return from Tibet to, 157, 173, 174; temples in, *165*, *166*, *175*, 176. *See also* Chengdu
Sino-Japanese War, Second, 207n33

Sino-Tibetan College (Hanzang xueyuan), 77
Sino-Tibetan Institute (Chongqing), 86, 113, 114, 244n84; Chaoyi as teacher at, 126; cross-cultural education at, 118; establishment of (1931), 123; Fazun as teacher at, 127
Six Banyan-Tree Temple (Liurongsi), 106
social media, 184
Society of the Restoration of Chinese Esoteric Buddhism (Zhendan mijiao chongxinghui), 77
Sørenson, Henrik H., 12, 213n20
soteriology, 21, 71, 98, 108; doctrinal study and, 137; vegetarianism and, 115
Southwest Peace Ceremony (Xinan heping fahui), 61
Special Issue on the Tianjin Golden Light Dharma Ceremony (Tianjin jinguangming fahui tekan), 80, 81, 82, 228n30
spiritual master (*a she li, ācārya*), 32, 77, 84, 105, 106–7, 111, 215n35
spirit writing, 65
Stael-Holstein, Alexander von, 153, 256n27
Standaert, Nicolas, 8, 205n19
"Standards for Preserving and Eliminating Gods and Shrines" (Shenci cunfei biaozhun), 63–64
Stūpa of the Efficacy of Piety [Xiaoganta] (Deyang), 174
Stūpa of the Rising Dragon [Longxingta] (Pengzhou), 174, *175*, 179, 261n99
Śubhakarasiṃha, 31, 32, 215n34
Sui dynasty, 98
Sun Chuanfang, 48, 53, 54, 58, 59, 211n2
Sun Jingfeng, 92–93, 234n104, 234n107
Sun Yat-sen, 30, 52, 150, 212n12
superstition: associated with outdated past, 63; Buddhism separated from, 23; campaigns against, 19, 47; esoteric rites criticized as, 50, 182;

INDEX

excluded from officially approved religious activities, 29; as "meaningless religious activities," 64; "true belief" (*zhengxin*) differentiated from, 65
Supreme Yoga tantras, 115
Sutra of Humane Kings, 157
Swidler, Ann, 2, 4
syncretism, 2, 78, 127

Taiping Rebellion, 31, 212n15
Taiwan, 2, 18, 86
Taixu, 6, 8, 121, 181, 183, 213n17; caution over ideas inconsistent with Mahāyāna teachings, 102; changing attitudes of, 35, 97, 235n5; Chinese and Japanese Buddhist schools criticized by, 126, 248n23; controversial interpretative decisions of, 96; disciples of, 35, 75, 95; as editor of *Voice of the Sea Trade*, 35, 215n33; on "humanistic Buddhism," 55; Hu Zihu's patronage of, 76; Japanese Buddhism and, 8–9, 22–23, 31–32, 33, 34, 46; "Kālacakra Ceremony in Contentious Debate," 69; on Kūkai's Buddhahood, 103, 240n41; *lamrim* literature and, 147, 183, 247n9; on meditation, 103, 239n40; modified vision of esoteric Buddhism, 36–37, 215n39; open but critical attitude toward esotericism, 119; on reincarnation, 117; religion demarcated from superstition, 64–65; "The Reorganization of the Sangha System," 22, 31; revival of esoteric Buddhism and, 95, 234n1; Sino-Tibetan Institute (Chongqing) and, 114, 123; on six ways of attaining Buddhahood, 103, 239n35; as student of Yang Wenhui, 31; Tantrism and, 208n43; Tibetan college in Beijing built by, 23, 37; Tibetan scholasticism and, 182; on transmission of esoteric teachings, 213n20; World Buddhist Institute and, 76; Wuchang Buddhist Seminary founded by, 113

Tang dynasty, 5, 14, 42, 70, 106, 119; Chengshi and Sanlun schools of, 124; eight mainstream Buddhist schools during, 22, 33–34, 95; Kaiyuan period, 32; tantras transmitted to China during, 98; "three esoteric masters of," 31, 34, 46

Tanner, Kathryn, 3
tantras/tantric practices, 11, 38–39, 144, 183, 207n33; Kālacakra, 70; sexual, 97; special authorization for access to, 121; Supreme Yoga, 115; translation of tantric manuals, 93; transmitted to China during Tang dynasty, 98
Tantrayāna (*misheng*), 130, 131, 132, 133
Tantric Buddhism, 14, 92, 207n35; meanings of, 12; as mixture of magic and Brahmanism, 13, 208n39. *See also* esoteric Buddhism
Tanxu, 76
Tao Xingzhi, 52–53
taxation, 64
Taylor, Charles, 18
technology, 19, 51, 184
Temple of Cloudy Fog [Yunwunsi] (Mianzhu County), 165, 166, *166*, 176, 259n76
Temple of Cypress Forest (Bailinsi), 76
Temple of Dharma Rain (Fayusi), 54
Temple of Dharma Treasure (Fazangsi), 177
Temple of Heavenly Merit [Tentokuin] (Japan), 234n3
Temple of Hidden Efficieny (Lingyinsi), in Hangzhou, 27, 68
Temple of Manifested Efficacy (Xiantongsi), 77
Temple of Numerous Jewels [Duobaojiangsi] (Sanmen, Zhejiang), *178*, 179
Temple of Precious Efficacy (Baotongsi), in Wuhan, 36
Temple of Saintly Immortals (Shengxiansi), in Shanghai, 36

[309]

INDEX

Temple of Silent Peace (Jingansi), in Shanghai, 36
Temple of the Three Righteousness (Sanyimiao), 151
Ten Abiding Stages, 99
Tendai school, 2, 101, 108, 237n17
Testament of Ba, 140, 252n71, 252n74
Thatched Cottage of Vast Salvation [Guangji maopeng] (Mount Wutai), 11
theology: contextual, 204n9; indigenization and, 204n13
Theravada Buddhism, 20–21
Thirteen Deities of Yamāntaka Tantra (*Daweide shisan zun yigui*), 158
"three mystical associations of body, speech, and mind" (*sanmi xiangying*), 65, 109, 110, 253n81
Thubden Geshe, 45
Tianjin, city of, 24, 80, 82
Tianjin lay Buddhist society, 82
Tianran, 218n88
Tiantai school, 9, 10, 24, 98, 99–100, 183, 250n51; Buddhahood in this very body and, 103, 240n41; Lotus Sutra as basis of, 235n8; meditation and, 144; on *shi* (appearance) and *li* (reality), 237n23; Taixu's criticism of, 248n23. *See also* Japanese Buddhism
Tibet, 1, 63, 254n2; Buddhism as link with China proper, 2; Chinese monks studying in Lhasa, 45, 218n88; isolation policy (1920s and 1930s), 217n72; map, xi; relations with Beiyang government, 43
Tibetan Book of the Dead, lay translations of, 73, 88–93
Tibetan Buddhism, 7, 22, 71; anti-superstition campaign and, 63; authenticity of, 27, 67, 70; deities in, 65; Han Buddhists' suspicion of, 23, 46, 49, 69, 90, 112, 114, 127, 207n37; as "Lamaism," 208n42; mixture with non-Buddhist elements, 33; popularity in the West, 88; post-war expansion in the West, 55; scholasticism, 15, 182; shift in interest from Japanese Buddhism to, 37–38, 39, 42; as state-approved religion, 67; systematic transmission of, 47; in Taiwan, 2, 86; tantras/tantric practices, 38; vegetarianism and, 115. *See also* esoteric Buddhism; Gelug (Wylie: Dge lugs) tradition
Tibetan College in Beijing, 23, 37, 113, 126; founding of, 37–42; language training course and, 42
Tibetan language, 7, 39–40, 41, 75, 77, 92, 153; Longlian's fluency in, 174; Nenghai's study of, 11; Romanized mantras, 82, 229n38; taught at Jinci Monastery, 179; training course at Tibetan College in Beijing, 42
Tibetan Yoga and Secret Doctrines, 91, 233n92
transfer of awareness (*powafa*), 86
Travagnin, Stephania, 86
Treatise on Bodhi-Mind (Nāgārjuna), 100
triad of hearing, thinking, and meditation (*wen si xiu*), 138, 146, 250n57
trikāya ("three bodies of Buddha"), 99, 236n11
"true belief" (*zhengxin*), 65
Tsongkhapa, 15, 76, 121, 125, 166, 179, 213n22; as founder of Gelug lineage, 122; instruction on meditation, 144; Nenghai's interpretation of *lamrim* and, 130, 133, 141; on triad of hearing, thinking, meditating, 138. *See also Lamrim Chenmo*; *Lamrim Dordu*
Tuttle, Gray, 63, 67, 88, 208n42

Vairocana Temple (Nanjing), 60
Vajrabodhi (Jingangzhi), 31, 32
Vajra Place of Practice [Jingangdaochang] (Chongqing), 176, 177
Vajraśekhara Sūtra, 109, 110
Vajra Vehicle, 209n52
Vasubandu, 238n25, 250n57

INDEX

vegetarianism, 16, 69, 115, 119, 172
Vihāra of Understanding and Practice (Jiexing jingshe), 78, 84, 106
Vinaya (monastic disciplinary codes), 69, 158, 160, 165, 167; Four-Part Vinaya, 16, 172–73, 260n91; Nenghai's knowledge in, 172–73, 174; Sarvāstivāda Vinaya, 154, 173
Vinaya Monastery of Auspice [Jixiang lüyuan] (Mt. Wutai), 148, 176, 177
visualization, 81, 82, 144, 165, 229n41, 253n81; *The Guide to Visualize the Three Refuges*, 143; guru yoga and, 144–45; of infinite light, 83; maṇḍalas and, 93
Voice of the Sea Tide, 27, 35, 69, 113, 215n33

Walls, Andrew, 3
Wang Hongyuan, 10, 34–35, 77–78, 95; consecrations conferred by, 84, 85, 106, 230n51, 242n61; on doctrinal superiority of esotericism, 10, 77, 102–3, 132, 182, 239n33, 242n66; family of, 85, 230n55–56; on Huayan and the three mysteries, 110; Kūkai and, 104; as lay ācārya, 84, 105, 106–7, 120, 215n35; support for Kūkai's authority, 111
Wang Huilan, 85, 230n59
Wang Jiaqi, 87
Wang-Toutain, Françoise, 14
Wang Yiting, 221n35
Wank, David, 29
warlords, 17, 29, 56; Golden Light ceremonies and, 58, 59; Sichuan military schools and, 150, 254n7
Weiyin, 61
Welch, Holmes, 1, 31, 149, 240n48; on balance of study and practice, 134; on government recognition of Buddhist property rights, 67
White Parasol (Baisangai) rituals, 67
"Why Should We Welcome Master Taixu?" [Weishenme yao huanying Taixu fashi] (booklet), 76
Womb Realm consecration rite, 84

women, 73, 219n12; Buddhist nuns, 83, 105, 106, 176, 259n62; foot-binding custom and, 85, 230n53; laywomen, 83–88; women's Buddhist seminary (*nüzi foxueyuan*), 75
World Buddhist Institute (Shijie foxueyuan), 76
Wuchang Buddhist Seminary, 113, 126, 235n5
Wuchang Uprising (Revolution of 1911), 75
Wuhan, city of, *xi*, 24, 48, 130
Wu Jingjun, 228n29
"Wuliangshoufo fa" (Manual of the Dharma of the Infinite Life Buddha), 82–83
Wu Peifu, 211n2
Wutai, Mount (Wutaishan), 7, 17, 45, 113, 163, 180; Dayong at, 237n18; Golden Light ceremony and, 222n49; history as sacred site, 148, 254n2; Nenghai's move to (1934), 77, 149; Nenghai's reform at, 156–58, 160–62, 173; Temple of Manifested Efficacy, 77; temples closed during Cultural Revolution, 177; Thatched Cottage of Vast Salvation [Guangji maopeng], 11; threatened by advance of Japanese troops, 162
Wuyi, 44, 45

Xia Chao, 59
Xianyin, 35, 39; in Japan, 97, 105, 234n3; Tiantai philosophy studied by, 237n18; Wang Hongyuan's consecration opposed by, 105, 241n54
Xiong Xiling, 52, 211n2
"Xizang fabao guanzhu" (Strings of jewels in Tibetan Buddhist teachings), 91
Xuanzang, 42, 154, 252n70
Xu Shichang, 80, 228n29

Yamāntaka, 174, 177; rituals, 67, 144, 153–54, 157, 256n30; as wrathful expression of Mañjuśrī, 161, 256n30

[311]

INDEX

Yamāntaka tantra, 153, 161, 165, 166, 176; completion stage of, 166; Mañjuśrī's association with Mount Wutai and, 176
Yang Mingchen, 75
Yang Wenhui, 12, 31, 212n16, 213n17, 240n48
Yao Taofu, 230n51
Ye Dequan, 49
Yellow Tara mantra, 229n41
yellow temples (*huangmiao*), 148
Yinguang, 54
Yinshun, 13
Yixing, 32, 70, 95, 215n34, 238n25; *Commentary on the Mahāvairocana Sūtra*, 100; "three vehicles" and, 238n24
yoga (*yuqie*), 32, 38
Yoginī tantra, 245n95
Yongyan, 218n88
Yongguang, 45, 218n88; stūpa of, *171*
Yonghe Temple [Yonghe Gong] (Beijing), 39, 40, 48, 58, 80
Yongleng, 218n88
Yoshihide Yoshizu, 251n59
Yuan dynasty, 32, 213n22
Yuanfang, 115
Yuan Shikai, 30, 51–52, 150, 228n29, 254n9
Yunnan Military School (Yunnan jiangwutang), 150
Yu Shayuan, 255n17

Zahler, Leah, 251n60
Zen Buddhism, 20–21, 55
Zeng Ziyu, 255n16
Zhang, Lady (Nengxing), 152, 255n18
Zhang Binglin, 228n30
Zhang Kecheng, 137, 151, 250n52–53
Zhang Miaoding, 89, 90, 93
Zhang Xinruo, 232n76
Zhang Xueliang, 211n2
Zhang Yuanming, 83
Zhao Hengti, 49, 59
Zhao Hongzhu, 90–91
Zhao Jianji, 78

Zhaotong, 160, 258n52
Zhejiang Province, 17, 48, 53; anti-superstition campaign in, 64, 224n82; Golden Light ceremonies in, 59; map, *xi*; Panchen Lama in, 54, 66
Zhengguo, 76
Zhenyan Lay Buddhist Society (Zhenyanzong jushilin), 78, 84
Zhenyan school (Zhenyanzong), 10, 22, 31, 77, 105, 112; Avataṃsaka Sūtra and, 107; debate over doctrines and practices of, 36, 96; in Hong Kong, 83–84; Mahāvairocana Sūtra and, 109; proposal to reestablish, 95; speedy attainment of Buddhahood and, 102–3; spread among Chinese Buddhists, 97; status as self-conscious sectarian institution, 213n20; turn to Tibetan Buddhism by adherents of, 123. *See also* Kaiyuan school; Shingon Buddhism
Zhenyi, stūpa of, *171*
Zhili Army, 52, 211n2
Zhili clique (Zhixi), 53
Zhimin, 179, 180
Zhipan, 32
Zhiyan, 235n6
Zhiyi, 235n6, 238n31
Zhong family, 150
Zhongyin jiudu mifa (The secret teaching of bardo liberation), 89
Zhongyou jiaoshou tingwen jietuo mifa [The secret teaching of liberation through hearing during the intermediate state] (Sun Jingfeng), 92
Zhongyou wenjiao dedu mifa (The secret teaching of liberation through hearing during the intermediate state), 90
Zhou Zhicheng, 78
Zhuang family, 151, 255n14
Zivkovic, Tanya, 245–46n106
Zuo chan sanmei jing (The Sūtra on the Samādhi of Sitting Meditation), 144, 253n84
Zürcer, Erik, 8

GPSR Authorized Representative: Easy Access System Europe, Mustamäe tee 50, 10621 Tallinn, Estonia, gpsr.requests@easproject.com